The Art of Negotiation in the Business World

The Art of Negotiation in the Business World

SECOND EDITION

Charles B. Craver
FREDA H. ALVERSON PROFESSOR OF LAW
THE GEORGE WASHINGTON UNIVERSITY
SCHOOL OF LAW

CAROLINA ACADEMIC PRESS
Durham, North Carolina

Library of Congress Cataloging-in-Publication Data

Names: Craver, Charles B., author.
Title: The art of negotiation in the business world / by Charles B. Craver.
Description: Second edition. | Durham, North Carolina : Carolina Academic
    Press, LLC, [2020]
Identifiers: LCCN 2019058613 | ISBN 9781531017774 (paperback) | ISBN
    9781531017781 (ebook)
Subjects: LCSH: Negotiation in business.
Classification: LCC HD58.6 .C737 2020 | DDC 658.4/052--dc23
LC record available at https://lccn.loc.gov/2019058613

Carolina Academic Press
700 Kent Street
Durham, North Carolina 27701
Telephone (919) 489-7486
Fax (919) 493-5668
www.cap-press.com

Contents

The Art of Negotiation in the Business World

Chapter 1

Introduction

§ 1.01. Importance of Bargaining Proficiency

Business persons negotiate regularly, even when they do not appreciate the fact they are negotiating. They negotiate with their own superiors, subordinates, and colleagues. They negotiate with people in different departments and divisions of their own firms. Proficient negotiators have good interpersonal skills. As a result, they are respected by their peers and liked by the persons they supervise. Individuals who lack such skills have less loyal and less productive subordinates who think they are not appreciated. As a person who regularly mediates controversies involving employment law issues, I am amazed how many claims concern rude managers who do not know how to interact effectively with the people around them.

Corporate representatives negotiate with suppliers of goods and services, and with parties seeking to acquire their own company's goods or services. They negotiate the terms of lease agreements and property purchases and sales. They negotiate with federal, state, and local government agencies regarding health and safety issues, employment terms, tax matters, economic policies, and similar issues. As the business world becomes increasingly global, they negotiate with related firms, government regulatory agencies, and other parties throughout the world.

Corporate representatives negotiate buy/sell arrangements, commercial property transactions, patent, copyright, and trademark licensing agreements, joint ventures, and similar business relationships. Effective negotiators know how to structure such arrangements in ways that will benefit their own companies—as well as the parties with whom they are interacting. Less proficient representatives often fail to consummate beneficial deals, or they generate terms that are not as efficient as what could have been achieved.

§ 1.02. Limited Educational Treatment

Many individuals employed in the business world have had minimal training with respect to this fundamental skill. For many years, neither business schools nor law schools taught negotiation courses. Although most business schools and law schools do so today, many other college departments continue to forgo such courses. They do not feel comfortable teaching such practical skills, and they seem to think that individuals will develop the necessary skills on their own, or once they become commercially employed. Since most negotiation courses are taught on a limited enrollment basis, a large number of business and law school graduates fail to take such classes.

Negotiation courses are both practical and theoretical, and they are quite interdisciplinary. People can read every book written on the negotiation process, and not improve their bargaining skills. They can conversely engage in various negotiation exercises without gaining a real appreciation of the factors that directly influence bargaining encounters. Negotiations involve *experiential endeavors* that must be learned through both an understanding of the applicable theoretical concepts and through the practical application of those concepts on exercises that are carefully designed to demonstrate the complex nature of such interactions.

Negotiators must appreciate the impact of psychological and sociological concepts, the importance of verbal and nonverbal communication, and the relevance of economic game theory. They have to appreciate the structured nature of bargaining interactions, to enable them to comprehend what they should be trying to accomplish during each separate stage of the process.

Proficient negotiators generally outperform less skilled bargainers. They know how to prepare thoroughly for such interactions, and they know what they should be doing during each stage of the process. They are familiar with different bargaining techniques, both to enable them to decide which tactics they should employ and to effectively counteract the techniques being used against them. This enables them to develop and exude an *inner confidence* that disconcerts less certain counterparts. When I ask less successful students in my Negotiation classes why they gave in to opposing party demands, they often indicate their counterparts were not great negotiators — they simply seemed so certain that they were entitled to what they were seeking that these individuals thought they were wrong. What these less successful bargainers did not appreciate was the fact that the carefully developed confidence of their counterparts caused them to doubt their own initial assessments and induced them to move in the direction of the persons on the other side.

§ 1.03. America Is Not a Bartering Culture

Most Americans are not naturally skilled negotiators. We are not a bartering culture. We rarely go to commercial markets and seek to negotiate the terms of our transactions. We usually pay the listed prices or refrain from purchasing the items in question. In many other cultures, however, these prices are negotiable. Individuals in these nations barter repeatedly with respect to almost everything they desire. As a result, they are comfortable with the bargaining process, and they eagerly anticipate negotiation opportunities. My mother was raised in such a bartering culture in a small farm community in Eastern Europe. When I was growing up in the United States, she regularly bartered with the produce persons at grocery stores, and they accommodated her by reducing the prices they were charging for different items. She even bartered with the salespersons at large department stores in New York City, and they almost always negotiated price reductions with her.

Several of my students have had their mothers visit them in Washington, D.C., and have accompanied them to the Middle Eastern bazar known as Nordstrom's Department Store at Tyson's Corner, Virginia. After each found something they wished to purchase, they politely asked the salespersons if that was the best price they could get. In both cases, their daughters became embarrassed by their effort to barter at such a respectable store. Nonetheless, after one mother got a twenty-five percent reduction and the other got a twenty percent reduction, their daughters were no longer embarrassed. These stories have encouraged a number of my Negotiation class students to seek such price reductions at commercial stores, and I am amazed by the many who have obtained significant price reductions.

Many individuals dislike the ***ritualistic nature*** of bargaining interactions. They do not appreciate the fact the negotiation process takes time to develop, with certain protocols required in many settings. One of the best stories of bargaining ritual comes from my friend Gerry Williams, who taught negotiation skills at the Brigham Young University Law School for many years, and is one of the leading scholars in this field. Many years ago, he spent several years in Afghanistan, where all consumer goods are negotiable. Being a knowledgeable expert in the field, he went to the markets to see how the local residents bartered. When they visited the potato merchant, they asked the price of a kilo of potatoes and were told twelve afs. They indicated that they did not look so good, and offered two afs. The merchant countered with ten afs, they suggested four, the merchant suggested eight, and the deal was concluded at six afs.

For many weeks, Professor Williams went through this ritual and paid six afs. One day when he was quite busy with other obligations, he went to the potato merchant and simply put six afs on the counter. The merchant said they were twelve afs. When Professor Williams replied that he had been paying six afs for a number of weeks, the merchant replied that there had been a drought in the North causing the price of potatoes to rise. Professor Williams then noted that the merchant had sold a kilo to the woman ahead of him for six afs. The merchant replied that he had done so out of sympathy for a person who had recently lost her husband and had to feed a number of children on a limited income. He said he took a loss on that transaction.

Professor Williams spent more time on that day with the merchant than on any previous occasion, and yet he departed with no potatoes. The merchant was not willing to sell for his opening offer, since that would be an insult to someone who expected customers to go through the bartering process, and Professor Williams was not willing to pay more than the six afs he had become accustomed to paying. He returned the following morning and asked: "How much are the potatoes?" He finally appreciated how crucial ritualistic behavior can be during bargaining interactions.[1]

Americans should not be afraid of bargaining encounters. They should view such situations as ***opportunities*** providing them with the chance to improve their situations.

---

1. For a perfect example of the bartering approach, go to youtube.com and type in "life of brian haggle." This will take you to a lovely five minute clip from a Monty Python movie demonstrating how individuals are supposed to haggle.

It is amazing how often persons politely asking if something is negotiable will obtain more beneficial terms. Students must appreciate this fact and view bargaining encounters as pleasant situations. They have been negotiating for many years with their parents, siblings, and friends—and even strangers—but have rarely thought about these regular occurrences. They were born with basic needs and limited communication skills. They quickly learned to make sounds to be fed, changed, and put down for naps. As their communication skills improved, they became even more manipulative negotiators. They learned something many adult bargainers seem to ignore— you get more with honey than you do with vinegar. They thus asked for things they wished to obtain in a nice manner, and they often played off one parent against the other. They were persistent, often asking for something several times before obtaining it. They also appreciated a critical fact that many adults do not understand; there is no such thing as bargaining power, but only the perception of it. No matter how much bargaining power someone might think they possess, if the opposite side is unaware of their power it becomes irrelevant. When parents negotiate with their children, they believe that they possess the superior bargaining authority. When their children simply ignore this factor, the parents begin to realize the fact that their objective power will not determine the outcome. After parents spend a substantial amount of money to educate their children, those persons forget everything they intuitively learned as children. They then have to take formal Negotiation courses to relearn what they knew before kindergarten!

§ 1.04. Ethical Considerations

Many individuals feel uncomfortable when they engage in bargaining interactions due to the seeming deception involved. Side A would like to sell its business, and will accept anything over $25 million. Side B is thinking of purchasing that business, and is willing to pay up to $30 million to get it. The parties thus have a $5 million *settlement range* between the lowest Side A will go and the highest Side B will go. They should thus be able to reach a mutually acceptable agreement. They have some small talk, and then the serious discussions begin. Side A says it will not accept anything below $35 million, and Side B indicates that it cannot go a penny over $20 million. Side A and Side B are pleased by the fact they have begun the negotiation process successfully, yet both have begun with barefaced lies! Have they engaged in unethical behavior?

Relatively strict ethical standards are imposed upon practicing lawyers by the American Bar Association Model Rules of Professional Conduct. Model Rule 4.1 expressly states that "a lawyer shall not knowingly: (a) make a false statement of material fact or law to a third person." What could be clearer—a lawyer may not lie. When Model Rule 4.1 was being drafted, it was actually intended to prohibit all dishonest behavior by attorneys. Persons who teach negotiation skills quickly pointed out the fact that almost all proficient lawyers misstate certain information when they engage in bargaining interactions due to the deceptive nature of such situations. They over- or under-state their client settlement intentions, and they often over- or under-state the value of the items to be exchanged for strategic purposes. For example, if Side A knows that Side B really wishes to obtain a term it does not particularly value, it may indicate that it does not wish to give up that item to enable it to obtain a significant concession from Side B. On the other hand, if Side A wants to obtain an item it does not believe Side B particularly values, it may under-state the degree to which it wishes to get that term to minimize what it will have to trade for that item.

To deal with these issues, the ABA added Comment 2 to Model Rule 4.1 which recognizes that a certain degree of deception is an inherent part of most legal—and even business—negotiations. "Under generally accepted conventions in negotiation, certain types of statements ordinarily are not taken as statements of material fact. Estimates of price or value placed on the subject of a transaction and a party's intentions as to an acceptable settlement of a claim are ordinarily in this category ..."[2] As a result of these exceptions, what is commonly regarded as "puffing" and "embellishment" during bargaining interactions is considered perfectly acceptable.[3] It is thus permissible for business attorneys to misstate the settlement intentions of their corporate clients and to misrepresent the degree to which their clients wish to obtain certain terms. Although non-attorney commercial negotiators are not governed by Model Rule 4.1, they do subject their firms to liability for fraud if they knowingly misrepresent *material fact* which opposing parties may reasonably rely upon. Courts have appropriately acknowledged the deception that is part of the bargaining process, and have allowed the same degree of "puffing" and "embellishment" permitted under Comment 2.[4]

Both attorneys and business persons are often shocked when I speak at forums and indicate that I have never participated in legal or business negotiations as an advocate or mediator where both sides did not lie, yet I have rarely encountered an attorney or corporate representative I thought was dishonest. I then explain the degree to which they over- and under-state how much their clients value the items being exchanged and the actual settlement intentions of those parties. I have almost never encountered someone I thought was misrepresenting relevant information of a different variety. When they talk about what the opposing side has the right to know, they almost always do so honestly. They appropriately recognize that if they misrepresent these areas, they may lose their reputations for honesty and subject their clients to suits for commercial fraud.

---

2. *See also* Section 98 of *The American Law Institute Restatement of the Law Third Governing Lawyers* Vol. 2, 58–69 (2000) (similarly recognizing the critical distinction between acceptable "puffing" and "embellishment" during bargaining interactions and the unacceptable misrepresentation of "material" fact).

3. *See generally* Charles B. Craver, "Negotiation Ethics for Real World Interactions," 25 *Ohio State Journal on Dispute Resolution* 299 (2010).

4. *See* Rex Perschbacher, "Regulating Lawyers' Negotiations," 27 *Arizona Law Review* 75 (1985). *See generally* Roy J. Lewicki & Robert J. Robinson, "Ethical and Unethical Bargaining Tactics: An Empirical Study," 17 *Journal of Business Ethics* 665 (1998); Alan Strudler, "Incommensurable Goods, Rightful Lies, and the Wrongness of Fraud," 146 *University of Pennsylvania Law Review* 1529 (1998).

Business representatives many never misrepresent *material* fact, economic issues, or business information which the opposing side has the right to rely upon during commercial interactions. If they do so, they and their firms can be sued for monetary damages under the law of commercial fraud. For example, if a real estate owner falsely tells a lessee that he has an offer from a third party for an overstated rental amount in an effort to induce the lessee to enter into a new lease at an excessive rental rate, he could be held liable.[5] Nonetheless, commonly accepted "puffing" and "embellishment" regarding the general value of the property in question would normally be acceptable.

It is common knowledge and may always be assumed that any seller will express a favorable opinion concerning what he has to sell; and when he praises it in general terms, without specific content or reference to facts, buyers are expected to and do understand that they are not entitled to rely literally upon the words.[6]

Business negotiators must appreciate the critical nature of their professional reputations. If they are ever caught lying about what opposing parties have the right to rely upon, those persons will never trust them again — and they will most likely communicate to others regarding the negative behavior of those deceptive individuals. They could even share this information with others via the Internet, and it would be almost impossible for the targets of such criticisms to recover from the negative consequences involved.

§ 1.05. Traits Possessed by Proficient Negotiators

For 40 years I have taught Negotiation courses to law students. During these classes, we explore the pertinent aspects of bargaining interactions, and the students engage in a series of negotiation exercises. The first few are solely for practice, to demonstrate the concepts being taught, and to allow the participants to experiment with different styles and techniques. The students are then assigned a series of exercises, the results of which are rank-ordered from high to low, with these results accounting for one half of their course grades. The other half is based upon course papers they prepare discussing what they have learned from their bargaining encounters.

During the years I have taught this course, I have sought to determine the factors that are possessed by effective negotiators. Successful bargainers are generally thoroughly prepared persons who can forcefully advance their own positions. They understand the negotiation process, and appreciate the different psychological factors that influence the decision-making of most individuals. Since many of these considerations might be possessed by students who do well academically, I decided to determine whether students with elevated GPAs achieve better negotiation exercise results than students with lower GPAs. In two separate studies, I found absolutely

---

5. *See Kabatchnick v. Hanover-Elm Bldg.Corp.*, 103 N.E.2d 692 (Mass. 1952).
6. *Restatement (Second) of Torts* § 542 Comment e (2009).

no statistically significant correlation between student GPAs and the results they achieved on my course exercises.[7]

Some like Daniel Goleman seem to think that if performance is not directly related to IQ, it must be correlated with EQ—emotional intelligence. Over the past several years, I worked with Dr. Allison Abbe, a clinical psychologist, to examine the impact of emotional intelligence on student negotiation performance. In our study, we found no statistically significant correlation between emotional intelligence scores and negotiation exercise outcomes.[8]

Since I used to be occasionally asked by senior partners at law firms whether I thought that minority students and women could negotiate as proficiently as their white male cohorts, I decided to explore these significant factors. I found absolutely no difference between the results achieved by minority and nonminority students.[9] I similarly found no significant differences with respect to the exercise results achieved by male and female students.[10]

What factors are possessed by skilled negotiators? I have found that they are persons who are *thoroughly prepared* for their encounters. They have established *elevated*, but *realistic, aspirations* for the items to be exchanged, and *confidence* in the positions being taken. They also do an excellent job of *placing themselves in the shoes of their counterparts* to enable them to estimate the goals and bottom lines of those individuals. They also *ask many questions* of their adversaries during the initial portions of their interactions to verify their pre-bargaining predictions regarding the desires of those persons. They work to expand the overall pie to be divided, recognizing the fact that the greater the joint surplus generated, the easier it is for them to claim more of what they want for their own side. They also tend to be personable individuals who work well with others.

§ 1.06. Scope of Book

This book will carefully explore the relevant aspects of bargaining interactions. Chapter 2 will focus on the impact of negotiator styles on their encounters. Chapter 3 will discuss what individuals must do when they prepare for their negotiations.

---

7. *See* Charles B. Craver, "The Impact of Student GPAs and a Pass-Fail Option on Clinical Negotiation Couse Performance," 15 *Ohio State Journal on Dispute Resolution* 373, 380–384 (2000); Charles B. Craver, "Clinical Negotiating Achievement as a Function of Traditional Law School Success and as a Predictor of Future Negotiating Performance," 1986 *Missouri Journal on Dispute Resolution* 63, 65–67 (1986).

8. *See* Charles B. Craver, "Emotional Intelligence and Negotiation Performance," http://ssrn.com/abstract=2259785.

9. *See* Charles B. Craver, "Race and Negotiation Performance: Does Race Predict Success as a Negotiator?" 8 *Dispute Resolution Magazine* 22–26 (Fall 2001).

10. *See* Charles B. Craver, "The Impact of Gender on Negotiation Performance," 14 *Cardozo Journal of Conflict Resolution* 339, 354–356 (2013); Charles B. Craver & David W. Barnes, "Gender, Risk Taking, and Negotiation Performance," 5 *Michigan Journal of Gender and the Law* 299, 339–344 (1999).

Chapter 4 will explore the way in which persons should use the Preliminary Stage to establish rapport with opposing parties and to create positive environments for their impending interactions. Chapter 5 will discuss the "value creation" which takes place during the Information Stage. Chapter 6 will cover the critical distributive aspect of bargaining encounters when the participants use the Distributive and Closing Stages to decide how to divide the surplus created during the Information Stage. Chapter 7 will talk about "value maximizing"—when parties should employ the Cooperative Stage to be sure they have generated efficient agreements that maximize the joint returns achieved.

Chapter 8 will explore the various bargaining techniques that are employed during most interactions, while Chapter 9 will cover nonverbal communication. Chapter 10 will focus on telephone and e-mail interactions and discuss how they differ from in-person dealings. Chapter 11 will explore the impact of gender-based differences in bargaining interactions. Chapter 12 will focus on transnational dealings and the reasons they may differ from wholly domestic encounters.

Chapter 13 will explore alternative dispute mechanisms that parties may employ to help them achieve initial accords and resolve disagreements that may arise under existing agreements. Chapter 14 will emphasize the benefits that can be derived from occasional post-negotiation assessments following more significant bargaining encounters, and Chapter 15 will discuss ethical issues frequently encountered by commercial negotiators.

Chapter 2

Impact of Different Negotiator Styles

Most negotiation books divide bargainers into two stylistic groups: (1) Cooperative/Problem-Solvers and (2) Competitive/Adversarials. *Cooperative/Problem-Solving (win-win) negotiators* are epitomized by the book *Getting to Yes*.[11] These "*win-win*" participants move psychologically *toward* each other, try to maximize the *joint returns* achieved through the bargaining process, begin with realistic opening positions, seek reasonable and fair results, behave in a courteous and professional manner, rely upon objective standards to guide their discussions, rarely resort to threats or other disruptive tactics, maximize the disclosure of relevant information, are open and trusting, work diligently to satisfy the underlying interests of themselves and their counterparts, are willing to make unilateral concessions where appropriate, and try to reason with the persons on the opposing side.

Competitive/Adversarial (win-lose) negotiators are epitomized by the book *Secrets of Power Negotiating*.[12] These "*win-lose*" persons move psychologically *against* their counterparts, try to maximize their *own returns*, begin with unreasonable opening offers favoring their own side, seek extreme results beneficial to themselves, behave in an adversarial and frequently offensive manner, focus primarily on their own positions rather than upon objective and neutral standards, often resort to threats, minimize the disclosure of their own information, are closed and untrusting, are only concerned about the interests of their own side, try to make minimal concessions, and manipulate their counterparts.[13] They often judge their own success less by what they have obtained for their own side and more by the degree to which their adversaries have lost.

Cooperative/Problem-Solvers do not hesitate to disclose their critical information, explore the underlying interests of the respective parties, and strive for results that are beneficial to both sides. They often look for ways to explore innovative alternatives that may enable the bargainers to expand the overall pie through tradeoffs that si-

---

11. Roger Fisher, William L. Ury & Bruce Patton, *Getting to Yes* (2d ed. 1991). *See also* Hal Abramson, "Fashioning an Effective Negotiation Style: Choosing Between Good Practices, Tactics, and Tricks," 23 *Harvard Negotiation Law Review* 319 (2018); Yasmin Davidds, *Your Own Terms: A Woman's Guide to Taking Charge of Any Negotiation* 53–68 (2015); Robert H. Mnookin, Scott R. Peppet & Andrew S. Tulumello, *Beyond Winning* (2000).

12. Roger Dawson, *Secrets of Power Negotiating* (3d ed. 2011). *See also* Jim Camp, *Start with No* (2002); Robert Ringer, *Winning Through Intimidation* (1973).

13. *See* Herbert M. Kritzer, *Let's Make a Deal* 78–79 (1991).

multaneously advance the interests of both parties. When money is being discussed, they may agree to future payments or in-kind payments that satisfy the underlying interests of everyone involved. When Side A is trying to purchase Side B's corporation worth $50 million, but it only has $40 million in cash, it might propose to provide Side B with $40 million in cash and $12 million in future goods and services. Side B is pleased that it was able to sell its firm for $52 million, while Side A is gratified that it only had to pay $47 million, due to the fact it only cost it $7 million to generate the goods and services valued for $12 million by Side B.

Competitive/Adversarials tend to engage in disingenuous games-playing. They conceal their negative information, and try to manipulate their counterparts into providing them with terms that maximize the returns for their own side. They may even ignore different options that might benefit their adversaries if those alternatives would not clearly enhance their own returns.

Which negotiator style is more prevalent in the legal and business worlds, and which is likely to be employed by effective bargainers? In 1976, Gerald Williams conducted an empirical study among legal practitioners in Phoenix to ascertain the percentage of Cooperative/Problem-Solving and Competitive/Adversarial negotiators. He asked respondents to describe how persons with whom they had recently interacted conducted themselves. The respondents indicated that 65 percent of their recent counterparts behaved in a Cooperative/Problem-Solving manner, 24 percent in a Competitive/Adversarial manner, and 11 percent did not fit in either category.[14]

In 1999, Andrea Kupfer Schneider replicated the Gerald Williams study among practitioners in Milwaukee and Chicago.[15] Although she similarly found that about two-thirds of attorneys are considered Cooperative/Problem-Solvers and only one-third are considered Competitive/Adversarials, her findings reflected changes that had occurred generally in the American society over the prior 24 years. People are less pleasant today than they were a quarter century ago, and many have become more impatient and less courteous. She found that "the competitive negotiator described by Williams was not nearly as unpleasant and negative" as the contemporary competitive bargainer.[16]

When I ask attorneys and business persons who attend my Effective Legal Negotiation training programs what percent of their counterparts fit in each category, they generally indicate that 50 percent or more behave in a Competitive/Adversarial manner. Why do they tend to over-estimate the percentage of individuals who bargain in that fashion? *Emotional contagion* — when we interact with others, we are influenced by their emotional states. We tend to recall negative experiences more than positive ones, and this factor causes us to over-state the percentage of Competitive/Adversarials compared with Cooperative/Problem-Solvers.

---

14. *See* Gerald R. Williams, *Legal Negotiation and Settlement* 19 (1983).

15. *See* Andrea Kupfer Schneider, "Shattering Negotiation Myths: Empirical Evidence on the Effectiveness of Negotiation Style," 7 *Harvard Negotiation Law Review* 143 (2002).

16. *Id.* at 187.

§ 2.01. Which Style Is More Effective?

When I ask Effective Legal Negotiation course participants to describe the attributes possessed by effective negotiators, they generally suggest that they are aggressive individuals who openly work to obtain better results for themselves than for their counterparts. They may even indicate that such persons regularly employ offensive and manipulative tactics designed to intimidate weaker adversaries. I then ask what these respondents would do if someone came to their office that afternoon, openly indicated that they wanted to clean them out, and exacerbated the situation with some gratuitous rudeness. Would they give into the demands of such persons or get up for the interaction in a manner that would enable them to avoid exploitation by such a manipulative adversary? I then ask them how they would react to someone who came to their office and politely indicated an interest in achieving a mutually beneficial agreement that would satisfy the underlying interests of both sides. At this point, they begin to appreciate the fact that negotiators get more with courteous and professional behavior than they do with rude and insulting conduct.

Professor Williams asked the respondents in his study which of their recent adversaries were "effective," "average," and "ineffective" negotiators. They indicated that 59 percent of the Cooperative/Problem-Solvers were "effective," while only 25 percent of the Competitive/Adversarials were. Only 3 percent of the Cooperative/Problem-Solvers were considered to be "ineffective" negotiators, while 33 percent of the Competitive/Adversarials were placed in this category.

One would certainly expect the less professional and more repugnant Competitive/Adversarial negotiators described by respondents in Professor Schneider's study to be less effective than the less negatively described Competitive/Adversarial bargainers in Professor Williams' study, and this is precisely what she found. The percentage of "effective" Competitive/Adversarial negotiators declined from 25 percent in the Williams study to 9 percent in the Schneider study.[17] On the other hand, the percentage of Cooperative/Problem-Solvers found to be "effective" negotiators dropped only slightly from 59 percent in the Williams study to 54 percent in the Schneider study.

The findings with respect to persons considered to be "ineffective" negotiators are even more amazing. Professor Schneider found almost no change in the percentage of Cooperative/Problem-Solvers who were considered to be "ineffective" negotiators—an increase from 3 percent to 3.6 percent.[18] On the other hand, while 33 percent of Competitive/Adversarials were found by Professor Williams to be "ineffective" bargainers, 53 percent of such individuals were found to be "ineffective" in the Schneider study. This significant increase in this group would most likely be attributable to their more unpleasant demeanors.

In the 40 years I have taught Negotiation courses, I have not found effective Cooperative/Problem-Solvers to be less successful than effective Competitive/Adversarials.

---

17. *Id.* at 167, 189.
18. *Id.* at 167.

The thought that a person must be uncooperative, manipulative, and even abrasive to achieve beneficial results is clearly incorrect. Negotiators who desire to achieve beneficial results must simply possess the ability to say "no" forcefully and credibly to convince other parties that they must increase their offers if accords are to be obtained. Professional and low key bargainers can accomplish this objective as effectively as more demonstrative persons.

I have found only three significant differences with respect to the results achieved by Cooperative/Problem-Solvers and Competitive/Adversarials in my Negotiation course exercises. First, if an extremely one-sided agreement is reached, the prevailing party will generally be a Competitive/Adversarial negotiator based upon the fact that Cooperative/Problem-Solvers are usually more fair-minded and do not try to take such advantage of less proficient counterparts. Second, Competitive/Adversarials generate far more *non-settlements* than Cooperative/Problem-Solvers, since the more extreme positions taken by Competitive/Adversarials and their greater use of manipulative and offensive tactics make it more likely that their counterparts will decide to accept the consequences associated with non-settlements.

The third factor concerns the fact that Cooperative/Problem-Solver negotiators tend to achieve more efficient *combined results* than Competitive/Adversarial bargainers. This is due to the fact that Cooperative/Problem-Solvers are more open and trusting persons who desire to achieve mutually beneficial terms, while Competitive/Adversarials are less open and endeavor to maximize their own returns.

§ 2.02. Interactions between Cooperative and Competitive Style Negotiators

Cooperative/Problem-Solvers are generally open and trusting when interacting with other Cooperative/Problem-Solvers, while Competitive/Adversarials tend to be manipulative and confrontational when they negotiate with either Cooperative/Problem-Solvers or Competitive/Adversarials. What happens when Cooperative/Problem-Solvers bargain with Competitive/Adversarials? If the Cooperative/Problem-Solvers are naively open and trusting with counterparts who are more closed and manipulative, information imbalances would favor the Competitive/Adversarials.[19] Cooperative/Problem-Solvers wishing to avoid such exploitation must adopt a more strategic approach. They cannot disclose significantly more confidential information concerning their side's values and settlement intentions than the other side, or they will end up with less beneficial terms.

When Cooperative/Problem-Solvers begin bargaining interactions with individuals they do not know well, they should release confidential information in a deliberate

---

19. *See* Roger Volkema & Cheryl Rivers, "Beyond Frogs and Scorpions: A Risk-Based Framework for Understanding Negotiating Counterparts' Ethical Motivations," 28 *Negotiation Journal* 379, 381–382 (2012).

manner. If their openness is being reciprocated, they can continue their openness. On the other hand, if their candor is not being reciprocated, they must be less forthcoming to avoid the information imbalance that would place them at a distinct disadvantage.

§ 2.03. Competitive/Problem-Solving (WIN-win) Negotiators

In their studies, Professors Williams and Schneider found that certain traits are possessed by both effective Cooperative/Problem-Solving negotiators and effective Competitive/Adversarial bargainers.[20] Proficient negotiators from both groups are thoroughly prepared, behave in an honest and ethical manner, are perceptive readers of others, and are analytical, realistic, and convincing. They also found that effective negotiators from both groups endeavor to *maximize* their *own side's returns*. This was the Number One objective for Competitive/Adversarial bargainers, and the Number Two objective (behind ethical behavior) for Cooperative/Problem-Solving negotiators. Since own-side maximization is the quintessential objective of Competitive/Adversarial negotiators, this common trait would clearly indicate that many proficient negotiators who are identified by their cohorts as Cooperative/Problem-Solvers are actually wolves in sheepskin. These are what Professor Williams and I have characterized as *Competitive/Problem-Solving negotiators*.[21] They exude a seemingly open and cooperative style when they interact with others, but use somewhat manipulative techniques to achieve competitive objectives. They employ an approach which Ron Shapiro and Mark Jankowski describe as: "*WIN-win*: big win for your side, little win for theirs."[22]

Competitive/Problem-Solvers appreciate the fact that the imposition of poor terms on their counterparts does not necessarily benefit their own side. Once they have achieved the terms they wish to obtain, they strive to maximize opposite side satisfaction. When they conclude bargaining interactions, they do not compare their results with those achieved by the other side. They instead ask whether they like what they have obtained, realizing that if they attained their own objectives they had successful encounters.

Individuals who bargain with Competitive/Problem-Solvers generally describe such persons as Cooperative/Problem-Solvers, since they think those persons have been completely open with them and have avoided the use of manipulative tactics. This would explain why Professors Williams and Schneider found a much greater percentage of effective Cooperative/Problem-Solving negotiators than Competitive/Adversarial negotiators. What the counterparts of Competitive/Problem-Solvers fail to appreciate

---

20. *See* Williams, *supra* note 14, at 20–30; Schneider, *supra* note 15, at 188.

21. *See* Gerald R. Williams & Charles B. Craver, *Legal Negotiating* 64–65 (2007).

22. Ron Shapiro & Mark Jankowski, *The Power of Nice* 5 (2001). *See also* James C. Freund, *Smart Negotiating* 24–27 (1992); Bob Wolf, *Friendly Persuasion* 34–35 (1990).

is the fact that such persons are not completely open, and they are willing to employ somewhat manipulative strategies to advance their own side interests.

Competitive/Problem-Solvers recognize the importance of **negotiation process.** Individuals who believe that the bargaining process has been fair and they have been treated respectfully tend to be more satisfied with objectively less beneficial terms than they are with objectively more beneficial terms achieved through a process they found to be less fair and less respectful.[23] It is thus critical for Competitive/Problem-Solvers to always treat their counterparts with respect and professionalism, and to leave those persons with the sense at the end of their interactions that they obtained "fair" terms.

Proficient negotiators do not work to maximize counterpart returns once they have obtained what they want for purely altruistic reasons.[24] They appreciate the fact that this approach is most likely to enable them to advance their own interests. First, they have to provide their adversaries with sufficiently generous terms to induce them to accept proposed accords. Second, they want to be certain their counterparts will honor the agreements achieved. If opposing parties experience post-agreement "buyer's remorse," they may refuse to honor those accords. Finally, these effective negotiators appreciate the likelihood they will encounter their current adversaries in the future. If those individuals remember them as courteous, professional, and seemingly cooperative bargainers, their future interactions are more likely to be successful.

In his insightful book *Give and Take*,[25] Adam Grant carefully distinguishes between *givers* and *takers*. Although some might think that takers, who like to claim value for themselves, would be the most successful negotiators, he demonstrates why givers tend to do better. Takers develop reputations for selfishness, which discourages others from assisting them. Givers endeavor to help others, and induce those persons to reciprocate their generosity. Nonetheless, "selfless givers," who simply work to satisfy the needs of others without seeking reciprocity for themselves tend to do poorly, because they give others far more than they get in return. "Otherish givers" work to advance the interests of others, but simultaneously strive to enhance their own gains.[26] These proficient interactors are analogous to "Competitive/Problem-Solvers" who work to maximize counterpart gains — but only after they have obtained what they really want for their own side.

---

23. *See generally* Rebecca Hollander-Blumoff, "Just Negotiation," 88 *Washington University Law Review* 381 (2010); Rebecca Hollander-Blumoff & Tom Tyler, "Procedural Justice in Negotiation: Procedural Fairness, Outcome Acceptance, and Integrative Potential," 33 *Law & Social Inquiry* 473 (2008).

24. *See* Marc-Charles Ingerson, Kristen Bell DeTienne & Katie A. Liljenquist, "Beyond Instrumentalism: A Relational Approach to Negotiation," 31 *Negotiation Journal* 31, 37–38 (2015).

25. Adam Grant, *Give and Take* (Viking 2013).

26. *See id.* at 155–185. *See also* Carsten K.W. De Dreu, Laurie W. Weingart & Seungwoo Kwon, "Influence of Social Motives on Integrative Negotiation: A Meta-Analytic Review and Test of Two Theories," 78 *Journal of Personality & Social Psychology* 889, 901–902 (2000) (finding that negotiators with a pro-social motive generated more efficient agreements than negotiators with an egoistic motive, but only when the participants had a high resistance to yielding).

Competitive/Problem-Solvers appreciate the fact that negotiators who work to advance their own interests are more likely to achieve jointly efficient results than bargainers who behave in an entirely cooperative manner.[27] I have observed this phenomenon in my own Negotiation course. Since part of course grades are determined by the comparable results students achieve on a series of bargaining exercises, they generally work to obtain beneficial terms for themselves. Nonetheless, they also learn to be incredibly efficient negotiators. They appreciate the fact that the larger the joint surplus they create, the more likely they will be able to claim a large share for themselves. At the conclusion of each exercise, I talk about what the participants should have agreed upon to maximize their joint returns. Almost always, the most successful students have agreed upon terms that are highly efficient, based upon the fact they recognize that if client satisfaction is left on the bargaining table, neither side is likely to obtain optimal results.

Although proficient negotiators frequently manipulate counterpart perceptions regarding their own side's values and settlement intentions, they almost never misrepresent *material* facts, economic data, or business information. They know that a loss of credibility would undermine their ability to achieve beneficial results. In my Negotiation class, I include the Model Rules of Professional Conduct in my course rules. If a student is accused of an ethics violation, a trial would be conducted in front of the uninvolved class members. If a breach was found, a penalty would be imposed. In all the years I have taught my course, I have never had a formal ethics charge filed. What the students opt to do instead is raise the issue informally where no penalty is sought. The students involved explain their own perceptions, and we open it up to class discussion. In most cases, the other students conclude that the behavior in question merely involved acceptable "puffing" or "embellishment." On rare occasions, however, class members suggest that improper conduct was involved. The persons described in this manner almost always end up with one or two non-settlements on future exercises, due to the fact their counterparts do not trust them. This phenomenon graphically demonstrates the importance of bargaining reputations.

In recent years, a number of litigator-lawyers have adopted the "cooperative law"[28] or the "structured negotiation"[29] approach in which they endeavor to avoid the need to file formal complaints. They agree to work together with each other and with their respective clients in an open and cooperative manner designed to enable them to generate mutually beneficial settlement agreements. This approach enables them to resolve most disputes without the need for any formal legal proceedings.

---

27. *See* Kathleen O'Connor & Peter Carnevale, "A Nasty But Effective Negotiation Strategy: Misrepresentation of a Common-Value Issue," 25 *Personality & Social Psychology Bulletin* 504, 512 (1997).

28. *See* John Lande, "Practical Insights From an Empirical Study of Cooperative Lawyers in Wisconsin," 2008 *Journal of Dispute Resolution* 203 (2008).

29. *See* Lainey Feingold, *Structured Negotiation: A Winning Alternative to Law Suits* (ABA Publishing 2016).

§ 2.04. Unprofessional Behavior Is a Substitute for Bargaining Proficiency

Over the past several decades, lawyers and business persons have become less polite toward one another. Many have become more win-lose oriented, seeming to believe that if their counterparts obtain what they want they will be unable to achieve their own objectives. Individuals who encounter rudeness and unprofessional behavior from opposing parties should appreciate the fact that such improper conduct is *not* a sign of bargaining proficiency, but just the opposite. Uncivilized behavior is a substitute for bargaining competence. Skilled negotiators do not engage in offensive conduct. They understand that such acts are unlikely to induce adversaries to give them what they want to achieve. When we dislike the persons on the other side and the way they are treating us, we want to punish them for their unacceptable actions. On the other hand, when we like adversaries, we want to satisfy their needs and dislike saying "no" to them.

Another reason why persons should behave professionally during bargaining encounters concerns the fact that individuals who begin such interactions in positive moods bargain more cooperatively, while people who begin in negative moods bargain more adversarially.[30] As a result, persons who begin bargaining interactions in positive moods achieve greater joint gains than those who begin in negative moods. Individuals who behave rudely and unprofessionally when they interact with others are likely to generate negative moods in such persons and increase the likelihood of ending up with no agreements.

§ 2.05. Conclusion

Experts tend to classify negotiators as either Cooperative/Problem-Solvers or Competitive/Adversarials. The former endeavor to generate reasonable accords that satisfy the underlying interests of both sides and maximize the joint returns achieved, while the latter seek more one-sided arrangements favoring their own sides. Far more Cooperative/Problem-Solvers are considered to be effective negotiators than Competitive/Adversarials. Highly proficient negotiators tend to employ a hybrid Competitive/Problem-Solving approach which combines the optimal traits from both groups. Although they wish to maximize their own returns, they simultaneously work to expand the overall pie and maximize counterpart returns once they have achieved their own objectives. They also realize that courteous conduct is more likely to generate positive moods in others and increase the probability of cooperative behavior and the achievement of efficient joint returns.

---

30. *See* Clark Freshman, Adele Hayes & Greg Feldman, "The Lawyer-Negotiator as Mood Scientist: What We Know and Don't Know About How Mood Relates to Successful Negotiation," 2002 *Journal of Dispute Resolution* 13, 15, 19, 22–23 (2002); Joseph P. Forgas, "On Feeling Good and Getting Your Way: Mood Effects on Negotiator Cognition and Bargaining Strategies," 74 *Journal of Personality & Social Psychology* 565, 566–568 (1998).

Chapter 3

Establishing Goals and Limits During the Critical Preparation Stage

§ 3.01 Introduction

> If you know the enemy and know yourself, you need not fear the result of a hundred battles. If you know yourself but not the enemy, for every victory gained you will also suffer a defeat. If you know neither the enemy nor yourself, you will succumb in every battle.[31]

When business persons prepare for bargaining encounters, they spend hours on the factual, economic, business, legal, and political issues, but usually no more than ten to fifteen minutes planning their *negotiation strategy*. Before they commence their interactions with opposing parties, they frequently have only three things in mind relevant to their bargaining strategy: (1) their planned opening position; (2) where they hope to end up; and (3) their bottom line. Between their opening offer and the completion of their encounter, most persons "wing it," thinking of the interaction as entirely *unstructured*.

Bargaining interactions are actually quite structured. The participants work through a series of stages until they achieve agreements or non-settlements. Individuals who understand the different stages and appreciate what they should be endeavoring to accomplish in each are far more likely to obtain better terms for their own side and more efficient overall terms than persons who lack such knowledge.

Many individuals do not begin to think strategically until they begin to interact with persons on the opposite side. They fail to appreciate the fact that the most important stage of the bargaining process takes place prior to this point. People who are thoroughly prepared for their encounters almost always achieve better results than those who are less prepared, based upon the fact that knowledge constitutes power at the bargaining table.[32] Well prepared negotiators possess the knowledge they need to value their im-

---

31. Sun Tzu, *The Art of War* 43 (J. Clavell ed., Delta, 1983).

32. *See* Lynn A. Epstein & Elena Marty-Nelson, *Empowering Negotiators* 9–28 (2019); Ronald M. Shapiro, *The Power of Nice* 81–111 (revised ed. 2015); Gavin Kennedy, *Essential Negotiation* 176–177 (2d ed. 2009); *Bargaining: Formal Theories of Negotiation* 10–11 (Oran R. Young ed., 1975).

pending interactions, and they exude a greater confidence in their positions which undermines the convictions of less prepared counterparts. As less well prepared adversaries subconsciously defer to the greater certainty exhibited by their more knowledgeable counterparts, they tend to make more frequent and larger concessions.

§ 3.02. Gathering Critical Information

When business persons are instructed to negotiate on behalf of their firms, they must initially ascertain the relevant factual, economic, and business information possessed by their superiors. They need to communicate with all of the persons who might possess pertinent information. When in doubt, it is preferable to have more, rather than less, knowledge. They must next ask the responsible firm managers what they hope to achieve through the bargaining process. If they are endeavoring to obtain future goods or services, how much are they willing to pay for such items, and where else might they obtain similar commodities from other companies? If they are seeking to hire someone, how much are they willing to pay that person, and what other terms might they offer to induce that individual to accept their compensation package? If they are contemplating a patent, copyright, or trademark licensing arrangement, would it be exclusive or non-exclusive? Would it be global or geographically limited?

If the firm is thinking about leasing or purchasing specific commercial property, the managers may focus entirely on that particular location. If they are asked probing questions regarding their intended use, it may become clear that alternate locations may be acceptable. Knowledge about these alternatives enhances this side's bargaining power by providing it with viable options if the current talks do not generate satisfactory agreements. Officers contemplating the investment of resources in other firms should be asked about their ultimate objectives. Are they willing to invest their assets in a single venture, or would they prefer to diversify their holdings? Are they willing to risk capital to achieve a higher return or would they accept a less generous return on an investment that would be more likely to preserve their initial investment? If they are considering the sale of a corporate division, would they be willing to accept future cash payments, shares of stock in the purchasing company, or in-kind payments in goods or services provided by the purchasing firm? It is especially important for negotiators to help firm officials appreciate their true underlying interests, such as their desire for respect when they believe they have been treated disrespectfully or their wish to obtain an apology from a business partner who may have behaved badly.[33]

As company negotiators explore firm interests and objectives, they must endeavor to ascertain the degree to which the deciding officials value the different items to be exchanged. Most negotiators try to divide agent goals into three basic categories: (1) essential; (2) important; and (3) desirable. *Essential terms* concern the items that must be obtained if accords are to be successfully achieved. *Important terms* concern

---

33. *See generally* William Ury, *Getting to Yes with Yourself* (2015).

things firm officials really wish to acquire, but which they would be willing to exchange for essential or more important items. ***Desirable terms*** involve items of secondary value which officials would like to obtain but which they would be willing to exchange for essential or important terms.

For each item to be negotiated, firm representatives must try to determine how much officials value different levels of attainment.[34] If the firm is thinking of selling a division, $5 million may be "essential," with amounts above that amount merely being "important." Negotiators must make these determinations for ***each item*** to be discussed, to enable them to appreciate the degree to which firm officials value different amounts of particular commodities.

Negotiators must similarly ascertain the relative values of the different items placed within each broad category. Do firm officials value Item 1 twice as much as Item 2, or two-thirds as much? How does Item 3 compare to Items 1 and 2? It can be of significant assistance for negotiators to mentally assign point values to the various terms to enable them to appreciate how they can maximize overall company satisfaction. Bargainers can use this relative value information to decide which items to seek and which to exchange for more valued terms.

When determining firm objectives, negotiators must avoid the substitution of their own values for those of the responsible company officials, appreciating the fact that the interests of those persons must guide their bargaining strategy. If they believe that company officials have unrealistic or illogical values, they can carefully explore the relevant items with those persons to induce them to reassess their true objectives.

§ 3.03. Determining Own and Counterpart Aspirations

Once negotiators have ascertained the relevant factual, economic, and business information and the underlying firm interests and objectives, they must begin to plan their bargaining strategy. They have to develop cogent theories to support the positions they plan to articulate, and anticipate the arguments they expect opposing parties to make to enable them to think of effective counter ploys.

While they are interacting with firm officials, negotiators must carefully determine their side's bottom line. How far are they willing to go in the other side's direction with respect to *each issue* before they decide to walk away and accept their non-settlement alternatives? Roger Fisher and William Ury call this their BATNA, for their Best Alternative to a Negotiated Agreement.[35] Economic game theorists often use the

---

34. *See* Howard Raiffa, *Negotiation Analysis: The Science and Art of Collaborative Decision Making* 129–147 (2003).

35. Fisher, Ury & Patton, *supra* note 11, at 101–111.

terms "reservation point" or "resistance point." It is crucial for bargainers to appreciate this point to enable them to avoid the entry into agreements that are actually worse than what would occur if no agreement was achieved.

It can be beneficial to try to use an objective basis to calculate the expected value of a particular transaction. Suppose a corporation is contemplating the sale of a division, and the managers think there is a 10 percent likelihood they will get $25 million, a 30 percent likelihood they will get at least $20 million, a 60 percent likelihood they will get at least $15 million, a 90 percent likelihood they will get at least $10,000,000, and a 100 percent likelihood they will get at least $5 million. What would be the expected value of that division?

0.10 (10%)	x	$25,000,000	$2,500,000
0.20 (30% − 10%)	x	$20,000,000	$4,000,000
0.30 (60% − 30%)	x	$15,000,000	$4,500,000
0.30 (90% − 60%)	x	$10,000,000	$3,000,000
0.10 (100% − 90%)	x	$5,000,000	$500,000
		Expected Value:	$14,500,000

Firm officials must now decide how much money they really must obtain to sell this division. If they are somewhat risk averse, they might decide to accept any amount over $12 million. On the other hand, if they are risk takers, they may decide to hold out for a minimum of $18 or even $20 million.

Once negotiators have determined their own side's expected value, they frequently make the mistake of thinking that they have completed this portion of the evaluative process. Individuals who come to this conclusion ignore an equally critical part of the Preparation Stage. They must carefully evaluate the expected value to the *opposing side*.[36] They must endeavor to place themselves in the shoes of prospective division purchasers and ask themselves how much they think those parties might be willing to pay. They have to do their best to estimate the needs and underlying interests of those entities. In addition, they must try to determine the alternative investments available to those parties if they were to forego the purchase of this company's division. If the non-settlement options available to those parties are worse than this firm's external options, this side possesses greater bargaining power. An appreciation of counterpart non-settlement alternatives also enables this side to put together a bargaining strategy designed to culminate in an offer that would be preferable to one of those entities compared with their non-settlement options.[37]

---

36. *See* Greg Williams (with Pat Iyer), *Body Language Secrets to Win More Negotiations* 108 (2016); Grande Lum, *The Negotiation Fieldbook* 58 (2d ed. 2011).

37. *See* Michael Wheeler, "The Fog of Negotiation: What Negotiators Can Learn From Military Doctrine," 29 *Negotiation Journal* 23, 26–28 (2013).

When negotiators seek to ascertain the strengths and weaknesses of their own side and of the opposing side, they have the tendency to over-estimate their own weaknesses and to under-estimate the weaknesses affecting the other side.[38] This phenomenon is generated by the fact they are intimately familiar with the positive and negative factors influencing their own side, but far less familiar with the weaknesses affecting their adversaries. They are usually relying on information provided by the other side which projects their strengths rather than their weaknesses. They must diligently seek to ascertain the true circumstances affecting that party. How much do they believe that side really needs the deal they are seeking to reach with them?

I can recall a friend who contacted me for advice regarding a critical negotiation his corporation was engaged in with another company. After he explained how their interaction had thus far developed, I asked him what would happen to his firm if no agreement was achieved. He told me they would be bankrupt. When I asked him how bad this would be, he was shocked and repeated that they would be bankrupt. I asked him if they could survive and reorganize. He thought about my inquiry and replied in the affirmative. I then asked him what would happen to the other company if they reached no agreement with his firm. He told me he had no idea. When I asked him to think about this issue, he indicated that they would also be bankrupt. I asked if they would be able to reorganize. Once he thought about it, he said "no." His firm was their primary customer, and without their continuing relationship, that company would go out of business entirely. Only at this point did he begin to appreciate the fact that he possessed greater bargaining power than the opposing party, since his corporation would survive a bankruptcy proceeding while the other corporation could not. This information enabled him to negotiate beneficial terms for his own company.

It can occasionally be beneficial for individuals preparing for difficult bargaining interactions to ask colleagues to act as their counterparts and engage in mock negotiations where those colleagues endeavor to advance the interests of the opposing sides. When their colleagues strive to generate beneficial terms for the parties they are representing, the advocates on this side can begin to appreciate the factors affecting their counterparts. What are the issues they especially value, and what are the issues they do not really care about? What strengths and weaknesses are likely to influence the bargainers on the other side? This approach can really help the negotiators on this side to appreciate the factors influencing their counterparts.

---

38. *See* Herb Cohen, *Negotiate This* 167–168 (2003).

§ 3.04. Elevated Goals Generate More Beneficial Results

Many persons commence bargaining interactions focusing primarily on their bottom lines, and they usually fail to achieve the beneficial terms that could have been obtained if they had established higher goals. They seem to fear that if they seek much more than those amounts, they will end up with no deals. This concern is not well founded. Studies show that negotiators obtain more satisfactory outcomes when they begin with elevated, rather than modest, aspirations.[39] Consistently successful negotiators take the time to establish raised aspirations before they commence interactions with others.[40] They carefully assess the relevant circumstances affecting both their own side and the opposing side and try to generate beneficial goals. How far do they believe their counterparts might be willing to move in their direction to obtain final accords? When multiple item negotiations are involved, it is important for participants to establish elevated goals for *each issue*, because if they fail to do this they would be likely to forfeit the items for which they have no such sights.

When persons establish their bargaining goals, they must create generous—but *realistically attainable*—objectives. If their targets are wholly unreasonable, they will greatly discourage their counterparts and increase the probability of non-settlements.[41] In addition, once they begin to appreciate the fact that their objectives are not attainable, they may give up on this important touchstone and fall quickly toward their bottom lines. Individuals who reach this point during bargaining encounters should temporarily terminate their present discussions to give themselves time to reassess their situations and establish lower—but still elevated—aspiration levels. Only after they do this should they continue their interaction with their adversaries.

Skilled negotiators use their *aspiration levels* as their guideposts when they interact with others, and they strive to achieve those objectives.[42] They articulate these positions as the interactions develop and provide logical explanations to support those proposals. This helps them exude confidence in these terms and may help to undermine counterpart confidence in their positions. Less skilled negotiators, however, tend to focus primarily on their bottom lines, and they relax when they attain those minimal objectives. As a result they rarely attain the generous terms they could have achieved if they had focused more on a set of elevated goals.[43]

---

39. *See* Dawson, supra note 12, at 16–17; Stuart Diamond, *Getting More* 15–19 (2010); Russell Korobkin & Joseph Doherty, "Who Wins in Settlement Negotiations?," 11 *American Law & Economics Review* 162, 175,183 (2009).

40. *See* David Lax & James Sebenius, *3-D Negotiation* 186–187 (2006); G. Richard Shell, *Bargaining for Advantage* 31–33 (1999).

41. *See* Russell Korobkin, "Aspirations and Settlement," 88 *Cornell Law Review* 1, 62–63 (2002).

42. *See* Deepak Malhotra & Max H. Bazerman, *Negotiation Genius* 48 (2007); Shell, *supra* note 40, at 28–29.

43. *See* Linda Babcock & Sara Laschever, *Ask For It* 268–269 (2008).

The most proficient bargainers frequently consummate deals that are not as good as the ones they hoped to achieve. They have established highly beneficial aspirations that they could not entirely achieve. They are disappointed and think they did not do very well. They have to appreciate the fact that the best negotiators regularly come up short due to their elevated objectives. On the other hand, their less successful cohorts are usually quite pleased when they consummate deals, since they are commensurate with the modest goals they created. This explains why I laugh when professional negotiators tell me they must be highly skilled based upon the fact they always get what they want when they interact with others. What they fail to appreciate is that there is only one way people can always get everything they want when they negotiate—establish unreasonably low aspirations! Individuals who always get what they want should raise their aspiration levels in 10 to 15 percent increments until they begin to come up short when they reach agreements. By that point, they would most likely be obtaining appropriately elevated accords.

§ 3.05. Planning Elevated Opening Positions

Many individuals like to begin their bargaining interactions with the articulation of modest proposals hoping to generate similar behavior by their adversaries that will lead to entirely cooperative win-win results. This may appear to be a completely rational approach, but it actually has the opposite effect due to a phenomenon known as *anchoring*.[44] When people receive better offers than they expected, they question their own preliminary evaluations, increase their own aspiration levels, and psychologically move away from their adversaries. This anchoring effect greatly disadvantages people who make excessively generous opening offers.[45] If their counterparts are induced to increase their own planned opening positions, it will likely cause the modest openers to make greater concessions during the interaction which will cause them to end up with terms much less beneficial than they hoped to attain. On the other hand, when individuals receive less generous opening offers, they tend to decrease their own expectations and plan to make opening offers that are more generous to their adversaries.

Proficient negotiators recognize the importance of elevated opening offers, and they carefully develop initial positions they can logically support. They anticipate that their adversaries would be likely to articulate similarly beneficial opening offers of their own, and they wish to develop an overall bargaining strategy that they hope will culminate in terms reflecting their raised aspirations. They also understand the

---

44. *See* Korobkin & Doherty, *supra* note 39, at 177–178; Dan Orr & Chris Guthrie, "Anchoring, Information, Expertise, and Negotiation: New Insights from Meta-Analysis," 21 *Ohio State Journal on Dispute Resolution* 597, 599–611 (2006). *See generally* Daniel Kahneman, *Thinking Fast and Slow* 219–228 (2011).

45. *See* Russell Korobkin & Chris Guthrie, "Psychology, Economics, and Settlement: A New Look at the Role of the Lawyer," 76 *Texas Law Review* 77, 101–107 (1997).

impact of **bracketing** which tends to generate final terms near the midpoint between the opening positions of the negotiators.[46] They thus endeavor to place themselves in the shoes of their counterparts to estimate what their opening positions and goals are likely to be, to enable them to begin with positions they believe will enable them to reach their actual objectives most effectively.

When negotiators develop their opening offers, they should concurrently develop *principled rationales* they can use to explain how they arrived at those points.[47] When they use this approach, they greatly enhance the validity of their initial positions. For example, if Side A is contemplating the purchase of a division of a firm owned by Side B, they should carefully demonstrate support for their opening offer of $25,549,000. They should value the real property, the building and equipment, the inventory, the accounts receivable, patents, copyrights, and trademarks, the sales records, the reputation of the target firm, and other relevant information in a seemingly objective manner that supports their offer. This provides them with a rational basis for their position, and helps them define the issues to be addressed.

§ 3.06. Multi-party Negotiating Teams

Persons involved in large corporate or governmental transactions are usually required to participate in negotiations that include a large number of persons—both on their own side and on the opposite side. If the interaction is to be successfully concluded, it is imperative for the people on the same side to develop unified goals and a common strategy. A large *intra-group* Preparation Stage is critical. All of the relevant interest groups must be included, and be encouraged to express their desired objectives and the means they believe should be employed to achieve the attainment of those goals. If the inter-organizational negotiations commence before a common team plan has been developed, adept counterparts will be able to exploit intra-group weaknesses. Substantive disagreements will undermine bargaining effectiveness, and strategic conflicts will preclude the presentation of a united front. If many persons are permitted to speak during the inter-organizational discussions, well organized counterparts will be able to discern and take advantage of internal conflicts. It is thus helpful to select the person or persons who will speak for the group. One individual may do all of the talking, or different persons may speak with respect to particular issues, with no one else on this side speaking without being requested to do so by their own team leader(s).

---

46. *See* Dawson, *supra* note 12, at 18–20.
47. *See* Malhotra & Bazerman, *supra* note 42, at 34–35.

§ 3.07. Choreographing the Impending Interaction

Once negotiators have established their bottom lines, their aspiration levels, and opening positions, they should take some time to plan their bargaining strategy. How do they visualize moving from where they commence their interaction to where they hope to end up? Do they plan to make a few position changes or a number of such modifications? What bargaining techniques do they expect to employ to get what they want? What tactics do they anticipate their counterparts will use, and how do they hope to counteract those actions? How do they plan to induce the opposing side to accept terms that both sides should find beneficial?

§ 3.08. Consideration of Relevant Psychological Factors

As they develop their bargaining strategy, it is important to put together a conclusion that will seem like a benefit to the persons on the opposing side due to the impact of *gain/loss framing*.[48] Individuals facing a *sure gain* or the possibility of a greater gain or no gain tend to behave in a *risk averse* manner and accept the sure gain to avoid the possibility of obtaining nothing. On the other hand, people facing a *sure loss* or the possibility of a greater loss or no loss tend to behave in a *risk taking* manner and accept the option that might provide them with no loss despite the risk of a greater loss. In most business transactions, both sides tend to view the outcomes as gains, rather than losses, whether they are the buyer or seller, lessor or lessee, licensor or licensee, new business partner, etc. As a result, both sides are more likely to be risk averse rather than risk taking. When individuals prepare for bargaining interactions, they should think of ways to make what they are going to offer to the opposing side clearly appear to be a sure gain to enhance the likelihood that party will work with them to generate definitive accords.

Many commercial negotiations involve a multitude of issues that must be mutually resolved if agreements are to be achieved. What complicates the situation concerns the fact that each term to be addressed may have various options that might be adopted. This factor can become an inhibiting force due to the *paradox of choice*.[49] When individuals have three or four choices, they tend to compare all of them together and select the one that best suits their particular needs. On the other hand, when they have fifteen or twenty alternatives, they find it impossible to compare all of them at once. They thus divide the items into smaller groups and make a series of separate comparisons. They select one from the first group, then another from the second

---

48. *See* Chris Guthrie, "Prospect Theory, Risk Preference, and the Law," 97 *Northwestern University Law Review* 1115, 1117–1127 (2003). *See also* Kahneman, *supra* note 44, at 316–318, 334–335 (2011).
49. *See generally* Barry Schwartz, *The Paradox of Choice* (2004).

group, and so forth. When they have completed this process, they should carefully compare all of the items they have selected from each of the separate groups and objectively decide the optimal one for them. Persons often fail to do this, however, because they tend to focus more on their more recent determinations rather than their earlier comparisons. Although the item they selected from the first or second group might be the best for them, they may actually choose the item they selected from the last or next-to-last group based upon the fact that term looked so good compared to the other items in that particular group. As a result of this phenomenon, they may select the incorrect item.

When negotiators know that they will have to make choices among many items on the bargaining table, they have to prepare to make their initial assessments on a group-by-group basis. Once they have made these determinations, they must be carefully to include all of the selected items together in a single final group to enable them to compare these items objectively with one another. They should seek to prevent their more recent group selections from overly influencing their final selections. When they think that the paradox of choice may be impeding the decision-making process being conducted by their counterparts, and they fear that this factor may induce those persons to make suboptimal decisions that may detract from the overall pie to be shared, they should not hesitate to assist them through the decision-making process in a manner designed to lead them to the optimal determination.

Another factor that may influence bargaining interactions concerns the ***endowment effect***.[50] When someone owns something someone else is thinking of buying, they tend to overvalue that item. This is especially true if the potential seller created the item in question, due to the fact they recall all of the time and effort that went into the development of that business, innovative technology, or other commercial property. On the other hand, potential buyers tend to evaluate such matters in a detached manner and seem to undervalue them. Negotiators should anticipate this phenomenon whether it is causing its own side to over value the items others are seeking or causing the other side to do so when they own the items being sought by this side.

One way for negotiators to minimize the impact of the endowment effect is to induce counterparts to focus primarily on what they are being offered, instead of what they are being asked to give up.[51] For example, someone thinking of purchasing a firm owned by another party should offer a realistic amount of money for that company, instead of asking that party what they would have to be paid in exchange for their business. If those persons can be induced to focus primarily of the money they are being offered, they tend to be less averse to selling what they own — and more

---

50. *See generally* Kahneman, *supra* note 44, at 289–299; Russell Korobkin, "The Endowment Effect and Legal Analysis," 97 *Northwestern University Law Review* 1227 (2003).

51. *See generally* Roman Trotschel, David D. Loschedler, Benjamin P. Hohne & Johann M. Majer, "Procedural Frames in Negotiations: How Offering My Resources vs. Requesting Yours Impacts Perception, Behavior, and Outcomes," 108 *Journal of Personality and Social Psychology* 417 (2015).

likely to sell for less money than if their primary focus was on what they were being asked to give up. On the other hand, when they are asked how much they would expect to be paid for their firm, they focus primarily on what they own and are more concession averse and more likely to expect greater compensation.

When individuals make decisions, they frequently act in ways that will enable them to avoid the likelihood they will subsequently discover that they made incorrect choices, due to a phenomenon known as *regret aversion*.[52] For example, someone considering the sale of a business may accept a current offer of $5 million despite the fact they might be able to obtain a higher figure if they held out longer, to avoid the possibility of ultimately finding out that they made the wrong decision and had to sell for less. When persons develop their negotiation strategies, they should plan to end the process with offers that regret-averse adversaries would be unlikely to reject due to the fact they might later discover they made the incorrect decision.

§ 3.09. Determining the Contextual Factors

The final issue to be contemplated concerns the *contextual factors*—the time, date, and location for the discussions. These matters can significantly influence bargaining interactions. Some negotiators may permit the opposing side to choose the location to demonstrate their cooperativeness. Nonetheless, most people feel more comfortable in familiar surroundings and prefer to negotiate at their own offices. The party that determines the date, time, and location for the interaction gains a psychological edge by obtaining such preliminary concessions from the other side.

If the discussions are to occur at your location, how do you plan to arrange the furniture? If there is a square or rectangular table, combative adversaries are likely to take seats on opposite sides of the table. Such a confrontational configuration heightens the anxiety level and lessens the possibility of a pleasant interaction. If a round or oval table is provided, and the participants are encouraged to sit more adjacent to one another, this more cooperative setting should enhance the talks. Even if a square or rectangular table must be used, if the participants can be induced to sit on adjacent sides, instead of directly across from one another, this can similarly enhance the bargaining environment. If a sofa is available, a more cooperative situation can be generated by having the parties sit next to one another.

If the discussions are to take place at your location, you should plan to provide appropriate food and drink. This can be done to make the visitors feel more comfortable—and to generate feelings of obligation that might cause them to become more reciprocal when the substantive exchanges begin.

---

52. *See generally* Kahneman, *supra* note 44, at 346–352; Chris Guthrie, "Better Settle than Sorry: The Regret Aversion Theory of Litigation Behavior," 1999 *University of Illinois Law Review* 43 (1999).

§ 3.10. Dealing with Internal Negotiator Conflicts

In their insightful article, Robert Bordone, Tobias Berkman, and Sare del Nido[53] discuss how "internal conflicts" experienced by individuals may affect and even undermine bargaining interactions with others. Individuals may initially establish elevated aspirations to advance the interests of their principals, but feel guilty about their establishment of such one-sided objectives. Someone else who plans to take a tough approach at the bargaining table may feel uncomfortable with respect to the negative impact such an approach may have on their reputation for fairness and their future dealings with their counterparts.

As persons prepare to negotiate with others, it is imperative that they recognize the existence of such internal conflicts and appreciate how such conflicts may affect their impending interactions. They must carefully decide how they should endeavor to resolve such internal conflicts and how they plan to behave. If they do so effectively, they should be able to project a definitive style and approach that should most effectively advance the interests of their own side. If they fail to resolve such conflicts, however, they may either fail to achieve agreements that would have been preferable to their non-settlement alternatives, or agree to final terms that are not as mutually beneficial as they could have been.

§ 3.11. Conclusion

During the Preparation Stage, negotiators must ascertain the relevant factual, economic, and business issues affecting their own side—and the opposing side. They then must determine their own bottom lines and goals—and those affecting the other party. They should develop elevated, but realistic, opening offers that will decrease, rather than increase, counterpart expectations due to anchoring. Their offers should appear to be gains, rather than losses, to adversaries, due to the impact of gain/loss framing. They must finally plan an overall bargaining strategy that should enable them to move effectively from where they begin to where they hope to end up.

———————

Table 3-1 sets forth a ***Negotiation Preparation Form*** that can be employed by individuals getting ready for bargaining interactions. It is designed to lead them through the areas they should focus on during the Preparation Stage.

———————

53. Robert Bordone, Tobias Berkman & Sare del Nido, "The Negotiation Within: The Impact of Internal Conflict Over Identity and Role on Across-the-Table Negotiations," 2014 *Journal of Dispute Resolution* 175 (2014).

Table 3-1 Negotiation Preparation Form

1. Your *bottom line*—minimum terms you would accept given your Best Alternative to a Negotiated Agreement (BATNA). Do not forget to include the monetary and nonmonetary transaction costs associated with both agreement and non-agreement.

2. Your *aspiration levels*—best result you hope to achieve. Be sure your goals are sufficiently elevated, and realistic. Never begin a negotiation until you have mentally solidified your ultimate objective with respect for *each item* to be negotiated.

3. Your estimate of *counterpart's bottom line.* Try to place yourself in the shoes of the other side and use their value system when estimating their bottom line.

4. Your estimate of *counterpart's aspiration levels.* Try to again use your counterpart's value system when estimating their goals.

5. Your factual, economic, and commercial *leverage* with respect to *each issue* (strengths and weaknesses). Prepare logical explanations supporting your strengths and anticipate ways in which you might minimize your own weaknesses. What is the best alternative result you could achieve through other channels if no agreement can be achieved through the current bargaining interaction? What are the monetary, psychological, tax-related, temporal, etc. costs associated with agreement and non-agreement?

6. Your *counterpart's leverage* with respect to each issue. What counter-arguments can you use to challenge the claims you expect the other side to make?

7. Your planned *opening position.* Due to the impact of *anchoring*, you are usually better off beginning with less generous, rather than more generous, opening offers. Plan rational explanations to support *each component* of your "*principled" opening offer.*

8. What *information* are you willing to disclose, and how do you plan to divulge it? It is best to disclose important information in response to counterpart questions to minimize the impact of *reactive devaluation.* How do you plan to prevent the disclosure of your sensitive information (*"Blocking Techniques"*)?

9. What *information* do you hope to elicit from your counterpart during the Information Stage to help you determine their underlying needs, interests, and objectives? What *information seeking questions* do you plan to use?

10. What is your *negotiation strategy: agenda and tactics*? How do you envision moving from where you begin the interaction to where you hope to end up? Plan your anticipated *concession pattern* carefully to disclose only the information you intend to divulge and prepare principled explanations to support each anticipated concession.

11. Your prediction of *counterpart's negotiation strategy* and your planned countermeasures. How may you neutralize your adversary's strengths and exploit their weaknesses?

12. What *negotiation techniques* do you plan to employ to advance your interests? Be prepared to vary them and to combine some for optimal impact.

13. What *negotiating techniques* do you expect your counterpart to use, and how do you plan to counter those tactics?

14. If a number of persons from your side must participate in the interaction, conduct an intra-organization meeting during which you can establish common goals and a common bargaining strategy. Which members of your bargaining team will be authorized to address the different issues involved?

Chapter 4

Using the Preliminary Stage to Establish Rapport and the Tone for the Interaction

§ 4.01. Establishing Rapport and Tone

When inexperienced persons commence bargaining interactions with others, they frequently make the mistake of immediately moving toward the substantive discussions. They fail to appreciate the importance of taking a few minutes to establish personal rapport with their counterparts and the tone for the encounter. If they have had many prior dealings with the individuals on the other side, they would most likely be familiar with their bargaining styles. Nonetheless, they should still take some time to reestablish relationships and cordial environments that should positively influence their impending encounters. Bargainers who have not had significant prior dealings with one another should endeavor to obtain information regarding such persons from others they know. They should ask if they are cooperative or competitive, pleasant or unpleasant, and trustworthy or untrustworthy.[54] They should then spend the initial period of their interaction establishing good personal relationships, their professional identities, and the tone for their substantive discussions.[55]

During the preliminary part of their encounter, the participants should look for common interests they share with each other.[56] When they first meet, a nice handshake and a warm smile can help to establish a good relationship and a positive environment.[57] Are they from the same state or metropolitan area, did they attend the same college, do their children attend the same schools, do they enjoy the same music or sports, etc.? They should avoid controversial issues such as politics. Individuals who

---

54. *See* Donald Dell, *Never Make the First Offer* 86 (2009).

55. *See* Raymond Saner, *The Expert Negotiator* 157–158 (3d ed. 2008).

56. *See* Daniel Shapiro, *Negotiating the* Nonnegotiable 175–191 (2016); Daniel Goleman, *Social Intelligence* 29–30 (2006); Roger Fisher & Daniel Shapiro, *Beyond Reason: Using Emotions as You Negotiate* 55–56 (2005).

57. *See* Marc O. Opresnik, *The Hidden Rules of Successful Negotiation and Communication* 43–44 (2013).

discover that they share common interests enhance the probability they will like each other and develop mutually beneficial relationships.[58]

Individuals who encounter seemingly cooperative adversaries should carefully endeavor to ascertain whether those persons' apparent predisposition toward open interactions is consistent with their actual behavior. They should be sure that their initial disclosures are matched by similar disclosures from those people. If their openness does not seem to be reciprocated, they need to behave more strategically and become less forthright. If they continue to be naively open when their candor is not being returned, they will almost always place themselves at a distinct disadvantage.

Studies have found that competitive individuals tend to behave competitively regardless of the behavior of their counterparts, while cooperative persons tend to behave like those with whom they are interacting. This phenomenon is caused by the fact that competitive people believe that others are similarly adversarial, while cooperative persons tend to view the world as being composed of both cooperative and competitive parties.[59] Naturally cooperative negotiators feel more comfortable interacting with other cooperative bargainers, since this enables them to employ their natural style. Nonetheless, when they have to interact with more adversarial persons, they appreciate the fact that they have to behave more competitively to avoid the exploitation that would result is they behaved in a naively open manner.

Negotiators must similarly work to establish positive atmospheres when they begin their interactions. Studies have demonstrated that individuals who commence bargaining encounters in positive moods negotiate more cooperatively, share more information, are more trusting of others, reach more agreements, and are more likely to use problem-solving techniques to maximize the joint returns achieved by the parties.[60] Individuals who begin such interactions in negative moods behave in a more adversarial manner, achieve fewer accords, and tend to generate less efficient terms. In addition, negative mood negotiators are more likely to employ deceptive tactics than are positive mood interactors.[61]

---

58. *See* Chris Guthrie, "Principles of Influence in Negotiation," 87 *Marquette Law Review* 829, 831 (2004); Christopher W. Moore, *The Mediation Process* 184–185 (3d ed. 2003).

59. *See* Jeffrey Rubin & Bert Brown, *The Social Psychology of Bargaining and Negotiation* 185 (1975).

60. *See* R.B. Lount, Jr., "The Impact of Positive Mood on Trust in Interpersonal and Intergroup Interactions," 98 *Journal of Personality & Social Psychology* 420, 421–422 (2010); Erin Ryan, "The Discourse Beneath: Emotional Epistemology in Legal Deliberation and Negotiation," 10 *Harvard Negotiation Law Review* 231, 269–270 (2005).

61. *See* Clark Freshman, Adele M. Hayes & Greg C. Feldman, "The Lawyer-Negotiator as Mood Scientist: What We Know and Don't Know About How Mood Relates to Successful Negotiation," 2002 *Journal of Dispute Resolution* 13, 22–24 (2002).

§ 4.02. Using Attidudinal Bargaining to Counter Negative Behavior

Negotiators who encounter overly competitive "win-lose" adversaries should endeavor to diminish the negative tendencies of such persons. They may employ friendly introductions and warm handshakes to establish more personal and professional relationships. They should use an extended Preliminary Stage to enhance the bargaining environment. They should endeavor to create a positive bargaining atmosphere by trying not to sit across the table from the people on the other side, which is a highly confrontational configuration. They might ask their counterparts about their families or their colleagues, and share similar information regarding themselves. I try to establish first name personal relationships, because it tends to be easier to be rude toward persons we do not think of personally.

When these preliminary endeavors fail to diminish the adversarial behavior of such persons, negotiators can employ "*attitudinal bargaining*" to encourage more cooperative and pleasant conduct.[62] They should indicate their unwillingness to view negotiations as a combative process, and suggest the need to establish preliminary ground rules designed to induce the participants to function in a more cooperative and cordial manner. They might also indicate that their firm is looking for an ongoing and mutually beneficial relationship, and does not wish to conduct business with anyone who behaves in a negative way.

If attitudinal bargaining fails to change negative counterpart conduct and the negotiations must continue due to operational necessities, individuals who have to interact with offensive adversaries should try to control their encounters in ways that minimize the degree to which such persons can offend them. They might conduct much of their transaction through telephone discussions. If the negative behavior of their counterparts begins to bother them, they can indicate that they have another call and temporarily end their talks. They may alternatively exchange important information electronically. If they receive an offensive reply, they should wait until they have calmed down before they respond.

§ 4.03 Turn Off Electronic Devices before You Commence In-Person Bargaining with Others

We have become a high-technology society in which many individuals are constantly checking their iPhones and Blackberries for calls or messages. When individuals engage in such behavior during in-person bargaining interactions with others, they

---

62. *See* Raiffa, *supra* note 34, at 300–301. See generally William Ury, *The Power of a Positive No* (2007); William Ury, *Getting Past No* (1991).

are likely to undermine the process.[63] Studies show that persons who interrupt in person discussions to check their electronic devices are perceived by others as being less professional and less trustworthy than persons who refrain from such behavior. In addition, due to the fact that individuals distracted by such devices tend to listen less effectively and to miss more nonverbal signals than negotiators focusing more intently on their bargaining interactions, such persons tend to generate less beneficial results for themselves.

If someone is expecting a critical telephone or text message while they are negotiating with someone else, they should tell that person about this situation and plan to take a short break when the call or message is received. This will enable them to concentrate on the external message, and prevent them from losing focus on their bargaining discussions. To avoid offending the other side, they should apologize for the interruption, and turn off their electronic devices once talks resume.

§ 4.04 Conclusion

Negotiators should employ the Preliminary Stage to establish rapport with the persons on the opposing side, and to generate positive bargaining environments. Such conduct increases the probability that agreements will be achieved and the likelihood the final terms will be jointly efficient. If counterparts commence interactions in offensive manners, people should use "attitudinal bargaining" to modify such behavior. They should also turn off their electronic devices during in-person negotiations to avoid being perceived as rude and untrustworthy.

---

63. *See* Aparna Krishnan, Terri R. Kurtzberg & Charles E. Naquin, "The Curse of the Smartphone: Electronic Multitasking in Negotiations," 30 *Negotiation Journal* 191 (2014).

Chapter 5

Creating Value through the Information Stage

Once negotiators have established their identities and the tone for their interaction, they enter the Information Stage. The participants can generally recognize when this portion of their interaction begins, as the discussions shift from small talk to questions regarding each other's needs and interests. During this portion of the encounter, the negotiators work to determine the items they have to share with one another. Each side hopes to discern the primary objectives and underlying interests of the other side. Skilled bargainers look for ways to expand to overall pie to be divided, recognizing that in most circumstances the parties do not value the different items identically and oppositely. The more effectively the participants can expand the pie, the more efficiently they should be able to structure a mutual accord.[64]

§ 5.01. Importance of Information-Seeking Questions

The most effective way to elicit information from counterparts is to *ask questions*.[65] During the early portion of the Information Stage, many individuals make the mistake of asking narrow questions that can be answered with minimal replies. As a result, they tend to merely confirm what they already know. It is more effective to *ask expansive, open-ended, information-seeking questions* that induce counterparts to talk. The more such persons speak, the more information they directly and indirectly disclose. Negotiators who suspect something about a particular area should formulate several expansive questions pertaining to that area. The responding parties frequently assume that the questioners know more about their side's circumstances than they actually do, and they over answer the inquiries being propounded. They thus provide more information than they would have in response to more narrowly phrased questions.

Only after negotiators have obtained a significant amount of information through general inquiries should they begin to narrow their questions to confirm what they

---

64. *See* Steve Gates, *The Negotiation* Book 86–87 (Capstone 2016); Mnookin, Peppet & Tulumello, *supra* note 11, at 11–43.

65. *See* Peter Stark & Jane Flaherty, *The Only Negotiating Guide You'll Ever Need* 32–45 (2017); Ronald M. Shapiro, *The Power of Nice* 81–111 (2015); Jeswald W. Salacuse, *The Global Negotiator* 48–52 (2003); Leigh Thompson, *The Mind and Heart of the Negotiator* 60–61 (1998).

believe they have heard. If counterparts endeavor to avoid direct answers to such inquiries to preclude the disclosure of specific information, the questioners should reframe their inquiries in a manner that compels more definitive responses.[66] Once individuals think they have obtained a good deal of counterpart information, they should shift to "what" and "why" questions. The *what questions* are employed to ascertain the real objectives of the other side. What do they really need to obtain? The *why questions* are designed to probe the *underlying interests* reflected in those goals. Why do they really wish to obtain what they are seeking?

Questioners should carefully listen for *verbal leaks* that inadvertently disclose important information. For example, a counterpart might say: "We're *not inclined* [or *do not wish*] to pay more than $10 million." The emphasized words suggest that they are actually willing to go over that figure. They do not feel comfortable lying about their side's settlement intentions, even though they may ethically puff about such issues. To assuage their consciences, they truthfully say that they are "not inclined" or "do not wish" to go higher — even though they will do so if necessary to consummate the deal. As the discussions continue, they might say: "We *have to have* Item 1, we *really want* Item 2, and would *like to get* Item 3." Item 1 is *essential* — they have to get it. Item 2 is *important* — they really want it, but would give it up for something more valuable. Item 3 is *desirable* — they would like to obtain it, but would exchange it for anything they consider essential or important.

Negotiators must listen intently and observe carefully during the Information Stage.[67] They should maintain supportive eye contact to encourage further counterpart disclosures, and to discern verbal leaks and nonverbal signals. Smiles and occasional head nods are likely to generate more open responses from people who feel they are being heard. Occasional "mm-hms" or "I see" can be used to encourage additional disclosures, as can silent periods following counterpart responses. Active listeners often summarize what they have heard to let the speakers know that they are paying close attention to what those persons are saying. Questioners should take few notes, since when they are taking such notes they miss much of what is then being said. Negotiators must not only listen carefully to what is being said by their counterparts, but should also be aware of what is not being covered, since omitted areas may suggest weaknesses their counterparts do not wish to address.

Once the negotiators have identified the different issues to be exchanged, they should begin to determine the relative value of each of those items to the other side. They should ask whether Item 1 is more important than Item 2 or Item 3. How much more does the other side value Item 1 versus Item 2 — twice as much or only fifty percent more? How do Items 1 and 2 compare to Item 3? Questioners should listen carefully for verbal leaks that may disclose the relative interests of their counterparts. Bargainers should also endeavor to identify *compatible terms* that both sides would

---

66. *See* Donald G. Gifford, *Legal Negotiation: Theory and Applications* 102–104 (2d ed. 2007).
67. *See* Jeff Weiss, *HBR Guide to Negotiating* 72–73 (2016).

like to have resolved in the same manner, to ensure that these items will be included in their final accords.

Negotiators should proceed patiently during the Information Stage. It takes time for the persons being questioned to decide what should be disclosed, when it should be disclosed, and how they should divulge it.[68] Impatient persons rush through the Information Stage, because they can hardly wait to begin the distributive portion of their interactions. Individuals who behave in this manner usually fail to obtain crucial pieces of information, and ultimately achieve agreements that are not as efficient as those they could have obtained through the use of more deliberate inquiries.

§ 5.02. Benefits of Inducing Counterparts to Make Initial Offers

Many negotiators prefer to make the first offer, because they believe that this approach will enable them to anchor the bargaining range and discourage unrealistic counterpart position statements. This can be an effective approach when both sides have a good understanding of the items to be exchanged, and they are relatively cooperative bargainers. When these factors are not present, however, most proficient negotiators prefer to induce their counterparts to go first.[69]

If one or both sides have miscalculated the value of the interaction, whoever goes first will disclose the mistake and place themselves at a distinct disadvantage. Even though skilled negotiators can often predict accurately the areas in which their counterparts would be likely to open, they can never be certain. Their adversaries may have over-estimated this side's strengths or over-estimated their own weaknesses, and their initial offer will usually disclose this error.

Persons planning to make the first offers during bargaining interactions should formulate proposals focusing on what they are offering to their counterparts, instead of focusing on what they are endeavoring to obtain from the persons on the other side. By inducing their counterparts to begin with a focus on what this side is willing to give up, they are more likely to induce their counterparts to be more amenable to concessions and enhance the likelihood the offerors will be able to obtain more of what they wish to obtain from the persons on the other side.[70] On the other hand, when the individuals on the other side articulate first offers, if those persons focus on what this side has that those people want to obtain, rather than on what that side possesses and is offering to this side, this similarly induces the individuals making the opening offer to be more amenable to concessions, and significantly enhances

---

68. *See* Chris Voss, *Never Split the Difference* 30 (2016).

69. *See id.* at 129–130.

70. *See generally* Roman Trotschel, David D. Loschelder, Benjamin P. Hohne & Johann M. Majer, "Procedural Frames in Negotiations: How Offering My Resources vs. Requesting Yours Impacts Perception, Behavior, and Outcomes," 108 *Journal of Personality and Social Psychology* 417 (2015).

the likelihood the recipients of such opening offers will be able to obtain beneficial terms for themselves. If such initial offerors announce positions focusing primarily on what they have and are attempting to trade for something possessed by their counterparts, the recipients of such offers should try to get those persons to focus primarily on what they wish to obtain.

A second reason to elicit opening offers from counterparts concerns the responding side's ability to use *bracketing* to advance its own interests. Once adversaries have articulated their initial offers, the respondents can bracket their objectives by adjusting their own opening offers to place their goals near the mid-point between their respective opening positions.[71] For example, if a firm seller hopes to obtain $25 million and a prospective purchaser initially offers $20 million, the seller can counter with an opening demand of $30 million to keep their $25 million target in the middle. As the parties move together toward the center of their initial positions, due to the presumed obligation to make reciprocal concessions, the party that went second is more likely to obtain the sum it desires.

An additional reason to get counterparts to make initial offers concerns the fact that negotiators who make the *first concessions* tend to obtain less beneficial outcomes than their adversaries.[72] Such persons tend to be anxious bargainers who make more and larger position changes than their counterparts. Individuals who induce their adversaries to make the initial offers usually find it easier to persuade them to make the first concessions.

In some commercial situations, the usual business practices suggest which side should make the first offer. For example, someone who has decided to sell her business may be expected to announce the price she hopes to obtain. On the other hand, someone wishing to obtain the right to use patented technology may be expected to make the opening offer. Despite these expectations, however, skilled negotiators who might otherwise be expected to go first may be able to induce less patient counterparts to articulate opening offers. By prolonging the Preliminary Stage discussions and the early portions of the Information Stage, they can frequently induce less patient adversaries to initiate the substantive talks through the announcement of initial positions.

§ 5.03. Never Accept Counterpart Opening Offers

Negotiators should never accept the opening offers articulated by their counterparts.[73] They should respond with counteroffers of their own and let their adversaries talk them up or down. Even when they believe that counterpart offers are wonderful,

---

71. *See* Dawson, *supra* note 12, at 124–125.

72. *See* Kritzer, *supra* note 13, at 68; Robert M. Bastress & Joseph D. Harbaugh, *Interviewing, Counseling, and Negotiating* 493 (1990).

73. *See* Dawson, *supra* note 12, at 26–31.

they should work to get those persons to move up or down somewhat before they accept definitive terms. This allows their counterparts to think that their bargaining efforts influenced the final outcomes, and helps to leave such persons with the belief they obtained good deals. When opening offers are quickly accepted, the opening bidders frequently experience "buyer's remorse" and endeavor to get out of what they now think are bad deals. It is critical to always remember the importance of the *bargaining process* and the degree to which negotiators want to think that process evolved in a fair manner.

§ 5.04. Multiple Item Negotiations

When a number of different terms have to be negotiated, the participants should seek to discover the degree to which each side values each item. They can sometimes ascertain this information from the manner in which the serious discussions commence. It is difficult to bargain about 20 or 30 terms simultaneously. As a result, negotiators usually begin the serious talks focusing on no more than four or five items.[74] Some individuals begin with their important issues, believing that if accords can be achieved with respect to these matters the remaining issues should not be difficult to resolve. This approach is risky, however, due to that fact that when parties begin their substantive talks on the major items, they frequently reach a quick impasse. The distance between their initially stated positions seems insurmountable, and they think no agreement is possible.

It is usually preferable to begin the serious discussions with a focus on some of the less significant items to enable the participants to expeditiously reach tentative agreements with respect to these items. Such preliminary agreements are contingent on final agreements on the remaining issues, but can be highly beneficial to the bargaining process. As the negotiators tentatively resolve 40, 60, and possibly 75 percent of the issues to be addressed, they become psychologically committed to the achievement of overall accords. When they get to the more controverted topics, they remember the success they have already achieved and work diligently to conclude their discussions successfully.

It is usually obvious whether their counterparts have begun with their more important or less important terms simply from the context involved. If they begin with five items, four of which are important to this side, it is almost certain that all five are critical to the opposing side. Similarly, if they begin with five items, four of which are of minimal value to this side, all five are probably insignificant to them. As the interaction develops, in the first instance this side should endeavor to trade the item they do not value to the other side for something this side does value. In the second instance, they should subtly work to get the one item they do value in exchange for one or two of the other four terms they do not consider important.

---

74. *See* Deepak Malhotra, *Negotiating the Impossible* 11–21 (2016).

§ 5.05. Disclosing and Withholding Important Information

When people prepare for bargaining interactions, they must carefully decide several things regarding their own information. First, what information are they going to disclose, and how should they divulge it? Second, what sensitive information do they wish to withhold, and how do they plan to accomplish this objective? If they resolve these issues before they have to work with persons from the other side, they are more likely to accomplish their objectives successfully.

Negotiators who openly disclose their important information are likely to encounter several problems. As they naively disclose their interests and objectives, their statements may not be heard by counterparts who are not listening intently to their statements as they internally contemplate their own responses. In addition, when adversaries do hear the information being divulged, they tend to discount it due to *reactive devaluation*.[75] They assume that the volunteered disclosures are manipulative and self-serving, and they discount much of what they hear.

Individuals who wish to have their critical information heard and respected should disclose that information slowly in response to counterpart questions. When they behave in this manner, their adversaries tend to hear more of what they say, because people listen more intently to the answers to their own questions. They also attribute these disclosures to their questioning ability, and accord what they hear greater respect.

What should bargainers do when adversaries ask them about areas they would prefer not to address? In some instances, they can respond with answers that do not really divulge anything of significance. Their counterparts may accept these responses and not propound further inquiries. On other occasions, however, such superficial replies are unlikely to work. When this occurs, the persons being questioned can employ *blocking techniques*.[76] Individuals wishing to observe the adroit employment of such tactics need only watch politicians being interviewed on talk shows. It is amazing how infrequently they actually answer the inquiries being propounded!

The first blocking technique involves an effort to ignore the question being asked. The recipient of the inquiry simply continues their discussion as if they never heard the question. If they do this effectively, they may be able to induce their naïve counterpart to get caught up again in their own talks, which may cause that person to not appreciate the fact no answer has been provided.

Someone who is asked a two- or three-part question should respond to the portion they like and ignore the rest. If they can induce their adversary to focus on the issues being addressed, that person may forget to restate the other parts of the initial inquiry. The person being asked may choose to over- or under-answer the question being articulated. For example, if she is asked a specific question, she can provide

---

75. *See* Mnookin, Peppet & Tulumello, *supra* note 11, at 165.
76. *See* Kritzer, supra note 13, at 68; Bastress & Harbaugh, *supra* note 72, at 493.

a general reply; if she is asked a general question, she can provide a narrow reply. The recipient of the inquiry may misinterpret the question and respond to the question reframed by her. For example, when politicians are asked if they are willing to raise taxes, they almost always suggest that the questioner must be concerned about the deficit, and they address that issue! By misconstruing the inquiry, the responding party can steer the discussion in the direction she would like to see it move. If they do this effectively, the initial questioner often fails to restate the original inquiry.

Negotiators are occasionally asked about privileged or confidential company information. Individuals asking such questions hope to catch the targets off-guard and induce them to reveal information that should remain private. When individuals prepare for bargaining encounters, they should think about the firm information they are unwilling to divulge. When they are asked about such areas, they should calmly indicate that they will not respond to such inquiries due to the confidential nature of the information being sought. Once their counterparts realize that such questions will not work, they will move on to other areas.

People should not use the same blocking technique over and over again. They must carefully employ them on a limited basis when truly needed, and they should vary the way in which they defer the inquiries in issue. They might ignore one question, partially answer another, over- or under-answer a third, misinterpret a fourth, and rule out of bounds a fifth. If they are able to do this effectively, most counterparts will not even realize the amount of information being withheld.

§ 5.06. Exploring the Underlying Needs and Interests

When less proficient negotiators interact, they tend to focus entirely on the items initially articulated. They assume a fixed pie, based upon their belief that both sides value the identical issues. If they operate in this manner, they either fail to achieve any agreement, due to their overt competition for the same terms, or they agree to inefficient accords which leave a substantial amount of party satisfaction on the bargaining room floor. To avoid this type of disaster, bargainers must learn to go behind the stated positions and endeavor to explore the interests underlying those terms. The optimal way to accomplish this objective is through the use of non-adversarial questions designed to elicit a greater degree of bargainer candor. One-sided leading inquiries should be replaced by more neutral questions that may enable the bargaining parties to explore the underlying interests of both sides in a manner that will enable them to look for areas that would generate joint gains.[77]

Even when negotiations concern primarily monetary considerations, they should not be considered zero sum endeavors. One side may value money far more than

---

77. *See* Raiffa, *supra* note 34, at 198–201; Mnookin, Peppet & Tulumello, *supra* note 11, at 11–44; Fisher, Ury & Patton, *supra* note 11, at 41–57.

the other, and that side should give up anything it can in nonmonetary areas to protect its focus on the money. The side seeking money may have to have a certain amount to consummate any deal, yet it may be happy to forego much more than that sum in exchange for other terms. The party seeking monetary results may be willing to accept payments over a number of years, or be amenable to in-kind payments such as the provision of goods and services instead of cash. If the other side does not have a substantial amount of cash available, this alternative may prove to be mutually beneficial.

Most business interactions involve a number of different issues, and they are almost always valued differently by the opposing sides. This allows bargaining parties to explore exchanges that will simultaneously benefit both sides. Which items does Side A consider essential that Side B only considers important or desirable, and which items does Side B consider Essential that Side A considers less valuable? For example, when two corporations are contemplating the creation of a joint venture, one company may really wish to have its own name associated with the new business, while the other wants to retain the exclusive patent rights to certain technologies it is contributing to the new enterprise. Alternatively, a firm endeavoring to license patent rights to a new technology may only wish to have the rights in a limited geographical area which is of substantial benefit to the patent holder that has other companies interested in the license rights in other areas. By agreeing to the terms that generate the best results for each side, the bargainers can achieve accords that maximize the joint returns generated.

Business representatives often think of themselves as entirely logical and unemotional persons who should deal with all issues in an objective manner. They forget that all individuals are emotional, and may be personally offended by the manner in which they have been treated by superiors, subordinates, or colleagues, or by business partners, suppliers, or customers. In such situations, it may be critical for the negotiating parties to acknowledge and address the underlying emotional issues if they hope to resolve the existing controversies.[78] One side may have to express its concerns in a cathartic fashion, while the other may need to offer an apology to let the other side know that it is concerned about these issues. Until these concerns have been addressed, it may be quite difficult to resolve the other objective matters that must be tackled.

§ 5.07. Conclusion

During the Information Stage, the parties should focus on the needs and interests of each side. It is initially beneficial to begin the discussions with open-ended, information-seeking questions designed to elicit expansive responses. Once the general information has been exposed, the parties should employ more "what" and "why"

---

78. *See* Daniel Shapiro, *Negotiating the Nonnegotiable* 172–173 (Viking 2016).

questions to identify the specific issues involved and the underlying interests of the parties. It is usually helpful to begin the serious talks by focusing on the less important terms, to enable the participants to begin to achieve tentative agreements with respect to those items. This helps to generate a joint psychological commitment to an overall accord which enhances the likelihood an agreement will be obtained. It is normally more effective for parties to disclose their important information in response to counterpart inquiries due to the "reactive devaluation" which occurs when such information is unilaterally volunteered. When negotiators are asked about sensitive areas, they should employ "blocking techniques" to avoid disclosing more than they wish to divulge.

Parties should not assume fixed pies in which the parties value the various terms identically. Negotiators should attempt to determine the items Side A values more than Side B and Side B values more than Side A, to enable each side to exchange the items they value less for the ones they value more. When particular demands are unacceptable to one side, it should try to explore the underlying interests of the party seeking those terms to see if there is another way in which it might satisfy their underlying objectives. If emotional issues are involved, these may have to be addressed carefully before the truly substantive terms can be resolved.

Chapter 6

Claiming Value through the Distributive and Closing Stages

The transition from the Information Stage to the Distributive Stage is generally obvious. The participants cease asking each other what they want and why they want it, and begin to indicate what they wish to obtain and what they might be willing to concede. During the Information Stage, the focus is almost entirely on the *other side*, as negotiators endeavor to determine the size of the surplus they have to share with each other and to ascertain the degree to which the other side values the items involved. When they enter the Distributive Stage, each side begins to focus on its *own needs*, as the participants begin to claim the items they have discovered.

During the Information Stage, Cooperative/Problem-Solvers have usually been quite open regarding their needs and interests, while Competitive/Adversarials have tended to be more closed and manipulative. They are more likely to have over- and under-stated the value of different items for strategic reasons. Competitive/Problem-Solvers have generally been more open and less manipulative than Competitive/Adversarials, but less candid than Cooperative/Problem-Solvers as they worked to create circumstances that would enable them to claim more of the joint surplus in the end.

Many academics like to put together negotiation exercises which include issues valued quite differently by the two sides involved, to enable them to generate mutually beneficial win-win accords without having to compete for terms valued by both sides. Such exercises ignore the fact that almost all business encounters concern some important terms which both sides want to obtain. Most candid business representatives admittedly hope to claim more of these distributive items for their own firm. Ron Shapiro and Mark Jankowski have forthrightly acknowledged this objective. "[W]e're out to achieve *all* (or most) of *our* goals, to make *our most desirable deal*. But the best way to do so is to let the other side achieve *some* of *their* goals, to make their acceptable deal."[79] It is critical for negotiators to appreciate the fact that during this portion of their interactions both sides are competing for these mutually desired terms.[80]

---

79. Shapiro & Jankowski, *supra* note 22, at 5 (emphasis in original).

80. *See* Charles B. Craver, "The Inherent Tension Between Value Creation and Value Claiming During Bargaining Interactions," 12 *Cardozo Journal of Conflict Resolution* 1 (2010).

§ 6.01. Need for Carefully Planned Concession Patterns

Proficient negotiators begin the Distributive Stage with the articulation of highly principled position statements that logically explain why they deserve the terms they are seeking. This approach bolsters their own confidence, and undermines the confidence of less prepared counterparts. They also have carefully prepared concession patterns in mind that will enable them to move from their opening offers to their true objectives.[81] They may have in mind a series of incremental position changes or the making of several larger concessions. They intend to make "*principled concessions*" that rationally explain why they are making the position changes being announced. This lets their counterparts know why they are making these precise modifications, and why larger position changes are not currently warranted. It also provides them with the confidence they need to remain at their new positions until they obtain reciprocal concessions from the other side.

The timing of position changes is critical, because of the messages associated with such actions. Anxious negotiators find it difficult to deal with the uncertainty associated with bargaining interactions, and they frequently make rapid concessions in an effort to generate agreements. Some of these are made without reciprocal position changes from the other side. Such persons forget the fact that 80 percent of concessions tend to occur during the last 20 percent of negotiations.[82] People who use such tactics to expedite the bargaining process usually pay a high price for their impatience by conceding far more to their counterparts than they receive in return.[83]

Concession patterns must be thoughtfully formulated and announced in a tactical manner. When properly employed, a position change can signal a cooperative attitude. It can also communicate the need for an opposing side counteroffer if the bargaining process is to continue to move forward. If impatiently issued in an illogical manner, however, a concession can signal a loss of control. This is particularly likely when a change is announced in a tentative and unprincipled manner by someone who continues to speak nervously and defensively after the concession has been provided. Such an approach signals that the speaker does not expect immediate reciprocity. When a proficient negotiator encounters such individuals, she should subtly encourage them to keep talking in the hope she may be able to generate additional, unreciprocated position changes. To avoid such circumstances, skilled individuals articulate their concessions with logical explanations, then become silent to shift the focus to their counterparts in a manner designed to indicate the need for those persons to reciprocate.

The exact amount and precise timing of each position change is crucial. Each successive concession should be smaller than the preceding one, and each should usually

---

81. *See* Freund, *supra* note 22, at 130–141.
82. *See* Dawson, *supra* note 12, at 172.
83. *See* Samfrits Le Poole, *Never Take No for an Answer* 72 (2d ed. 1991).

be made in response to an appropriate position change by the opposing side. If a change is larger than the preceding ones, this is usually a sign of anxiety and ineptitude.

Even though negotiators should carefully plan their concession patterns in advance, they must remain flexible in recognition of the fact they may encounter unanticipated counterpart behavior. As they obtain new information regarding adversary strengths, weaknesses, and interests, they must be prepared to modify their initial plans.[84] On the other hand, they must remain patient, recognizing that many interactions take longer to complete than they may have originally anticipated. When position changes are modest and the issues are numerous and/or complex, negotiators must permit the process to unfold deliberately. Persons who rush the process generally place themselves at a tactical disadvantage.[85]

During the Distributive Stage, negotiators should primarily focus on their *aspirations*, instead of their bottom lines, to enable them to seek the results they really hope to obtain. Nonetheless, they must always be aware of their current non-settlement alternatives, especially as they approach their bottom lines. They need to appreciate the fact that it is irrational to agree to terms that are less beneficial than their external options. As this stage unfolds and participants approach their resistance points, many persons feel greater pressure to achieve agreements, when the opposite should be true. When the terms being offered by adversaries are not much better than their non-settlement options, the participants approaching their bottom lines possess more—rather than less—bargaining power due to the fact they have little to lose from non-settlements. Due to the fact they have little to lose if no accords are generated, they should not be afraid to reject the disadvantageous proposals currently on the table. Since at this point their counterparts are likely to lose more from non-settlements than they would lose, these persons should confidently demand further concessions as a prerequisite to additional discussions.

During the Distributive Stage, negotiators frequently hide their non-settlement alternatives to avoid letting their counterparts know their likely bottom lines. When individuals possess truly viable external options, they should not hesitate to disclose—to at least some degree—this fact. The more their adversaries appreciate the availability of these alternatives, the more likely they will understand the need for them to be more accommodating.

When specific position changes are met with unreceptive counterpart responses, negotiators can use their questioning skills to direct the attention of those persons toward the areas that may enable the parties to generate joint gains. These inquiries may enable them to elicit information from their counterparts regarding their underlying needs and interests.[86] As they obtain insights pertaining to the other side's value system, they should disclose information regarding their own side's objectives.

---

84. *See* P.H. Gulliver, *Disputes and Negotiations: A Cross-Cultural Perspective* 100 (1979).
85. *See* Rubin & Brown, *supra* note 59, at 145.
86. *See* Max H. Bazerman & Margaret A. Neal, *Negotiating Rationally* 90–95 (1992).

This helps the parties generate a certain degree of trust, and encourages them to employ a problem-solving approach.

As they move through the Distributive Stage, negotiators should listen carefully for *verbal leaks* that may clearly indicate the willingness of their counterparts to modify their present positions. For example, that person may say that she "does *not want* to go higher," which is a clear indication she will do so. They should similarly look for *nonverbal signals* that might suggest greater counterpart flexibility or interest.[87]

Even proficient negotiators may find themselves moving toward premature impasses. Before they allow this phenomenon to sever their talks, they should look for alternatives that might enable them to keep the discussions going.[88] They might reframe particular issues—especially emotional ones—to find more neutral language that would be acceptable to both sides. One—or both—sides may issue apologies that could significantly diminish hard feelings. The bargainers might also take a short break from their substantive discussions and talk about sports, weather, mutual friends, or similar topics hoping to diminish the present tension. It can be helpful for someone to recount a humorous story that will remind the participants not to take the present situation too seriously. They might even take a recess to allow both sides to calm down and to consider their current positions.

§ 6.02. Resort to Power Bargaining Tactics

Once negotiators move into the Distributive Stage, both competitive and cooperative negotiators usually employ some degree of power bargaining as they endeavor to claim for their own side some of the items both sides value.[89] They use this approach to convince their counterparts that they have to provide them with more generous terms than they actually must provide. This objective is most easily accomplished by inducing those persons to reassess their own circumstances. Have they over-estimated their own side's strength? Have they under-estimated this side's power? Negotiators can greatly expand their own power by convincing adversaries that they possess either greater strength or less vulnerability than their counterparts believe they do.[90] They may casually refer to non-settlement alternatives their counterparts might not realize could be available to them, or suggest ways in which they could avoid negative consequences the other side thinks they would suffer if no agreement was reached.

Self-confidence is one of the most important attributes possessed by proficient negotiators. They exude an inner peace, and always seem to be in control of the cir-

---

87. *See* Chapter 9, *infra.*
88. *See* Dawson, *supra* note 12, at 67–74.
89. *See generally* Gerald B. Wetlaufer, "The Limits of Integrative Bargaining," 85 *Georgetown Law Journal* 369 (1996).
90. *See* Samuel B. Bacharach & Edward J. Lawler, *Bargaining: Power, Tactics and Outcomes* 60–63 (1981).

cumstances. They do not appear to fear the consequences of non-settlements. They also employ a variety of techniques to further their interests. Some are employed in isolation, while others are employed together. It is critical for bargainers to carefully plan the power bargaining techniques they expect to use, and to anticipate and prepare to counter the tactics they think their adversaries are likely to use.

A. Argument

The power bargaining technique employed most frequently during serious business interactions concerns the use of factual, economic, business, and legal argument. Individuals focus on the areas that enhance their own positions and articulate them to their adversaries as persuasively as possible. Although they appear to be using these discussions to educate their counterparts in an objective manner, they selectively choose the claims that will most effectively advance their interests.[91] Individuals who possess greater bargaining authority tend to argue in favor of *equitable distributions* that favor their own side, while persons with less power usually argue for *egalitarian distributions* that will generate more equal final results.[92]

Persuasive arguments must be presented in a relatively fair and objective fashion if they are to appeal to opposing parties.[93] They are most effective when they are presented in a logical and orderly sequence designed to have a cumulative impact upon the recipients. It is also beneficial to develop innovative assertions that have not been anticipated by their counterparts. Once adversaries are induced to internally question their previously developed rationales supporting their own positions, they begin to experience a loss of bargaining confidence.

Negotiators should never ignore the potential persuasiveness of well-crafted emotional appeals. Although most business persons are logical and intelligent people who can easily counter logical assertions, they often find it difficult to reject emotional claims that generate feelings of guilt or compassion. If individuals can create assertions that make the situation seem like a matter of right and wrong, with themselves on the side of right, this can significantly advance their interests.

B. Threats, Warnings, and Promises

Almost all serious business interactions involve the use of overt or implicit threats. Individuals suggest that they will do business with other parties if the opposing side does not enhance its current offer. Such statements are employed to convince adversaries that their cost of disagreeing with proposed offers by this side transcends the

---

91. *See* Robert Condlin, "Cases on Both Sides: Patterns of Argument in Legal Dispute Negotiation," 44 *Maryland Law Review* 65, 73 (1985).

92. *See* Richard Birke & Craig R. Fox, "Psychological Principles in Negotiating Civil Settlements," 4 *Harvard Negotiation Law Review* 1, 41 (1999).

93. *See* Bastress & Harbaugh, *supra* note 72, at 437–438.

cost of acquiescence. Negotiators should never threaten negative consequences they are not prepared to carry out, because if their counterparts challenge them and they fail to effectuate what was threatened, they will lose their credibility.

Less confrontational bargainers try to avoid the use of direct *threats* regarding negative consequences they will personally impose, preferring to use less challenging *warnings* which suggest what their superiors, their firms, or the market place would do if accords are not achieved.[94] By suggesting that these actions will be taken by others beyond their control, it makes it seem that their assertions are less personal and more objective.

At the opposite end of the spectrum from negative threats and warnings are affirmative *promises*.[95] Instead of suggesting negative consequences, the promisor expresses "an intention to behave in a way that appears beneficial to the interests of another."[96] For example, the promisor foregoes the suggestion of possible legal action or the termination of an existing relationship, and indicates that if the other side would be willing to articulate a more generous position, this side would reciprocate with a new position of its own. Such an affirmative promise provides a face-saving way for adversaries to move jointly toward each other, because it promises reciprocal action in response to favorable position changes by the other party.

Individuals who contemplate the use of threats or warnings to advance their bargaining positions should carefully communicate their intentions to opposing sides, and the threatened actions must be proportionate to the position changes the communicators are seeking. Insignificant threats are generally ignored as irrelevant, while excessive threats tend to be dismissed as irrational and unlikely.[97]

Negotiators threatened with negative consequences if they fail to alter their current positions must always ask themselves a critical question. What is likely to happen to their side if no agreement is reached with the other side? If their external alternatives are preferable to what would be the result if they gave in to the other side, they should not be afraid to maintain their current positions. If they hope to remain firm but allow the bargaining process to continue in a positive manner, they can simply ignore the threat as if they never received it. This may allow the threatening party to continue the discussion in a face-saving manner.

C. Ridicule and Humor

Humor can effectively be employed by persons during the Preliminary Stage to help them establish rapport with their adversaries and a positive bargaining environ-

---

94. *See* Freund, *supra* note 22, at 212–213; Robert Mayer, *Power Plays* 64–65 (1996).
95. *See* Dean G. Pruitt & Jeffrey Z. Rubin, *Social Conflict* 51–55 (1986).
96. *See* Rubin & Brown, *supra* note 59, at 278.
97. *See* Richard Ned Lebow, *The Art of Bargaining* 92–93 (1996); Gary T. Lowenthal, "A General Theory of Negotiation Process, Strategy, and Behavior," 31 *Kansas Law Review* 69, 86 (1982).

ment. The use of humor can enhance the likeability of the communicators.[98] As the interaction develops, humor can also be used to calm the parties down when the discussions become unusually tense. An appropriate one-liner can remind everyone not to take the situation too seriously.

Ridicule and humor can also be employed by negotiators during the Distributive Stage to indicate how unacceptable opposing side offers might be. A derisive smile or sarcastic comment may be used to counter an especially one-sided offer to demonstrate how inappropriate it is. If used effectively, such behavior may embarrass their counterpart and induce that person to make a more reasonable offer. Nonetheless, individuals who do not feel comfortable employing humor should not use such an approach, since it would be likely to fail and create an even more negative environment.

D. Silence

Silence is an unusually effective bargaining technique that is often overlooked by participants. Less confident negotiators fear silence. They are afraid that if they cease talking, they will lose control of the interaction. They remember the awkwardness they have experienced in social settings during prolonged pauses, and they feel compelled to speak. When they do so, they tend to disclose, both verbally and nonverbally, information they did not intend to divulge, and they frequently make unintended position changes.[99]

When negotiators have something important to convey, they should do so in a succinct manner and become silent. They need to give their listener the chance to absorb what they have said. This is especially critical when concessions are being exchanged. Bargainers should announce their new positions, and quietly and patiently await reciprocal responses from the receiving parties. If prolonged silence from the other side makes them feel uncomfortable, they should review their notes or look out the window. Their calm patience will clearly indicate to the other side that they expect a response before they continue the discussions.

E. Patience

Individuals involved in bargaining interactions must appreciate the fact that such endeavors take time to develop. Persons who seek to rush the process generally obtain less beneficial results than they would have achieved had they been more patient. Offers that might have been acceptable if conveyed during the latter stages of a negotiation may not be so attractive when conveyed prematurely. The participants have

---

98. *See* K. O'Quin & J. Aronoff, "Humor as a Technique of Social Influence," 44 *Social Psychology Quarterly* 349 (1981).

99. *See* Mark McCormack, *What They Did Not Teach You at Harvard Business School* 108–111 (1984).

not had time to appreciate the fact that a negotiated deal is preferable to their external alternatives.

All negotiators experience anxiety created by the uncertainty that is an inherent aspect of all bargaining encounters. Persons who can control the tension they feel and exude a quiet inner confidence are generally able to achieve far better results than their less patient cohorts. They exhibit a stamina indicating that they are prepared to take as long as necessary to obtain their objectives.

Bargainers who wish to use their own patience and stamina to wear down less patient adversaries should develop patient styles that help them keep the process going when circumstances become difficult. If the bargaining environment becomes unusually tense, they might take short breaks to alleviate the tension. If they convince their adversaries that they will continue the process until they achieve their goals, they will often obtain capitulations from less committed adversaries.

F. Guilt and Embarrassment

Some negotiators work to generate feelings of guilt or embarrassment in their counterparts, for the purpose of inducing those persons to accede to their demands. They cite seemingly insignificant transgressions, such as someone showing up late for a meeting or forgetting to bring unimportant documents, hoping to disconcert such people. They hope to make the others feel so uncomfortable that those individuals will try to regain social acceptability by doing something nice for them. When someone tries to place a bargaining participant at a disadvantage over a small oversight, that person should simply apologize and move on without feeling the need to give up anything of substance.

G. Loud Voice and Intense Language

Some negotiators are afraid to raise their voices during their interactions with others for fear of offending their counterparts. They fail to appreciate the beneficial impact that can be achieved through the strategic use of loudness. Controlled voice volume can be a characteristic of persuasiveness. When people talk in a louder voice, others tend to listen. So long as the raised voice is not considered inappropriately aggressive or outright offensive, it does not hurt to communicate with more elevated volume when someone wishes to be heard.

Many persons believe they will be more persuasive negotiators if they use more intense language during their interactions. Studies show, however, that low intensity discussions are usually more persuasive than high intensity presentations.[100] This seeming anomaly is due to the negative reaction most people have toward such high

---

100. *See* Roy J. Lewicki, Joseph A. Litterer, John W. Minton & David W. Saunders, *Negotiation* 54–55 (2d ed. 1994).

intensity persuasive efforts. High intensity speakers appear to be manipulative and offensive, while low intensity presenters tend to induce counterparts to be less suspicious of and more receptive to their entreaties.

§ 6.03. Negotiators Must Always Remember Their Non-Settlement Alternatives

Throughout the Distributive Stage, negotiators must always remember their *current non-settlement alternatives*. It is no longer relevant what they may have been six months or a year ago, when individuals had to prepare for the present discussions. The passage of time has frequently affected the options that were previously available, and helped to generate new alternatives. Has the market improved the value of the firm being purchased or sold? Are the technology rights being licensed worth more or less than they were a year ago?

Bargainers who fail to appreciate the changes in the value of their current interactions may make the mistake of entering into arrangements that are worse than what they would have had with no agreement. They must always remember that bad deals are worse than no deals.[101] When their non-settlement alternatives are presently more beneficial than the terms being offered by their adversaries, they should not hesitate to walk away from the current discussions. They should always do this as pleasantly as possible, for two reasons. First, once their adversaries realize that they are really willing to end the interaction, they may reconsider their positions and offer them more beneficial terms. Second, even if the current negotiations are not regenerated and no accord is achieved, the parties are likely to see each other again in the future. If both sides remember these talks favorably, even though they were not successful, future negotiations would be likely to progress more smoothly than if these talks concluded on an unpleasant note.

§ 6.04. Using the Closing Stage to Solidify the Deal

Near the end of the Distributive Stage, the participants appreciate the fact that a mutual accord is likely to be achieved, and they enter a delicate part of their interaction. They feel a sense of relief, because the anxiety generated by the uncertainty of the bargaining process is about to be alleviated by the attainment of a definitive agreement. Careful observers can usually see signs of relief around the mouths of the negotiators, and the fact such persons are in more relaxed postures. As the bargainers become psychologically committed to a deal, they may move too quickly toward the conclusion of the transaction.

---

101. *See* Lum, *supra* note 36, at 54–55.

The Closing Stage represents a crucial part of the bargaining process. The majority of concessions tend to be made during the final portion of the interaction.[102] As a result, overly anxious participants may forfeit much of what they obtained during the Distributive Stage if they are not cautious. They must remain patient and allow the Closing Stage to unfold in a deliberate manner.

By the conclusion of the Competitive Stage, *both sides* have become mentally committed to a joint deal. Neither wants to see their prior efforts culminate in failure. Less skilled negotiators focus on their own side's desire for an agreement, and they disregard the settlement pressure affecting the other side. Since *both sides* wish to generate final terms, they should be expected to move jointly toward this objective. Negotiators should be careful not to make unreciprocated concessions, and to avoid excessive position changes. They should only consider larger concessions than they are receiving from the other side, when it is clear that their adversaries were overly accommodating during their earlier exchanges, and the verbal statements and non-verbal signals emanating from those participants indicate that they are approaching their resistance points.

The Closing Stage is not a time for swift action; it is instead a time for *patient perseverance*. The participants should continue to employ the techniques that got them this far, and they should be fully aware of their prior and current concession patterns. They should endeavor to make smaller, and, if possible, fewer position changes than their counterparts. If they fail to adhere to this practice and move too expeditiously toward a conclusion, they are likely to close most of the distance remaining between the parties.

Patience and *silence* are two of the most effective tactics during the Closing Stage. Negotiators should use "principled" concessions to explain the reasons for their precise position changes. After each change, they should become silent and patiently wait for the other side's response. They should be careful not to prattle on and demonstrate their anxiety, and should not consider additional movement until they have received reciprocity from the other side. They must continue to remember that their counterparts are as anxious to achieve final terms as they are.

Proficient negotiators can frequently obtain a significant advantage during the Closing Stage by exhibiting calm indifference. If they can persuade their more anxious adversaries that they do not care whether final terms are achieved, they may be able to induce those persons to make more expansive and more frequent position changes—all to the benefit of these individuals.

Even though the participants think they are nearing the end of their interaction, the Closing Stage can be a highly competitive portion of the bargaining process. It tends to involve a number of position changes, and a significant amount of participant movement. Negotiators who naively think that this part of their interaction consists primarily of cooperative behavior are likely to end up with less beneficial results than

---

102. *See* Dawson, *supra* note 12, at 194–198.

strategic counterparts who use this stage to induce them to close most of the outstanding distance between the two sides. Individuals who carefully monitor the concession patterns and make sure they do not make excessive or consecutive position changes should be able to avoid such exploitation by manipulative adversaries.

Negotiators who believe their counterparts may be approaching their bottom lines should listen carefully for **verbal leaks** suggesting that they are not. For example, their counterpart might say "that's **about as far** as I can go" or "I don't have **much more room**"—both of which suggest that the speaker has more room. When bargainers get to their true bottom lines, they say something like "that is as far as I can go," and they tend to exhibit an open, palms-up posture supporting their representation that they are really at their reservation point.

§ 6.05. Conclusion

During the Distributive Stage, the participants work to *claim* the joint surplus they generated during the Information Stage. This is a highly competitive portion of bargaining interactions, as most skilled negotiators endeavor to claim more of the pie than they concede to the other side. Persons should have thoughtful concession patterns in mind when they enter this portion of their interactions, and they must have rational explanations for each position change. Parties use power bargaining techniques to advance their positions, such as argument, threats, warnings, promises, humor, ridicule, silence, patience, guilt, embarrassment, and appropriate voice and language.

Near the end of the Distributive Stage, the parties see an agreement on the horizon, and they enter the delicate Closing Stage. By this time, both sides are usually psychologically committed to the attainment of final terms, but if one side feels more anxious, it is likely to make larger and more frequent position changes. Skilled negotiators move slowly, and make sure their concessions are matched by reciprocal counterpart position changes. If they are patient, they can frequently induce apprehensive adversaries to close an excessive part of the gap remaining between them.

Chapter 7

Value Maximizing through the Cooperative/Integrative Stage

By the conclusion of the Closing Stage, the parties have usually achieved mutually acceptable terms, and many erroneously think that the negotiation process is over. Although this belief may be correct with respect to truly zero sum problems, such as those involving the immediate exchange of money, where neither party could improve its present circumstances without generating a corresponding loss to the other side,[103] it is definitely not true for multiple issue encounters. Nevertheless, a number of participants involved with multiple issue interactions assume a fixed pie that cannot be expanded. This is rarely correct, due to the different party preference curves involved.[104] As a result, it is often possible for the negotiators to formulate innovative terms that allow them to expand the overall pie and simultaneously improve their respective interests.

§ 7.01. Explore Ways to Expand the Overall Pie

Once a tentative accord has been reached through the distributive process, the negotiators should contemplate alternative trade-offs that might concurrently enhance the interests of both sides. The bargainers may be mentally, and even physically exhausted from their prior discussions, but they should at least briefly explore alternative formulations that might prove to be mutually advantageous. During the Information Stage, the parties frequently over-state and under-state the actual value of different items for strategic purposes. During the Distributive and Closing Stages, they tend to employ various bargaining tactics to enable them to claim more of the surplus for themselves. Because of the disingenuous nature of this part of the bargaining process, Pareto superior arrangements are rarely attained by this point. The parties have

---

103. Even when the only issue to be negotiated concerns the payment of money, there may be room for cooperative bargaining. The parties may be able to agree to in-kind payments involving the provision of goods or services in lieu of cash, or to the payment of money over a number of months or years, which would enable the receiving party to get what it desires at less cost to the other side. It thus behooves even money traders to explore alternative payment schemes that might prove to be mutually beneficial.

104. *See* Jeanette Nyden, Kate Vitasek & Dana Frydlinger, *Getting to We: Negotiating Agreements for Highly Collaborative Relationships* 155–179 (2013).; Mnookin, Peppet & Tulumello, *supra* note 11, at 14–16.

achieved "acceptable" terms, but if they conclude their encounter at this point, they may leave a substantial amount of untapped joint satisfaction on the bargaining table.

Through the use of simulation exercises, it is easy to demonstrate the degree to which negotiators have successfully employed the Cooperative Stage. By comparing the aggregate point totals attained by the two sides, one may ascertain the degree to which they maximized their joint results. For example, where two counterparts might potentially divide 1000 points between themselves, some participants with proficient cooperative skills may have achieved agreements with combined totals of 950 to 1000 points. On the other hand, more competitive groups may have ended up with joint totals of only 600 or 700 points. Such results graphically show the participants the benefits to be derived from effective use of the Cooperative Stage. If the latter groups had been able to discover the 300 or 400 points they missed, both sides could have left the table with far more generous final terms.

If the Cooperative Stage is to be successful, several prerequisites must be established. First, the parties must have achieved a tentative accord. Second, at the conclusion of the Closing Stage, one or both parties should suggest movement into the Cooperative Stage. If one side is concerned that the other party might be reluctant to move in this direction until a provisional agreement has been established, it can suggest that both sides initial the terms already agreed upon. Even though some negotiators merge the latter part of the Closing Stage with the initial portion of the Cooperative Stage, most bargainers only move into the Cooperative Stage after they have achieved a mutually acceptable division of the relevant terms.[105]

§ 7.02. Both Sides Must Recognize Transition from the Closing Stage to the Cooperative Stage

It is vital that both sides recognize their transition from the Closing Stage to the Cooperative Stage, to avoid problems that might arise if one party attempted to move into the Cooperative Stage without the understanding of the other side. If the alternative proposals suggested by one party are less advantageous to the other side than what has already been attained, the recipient of such proposals may think that the proposing party is engaging in disingenuously competitive tactics. It is thus imperative for both sides to understand that they are beginning to consider various options that may — or may not — improve their respective circumstances.

During the Cooperative Stage, the negotiators must look for previously undiscovered alternatives that might prove to be mutually beneficial. They have to see if there is any way they can expand the overall pie by looking for options that would more effectively satisfy the underlying needs and interests of one side with less cost to the

---

105. *See* Dawson, *supra* note 12, at 173–174.

other party. To accomplish this objective, the participants must be willing to disclose their underlying interests with a significant degree of candor.

Both sides must be quite open during the Cooperative Stage, if the process is to function effectively. They should employ objective and relatively neutral questions to explore their underlying needs and interests. They should use brainstorming techniques to see if they can develop alternatives not previously considered. They should not be constrained by the need to formulate conventional business arrangements, but should be willing to think outside the box.[106] When one side asks the other if a different resolution would be preferable for that party than what they have already agreed upon, the respondent must answer in a completely forthright manner. It is only where the participants effectively explore all of the possible alternatives that they can really determine ways to enhance their initial agreements.

When the parties enter the Cooperative Stage, it is critical for them to preserve their credibility. They have probably been somewhat deceptive during the Information, Distributive, and Closing Stages with respect to their actual needs and interests. In the Cooperative Stage, they hope to correct the inefficiencies that may have been generated by their previous disingenuousness. If they are now too open regarding their prior misrepresentations, their counterparts may begin to question the accuracy of all of their previous statements and try to renegotiate the entire accord. This would be a disaster. It is thus imperative that negotiators not overly undermine their basic credibility while they seek to improve their respective circumstances during the Cooperative Stage.

It is important for persons participating in the Cooperative Stage to appreciate the competitive undercurrent that is often present even during these seemingly win-win discussions. Even though the participants are using cooperative techniques to expand the overall pie and improve the results achieved by both sides, some may also employ subtly competitive tactics to enable them to claim more than their share of the newly discovered areas for mutual gain. For example, if the participants discover an additional "250 points"[107] of party satisfaction that can be divided between them, there is nothing that requires them to allocate 125 points to each side. If one party realizes that a proposed change in the existing terms could increase her side's situation by 150 or even 200 points, she might disingenuously indicate that the new proposal would be a "slight improvement," to enable her to make her adversary think that the new terms would only expand the overall pie by 100 or 150 points. She would then give her counterpart 50 to 75 points, and retain the other 175 to 200 points for her own side.

---

106. *See generally* Tom Kelley, *The Art of Innovation* (2001).

107. In my Negotiation course, I assign point values to each item to be negotiated to apprise the students of the relative values placed on the different terms from their respective perspectives. When representing real parties, negotiators should mentally do the same thing, as they probe their own side's underlying needs and interests. The "essential" terms should have higher values than the "important" terms, which should be valued more than the "desirable" issues. This enables the bargainers to appreciate the comparative values of the different terms being exchanged.

§ 7.03. Be Sure to Confirm Terms Agreed upon and Review Accords Drafted by Other Side

Once truly final agreements have been achieved, negotiators frequently hang up the telephone or depart for home, thinking that they are done. As a result, they may fail to be certain that they have reached a complete meeting of the minds. Before they conclude their interaction, the participants should briefly review the specific terms they believe have been agreed upon. During the final stages of the bargaining process, changes take place expeditiously, and one side may believe that the other had either moved further than it actually intended to move or removed an item from the table it did not intend to remove. If they discover such a misunderstanding now, when they are both psychologically committed to a deal, they are likely to find a way to resolve it amicably. On the other hand, if they did not discover the misunderstanding until one side drafted the accord, there might be claims of dishonesty and recriminations.

On some occasions, the negotiators on one side may suspect that their counterparts may have difficulty selling the deal to their own principals. In such circumstances, it can be beneficial for the representatives on Side A to help their Side B counterparts in this regard.[108] They might provide them with arguments they could employ. They could make public statements suggesting that their own side did not get as good a deal as it had hoped to obtain. They could even encourage the Side B representatives to put on a demonstration of toughness designed to show their own principals how hard they worked to generate beneficial terms for their own side.

Most negotiators prefer to draft the terms of agreements achieved, believing that they will do a better job of reflecting their own side's understanding than their adversaries would. They clearly have an ethical duty to include precisely what was agreed upon. When counterparts draft the agreements, the recipients of such documents should review the terms carefully to be sure they reflect what was actually agreed upon. If they do not like particular language provided, they should not hesitate to suggest alternative wording. Was anything included that was not clearly agreed upon? For example, the other side may have included a dispute resolution procedure without the consent of this side. If they do not like that provision, they should contact the other side and discuss other options. Finally, they should be careful to ensure that nothing agreed upon has been omitted. When individuals draft the terms of tentative accords, they tend to focus on the issues of significance to their own side. They sometimes fail to include terms they do not consider important, forgetting that the other side may value those items. When persons review drafts prepared by their counterparts, they should check off each issue in their notes as they come across those terms in the draft agreement. When they are done, they should look carefully at their remaining notes to see if anything has been left out. If they discover such an

---

108. *See* James K. Sebenius, "Level Two Negotiations: Helping the Other Side Meet Its 'Behind the Table' Challenges," 29 *Negotiation Journal* 7 (2013).

omission, they should not automatically suspect dishonesty by the other side. They should simply contact that party and ask him about the term in question. In almost all cases, the other side will apologize and correct their mistake.

§ 7.04. Using Tit-for-Tat Approach to Encourage Cooperative Behavior

Persons who recognize that competitive/adversarial behavior tends to generate less efficient agreements than cooperative/problem-solving conduct may employ the "tit-for-tat" approach developed by Professor Anatol Rapoport to encourage cooperative interactions.[109]

A. Don't Be Envious of Opposing Side

Negotiators should not judge their own success by how well they believe their adversaries have done, because the persons on both sides rarely possess equal bargaining power and equal skills. The party with greater strength and ability should be able to obtain more favorable terms than their weaker counterparts. If the side with less power gets results that are beneficial to their principals, they should be pleased with the results.

B. Be Nice at the Outset

Individuals who wish to promote cooperative behavior should make it clear at the outset that they do not plan to employ competitive/adversarial tactics, unless they are forced to do so to counteract such conduct by their counterparts. This would undoubtedly encourage Cooperative/Problem-Solvers and Competitive/Problem-Solvers to behave cooperatively, and it may even induce Competitive/Adversarials to tone down their usually adversarial tactics.

C. Be Provokable in Response to Uncooperative Behavior

Many Cooperative/Problem-Solving negotiators do not know how to respond to competitive/adversarial behavior. They remain open and accommodating, placing themselves at a disadvantage. More proficient Cooperative/Problem-Solving bargainers appreciate the fact that overtly competitive behavior must be confronted and dealt with when it occurs. For example, after a final agreement has been achieved, a manipulative adversary might employ the "nibble technique" to obtain one last unreciprocated concession. They may indicate that their side is dissatisfied with a particular term and insist upon a modification of that provision. A naïve person might be afraid to let the entire deal unravel and concede the requested item. A provokable negotiator

---

109. *See* Robert Axelrod, *The Evolution of Cooperation* 109–124 (1984).

would appreciate the fact that both sides want the final accord and that the other party is not entitled to such a unilateral concession at this stage. She would thus demand a reciprocal concession in return for any modification to be made by her side. If her adversary truly requires the requested change, he would recognize the need for reciprocity and offer something in exchange for the change being sought. On the other hand, once a manipulative "nibbler" realizes that he cannot get the modification without reciprocity on his part, he would insist upon the original terms agreed upon.

D. Be Forgiving

Once the provoked negotiator makes it clear that her side will not alter the agreed-upon terms without reciprocity from the other side, and the other side has agreed to follow the original terms, she should not hold a grudge. She should not take this tactic personally, but realize that the other person was simply trying to obtain a final concession for his own side. She has made it clear that this type of conduct will not be accepted in the future, and should not permit the current situation to negatively influence their subsequent interactions.

E. Be Transparent and Establish a Clear Reputation

Cooperative negotiators who wish to encourage cooperative behavior in others should always try to project a cooperative image. On the other hand, they should also make it clear that they will not yield to inappropriate tactics. If their counterparts know that these persons are cooperative — but also provokable — they would be unlikely to resort to such manipulative tactics when they interact with each other in the future.

§ 7.05. Conclusion

At the end of the Closing Stage, many negotiators erroneously believe they are done with their interactions. They fail to appreciate the fact they should move into the Cooperative Stage to see if they can expand the overall pie and simultaneously improve their respective positions. Due to somewhat deceptive tactics employed during the Information, Distributive, and Closing Stages, the parties have often agreed to terms that do not maximize their joint returns. Once they are sure they have reached tentative accords, they should explore options that might benefit both sides. They should think outside the box and use brainstorming techniques to seek ways that might better serve their respective underlying needs and interests. Even this part of bargaining encounters may be somewhat competitive, due to the fact that nothing requires the parties to divide newly discovered alternatives on an equal basis.

Once they have reached final agreements, the participants should quickly review the actual terms to be sure they have no misunderstandings. If possible, they should seek to draft the agreement to reflect their own side's interests. When the other side drafts the accord, they should carefully review the language selected, look for any term included that was not previously agreed upon, and see if any item agreed upon has been erroneously omitted.

Negotiators who hope to minimize questionable tactics by adversarial individuals should use the tit-for-tat approach. They should not judge their success by what their counterparts have obtained. They should be cooperative when they interact with others, but be provokable when inappropriate behavior is employed. If they establish reputations for being provokable under such circumstances, they would minimize the likelihood their counterparts would employ inappropriately manipulative techniques.

Chapter 8

Negotiating Techniques

§ 8.01. Benefits Derived from Understanding the Different Techniques

There are a relatively finite number of techniques that may be employed by bargainers. It is thus possible to categorize and explore the various tactics negotiators might decide to use themselves, and encounter when they interact with others.[110] If individuals acquaint themselves with the commonly employed approaches, they can more readily identify the bargaining tactics being used against them. This facilitates their capacity to counteract those techniques, and it enhances their bargaining confidence and improves their chances of achieving beneficial results.

Some of these tactics are natural extensions of the individuals using them. For example, persons with aggressive personalities may intuitively adopt aggressive negotiating styles, while calm bargainers may use laid-back approaches. Whether negotiators embrace a Cooperative/Problem-Solving, Competitive/Adversarial, or Competitive/Problem-Solving style, they must employ different techniques that are designed to advance their positions. This reflects the fact they must select an approach that is consistent with their own personalities, the personalities of their counterparts, and the particular circumstances involved.

It is fairly easy to keep track of the tactics being used by negotiators who either employ one approach most of the time or use different techniques one at a time in sequence. It is more difficult to identify the devices being used by negotiators who employ various maneuvers simultaneously (e.g., "Mutt and Jeff," "Anger," and "Limited Authority"). Participants adopt such diverse approaches to keep their counterparts off balance. Individuals interacting with such persons should carefully monitor and respond to the particular tactics being employed during the various portions of their interactions, so they can most effectively counteract those bargaining games.

On some occasions, negotiators may counteract adversary tactics by indicating they are aware of the techniques being employed and suggesting that those approaches are not working.[111] If a particular tactic is considered offensive, the affected party

---

110. *See generally* Stark & Flaherty, supra note 65, at 131–236; Saner, *supra* note 55, at 135–152; Jay Conrad Levinson, Mark S. Smith & Orvel Ray Wilson, *Guerilla Negotiating* (1999).

111. *See* Deborah Kolb & Judith Williams, *Everyday Negotiation* 133–135 (2003).

may politely indicate that this strategy is actually undermining the discussions.[112] Once the actor realizes that his strategic behavior is not advancing their interests, he will usually consider less disruptive alternatives.

Seemingly ingenuous comments that disguise ulterior motives are common to almost all negotiations. For instance, individuals may attempt to convince their counterparts that they possess more beneficial alternatives to non-settlement than they actually do. The purpose of this tactic is to make the adversaries think they are not under great pressure to reach immediate accords. If their representations in this regard are believed, their bargaining power is meaningfully enhanced. Other advocates may resort to false flattery to soften strong counterparts or use feigned weakness or apparent ineptitude to evoke sympathy from their adversaries.

Some communications contain dual messages—one seemingly objective and forthright and the other subtle and ulterior.[113] For example, a company seller might suggest to someone who would apparently like to purchase a firm that he could barely afford to buy that "you probably can't afford this business." Even though this overtly "adult"-to-"adult" statement may be objectively correct, the seller does not wish to convince the prospective purchaser of this fact, because that would preclude sale of the firm in question. The ulterior message is surreptitiously conveyed in a "parent"-to-"child" fashion, with the "parent"-seller instructing the "child"-prospective buyer that he cannot do something. If the desired response is precipitated, the prospective purchaser will respond with a child-like "Yes, I can!"[114] If this device functions properly, the salesperson will be able to sell a company to someone who was not planning to select such an expensive property.

Negotiators should normally be suspicious of statements suggesting that a contemplated transaction cannot or should not be consummated. If the transmitters of such messages truly believed this fact, they would not have any reason to participate in the bargaining process. If, despite such communications, the speakers exhibit a desire to engage in further discussions, it is likely that they are endeavoring to shame or subconsciously entrap the unsuspecting respondents into accepting what are probably disadvantageous arrangements.

§ 8.02. Common Negotiating Techniques

A. Numerically Superior Bargaining Team

Many business negotiations are conducted on a one-on-one basis. In some instances, however, parties attempt to obtain a tactical and psychological advantage by including extra people on their bargaining team. They hope that the additional participants will intimidate their lone adversary. The added participants also make the

---

112. *See id.* at 135–141.
113. *See* Lothar Katz, *Principles of Negotiating International Business* 158–159 (2008).
114. *See* Eric Berne, *Games People Play* 33–34 (1964).

team more capable of discerning the verbal leaks and nonverbal messages being emitted by that individual.[115] These extra participants may monitor the signals while one of their partners is speaking. Parties with expanded negotiating teams also think that since a lone counterpart has to observe, listen, plan, and speak simultaneously, they can confuse that person with excessive verbal and nonverbal stimuli. Furthermore, the additional participants provide their group leader with someone to consult during separate caucuses.

Some of the exercises used in my Negotiating Class are conducted on a two-on-two basis. One of the students is occasionally unable to participate due to illness or personal obligations. In almost every such instance, the lone negotiator finishes in the bottom third of the class. In a number of such cases, that person has been dead last.

The addition of even a single negotiating partner can significantly diminish the advantage that counterparts may derive from an expansive group. Even if the extra person does not speak, she can carefully monitor nonverbal clues and verbal messages while her colleague is more actively interacting with the various counterparts. I prefer to have a partner who actively participates in the interaction, because they may see a fleeting opportunity I might miss. If they were unable to speak, this opening would be lost. In addition, when the bargaining groups conduct separate caucus sessions, this team has at least two people who can jointly evaluate recent developments.

When adversaries attempt to overload their bargaining teams in an unconscionable fashion, it would not be inappropriate for someone to refuse to meet with that group until it is reduced to a more manageable size. If such a reduction could not be achieved due to the various constituencies that must be represented on the opposing team, it may be necessary to bring additional people to the sessions to counterbalance the sheer size of that group. It may also be possible to counteract this technique by conducting telephone or e-mail interactions that decrease the impact of multiple counterparts.

In rare instances, institutional considerations require opposing bargaining teams to include a number of representatives from diverse constituencies. This is typical of negotiations with expansive corporations, labor unions, and governmental agencies with different departments. During these interactions, one side may have only two or three representatives, while the opposing team consists of ten, fifteen, or even twenty participants. On these occasions, the smaller group may actually enjoy an advantage. Unless the more expansive opposing team members have carefully coordinated their goals and developed a united approach through detailed intra-group negotiations conducted during the Preparation Stage, the members of that group may emit mixed signals that undermine group solidarity.[116] Individuals dealing with

---

115. *See* James Day Hodgson, Yoshihiro Sano & John L. Graham, *Doing Business with the New Japan* 25 (2000).
116. *See* Susan Brodt & Leigh Thompson, "Negotiating Teams: A Levels of Analysis Approach," 5 *Group Dynamics: Theory, Research, and Practice* 208, 212 (2001); LePoole, *supra* note 83, at 98–101.

enlarged bargaining groups should not hesitate to employ tactics that are designed to divide and conquer disorganized counterparts.

Organizations that must conduct negotiations through expanded group participation may be disadvantaged by a lack of intragroup preparation, and the resulting lack of group cohesiveness. If they lack common objectives and a unified strategy, proficient counterparts may exploit their weaknesses. On the other hand, well prepared groups may actually outperform smaller teams if they can take advantage of their capacity to look more carefully for verbal leaks and nonverbal cues emanating from the other side. Well-coordinated groups can reinforce their common beliefs and their jointly developed objectives. It is usually beneficial to have one or two persons do all of the talking for such large groups or to assign different issues to one or two main speakers, in recognition of the fact that if everyone could speak when they felt motivated, it would be impossible to present a truly united front.

Larger negotiation groups often behave more competitively, and they are less likely to employ cooperative strategies due to pressure to achieve beneficial group returns.[117] This approach may generate optimal results with respect to distributive interactions that involve primarily monetary issues, but it can create problems when integrative terms are involved. If group dynamics inhibit cooperative bargaining designed to expand the overall pie and enhance joint returns, both sides may suffer from an inability to generate efficient resolutions that may have been achieved through more integrative discussions.

B. Use of Asymmetrical Time Pressure

During the Preliminary Stages of an interaction, negotiators occasionally discover the existence of time constraints that affect the other party more than they influence their own side. Japanese bargainers frequently employ this factor to their advantage when they are visited by foreign corporate representatives. They initially ask about the return flight schedule of their guests — ostensibly to allow them to reconfirm those flights. They then use generous hospitality to preclude the commencement of substantive discussions until a few days before their visitors are planning to return home. The Japanese negotiators recognize that their foreign agents do not want to return home without agreements. This forces those visitors to consider extra, last-minute concessions in an effort to achieve final accords while they are still in Japan.

Whenever possible, negotiators should try to withhold information that might suggest the existence of an asymmetrical time constraint.[118] For example, individuals traveling to another country to discuss a possible business venture should refrain from booking a definite return flight. When their hosts ask them when they plan to return

---

117. *See* Brodt & Thompson, *supra* note 116, at 213.
118. *See* Dawson, *supra* note 12, at 175–176.

home, they should reply that they are prepared to remain as long as it takes to fully explore the possibility of a mutually beneficial relationship. If they can exhibit a calm patience, they can increase the likelihood of achieving an expeditious and beneficial agreement. If they can convince their counterparts that they are not being influenced by the time factor, they can substantially enhance their bargaining posture.

Negotiators feeling time pressure frequently fail to appreciate the time pressure affecting the other side, and they thus concede the time advantage to their adversaries. They must remember that superiors regularly impose real and artificial time constraints. Such persons regularly telephone their negotiators for progress reports, and corporate and government agency administrators make similar requests. By acknowledging the fact that time pressure affects *both sides*, negotiators can diminish the impact of this factor on themselves.

When transactional bargainers have certain deadlines that must be met and their counterparts are not operating under a similar constraint, they may take preemptive action to neutralize the time factor. They can announce at the beginning of discussions that everything must be concluded by their deadline if a mutual accord is to be achieved.[119] Through this approach, they can impose their time constraint on their adversaries and deprive them of the opportunity to use this factor to their advantage. Negotiators should only make statements of this kind when they truly have deadlines that must be satisfied if agreements are to be attained, since a misrepresentation regarding this issue could easily preclude any agreement and destroy the deceitful person's future credibility.

I am frequently asked how negotiators can induce their counterparts to make generous offers early in the bargaining process. In most cases, they cannot do so. It is the immediacy of deadlines that generates action.[120] Most bargainers only begin to feel pressure to compromise when they see a deadline looming in the immediate future. It thus behooves participants to be patient during the preliminary stages, lest they concede too much during the early part of the interaction. As a deadline approaches, both parties will feel pressure, and they should move simultaneously toward closure.

C. Extreme Initial Demands

Empirical studies have demonstrated that people who enter negotiations with high aspiration levels generally obtain more beneficial results than those who begin with less generous expectations. It thus behooves bargainers to commence their interactions with high demands or low offers.[121] Bargainers who can rationally defend their seemingly excessive opening demands or apparently parsimonious offers may be able to *anchor* the discussions and induce careless adversaries to reconsider their own pre-

---

119. *See* Freund, *supra* note 22, at 148–149.
120. *See* Cohen, *supra* note 38, at 75–77.
121. *See* Dawson, *supra* note 12, at 16–21; Kritzer, *supra* note 13, at 54, 78–79.

liminary assessments.[122] Once those individuals begin to doubt the propriety of their own positions, they are in trouble. They may even lose touch with reality and accept the skewed representations being advanced by their avaricious counterparts.

When Individuals formulate their initial demands/offers, they should not make them so obviously unreasonable that they cannot be rationally defended. Clearly absurd opening demands/offers will suffer from a lack of legitimacy, and may create unintended difficulties. If the recipients of outlandish proposals conclude that the matters in issue cannot reasonably be resolved through the negotiation process, they may terminate the present discussions. Even when interactions are not discontinued, the participants who articulated the extreme positions may find it impossible to make the necessary concessions in an orderly manner. They may thus be forced to make large, irrational position changes, causing a concomitant loss of control.

Persons confronted by truly unreasonable initial demands/offers should not casually indicate their displeasure with those positions, because this response may lead their counterparts to think that their demands/offers are not wholly unrealistic. This may induce those people to raise their aspiration levels in a way that would be likely to generate non-settlements. Recipients of outrageous opening demands/offers should immediately and unequivocally express their displeasure with those positions, to disabuse the offerors of any thought their entreaties are not absurd. For example: "You know and I know how utterly unrealistic your position is. If that is the area you wish to explore, we have nothing to discuss." Individuals who begin with extreme positions are often unsure of their situations. To protect themselves, they start with what they suspect are unreasonable proposals. They expect their counterparts to react with disapproval, and actually feel better when their adversaries do so. This confirms their preliminary view that their starting positions were excessive, and allows them to place greater faith in their preliminary assessments.

Once the recipients of extreme offers have indicated how unrealistic those positions are, they may respond in one of several ways:

(1) They may indicate that they do not plan to articulate their own initial offer until the other side sets forth a reasonable position. The primary difficulty with this approach is the fact it requires the unreasonable participants to "bid against themselves" — *i.e.*, to make consecutive concessions. Proficient negotiators hate to make unreciprocated position changes, and would be unlikely to make a series of opening concessions as a prerequisite to counterpart participation in the process.

(2) Some individuals counter extreme demands/offers with their own outlandish initial positions. When challenged by their counterparts, they smile and indicate that their initial offer is no more unreasonable than that of the other side. They can then use the promise technique and suggest their willingness to provide a realistic offer, *if* their counterpart articulates a credible position. Such

_____

122. *See* Katz, *supra* note 113, at 148–150.

"attitudinal bargaining" is always an appropriate way to induce unreasonable adversaries to contemplate more realistic opening entreaties.

(3) A few negotiators try to ignore unreasonable opening offers by their counterparts and articulate realistic offers of their own, hoping to embarrass their adversaries into more accommodating behavior. This approach may create unanticipated difficulties if their adversaries do not significantly modify their initial positions. After a number of concessions have been made by both sides, the party that started with the extreme position is likely to emphasize how far it has moved compared to the side that began with the reasonable figure. In many instances, the persons who started with realistic positions are likely to give up more or accept less than they should, because of the guilt they experience when they attempt to induce their unreasonable counterparts to make concessions on a ten- or twenty-to-one basis throughout the entire interaction.

D. Use of Probing Questions

Negotiators confronted by wholly unreasonable positions may generate a more flexible atmosphere through the use of probing questions.[123] Instead of directly challenging those positions—a tactic that would probably cause the other side to become more resolute—they separate the different items into definitive components. They then propound a series of questions—beginning with the more finite items that do not lend themselves to excessive puffing—designed to force their counterparts to reassess each aspect of their offer. For example, if a participant in a corporate buy out were to make a wholly unrealistic offer or demand, the recipient could ask that person how much he allotted for the real property. If the questioner receives a realistic response, she writes it down and goes on to the next item. If the figure mentioned is unreasonably high or low, the questioner may cite a recent appraisal and ask how the respondent calculated his figure. Once a realistic amount is obtained for this term, the questioner moves on to the proposed figures for the building and equipment, the inventory, the accounts receivable, the patent, trade, or copy rights, the corporate good will, and other relevant considerations.

If these inquiries are carefully formulated in a relatively neutral and nonjudgmental manner, they may induce the other side to examine the partisan bases underlying their position statement. As each component is addressed, the counterparts must either articulate rational explanations or begin to recognize the lack of any sound foundation for that aspect of their offer. When adversaries do not respond thoughtfully to queries that are posed, they should be reframed and asked again. When this process is finished and the different amounts are totaled, the sum is usually four or five times what was originally offered or one-fourth or one-fifth what was initially demanded. This is due to the fact that negotiators who begin with truly unrealistic offers have made them up and have no idea how to defend them on a component-by-component basis.

---

123. *See* Katz, *supra* note 113, at 167–168; Mayer, *supra* note 94, at 68.

E. Boulwareism/Best Offer First Bargaining

This technique derives its name from Lemuel Boulware, a former Vice President for Labor Relations at General Electric. Mr. Boulware was not enamored of traditional "auction" bargaining that involved the use of extreme initial positions, the making of time-consuming concessions, and the achievement of final collective bargaining agreements similar to those the parties initially knew they would reach. He thus decided to determine ahead of time what the company was willing to commit to wage and benefit increases. He surveyed the employees to ascertain the areas in which they wanted the increases to be granted, and formulated a complete "best-offer-first" package. This was presented to union negotiators on a "take-it-or-leave-it" basis. He informed the labor representatives that the company would only modify its initial offer if they could convince it that some miscalculation had been made or changed circumstances had occurred. This approach precipitated a costly work stoppage and resulted in protracted unfair labor practice litigation.

The term "Boulwareism" is now associated with "*best-offer-first*" (offeror's perspective) or "*take-it-or-leave-it*" (offeree's perspective) bargaining.[124] The people who employ this approach frequently are insurance adjusters. They endeavor to establish reputations as people who make one firm, fair offer. If that proposal is not accepted by the claimant, they do not plan to alter their position. A few individuals are able to employ this technique effectively. They make reasonable offers in a relatively non-threatening manner, and many of their firm offers are accepted. On the other hand, individuals using Boulwareistic tactics must recognize that this approach may actually cost their side money. Had they been willing to engage in more conventional auction bargaining, they may have been able to resolve their differences for less than they were initially willing to pay. In addition, they may have avoided the rejection of what might otherwise have been acceptable agreements—but were rejected because of the patronizing way in which they were presented.

Rarely can the representatives on one side definitively determine the true value of an impending bargaining transaction *before* they meet with their counterparts. No matter how thoroughly they review the information preliminarily available to them, they must remember that it is impossible to ascertain the real value of a prospective deal prior to discussions with the people representing the other side. Only through these inter-party exchanges can they learn how much their adversaries desire an agreement. They must assess how risk-averse their counterparts are, and the degree to which time pressure may be influencing those people. Without such critical information, it is not possible to calculate accurately what is truly required to satisfy counterpart needs and interests. If an insurance adjuster willing to pay

---

124. *See* Katz, *supra* note 113, at 129–131; Robert S. Adler & Elliot M. Silverstein, "When David Meets Goliath: Dealing with Power Differentials in Negotiation," 5 *Harvard Negotiation Law Review* 1, 97–98 (2000).

$50,000 begins the negotiation process with an offer of $20,000 or $25,000 and be-comes difficult once he gets to the $40,000 to $45,000 range, he may be able to resolve the claim for $42,000 or $43,000 — saving his company $7,000 or $8,000! Moreover, the claimant would probably be more satisfied with the $42,000 or $43,000 obtained through the auction process than with $50,000 offered in a Boulwareistic fashion.

Negotiators should also be extremely hesitant to adopt a Boulwareistic approach because of the impact of this tactic on counterparts. It exudes a paternalistic arro-gance, with offerors effectively informing offerees, in a "parent"-to-"child" inter-action, that they know what is best for both sides. Few bargainers are willing to defer so readily to the superior knowledge of opposing parties. This technique also deprives adversaries of the opportunity to participate meaningfully in the bargaining process. Even if the claimant would initially have been pleased to resolve her case for $50,000, she may not be satisfied with a take-it-or-leave-it first offer of $50,000. She wants to explore the matter through the Information Stage and to exhibit her negotiating skill through the Distributive and Closing Stages. When the process has been completed, she wants to think that her own personal ability influenced the final outcome.

People contemplating the use of Boulwareism must realize that this approach may only be employed effectively by negotiators who possess significant power. If weak participants attempt to use this technique, their take-it-or-leave-it demands are likely to be unceremoniously rejected. When bargainers enjoy a clear strength advantage, there is no reason to use this approach — except to avoid the need to en-gage in any real give-and-take negotiating. The more power negotiators have, the more generous they should be with *process* — not substance. They should permit counterparts to participate meaningfully in the interaction and let them think they influenced the outcome. Studies have shown that individuals who believe that the negotiation *process* has been fair are more satisfied with objectively less beneficial terms than are persons who obtain objectively better terms through a process they did not believe to be fair.[125] The use of more traditional auction bargaining techniques increases the likelihood the parties will reach mutual accords. It simultaneously pro-vides individuals employing conventional negotiating tactics with the opportunity to achieve final terms that are better from their own side's perspective than they were initially willing to offer.

F. Settlement Brochures

Some business representatives attempt to enhance their bargaining posture through the preparation of pre-negotiation settlement brochures. These consist of written documents that specifically articulate the factual, economic and business bases for

---

125. *See* Hollander-Blumoff, *supra* note 23; Hollander-Blumoff & Tyler, *supra* note 23, at 489–493.

the positions being articulated. Each monetary item is separately listed and explained in an attempt to establish highly "principled" opening positions.[126] Transactional negotiators who represent corporate clients frequently employ settlement brochures. They formulate detailed opening positions in writing that carefully explain the way in which they have valued the various items to be exchanged. Labor and management representatives also use this technique when they bargain with each other. It can be a particularly effective approach, if it induces their counterparts to afford these documents more respect than they objectively warrant.

Settlement brochures may subconsciously be accorded greater respect than would verbal recitations, due to the aura of legitimacy associated with printed documents.[127] The use of this technique may bolster the confidence of individuals using them, and may enable them to seize control of the negotiating agenda at the outset of the bargaining process. Although some negotiators do not provide counterparts with copies of settlement brochures until their first formal meeting, others have them delivered several days in advance of initial sessions to enable their counterparts to review these documents before they meet.

Individuals who are presented with settlement brochures should be careful not to accord them greater respect than they deserve. The recipients should treat the factual, economic, and business representations set forth in those documents as they would identical verbal statements. While few proficient bargainers would think of making deliberate factual or economic misrepresentations in writing, most would not hesitate to engage in "puffing" or "embellishment." If recipients are provided with these instruments before the first bargaining session, they should thoroughly review the assertions made by their counterparts and prepare effective counter arguments that they can express during their negotiation discussions. They should be cautious not to allow their adversaries to use their settlement brochures to control the agenda of their interaction.

Advocates who prepare settlement brochures frequently use charts, tables, or graphs to support their positions. Individuals presented with these claims should carefully review the assumptions underlying those projections. Have the document preparers assumed economic and business developments that have no objective support? Once these underlying assumptions are accepted, the brochure presentations logically follow. This is why the basic assumptions must be perused.

G. Multiple/Equal Value Offers

When multiple issue negotiations are involved, some participants attempt to disclose their own relative item values and elicit similar information regarding their

---

126. *See* Dawson, *supra* note 12, at 137–38; Leigh Steinberg, *Winning With Integrity* 70–71 (1998).
127. *See* Gavin Kennedy, *Essential Negotiation* 48–53 (2009).

counterparts through the use of multiple/equal value offers.[128] They formulate several different offers that vary what they are seeking and what they are willing to give the other side. These diverse offers have a common theme. Each one provides the offeror with a relatively equal level of satisfaction. People who use this technique hope to let the other side understand the different amounts of the various items they must obtain to create equal client satisfaction.

Multiple/equal value offerors hope to induce their counterparts to let them know which of these diverse offers is preferable from their perspective. They want their adversaries to indicate in their counter-offers the terms they prefer to obtain and the issues they are willing to concede to the initial offerors. The parties can then work to generate efficient agreements that maximize the joint returns achieved by the bargaining parties.

When employed carefully with trustworthy counterparts, this approach allows the offerors to let the opposing side know which term combinations they value equally. The offerors thus disclose the relative priorities associated with their underlying needs and interests. They hope their adversaries will share their underlying priorities through their critiques of the initial offers and their own counter-offers.

As the parties explore their respective bundled offers and counter-offers, they can discard less efficient formulations, and focus on the mutually beneficial packages. If the use of multiple/equal value offers is to function effectively, the negotiating participants must indicate, with some degree of candor, which items are essential, important, and desirable, and how much of each they hope to obtain. This allows each side to appreciate the other's basic interests and encourages the development of mutually beneficial accords.

Parties initiating the use of multiple/equal value offers are counting on reciprocal candor from the other side. The offerors, have to a significant degree, disclosed their relative values. If the other side counters with manipulative and disingenuous offers designed to exploit the original offerors' openness, it may be able to claim an excessive share of the joint value created.

A second risk concerns the articulation of an excessive number of package offers. Individuals who are presented with two, three, or even four options usually do a good job of determining which alternative is preferable. On the other hand, persons presented with a greater number of options often become confused. They fail to evaluate all of the options together, but instead make comparisons among finite groups.[129] As a result, even though Package 2 may be optimal, one side may only compare Pack-

---

128. *See* Malhotra & Bazerman, *supra* note 42, at 100–101; Lax & Sebenius, *supra* note 40, at 209–210; Victoria Husted Medvec & Adam D. Galinsky, "Putting More on the Table: How Making Multiple Offers Can Increase the Final Value of the Deal," 8 *Negotiation* 4 (2005); Brian J. Dietmeyer & Rob Kaplan, *Strategic Negotiation* 131–141 (2004).

129. *See generally* Shenna Iyengar, *The Art of Choosing* 183–215 (2010); Schwartz, *supra* note 49.

ages 3, 4, and 5 and select the preferable one from this group. They fail to compare the one picked with Package 2 and end up with an inferior choice. It thus behooves negotiators using multiple/equal value offers to limit the number articulated at one time to a manageable number the recipients can assess together. This is especially important when many items are involved and offer recipients must compare expansive packages with one another. Offerors who suspect that the "paradox of choice" may be affecting the assessments of offer recipients may minimize this phenomenon by asking those parties if they have compared the offer they said they preferred with all of the other packages which have been tendered.

H. Contingent Concessions

When negotiators begin to find it difficult to make additional position changes, the discussions may approach an impasse. Each side is afraid to make a concession, fearing that its position change will not be matched by the other side. One way to get past this concern is to suggest a concession that is conditioned upon an equal value position change by the other party.[130] For example, one side may be demanding $27 million for its company, while the other is offering $23 million. It may have taken a number of interactions to get the parties this close together. Neither seems willing to move. The prospective buyer may indicate that it would be willing to increase its offer to $24 million if the prospective seller could come down to $26 million. If this conditional concession is accepted, the $4 million gap is reduced to $2 million.

If the party receiving the contingent concession recognizes the face-saving way for the two sides to move closer together, it may accede to the offeror's suggestion. Once the parties are only $2 million apart, one may make another position change, or another contingent concession might be proposed to bring the parties even closer together. As their respective positions begin to merge, the likelihood of an agreement increases dramatically.

The use of a contingent concession provides a face-saving way for temporarily recalcitrant parties to move together. If either made a concession and it was not reciprocated, that side would feel embarrassed and angry. When the two sides agree to make simultaneous position changes, neither appears weak in the eyes of the other. In addition, neither is afraid of making an unreciprocated position change.

The first risk associated with contingent concession offers concerns the fact the conditional position change may be rejected. Although the offeror will then remain at her current position, this technique clearly signals to the other side the willingness of this party to change its position. A more recalcitrant counterpart may use this information to get the initial offeror to ultimately make a unilateral position change. To avoid this likelihood, the party offering a contingent concession should indicate

---

130. *See* Malhotra & Bazerman, *supra* note 42, at 66–71.

her hesitancy to make another position change. She could acknowledge the likelihood that the other side is experiencing similar feelings. She can then suggest contingent concessions as a way for both sides to move closer together.

The second risk associated with contingent concessions concerns the fact that parties making such concessions tend to move toward the mid-point between their present positions. One side may have already conceded more than it should have, and it may be completely unwilling to achieve agreement by splitting the remaining difference. This difficulty can be addressed by this party suggesting an unwillingness to make an equal contingent concession—but a willingness to make a position change that is one-half of the position change being offered by the other side. This party should carefully indicate why he believes that it would inappropriate for him to match the offeror's suggested concession. He might point to prior concessions he has already made, and indicate that he is not in a position to match the exact size of the proposed joint concessions. This approach might enable him to move up $1/2 million in response to the offeror's willingness to come down $1 million. If this suggestion is accepted, the parties can continue to use similar position changes to move toward agreement.

I. Range Offers

Negotiators occasionally phrase their monetary offers in terms of a range rather than as a single figure—*e.g.*, "we would expect something in the $1,000,000, 1,500,000, or 2,000,000 area." This approach frequently indicates uncertainty in the mind of the offeror. A more carefully prepared individual would have determined the precise number to be mentioned. Advocates who hope to establish a conciliatory bargaining atmosphere may use range offers to evidence their receptivity to compromise.[131] Recipients of range offers should focus on the most beneficial end of the spectrum— *i.e.*, business sellers should discuss the $2,000,000 figure, while buyers should explore the $1,000,000 demand.

Bargainers should usually avoid range offers, since this approach tends to undermine the persuasiveness of their presentations. When they make "principled" opening offers, the figures provided should be definitive, based on the underlying rationales provided. When "principled" concessions are articulated, they should be similarly related to the precise explanations given for those particular position changes. Nonetheless, when individuals are dealing with persons they know well and with whom they have good relationships, range offers can be used to induce their counterparts to begin with realistic offers and to encourage positive interactions.[132]

---

131. *See* Daniel R. Ames & Malia F. Mason, "Tandem Anchoring: Informational and Politeness Effects of Range Offers in Social Exchanges," 108 *Journal of Personality and Social Psychology* 254 (2015).

132. *See* Ames & Mason, *supra* note 131.

J. Limited Client Authority/Lack of Client Authority

Many negotiators like to indicate during the preliminary stages of a negotiation that they do not possess final authority from their firms regarding the matters being discussed.[133] Some people who possess real authority employ this technique to reserve the right to check with their absent superiors and reassess the terms agreed upon before tentative agreements formally bind their side. Other negotiators really do have constituencies that must ultimately approve preliminary accords before they become operative. For example, labor organizations must generally have collective contracts ratified by members. Representatives of federal, state, and municipal government entities must usually obtain legislative or departmental approval before their agreements become effective.

The advantage of a limited authority approach — whether actual or fabricated — is that it permits the participants using this device to obtain psychological commitments from counterparts who are authorized to make binding commitments on behalf of their firms. The unbound bargainers can thereafter seek beneficial modifications of negotiated contracts based upon "unexpected" demands of their superiors. Once counterparts became familiar with this tactic, they begin to hold back some of the items they were initially prepared to commit. This allows them to increase their final offers after the first contracts are rejected by their counterparts. As it becomes apparent to individuals who use limited authority to obtain additional concessions at the end of transactions that their adversaries are effectively countering this approach, they begin to recognize the futility of this technique.

Bargainers who encounter counterparts who initially indicate that they lack the authority to bind their firms frequently find it advantageous to state that they similarly lack final authority over the issues being discussed. This permits them to "check" with their own absent principals before they make final commitments. If they are unable to claim limited authority of their own, they may alternatively refuse to bargain with agents who do not possess a meaningful degree of final control. A counterpart's alleged lack of authority may occasionally be an impediment to a final agreement. That person may have specifically indicated that she is not empowered to accept a certain offer that is really within the scope of her actual authorized limits. It is rarely helpful to directly challenge that person with respect to this issue, because she is unlikely to admit overt prevarication. It is far more productive to provide that individual with a face-saving escape. By suggesting that she privately contact her superior and request permission to agree to the offer on the table, a final accord may be achieved without the need for unnecessary accusations or recriminations. This approach best serves party interests by maximizing the likelihood of an ultimate settlement.

Advocates who disingenuously inform their counterparts that they have limited authority and must obtain superior approval before agreements are final may occa-

---

133. *See* Dawson, *supra* note 12, at 49–60; Katz, *supra* note 113, at 124–26; Adler & Silverstein, *supra* note 124, at 98–100.

sionally find themselves with a dilemma. They have achieved outstanding terms and fear that their adversaries may reconsider their circumstances and reopen the negotiations prior to the perfection of mutually binding commitments. To deprive their counterparts of the opportunity to reflect on the provisions that have been tentatively agreed upon, these advocates can ask for a brief recess prior to the conclusion of the current talks to enable them to "consult with their absent principals." They can then return to the bargaining table with definitive acceptance and procure binding commitments from their adversaries.

Negotiators occasionally receive telephone calls from counterpart agents who would like to know their thoughts regarding the issues at hand. The caller asks what the recipient hopes to achieve from the impending interaction. When these targets openly disclose their initial positions, they are told that the suggested terms are outrageous and wholly unacceptable. The callers even indicate that they could not possible convey those proposals to their superiors. If the callers are asked what their side would be willing to provide, they indicate that they lack the authority to put any offer on the table. This technique is designed to make naive respondents feel guilty about their "extreme demands" and induce them to unilaterally modify their opening offers to the benefit of their adversaries.

It is impossible to bargain meaningfully with people who lack the authority to speak for their own organizations. The participants who possess real client authority can only bid against themselves by articulating consecutive opening offers. When unauthorized counterparts telephone, it is apparent that they do not plan to conduct serious negotiations. They hope to obtain several concessions as a prerequisite to participation by the people on their side. Negotiators should not succumb to this approach. If they are willing to do so, they should disclose their initial offers. When the unauthorized callers criticize their position statements, the call recipients should ask the callers to state their own positions. If they indicate that they lack the authority to do so, they should be told to get some authority and to state their own positions to enable the participants to discuss their respective positions. If they indicate that they cannot get such authority, they should be instructed to have someone with actual authority contact the call recipients with offers from their side. Only when the representatives of both parties possess the authority to articulate meaningful offers can real bargaining occur.

K. Flinch/Krunch

When negotiators receive opening offers from the other side, they often generate consecutive opening offers through the use of the Flinch or Krunch[134] As soon as they receive the opposing party's offer, they work nonverbally to generate unreciprocated opening offers. Sometimes they say nothing. They simply pull back and look disappointed with the clearly inadequate opening offer. On other occasions,

---

134. *See* Dawson, *supra* note 12, at 32–35; Jim Thomas, *Negotiate to Win* 86–100 (2005).

they orally indicate their disappointment in such a parsimonious opening. They hope to induce the party who initiated the bargaining process to bid against himself or herself.

If their initial Flinch/Krunch is effective and they receive another opening offer, they can continue this tactic to induce additional unreciprocated position changes. They can indicate that the new offer is "a step in the right direction" but still insufficient. If they are effective, they may generate three or four opening offers from the opposing side before they have to articulate any position of their own. They can also employ this tactic during later discussions following counterpart position changes to induce the other side to make consecutive concessions.

The Flinch/Krunch can be an especially effective technique when employed by individuals who can appear to be sincerely shocked by the inadequacy of the other party's initial position. If the users of this tactic seem to be disingenuously attempting to take advantage of naive counterparts, they may create hostility and a negative reaction.

What should someone do if their opening offer is countered by a Flinch/Krunch? They should be careful not to bid against themselves by announcing another offer. They could remain silent and look to the other side to articulate its opening position. They could also ask that party if they are contemplating an opening offer of their own or ask them what they think would be the appropriate result.

The Flinch/Krunch does not have to be confined to opening offers. When counterparts make concessions, this tactic can be employed to suggest the obvious inadequacy of their concessions. The concession recipients may again remain silent hoping to induce the other side to bid against themselves, or they may orally indicate their disappointment with the small position change. If they use this technique adeptly, they may be able to frequently generate consecutive concessions during their bargaining interactions. This should enable them to achieve final results that favor their own side.

Individuals who make concessions should be certain not to permit use of the Flinch/Krunch to induce them to bid against themselves. They should not announce additional concessions until they have received reciprocity from the other side. When the opposing party shows no indication of a willingness to change their current position, they should make it expressly clear that no further position changes will be forthcoming without reciprocal movement from the other side.

L. Real or Feigned Anger

Resort to real or feigned anger during the critical stages of a negotiation may effectively convince their counterparts of the seriousness of one's position.[135] It may also intimidate adversaries and convince them of the need to make concessions if the bargaining process is to continue.[136] Empirical evidence indicates that negotiators facing

---

135. *See* Katz, *supra* note 113, at 150–151.
136. *See* Adler & Silverstein, *supra* note 124, at 95–96.

angry counterparts tend to lower their expectations and make more generous concessions, especially when they do not possess beneficial non-settlement alternatives.[137]

Although true anger is occasionally displayed during bargaining encounters, proficient negotiators almost never lose their tempers. They use carefully orchestrated anger that is designed to intimidate anxious counterparts. I have seen collective bargaining agents shout, swear, pound the table, and walk out. As soon as they enter their side's private caucus room, they calmly ask: "How did I do? Wasn't I more believable than last year?"

The use of real anger can be dangerous, because people who permit bargaining frustration and anxiety to precipitate unplanned diatribes frequently disclose more information during their outbursts than they intended. For example, a prospective firm buyer who has offered $7,500,000 to a corporate seller who is steadfastly demanding $10,000,000 might finally explode with a statement indicating that "this firm cannot be worth more $8,000,000!" This exclamation would strongly suggest to the selling company representative that the prospective purchaser is willing to pay at least $8,000,000, but little above that figure. This is critical information, because it provides the seller with a good approximation of the buyer's resistance point. If the seller was hoping to achieve a result in excess of $8,000,000, he should realize that this result is unlikely during the current negotiation. It may thus be necessary to plan subsequent discussions, with the expectation that greater time pressure may ultimately induce the purchaser to reconsider its current upper limit.

Individuals who wish to employ feigned anger to advance their position should plan their tactic with care. They should decide which words would be most likely to influence their counterpart's assessment of the transaction, and try to limit their apparent outburst to those comments. They should simultaneously watch for signs of increased frustration and anxiety on the part of their adversary (*e.g.*, clenched teeth, wringing of hands, or placing of open hands in front of self as defensive measure against the verbal onslaught), to be certain not to provoke an unintended reaction such as the cessation of talks.

People who find themselves berated by an angry counterpart may be tempted to respond with their own retaliatory diatribe to convince their adversary that they cannot be intimidated by such irrational tactics. This quid pro quo approach involves obvious risks. At a minimum, the vituperative exchange would probably have a deleterious impact upon the bargaining atmosphere. It may even cause a cessation of meaningful discussions and force the participants to resort to their non-settlement alternatives. While this response may be appropriate to counteract the conduct of an unreasonably angry counterpart or an aggressive bully, there is a more productive way to react to contrived counterpart anger. The targets of these outbursts should remain silent and listen intently for inadvertent verbal leaks and watch for informative

---

137. *See* Gerben Van Kleef, Carsten K. De Dreu & Anthony S. Manstead, "The Interpersonal Effects of Anger and Happiness in Negotiations," 86 *Journal of Personality and Social Psychology* 57 (2004).

nonverbal signals. They should look at their raging counterparts as if they are behaving like petulant children. Their quiet styles may disconcert manipulative adversaries who are using feigned anger to advance their cause.[138]

Negotiators with sincere demeanors may effectively counter angry eruptions by indicating that they have been personally offended by the ad hominem attack. They should indicate that they cannot understand how their reasonable and fair approach can be subject to such an intemperate challenge. They may recite several of their most recent position changes to demonstrate their sincere efforts to accommodate counterpart needs. If they are successful in this regard, they may create feelings of guilt and embarrassment in the attacking party. This technique may even shame that person into a conciliatory concession.

M. Aggressive Behavior

Aggressive behavior is usually intended to have an impact similar to that associated with real or feigned anger.[139] It is employed to convince counterparts of the seriousness of one's position. It can also be used by anxious individuals to maintain control of the bargaining agenda. By being overly assertive, aggressive negotiators may be able to dominate the interaction. This technique is most effectively employed by naturally aggressive individuals. Less assertive persons who try to adopt an uncharacteristically aggressive approach do not feel comfortable with this style, and they may be unable to project a credible image.

Some highly combative negotiators attempt to augment their aggressive style with gratuitous sarcasm. Their goal is to make their counterparts feel so uncomfortable that they will be induced to make excessive concessions in an effort to end their unpleasant interaction. I once worked with such an individual. He was constantly insulting and belittling those around him. Although his tactics caused many adversaries to breakoff settlement talks in circumstances in which accords might otherwise have been achieved, there were numerous occasions when he was able to obtain beneficial results from counterparts who wanted to conclude the interactions quickly to avoid further contact with this abrasive person. Individuals who use this approach risk needless non-settlements from counterparts who refuse to tolerate their offensive behavior. They also tend to generate accords that are not as efficient as the ones they may have achieved if the parties had developed more cordial and trusting relationships.

Aggressive negotiators, particularly those who use abrasive tactics, should carefully monitor their counterparts for nonverbal indications of excessive frustration and stress. They should look for clenched teeth, crossed arms and legs, increased gross body movement, and similar signals. If they are unaware of these signs, they may generate unintended bargaining breakdowns.

---

138. *See* Shapiro & Jankowski, *supra* note 22, at 178.
139. *See* Katz, *supra* note 113, at 146–148.

Well-mannered negotiators who attempt to counter offensively aggressive bargainers with quid pro quo attacks are likely to fail, due to the capacity of those individuals to out-insult almost anyone. People who encounter these adversaries should diminish the aggregate impact of their demeaning techniques through the use of short, carefully controlled interactions. Telephone discussions or e-mail exchanges may be used to limit each interaction. When telephone discussions become tense, the targets of aggressive counterparts can indicate that they have to take care of other business and terminate their immediate interactions. They can thereafter re-phone their adversaries when they are more inclined to tolerate their behavior. When people receive nasty e-mail messages, they can take their time to reply. Personal meetings should, if possible, be restricted to sessions of less than one hour in duration. These abbreviated discussions can prevent abrasive advocates from building momentum with the effect of their sarcasm. It also makes it easier for the objects of such insults to retain control over their own emotions.

Negotiators must unfortunately recognize that people still view aggressive and abrasive behavior by male and female advocates differently (*see* Chapter 11, *infra*). When women employ a loud voice and crude language to intimidate male counterparts, those recipients are likely to find that conduct more offensive than they would if identical tactics were employed by men. This fact would certainly suggest that female bargainers who adopt aggressive styles do not need to be as offensive as their male cohorts to achieve the same impact. My classroom observations have similarly indicated that male recipients of aggressive female behavior are less likely to respond in kind than they would if similar conduct were emanating from other males. This fact may enable female negotiators to obtain a psychological advantage over male recipients who are unable to respond to aggressive female adversaries as they would against male adversaries.

N. Walking Out/Hanging Up Telephone

This technique is frequently employed by demonstrative negotiators who want to convince their counterparts that they are unwilling to make additional concessions.[140] Once the parties have narrowed the distance between their respective positions, these individuals storm out or slam down the telephone receiver in an effort to induce risk-averse adversaries to close all or most of the remaining gap. This approach may induce overly anxious counterparts to cave in.

Bargainers should not permit this type of bullying conduct to intimidate them into unwarranted and unreciprocated concessions. Targets of such behavior should *never* run after their departing counterparts or immediately re-telephone people who have deliberately terminated their present interactions. This would be viewed as a sign of weakness to be exploited. They should instead give their demonstrative counterparts time to calm down and reflect on the current positions on the table. They

---

140. *See id.*, at 153–155.

should also reevaluate their own non-settlement options to be certain they do not succumb to unreasonable counterpart demands. If targets of these intimidating techniques are able to maintain their resolve, their bullying adversaries are likely to resume negotiations and make new counter offers.

O. Irrational Behavior

A few negotiators attempt to gain a bargaining advantage through seemingly irrational conduct.[141] Some of these persons attribute the irrationality of their positions to their absent superiors (*see* "Mutt and Jeff" approach, *infra*), while others exhibit their own bizarre behavior. These individuals hope to convince their counterparts that their side cannot be dealt with logically. Adversaries must either accept their one-sided demands or face the consequences associated with the lack of any accord.

People who encounter aberrant counterparts tend to become frightened by their unusual behavior. They fear that these irrational bargainers will destroy both sides. To avoid these dire consequences, they frequently accept the dictates of their seemingly illogical adversaries. As a result, they end up with agreements that are worse than their non-settlement options.

Few negotiators or their corporate superiors are truly irrational. If they were, they would be unable to achieve consistently successful results in a highly competitive world. In most instances in which bizarre behavior is encountered, the actors are crazy like a fox — using *feigned irrationality* to advance their bargaining objectives. The most effective way to counter contrived preposterousness is to ignore it and respond in an entirely rational manner. As soon as these manipulative counterparts caucus to consider proposed terms, they cease their illogical conduct and rationally evaluate the proposals on the table. Once they realize that their strange conduct is not having its expected impact, they are likely to forego this approach.

On rare occasions, truly irrational counterparts are encountered. While these individuals may be the negotiators themselves, they are more frequently the principals involved. When such people participate in negotiations, it is impossible to deal with them logically. They are incapable of evaluating bargaining proposals and non-settlement options in a realistic manner. They continue to reiterate their unsound proposals in an unthinking fashion no matter the risks involved. counterparts must either give **in** to their positions or accept their non-settlement alternatives.

When negotiators are forced to interact with truly bizarre adversaries, they must carefully reassess their own non-settlement alternatives. They should avoid agreements that are less beneficial than their external options. They should only accept the dictates of unstable counterparts when those terms are clearly preferable to continued disagreement. Even when agreements are consummated with irrational adversaries, bar-

---

141. *See id.*, at 126–127.

gainers should recognize the subsequent difficulties that may be encountered during the performance stages of their relationship. To protect firm interests, bargainers who enter into contracts with unstable counterparts should try to minimize the risks associated with non-performance or partial performance.

P. False Demands

Alert negotiators occasionally discover during the Information Stage that their counterparts really desire several items that are not valued by their own side. When this knowledge is obtained, many bargainers endeavor to take advantage of the situation. They try to avoid providing the other side with these terms in exchange for insignificant issues.[142] They instead endeavor to extract more substantial concessions. To accomplish this objective, they mention how important those subjects are to their side and include them with their initial demands. If they can convince their counterparts that these issues are of major value to their side, they may be able to enhance their firm's position with what are actually meaningless concessions on their part.

One serious risk is associated with false demands. If individuals employing this technique are too persuasive, they may find themselves the tragic beneficiaries of unwanted bargaining chips. It would be disastrous for them to attempt to rectify this tactical error with a straightforward admission of deception, since this confession would probably impede further negotiation progress. They should tentatively accept the items in question. As the interaction evolves, they should be able to exchange these terms for some other more useful topics. Even if their counterparts recognize their predicament, they should generally permit them to employ this face-saving escape route. Little would be gained by an overt challenge to the manipulative individual's personal integrity, and the risk to the bargaining process would be substantial.

Q. Alleged Expertise/Snow Job

A few individuals attempt to overwhelm bargaining counterparts with factual, economic, and/or business details that are not particularly relevant to the basic interaction. They cite factual, economic, and business matters that are of no meaningful concern to the negotiating parties. They hope to bolster their own bargaining confidence through demonstrations of their thorough knowledge, and hope to intimidate adversaries who have not developed such expertise.

People should not permit their counterparts to overwhelm them with factual or business minutiae. When someone tries to focus upon marginally relevant details, they should be praised for their thorough preparation and be asked to concentrate on the more salient items. If necessary, they should be asked to summarize their po-

---

142. *See id.*, at 119–121.

sitions without the need for repeated reference to superfluous data. Skilled counterparts may even be able to make these "experts" appear silly, and induce them to become more cooperative in an effort to overcome their resulting embarrassment.

R. Bracketing

Some negotiators, especially in transactions pertaining primarily to money, use a technique designed to lead counterparts to the figure they hope to achieve. The work to elicit opening offers from the other side, then begin with an offer or demand that is as far away from their goal as is the other side's initial offer. For example, if a prospective firm buyer begins with an offer of $10,000,000 and the company owner hopes to get $12,500,000, the seller counters with a demand of $15,000,000. If the purchaser moves to $11,500,000, the seller reduces her demand to $13,500,000, carefully keeping her $12,500,000 objective between the two sides' current positions. When the buyer goes up to $12,000,000, the seller comes down to $13,000,000. As the participants move toward the center of their positions, the seller can steer the buyer toward her $12,500,000 goal.

When one party appears to be employing Bracketing, the other may occasionally respond with "*Double Bracketing*."[143] When the seller reduces her demand to $13,000,000 in response to a buyer offer of $12,000,000, the purchaser indicates that he is unable to go as high as the $12,500,000 midpoint between their current positions. He then suggests a deal at $12,250,000 — half way between the seller's apparent objective of $12,500,000 and the buyer's current $12,000,000 offer. If the buyer can induce the seller to succumb to this entreaty, the parties will settle $250,000 below the seller's preliminary goal.

S. Disingenuous Consecutive Concessions

Whenever bargainers lose track of the offers and counteroffers being made and inadvertently make consecutive concessions, they place themselves at a disadvantage. They have probably become confused due to negotiating anxiety and pressure, and they are moving aimlessly toward the position being taken by their counterparts. They normally do not realize that they are making these unreciprocated position changes. counterparts of these individuals should encourage further concessions by challenging the sufficiency of their position changes or though patience and prolonged silence following each concession.

Other negotiators use contrived consecutive concessions to create feelings of guilt and obligation in their adversaries. For example, they may be contemplating a move from their current demand of $500,000 to a new demand of $400,000. Instead of making a "principled" $100,000 concession, they adopt a different approach. They first move to $450,000, with an appropriate explanation for their action. After a rea-

---

143. *See* Richard G. Halpern, "Negotiation Blunders: Allowing Yourself to be Double-Bracketed," *Negotiator Magazine* (Oct. 2003) (http://www.negotiatormagazine.com).

sonable amount of discussion, they then mention $420,000, accompanied by a suitable rationale. They finally move majestically to $400,000. At this point, they indicate that they have made three unanswered concessions. They hope to induce unsuspecting counterparts to respond with a greater counteroffer than would have been produced by a direct move from $500,000 to $400,000. They not only plan to accomplish this result through guilt and obligation, but also from the fact that their successive $50,000, $30,000, and $20,000 position changes suggest that they are rapidly approaching their bottom line.

Recipients of consecutive concessions should immediately become suspicious when they are specifically apprised of their occurrence by counterparts who have made them. Sincerely confused concession-makers are not aware of the fact they have made consecutive concessions. If they are clearly cognizant of their behavior, the recipients of their apparent largesse should realize that this technique is probably being deliberately used as a bargaining strategy. They should not be overly impressed by the consecutive nature of the concessions, but should instead focus upon the aggregate movement involved. They should then respond as they would have if they had been given a direct $100,000 position change.

T. Uproar — "Chicken Little"

Negotiation participants occasionally threaten dire consequences if mutual accords are not achieved. They then indicate that the predicted havoc can be avoided if the other side agrees to the terms they are offering. Careless bargainers may be influenced by this devious technique, if they focus entirely on the damage they will suffer if the extreme consequences occur. For example, a school district may attempt to enhance its bargaining power by threatening to lay off all of the untenured teachers if their representative labor organization does not moderate its demands. The pink-slipped teachers and their tenured colleagues may panic and immediately reduce their requests. When they behave in this manner, they ignore the fact that the threatened layoffs would eliminate most of the English department or create such under staffing that the local school district would no longer be eligible for state education funding.

When extreme consequences are threatened, the affected party should ask two fundamental questions. First, what is the probability that the promised havoc would occur if no accord were attained? In many instances, they would realize that no devastation is likely to result from their refusal to give in to counterpart demands. Second, if there is a possibility that the promised cataclysm may take place, how would that event affect the *other side*? A detached assessment may indicate that the negative consequences would be far greater for the threatening party than they would be for the party being threatened. If this were true, the threatening party would have more to lose if no agreement were achieved, and it would be under greater pressure to avoid a non-settlement. If the threatened participants can be patient, they should be able to benefit from this favorable power imbalance.

U. Brer Rabbit (Reverse Psychology)

In *Uncle Remus, His Songs and His Sayings* (1880), Joel Chandler Harris created an unforgettable character named Brer Rabbit. The story involves a rabbit who is captured by the fox. The rabbit employs reverse psychology to effectuate his escape. While the fox is contemplating his fate, Brer Rabbit says:

> I don't care what you do with me, so long as you don't fling me in that brier-patch. Roast me, but don't fling me in that brier-patch....Drown me just as deep as you please, but don't fling me in that brier-patch....Skin me, snatch out my eyeballs, tear out my ears by the roots, and cut off my legs, but don't fling me in that brier-patch.

Since the fox wanted to punish Brer Rabbit, he chose the one alternative the rabbit appeared to fear most. He flung him in the brier-patch, and Brer Rabbit escaped!

Adept negotiators frequently employ the "Brer Rabbit" approach to obtain beneficial terms from retributive, *win-lose counterparts* who irrationally judge their "success" not by how well they have done, but by how poorly they think their adversaries have done.[144] Brer Rabbit bargainers subtly suggest to such counterparts that they or their firms would suffer greatly if certain action were either taken or withheld, when they actually hope to obtain the very results being eschewed. They then ask for other items they do not really wish to attain. Their adversaries are so intent on ensuring their complete defeat that they force on the Brer Rabbit negotiators the items they appear to want least (*i.e.*, their *real first choices*). They have to play the game until the end by asking if their counterparts could possibly give them something else, suggesting that their superiors will be so disappointed if this is all they get. Their counterparts will smile and absolutely refuse to make another concession.

The Brer Rabbit technique may be successfully used by bargainers to obtain favorable results from win-lose adversaries. Nonetheless, this approach involves serious risks. If it is employed against win-win counterparts, they may be induced to agree to terms that the manipulative participants do not really desire. When their counterparts grant them their verbally preferred choices, they may be forced either to admit their devious conduct or to accept the less beneficial terms granted to them.

V. Mutt and Jeff (Good Cop/Bad Cop)

The Mutt and Jeff routine constitutes one of the most common—and effective— bargaining techniques.[145] One seemingly reasonable negotiator softens counterpart resistance by professing sympathy toward the "generous" concessions being made by the other side. When the counterparts begin to think a final accord is on the horizon, the reasonable person's partner summarily rejects the new offer as entirely insufficient.

---

144. *See* Katz, *supra* note 113, at 127.

145. *See* Greg Williams (with Pat Iyer), *Body Language Secrets to Win More Negotiations* 159–161 (2016); Dawson, *supra* note 12, at 80–84; Lum, *supra* note 36, at 163; Katz, *supra* note 113, at 122–24.

The unreasonable participant castigates their counterparts for their parsimonious concessions and insincere desire to achieve a fair accord. Just as the counterparts are preparing to explode at the unreasonable participant, the reasonable partner assuages their feelings and suggests that if some additional concessions are made, she could probably induce her seemingly irrational partner to accept the new terms. It is amazing how diligently many people interacting with Mutt and Jeff bargainers strive to formulate proposals that will satisfy the critical participant.

Devious negotiators occasionally employ the Mutt and Jeff approach with the truly unreasonable person assuming the role of the "reasonable" party. That individual instructs his partner to reject every new counterpart offer in an outraged and belittling manner. The "unreasonable" participant then suggests that no settlement is possible, so long as the counterparts continue to evidence such an unyielding attitude. The "unreasonable" partner is occasionally expected to get up and head toward the exit — only to be prevailed upon to reluctantly return to the bargaining table through the valiant efforts of her "conciliatory" partner.

Mutt and Jeff tactics may even be used by single negotiators. They can claim that their absent superior suffers from delusions of grandeur that must be satisfied if any agreement is to be reached. These manipulative bargainers repeatedly praise their counterparts for the munificent concessions being made, but insist that greater movement is necessary to satisfy the excessive aspirations of their irrational principal. It is ironic to note that their absent superior may actually be highly receptive to any fair resolution. Since the counterparts have no way of knowing this, they usually accept the representations regarding extravagant principal intransigence at face value. The adversaries then endeavor to satisfy the alleged needs of the missing party.

Negotiators who encounter Mutt and Jeff tactics should not directly challenge the apparently devious scheme being used against them. It is possible that their counterparts are not really engaged in a disingenuous exercise. One counterpart may actually disagree with his partner's assessment of the situation. Allegations regarding the apparently manipulative tactics being used by those individuals would probably create a tense and unproductive bargaining environment — particularly when the counterparts have not deliberately adopted a Mutt and Jeff style. Such allegations may also induce truly Machiavellian adversaries to embrace some other devious approach. Since it is generally easier to counter techniques that have already been identified, there is no reason to provide deceptive adversaries with the opportunity to switch to other practices that might not be so easily recognized and neutralized.

Individuals who encounter Mutt and Jeff bargainers tend to make the mistake of allowing the seemingly unreasonable participants to control the entire interaction. They direct their arguments and offers to those persons in an effort to obtain their reluctant approval. It is beneficial to include the reasonable participants in the discussions in an effort to obtain their acquiescence — before attempting to satisfy their irrational partners. Ask those persons if they would be satisfied with the terms they have indicated are reasonable. In a few instances, the more conciliatory counterparts may actually indicate a willingness to accept particular proposals that will be characterized as unacceptable by their associates. If the unified position of the counterparts can be shattered in this fashion, it may be possible to whipsaw the reasonable individuals against their excessively demanding partners.

If the persons representing the other side are truly employing a Mutt and Jeff approach, the reasonable participants will never suggest their willingness to assent to the particular terms being offered. Those individuals will instead reiterate a desire to obtain the acquiescence of their unreasonable partners. When this occurs, the reasonable participants should again be asked—not if their partners would be likely to accept the terms being proposed—but whether *they* would be willing to accept those conditions. Proficient "reasonable" participants will never indicate their acceptance of the proffered terms, without the concurrence of their partners, and it will become clear that the counterparts are using wholly manipulative tactics.

It is always important when dealing with seemingly unreasonable counterparts to remember what would likely occur if no mutual accords were achieved. If the overall cost of surrendering to the one-sided demands of those adversaries would clearly exceed the costs associated with non-settlements, the interactions should not be fruitlessly continued. The counterparts should be informed that they will have to substantially modify their assessments before further bargaining can meaningfully occur.

W. Belly-Up ("Yes . . . , but . . .")

Some individuals use a bargaining style that is particularly difficult for counterparts to counter.[146] They act like wolves in sheepskin. They wear bedraggled outfits to the offices of their adversaries and indicate how commodious those environments are. They then profess their lack of negotiating ability and economic and business knowledge in an effort to evoke sympathy and to lure unsuspecting adversaries into a false sense of security. They readily acknowledge the superior competence of their counterparts, and shamelessly exhibit a complete lack of ability. They then ask their adversaries what those people think would constitute fair terms.

The epitome of the Belly-Up style was artfully created by actor Peter Falk in his Lt. Columbo police detective character. That inspector seemed to bumble along during criminal investigations with no apparent plan. When he interviewed suspects, he did so in a wholly disorganized manner. By the time the suspects realized that Lt. Columbo really understood what was happening, they had already confessed and were in police custody! Another example of this type of person was provided by the late Senator Sam Ervin of North Carolina. During the Senate Watergate Hearings, the general public became well acquainted with his masterful, down-home style. This casual "country lawyer" quoted Biblical parables and recited southern homilies while adroitly obtaining confessions to High Crimes and Misdemeanors from perspicacious administration witnesses who thought they could easily outsmart this innocuous old

---

146. *See* Katz, *supra* note 113, at 115–117.

man. One should be especially suspicious of any self-proclaimed "country lawyer" who graduated from the Harvard Law School!

Especially devious Belly-Up negotiators may resort to more manipulative conduct. When counterparts take tough positions, they place their hand over their heart and display pained facial expressions. If their adversaries continue to push for beneficial terms, these participants may reach into their desk drawer and extract a nitroglycerin vial! I have met several people who have bragged about the effectiveness of this tactic. If you are certain these counterparts do not suffer from chest pains, you can continue your aggressive approach. If, however, you were to suspect real heart problems, you should recess your discussions and contact a senior official in the opposing entity. Explain to that person that you are engaged in a difficult interaction with X, and indicate that you are concerned about that individual's physical or emotional capacity to participate. If the official downplays that person's condition, you can assume that he is using the Belly-Up approach to take advantage of you. On the other hand, if the official suggests the participation of another firm representative, you should be pleased to interact with that person. Never continue negotiations with someone you think may suffer serious health consequences as a result of your interactions.

Belly-Up bargainers are difficult people to deal with, because they refuse to participate in the normal negotiation process. They ask their counterparts to permit them to forego traditional auction bargaining due to their professed inability to negotiate competently. They merely want their respected and honorable adversaries to formulate fair and reasonable arrangements that will not unfairly disadvantage the unfortunate business owners who have chosen such pathetic representatives. Even though their thoroughly prepared counterparts have established high aspiration levels and "principled" opening positions, the Belly-Up negotiators are able to induce them to significantly modify their planned approach.

By the conclusion of their interaction, the Belly-Up bargainer has usually achieved a magnificent accord for his firm, while the opposing party has been left figuratively naked. The extraordinary aspect of this transaction is that the opposing negotiator feels truly gratified that she has been able to satisfy the underlying needs of the other person's poor principal. It requires unbelievable skill to be able to fleece an adversary and leave that person with a feeling of accomplishment and exhilaration.

Negotiators should never permit seemingly inept counterparts to evoke such sympathy that they concede everything in an effort to formulate solutions that are acceptable to those pathetic souls. It is not fair for those devious individuals to force their adversaries to do all of the work. Instead of allowing Belly-Up bargainers to alter their initially planned approach, negotiators should begin with their originally formulated "principled" offers and require those people to participate actively in the process. When Belly-Up participants challenge these opening proposals, they should be forced to articulate their own proposals, so they can be evaluated and challenged. It is generally painful for Belly-Up bargainers to interact in such a traditional manner. They are not used to formulating and defending their own proposals. They are much more comfortable trying to evoke sympathy by criticizing the offers being made to them. Once these individuals are induced to participate in the usual give-and-take, they tend to lose much of their bargaining effectiveness.

X. Passive-Aggressive

Passive-aggressive negotiators are frequently as difficult to deal with as Belly-Up bargainers. Instead of directly challenging the tactics and proposals of their counterparts, they employ oblique, but aggressive, forms of passive resistance. They tend to pout when they are unable to obtain favorable offers, and they resort to obstructionism and procrastination to achieve their objectives. For example, they may show up late for scheduled bargaining sessions or appear with incorrect files or documents. They may exhibit personal ineptitude in an effort to frustrate the negotiation progress and to generate concessions from impatient counterparts. They may even conveniently misplace unsatisfactory proposals that were sent to them and act as if they never arrived. When they are expected to draft final accords, they often take an inordinate amount of time to accomplish their task and may even fail to prepare any written document.

Since passive-aggressive individuals tend to react to problems and confrontations in an indirect manner, it is particularly frustrating to interact with them. Instead of expressing their actual thoughts directly, they employ passive techniques to evidence their displeasure. People who deal with them should recognize the hostility represented by their passive-aggressive behavior. They are usually individuals who really dislike the negotiation process. They may not feel comfortable engaging in the conventional give-and-take. They may dislike their immediate circumstances or current counterparts. Since these factors can rarely be altered, it is more productive to take steps that will beneficially modify the actual behavior of these Passive-Aggressive participants.

Copies of important papers should be obtained through other avenues in case they claim an inability to locate their own copies. Since passive-aggressive individuals do not say no easily — an overtly aggressive act — it is beneficial to present them with seemingly realistic offers they cannot reject. When they are given these proposals, they tend to acquiesce in a predictably passive manner. Once agreements are reached, persons bargaining against them should always offer to prepare the necessary documents. Even when the Passive-Aggressive participants insist upon the opportunity to draft the accord, as they usually do, their counterparts should prepare their own draft agreements in anticipation of their failure to do so. Once Passive-Aggressive negotiators are presented with fait accomplis, they usually accept their fate and execute the proffered agreements. In those infrequent cases in which Passive-Aggressive counterparts do not respond, it may be necessary to have messengers personally deliver the final documents to them and wait for those papers to be duly executed.

Y. Splitting the Difference

One of the most common techniques used to achieve final agreements following detailed auction bargaining that has brought the parties close together involves splitting the remaining difference between their most recent offers. Instead of threatening counterparts with non-settlement consequences if final terms are not achieved, the moving parties use the face-saving "promise" technique to generate simultaneous movement. For instance, parties may have commenced their interaction with a firm seller demand for $10,000,000 and a prospective buyer offer of $7,000,000. After various concessions and counter offers have been exchanged, the seller is requesting $9,000,000, and the buyer is offering $8,000,000. One of the two participants is likely to suggest that they "split the difference" and agree to $8,500,000. This is an expeditious method of reaching the point these negotiators would probably have attained had they continued to rely upon other traditional bargaining techniques.

Persons who are asked to split the outstanding difference to achieve final accords should consider the previous bargaining sequence before they too readily assent to this proposal.[147] They must first decide whether their counterparts were able to unfairly skew the apparent settlement range in their favor through a biased opening offer. If an unreasonably skewed initial offer has been made, it is important to be certain that the negotiation process has effectively negated the unfair advantage associated with that proposal *before* the parties contemplate a splitting of the remaining difference to achieve a final settlement.

Individuals who are contemplating use of the split-the-difference technique to resolve the remaining area of disagreement should similarly review the prior concessions which have been made by both parties. If one has already made six concessions while the other has only made five, it would normally be inappropriate to split the remaining difference until the second party has made one more reciprocal concession. The final result would otherwise be biased in favor of that person's side.

Some experts believe that it is beneficial to let counterparts offer to split-the-difference first.[148] This provides the recipient of this offer with the opportunity to decide whether it is tactically advantageous to accede to this request. It also gives the recipient the chance to obtain one last bargaining edge. Once the counterpart offers to split the distance remaining between the parties, the offeree can treat the midpoint between the parties' existing positions as a new counterpart offer and suggest that they split the distance that *remains* between that new counterpart position and her most recent proposal.

---

147. *See* Freund, *supra* note 22, at 158–159.

148. *See* Alan McCarthy & Steve Hay, *Advanced Negotiation Techniques* 37–38 (2015); Dawson, *supra* note 12, at 64–65.

Z. "Nibble" Technique

Some negotiators "agree" to final accords with apparent principal authority. Their counterparts are pleased with the agreements and contact their superiors to give them the good news. Several days later, these bargainers contact their counterparts with seeming embarrassment and explain that they did not really possess full authority to bind their firms. They sheepishly indicate that their principals are dissatisfied with what was negotiated and require several additional concessions before they will accept the other terms of the agreements.[149] Since the unsuspecting counterparts and their clients are now psychologically committed to final accords and do not want to permit these items to negate their previous efforts, they normally agree to the requested modifications. This "nibble" technique is frequently employed by car salespeople who induce prospective buyers to agree to pay a certain amount for a particular automobile. The salesperson thereafter checks with the "sales manager"—who may not even exist—and contritely informs the psychologically committed customers that several hundred additional dollars are required to consummate the sales transaction. It is amazing how frequently this tactic is successfully employed.

Individuals who are challenged by "nibbler" counterparts often make the mistake of focusing entirely on the desire of their *own side* to preserve the final accords previously reached. They are afraid to let their agreements fall through over the changes being sought. They fail to direct their attention to the *opposing parties*. If they were to ask themselves whether their coun*terparts* would be willing to forego the agreements reached over these items, they would realize that those people also want to retain the terms already agreed upon. If they did not have that similar objective, they would not have participated in the antecedent negotiations. Persons who are asked for additional concessions to cement deals must not be afraid to demand reciprocity for the requested position changes.

When negotiators suspect that they are interacting with counterparts who may try to use disingenuous client disgruntlement to obtain post-agreement concessions, they need to behave in a *provocable manner* and demand reciprocal concessions. They should mentally select the particular terms they would like to have modified in their favor. When their adversaries request the anticipated changes, they can indicate how relieved they are to address this matter, because of the dissatisfaction of their own principals regarding other provisions agreed upon. If their counterparts are acting in good faith and are sincerely upset about the topics raised, they will acknowledge the need for reciprocity and address the proposed exchanges. On the other hand, individuals who are disingenuously using the "nibble" technique to "steal" items will be reluctant to do so. They will usually reject further discussions and insist upon the terms that were initially agreed upon! When "nibblers" put their hands in your pocket in an effort to pick it, you should remember to reach into *their pocket* to extract reciprocal benefits.

---

149. *See id.*, at 85–92; Katz, *supra* note 113, at 140–141; Thompson, *supra* note 65, at 103–109.

§8.03. Conclusion

During negotiation interactions, the parties employ various techniques to further their interests. Each side must decide which tactics they should employ, based upon their own personalities, the personalities of their counterparts, and the particular bargaining circumstances involved. It is also important for negotiators to recognize the techniques being used by their adversaries, to enable them to effectively counteract those tools.

Chapter 9

Verbal Leaks, Posture/ Speech Pattern Mirroring, and Nonverbal Communication

§ 9.01. Verbal Leaks

When individuals interact with one another, their choice of words can be significant. Various verbal expressions can convey quite different messages, even when they seem to be saying the same thing. Negotiators must carefully consider the precise words being expressed to determine whether the speakers mean what they seem to be saying. When an unambiguous statement is uttered, the speaker's meaning is usually clear. On the other hand, when "verbal leaks" are included, these may undermine the seemingly definitive nature of the representation involved.[150]

Negotiators must also monitor their own language to avoid the conveyance of information they do not intend to convey. During the critical stages of interactions, they should employ more definitive terms that do not include verbal leaks. This makes their representations more persuasive. They should avoid modifiers that undermine what they intend to convey.

Classic verbal leaks involve statements such as "I am *not inclined* to go higher" or "I do *not want* to go higher," both of which suggest the speaker is actually willing to go higher. When someone says "I *must have* Item 1, I *really want* to have Item 2, and I *would like* Item 3," they have clearly indicated the degree to which they need the items in question. Item 1 is *essential*, because they "must have" it. Item 2 is *important*, because they "really want" it. Item 3 is *desirable*, because they "would like" to get it. When someone gets near the end of a bargaining interaction and says "that is *about as far* as I can go" or "I don't have *much more* room," they almost always have more to concede. When they reach their actual bottom lines, they will employ direct language with no such modifiers included.

---

150. *See* LePoole, *supra* note 83, at 34.

§ 9.02. Body Posture/Speech Pattern Mirroring

When persons interact with others, they tend to respond more favorably to individuals who exhibit body postures and speech patterns similar to their own.[151] Negotiators who wish to take advantage of this factor can endeavor to mirror the body postures of those with whom they are interacting. If their counterpart leans back in her chair, they can lean back in their own chair. If that person crosses one leg over the other, they can cross the same leg over their other leg. If their adversary leans forward in her chair, they can lean forward in a similar manner.

They may also mirror the speech patterns of their counterpart by speaking more slowly when he does so and speaking more rapidly when he does so.

When individuals speak, they tend to employ one of three sensory preferences.[152] Some have a *visual* orientation. Their words describe visual images of what they are discussing. They may ask if you can *picture* what they are proposing, or may indicate that they *see* what you want. Such visual persons respond more favorably to people who respond in a similarly visual fashion. Other persons have an **auditory** orientation. They may ask counterparts to *listen to* what they are saying, or respond by indicating that they *hear* what was said. Such individuals tend to respond most receptively to others who use similar auditory references. The third group of people have a **kinesthetic/feeling** orientation. These persons like to *feel* or *sense* things. They might suggest that something has a *bad taste*, or indicate that something has left them with a bad *gut feeling*. counterparts should respond to such persons with a similar kinesthetic or feeling orientation to enhance their persuasiveness. For example, they may say that they are comfortable with the offer they just received.

§ 9.03. Reading and Interpreting Nonverbal Signals

Nonverbal communication, one of the most important sources of information available to negotiators, is frequently overlooked, even though it constitutes a substantial portion of the communication being conveyed.[153] Participants generally concentrate on what is being verbally communicated by their counterparts. Bargainers who ignore nonverbal stimuli are only cognizant of the most controlled communi-

---

151. *See* Greg Williams (with Pat Iyer), *Body Language Secrets to Winning More Negotiations* 150–151 (2016); Noah J. Goldstein, Steve J. Martin & Robert B. Cialdini, *YES! 50 Scientifically Proven Ways to Be Persuasive* 134–135 (2008); Allan Pease & Barbara Pease, *The Definitive Book of Body Language* 250–264 (2006).

152. *See* Barbara G. Mandonic, *I Hear What You Say, But What Are You Telling Me?* 24–31, 128–129, 160–161 (2001).

153. *See* Kennedy, *supra* note 127, at 153–154; Anne E. Beall, *Reading the Hidden Communications Around You* 1–2 (2009); Pease & Pease, *supra* note 151, at 10; Peter B. Stark & Jane Flaherty, *The Only Negotiating Guide You'll Ever Need* 45 (2003).

cation being sent by opposing parties.[154] They also miss nonverbal messages that are being conveyed while adversaries are not speaking. Unless they can train themselves to appreciate the subtle nonverbal signs that significantly influence the negotiation process, advocates will rarely have a comprehensive understanding of the transaction. Through their oversight of nonverbal communication, they may miss the most trustworthy messages that their adversaries convey. They may also fail to appreciate the nonverbal messages they are conveying to the other side.[155]

Nonverbal signs are employed for different purposes.[156] Some nonverbal signals are used as *illustrators* to punctuate what the person is saying verbally. Examples of this phenomenon may include finger pointing and head bobbing. *Regulators* are used to regulate the speech of others. Examples might include putting up one's hand like a stop sign, rotating one's hand quickly to encourage the speaker to move more quickly, or putting one's fingers to one's lips to ask for silence. *Adaptors* include gestures employed to relieve stress. These may include hand-wringing and neck rubbing. *Barriers* are signs of discomfort. Someone may turn sideways in a defensive posture or cross their arms during their conversation.

Should negotiators try to fake their nonverbal signals to confuse their counterparts? Rarely can persons manipulate their own signals in a credible manner.[157] Although most people can tell credible lies verbally, few individuals who have not studied acting and become proficient performers are able to convey disingenuous nonverbal messages in a believable way.

During their formal college education, students are forced to think in a logical and abstract fashion. They are often instructed to disregard emotional considerations that do not have an empirically verifiable foundation.[158] The truly personal aspect of relationships is viewed as irrelevant. Mere intuitive "feelings" are to be accorded little or no respect.

People with negotiating experience can all recall circumstances in which they sensed that their adversaries were being disingenuous. Numerous "last offers" have been rejected, along with "final last offers" and even "absolutely final last offers" as preludes to more generous proposals that were subsequently accepted. What induced these persons to sense that the allegedly "final" position statements were merely intermediate steps in the overall process? These suppositions are generally based upon the reading of nonverbal signals which are not congruent with the verbal messages being conveyed.[159]

---

154. *See* Susan Quilliam, *Body Language* 9 (2004); Paul Ekman & Wally Friesen, *Unmasking the Face* 135–136 (1975).

155. *See* Quilliam, *supra* note 154, at 11–13.

156. *See* Gregory Hartley & Maryann Karinch, *I Can Read You Like a Book* 67–68 (2007).

157. *See* Beall, *supra* note 153, at 2; Peter A. Anderson, *The Complete Idiot's Guide to Body Language* 5 (2004).

158. *See* Erin Ryan, "The Discourse Beneath: Emotional Epistemology in Legal Deliberation and Negotiation," 10 *Harvard Negotiation Law Review* (2005).

159. *See* Henry Calero, *The Power of Nonverbal Communication* 89–90 (2005).

True final offers are not casually transmitted from persons who are sitting back in their chair with their arms folded across their chest. The speakers are likely to be leaning slightly forward in the chair with their arms extended and their palms facing outward to demonstrate the openness and sincerity of their positions. It is only when the nonverbal signals are consistent with the words being expressed that the verbal representations become credible.

Negotiators must learn to seriously consider the tentative "feelings" they experience.[160] When they have the sense that their counterpart is making a misrepresentation or is receptive to their most recent offer despite oral protestations to the contrary, they should endeavor to understand the reasons for their suspicions. They may well be based upon their subconscious interpretation of nonverbal messages that provide an accurate impression of the counterpart's true situation. These interpretive "feelings" should not be rejected until it can be established that they are not premised on rational considerations.

Most bargainers fail to observe many of the nonverbal signs emanating from their counterparts. Some naively believe that there is no need to look for these messages, because no competent negotiator would be so careless as to divulge important information in such an inadvertent manner. Anyone who harbors this opinion should consider theatrical performances by well- known actors. Rarely can actors eliminate all of their own involuntary gestures and mannerisms and portray only those attributable to their characters. If these professionals are unable to avoid unintended nonverbal disclosures, surely untrained negotiators will experience less success in this regard.

Other negotiation participants focus so intently upon the responses they are formulating that they miss direct verbal as well as nonverbal messages sent by counterparts. This problem is compounded by the fact that negotiations involve stressful settings that tend to decrease the cognitive abilities of the participants. Bargainers must force themselves to observe their adversaries more diligently, even while planning their own internal strategies. People who find such a bifurcated approach too difficult may wish to have other persons participate on their negotiation teams as observers. These assistants could carefully listen to and observe opposing parties. They could also determine if any unintended information is being inadvertently disclosed by their own spokespersons.

Some individuals tend to be more adept readers of nonverbal communication than others. People trained in psychology, counseling, and theatrics are usually more cognizant of nonverbal stimuli. A number of empirical studies have found that women are typically more sensitive to nonverbal messages than their male cohorts.[161] Studies have also found that African-Americans are more attuned to nonverbal signals than Caucasians.[162] These gender and racial differences may reflect the fact that members

---

160. *See* Beall, *supra* note 153, at 6; Ryan, *supra* note 158, at 275–76.

161. *See* Pease & Pease, *supra* note 151, at 13–14; Charles V. Ford, *Lies, Lies, Lies!!!* 208–209 (1996).

162. *See* Judith A. Hall, *Nonverbal Sex Differences* 41–42 (1984); Nancy Henley, *Body Politics: Power, Sex, and Nonverbal Communication* 14 (1977).

of groups that have historically had less societal empowerment have learned to be more perceptive with respect to nonverbal clues as a means of counterbalancing their power imbalance.[163]

Persons who are not especially sensitive to nonverbal stimuli can easily enhance their ability in this regard. Various books have thoughtfully explored the nonverbal communication area in a manner that is comprehensible to people who have not formally studied this important topic.[164] By reading several of these books and concentrating more intently on the nonverbal behavior of others in social as well as business settings, less skilled nonverbal readers can significantly improve their capabilities. They should carefully observe the facial expressions, hand movements, and body postures of those with whom they interact, and they should ask themselves what these movements say about the individuals being watched.

§ 9.04. Common Nonverbal Signals

One of the most obvious forms of nonverbal communication involves *facial expressions*. A derisive smile may be employed to demonstrate disdain for a wholly unacceptable proposal. Conversely, a subtle smile or other sign of relief in response to a person's fourth or fifth proposal may indicate that this offer is almost acceptable. Such a supposition may be reinforced by the fact that the responding negotiator did not reject this offer with the same alacrity with which previous submissions were declined. It may also have been renounced through the use of a "signal" phrase such as "to be candid" or "to be honest." On the other hand, if a few proposals have been exchanged and a bargainer's effort to make a suggestion believed to be quite reasonable is received with a pained expression (*e.g.*, taut lips and/or the gnashing of teeth evidenced by the visible expansion and contraction of the jaw muscles on both sides of the face), it should be apparent that either or both participants have incorrectly assessed the true value of this transaction.

Negotiators should always look for "*double messages*" that emanate from adversaries. For example, individuals may, while stating how disappointed they are regarding some unfortunate developments, accompany their sad words with inappropriate signs of pleasure (*e.g.*, smiles). These contradictory facial expressions would strongly suggest that these speakers are not really as disconsolate as their unembellished statements might otherwise indicate. These persons most likely enjoy their current plight and do not want to have their problem alleviated too expeditiously.

Persons who negotiate in teams need to establish specified means to communicate with one another during bargaining sessions without inadvertently divulging confidential information. If they fail to resolve this problem beforehand, the may disclose

---

163. *See* Henley, *supra* note 162, at 14–15.

164. *See, e.g.*, Joe Navaro (with Marlin Karllins), *What Every Body is Saying* (2008); Pease & Pease, *supra* note 151; Henry Calero, *The Power of Nonverbal Communication* (2005); Anderson, *supra* note 157.

their thoughts through a casual sideways glance or a slight nod toward a partner following a particular offer. They may communicate a similar message when they decide to caucus over an offer under circumstances in which the five prior proposals had been summarily rejected without the need for any conference. When several individuals plan to represent the same party it is frequently advantageous to designate a single speaker to make the immediate decisions necessary during the bargaining meetings. This member would be authorized to do so without consulting the other team members first. To avoid letting their counterparts know how interested they are in particular offers, this speaker can initially announce an intention to caucus every hour or two to discuss developments.

Negotiators must remember that facial expressions are generally controlled more readily than are less voluntary body movements. Contrived smiles or frowns may be carefully orchestrated to convey deceptive messages, while less voluntary arm, leg, and upper body movements are more likely to communicate true feelings. It is thus imperative for bargaining participants to observe as many informative body movements as possible. They should not merely focus on facial signals. Furthermore, no isolated signal should be given a definitive interpretation. People must look for *changes in the behavior of others* and predictable *patterns of conduct.*[165]

A. Classic Signs

1. Facial Expressions

Even though facial expressions are generally the most easily manipulated form of nonverbal communication, subtle clues may frequently be perceived by careful observers. Taut lips may indicate anxiety or frustration. A subtle smile (usually hidden by a bowed head) or brief signs of relief around the corners of a counterpart's mouth when a new offer is being conveyed may indicate that the offer is approaching or has entered that person's settlement range. The nonverbal indication of relief evidences that individual's belief that a final settlement is likely.

2. Pursed Lips — Lips Rotate in Outward Manner

This is a classic indication that the person does not agree with what is being said.[166] This is a clear sign of resistance to what that individual feels are unattractive ideas.

3. Flinch — Pained Facial Expression

This may be an uncontrolled response to a surprisingly inadequate opening offer. An uncontrolled flinch sincerely indicates to the offeror the wholly unacceptable nature of his or her initial position. Adroit negotiators may employ a contrived

---

165. *See* Navaro, *supra* note 164, at 12–13; Pease & Pease, *supra* note 151, at 21; Calero, *supra* note 164, at 73.
166. *See* David Givens, *Your Body at Work* 12–13 (2010).

"flinch" to silently challenge opposing party opening offers without having to engage in verbal discourse.[167] Skilled use of the "flinch" may subtly undermine counterpart confidence in their position, and it may induce careless adversaries to modify their initial offers before they obtain opening position statements from their flinching adversaries.

4. Raising of One Eyebrow

The involuntary raising of a single eyebrow generally connotes skepticism.[168] This signal may sincerely indicate that the actor is suspicious of counterpart overtures. It may be disingenuously employed by manipulative negotiators to suggest their disappointment with counterpart offers or concessions.

5. Raising Both Eyebrows/Widening of Eyes

This is a clear indication of surprise.[169] It is often visible when a negotiator's opening offer or subsequent position change is more generous than the recipient anticipated. It may similarly follow the disclosure of wholly unanticipated information. When negotiators observe such signs, they should suspect potentially serious tactical errors on their part. They should quickly reassess their present situations and try to determine whether they have made inadvertent tactical mistakes.

6. Scratching Head/Brushing Cheek with Hand

These are usually indications of puzzlement.[170] Such behavior may suggest that the actor is having difficulty comprehending the counterpart's negotiating behavior. The actor is likely to believe that the bargaining process is not moving in the right direction.

7. Wringing of Hands

This is frequently an indication of frustration or tension. Particularly distraught people are likely to twist their hands and fingers into seemingly painful contortions. This message usually emanates from people who are unhappy with substantive developments or anxious about the aggressive tactics being employed by their counterparts.

8. Tightly Gripping Arm Rests/Drumming on the Table

People who are impatient or frustrated often tightly grip the arm rests of their chair or drum their fingers on the table in front of them.[171] Negotiators who are displeased by a perceived lack of progress may engage in this kind of conduct.

---

167. See Dawson, *supra* note 12, at 32–35.
168. See Hartley & Karinch, *supra* note 156, at 77–78; Desmond Morris, *Bodytalk* 51 (1994).
169. See Givens, *supra* note 166, at 42–43.
170. See *id.*, at 60–61; Morris, *supra* note 168, at 16, 143.
171. See Elizabeth Kuhnke, *Body Language for Dummies* 162 (2007).

9. Shoulder Shrug

This is a clear indication of helplessness or powerlessness.[172] When a counterpart indicates that they cannot agree to something, a shoulder shrug may suggest that the person's position is not final and that greater movement is likely. On the other hand, when someone says "no" and maintains rigid shoulders, they are unlikely to change their position now.

10. Biting Lower Lip/Biting Fingernails/Running Fingers through Hair/Rubbing Forehead

These signs usually indicate stress or frustration. They tend to emanate from individuals who are disappointed by the lack of negotiation progress or by perceived counterpart intransigence. As they feel greater frustration, these signals tend to become more intense.

11. Beady Little Eyes/Snake Eyes

These are signs of disagreement or disapproval.[173] When exhibited during bargaining interactions, these indicate displeasure with what the person is hearing from the other side.

12. Eyes Wandering/Looking at Watch/Crossing and Uncrossing Legs/ Doodling/Head Resting in Hand/Sighing

These are signs of boredom and/or disinterest.[174] These signals would indicate that you're your counterpart is not interested in your presentation. You may wish to ask some questions that are designed to get your adversary more actively involved in the discussions and to elicit their real concerns.

13. Sitting or Standing Face-to-Face or at an Angle

Persons sitting or standing face-to-face tend to like each other more and be more interested in their interaction than individuals sitting or standing at an angle to one another.[175] This factor can be influenced by gender, since women are more likely to sit or stand face-to-face than men, with males being more likely to sit or stand at an angle. If another person moves from a face-to-face posture to a more distant posture, it may help to ask that person several questions to induce him or her to become more involved in the interaction.

---

172. *See* Givens, *supra* note 166, at 66–73.
173. *See* Kuhnke, *supra* note 171, at 79.
174. *See* Jo Ellan Dimitrius & Wendy Patrick Mazzarella, *Reading People* 62 (1998).
175. *See* Beall, *supra* note 153, at 17–19.

14. Shifting Back and Forth in Chair/Tilting Head from Side to Side/ Opening and Closing Mouth without Speaking

These are indications of indecision.[176] The message sender is not sure how to proceed and is contemplating his or her options. You should patiently and silently wait to give this person the time they need to formulate an opinion they can express.

15. Hands Neatly Folded in Lap

This often denotes contrite penitence and possibly even submissiveness.[177] This posture tends to be exhibited more by females than by males. If this information appears to be consistent with other signals emanating from the negotiator, the opposing party should certainly endeavor to encourage this attitude and take advantage of it. However, some people who have been carefully raised to be "good little boys and girls" might sit in this fashion merely because of their prior upbringing. Negotiators should normally avoid such a seemingly submissive posture — unless they are deliberately attempting to induce over-confident counterparts to take them lightly.

16. Sitting on the Edge of One's Chair

When this action appears to occur involuntarily following a recent proposal and the posture did not accompany the receipt of previous offers, this may suggest increased interest on the part of the actor.[178] If this interpretation is correct, it may indicate that the offeror is approaching the offeree's zone of expectation. Most persons do not sit literally on the front of their chair. They only move slightly forward in their seat. A few individuals, however, are more demonstrative. They lean so far forward that they place their elbows on the table in front of themselves. This gesture is often made by individuals who are preparing to disclose important information or to make concessions.[179]

17. Hands Touching Face/Stroking Chin/Playing with Glasses/ Playing with Papers or Notes

These acts are often indications of meditative contemplation. Since people feel awkward regarding the prolonged silence while they are considering proposals and formulating appropriate responses, they frequently resort to these artifices to camouflage their thinking. This conduct may suggest that their counterpart's most recent proposal has finally forced them to think seriously about the proper reply. They plan to reject the new offer, but do so in a more positive manner. It may take twenty or thirty seconds for them to formulate their revised rejection statement. To disguise the resulting silent pause, they play with their glasses, stroke their cheeks, or look at

---

176. *See* Dimitrius & Mazzerella, *supra* note 174, at 67–68.
177. *See* Jay Folberg & Allison Taylor, *Mediation* 122 (1984).
178. *See* Kuhnke, *supra* note 171, at 119–120.
179. *See* Calero, *supra* note 164, at 84–85.

their notes. If they did not employ these diversionary actions when they considered prior offers, this probably demonstrates that they perceive the instant proposal to be quite reasonable.

18. Steepling Gesture (Hands Pressed Together with Fingers Uplifted or Hands Together with Interlocked Fingers Also Uplifted, with Elbows Out in Expansive Manner)

This conduct usually indicates that the actor feels confident.[180] Negotiators who observe this behavior should be certain that they are not conceding more than is necessary, since their counterparts appear to be pleased with developments. Individuals being interviewed on television frequently display steepling signs when they think they are doing well.

19. Leaning Back in Chair with Hands on back of Head

This posture is adopted more by males than by females. It is usually an indication of confidence and contentedness.[181] When men who are interacting with women adopt this posture, it is not only a sign of confidence but an indication of perceived domination. Female negotiators who observe this behavior in male counterparts should be especially cautious, because those people may think that things are going their way. This action is also an indication of power and authority, and is frequently employed by superiors when they interact with subordinates.

20. Placing One Hand Behind Head/Massaging and Stroking Neck

When someone uses one hand to clasp the neck behind their ear, this is usually an indication of distress.[182] It is as if the person is psychologically giving himself or herself a consoling hug to offset the negative consequences being experienced.[183] During bargaining interactions, such a posture is likely to indicate that the actor sees negative developments ahead. Such action can also be an indication of uncertainty. A similar indicator of stress involves the massaging and stroking of one's neck.[184]

21. Extending Hands toward Counterpart with Fingers Pointed Upward and Palms Facing Out

This is common behavior by individuals who are being verbally assaulted by aggressive bargainers. It is a defensive posture used to symbolically (but ineffectively) protect the actors against the oral onslaught emanating from their counterparts.[185]

---

180. *See* Navaro, *supra* note 164, at 147–148; Pease & Pease, *supra* note 151, at 132–135; Calero, *supra* note 164, at 78–82.

181. *See* Pease & Pease, *supra* note 151, at 245–246.

182. *See* Givens, *supra* note 166, at 46–47; Morris, *supra* note 168, at 168.

183. *See* Kuhnke, *supra* note 171, at 129.

184. *See* Navaro, *supra* note 164, at 42–43.

185. *See* Givens, *supra* note 166, at 49–50; John Ilich, *Dealbreakers and Breakthroughs* 161–162 (1992).

22. Rubbing Hands Together in Anticipatory Manner

This behavior is often exhibited by anxious negotiators who anticipate beneficial offers from their counterparts.[186] This conduct usually suggests an over-eagerness that may be satisfied with a minimal position change.

23. Placing Palm of Right Hand over Heart

Some people voluntarily or involuntarily place the palm of their right hand over their heart when attempting to appear sincere or credible. If this behavior seems inadvertent, it may be a sign of true sincerity. If this action occurs in a deliberate manner, however, it is likely to be a disingenuous effort to mislead their counterpart.

24. Open or Uplifted Hands with Palms Facing Out

This technique is generally used to demonstrate openness and sincerity.[187] It is a posture one normally expects when being given true final offers. The posture may be very open—with the hands far apart—or more subtle—with the hands closer together. If the gesture appears stilted, it is probably a deliberate attempt to deceive the observer.

25. Crossed Arms/Crossed Legs

This may constitute an aggressive, adversarial posture or a defensive position, depending on the particular position involved.[188] If the arms are folded high on the chest and the legs are crossed in a "figure-four" position (with the ankle of one leg placed on the knee of the other leg in a typically masculine fashion), this represents a competitive or combative posture. This is especially true if the arm-crosser's fists are also in a closed position.[189] If the arms are folded low on the chest and one leg is draped across the other, this tends to be a defensive position. The intimidated actor is likely to be leaning back in their chair in a subconscious effort to escape the verbal onslaught of their counterpart. Both of these crossed arms/crossed legs postures constitute unreceptive poses.[190]

If an adversary commences negotiations with arms folded and legs crossed, it is beneficial to try to establish sufficient rapport with this person to soften his or her stance prior to the commencement of formal discussions. Serious final offers should never be made when one's arms are folded and one's legs are crossed, because this does not present a credible appearance.

26. Standing with Hands on Hips

This is a rather aggressive posture that tells others to stay away from the actor.[191] It is often exhibited by angry individuals who do not wish to interact with those

---

186. *See* Kuhnke, *supra* note 171, at 146; Pease & Pease, *supra* note 151, at 128–130; Morris, *supra* note 168, at 197.

187. *See* Givens, *supra* note 166, at 56–58; Kuhnke, *supra* note 171, at 140–142.

188. *See* Kuhnke, *supra* note 171, at 126–128.

189. *See* Pease & Pease, *supra* note 151, at 95–96.

190. *See id.*, at 91–94; Calero, *supra* note 164, at 84–85.

191. *See* Pease & Pease, *supra* note 151, at 237–239; Morris, *supra* note 168, at 4.

around them.[192] People who do not like to negotiate may greet new counterparts in this position.

27. Gnashing of Teeth

This is a frequent indication of anxiety or anger, and is evidenced by the contracting and relaxing of the jaw muscles on both sides of the face. Aggressive negotiators should carefully watch for the gnashing of teeth, the wringing of hands, and other reactions that may suggest the person is experiencing substantial stress, in recognition of the fact that continued combative conduct may precipitate a cessation of the talks.

28. Covering and Rubbing One Eye

It is not uncommon for individuals to casually cover and rub one eye when they find it difficult to accept something being expressed to them.[193] This is the nonverbal equivalent of the expression "my eye" that may be uttered by someone who doubts the veracity of a speaker's comments. Negotiators who encounter this signal when they are making crucial representations should recognize the substantial possibility that their statements are not being accorded much respect. They may wish to rephrase their communication in a more credible manner.

29. Massaging the Pain Muscles between the Eyes

This is an indication of high stress.[194] The actor is subconsciously endeavoring to relieve the tension they are feeling.

30. Rubbing Chin in Inquisitive Manner

This is another nonverbal sign of disbelief.[195] While the actor may be unwilling to express his or her disbelief verbally, this nonverbal conduct conveys a similar message.

31. Picking Imaginary Lint from One's Clothing

People who disapprove of or are made particularly uncomfortable by shocking or outrageous statements being made by others may begin to pick imaginary lint from their clothing "especially when they are hesitant to express their disapproval or discomfort directly."[196] This behavior is common in response to graphic descriptions of severe injuries or gory medical procedures.

---

192. *See* Givens, *supra* note 166, at 11.
193. *See* Morris, *supra* note 168, at 49; Alice Scheflen, *Body Language and the Social Order* 79 (1972).
194. *See* Hartley & Karinch, *supra* note 156, at 72.
195. *See* Morris, *supra* note 168, at 31.
196. *See* Pease & Pease, *supra* note 151, at 236; Scheflen, *supra* note 193, at 109.

32. Casual Touching (e.g., Prolonged Handshake; Hand or Arm on Counterpart's Shoulder or Forearm)

This device can be effectively used to indicate one's sincerity and to establish some rapport.[197] A warm handshake at the commencement of a bargaining interaction can often reduce the likelihood of needless interpersonal conflict. Even during negotiation sessions, casual touching of the other participant's hand or forearm can be used as a "personal touch" to maintain harmonious relations and to encourage the other person to respond favorably to our entreaty. Even though Americans are not as touching as some cultures, we tend to touch each other during interactions more frequently than most of us realize, even when talking with relative strangers. This is true whether we communicate with persons of the same or the opposite gender. Women tend to engage in casual touching with others more often than men.[198]

On rare occasions, a negotiator may try to place an arm over the shoulder of the other party in a condescending fashion to denote a superior-subordinate relationship. This tactic may be used by a larger individual toward a smaller person or by a male toward a female. Since the speculative benefits that might be derived from such patronizing conduct would be minimal and this behavior could easily offend the recipient, the use of this approach is definitely not recommended.

33. Direct Eye Contact

People who make regular eye contact with others are often perceived as being more personable and forthright than those who lack this trait.[199] Negotiators who can maintain nonthreatening eye contact with counterparts can frequently enhance their apparent credibility. They are also likely to be more cognizant of the nonverbal messages emanating from their adversaries. On the other hand, intensive staring is usually perceived as intimidating and combative. Women tend to look at others during their interactions more frequently and for longer periods than men.[200]

34. Head Nodding

Casual head nodding is generally employed by active listeners to indicate their comprehension of what is being said.[201] Head nodding by listeners is occasionally misinterpreted by speakers as a sign of agreement. Rapid nods, however, may indicate a lack of interest or may be employed by impatient individuals to encourage speakers to get to the point more expeditiously.

---

197. *See* Beall, *supra* note 153, at 40–49; Kuhnke, *supra* note 171, at 133 — 138; Pease & Pease, *supra* note 151, at 104–106.

198. *See* Beall, *supra* note 153, at 46–48.

199. *See* Kuhnke, *supra* note 171, at 76–77.

200. *See* Beall, *supra* note 153, at 60.

201. *See* Kuhnke, *supra* note 171, at 51–52.

35. Tilted or Straight Head

When persons are paying close attention to what is being said to them, they often have a slight tilt in their heads.[202] On the other hand, when their head is perfectly straight, they are not usually as interested in what is being said.

36. Turning around in Chair and Looking Away from Counterpart after Making New Offer

This behavior is often expressed by individuals who hate to compromise. They cannot stand to look at their counterparts after they make concessions. People interacting with these bargainers should not be personally offended by this seemingly disrespectful conduct, but should expect to see it after other position changes.

B. Nonverbal Signs of Deception

The preceding part of this section covered various nonverbal clues that do not pertain specifically to the discovery of deliberate deception. This section explores those inadvertent signals that often indicate the employment of intentional misrepresentations. Readers should not, however, be induced to think that they can discern all or even most of the dishonest statements uttered during their negotiations. Few can hope to be so perceptive.[203]

In his book *Telling Lies*, Psychologist Paul Ekman noted that people are surprisingly inept at discovering when they are being told lies.[204] This phenomenon may be partially due to the fact that mendacity occurs in different forms ranging from mere "puffing" to unabashed prevarication. It must be acknowledged that many of the stereotypically accepted indicia of deceit have little empirical support. Bargainers who endeavor to rely upon the traditionally cited indicators of deception will undoubtedly reject many generous offers from seemingly untrustworthy fidgetors and accept many disingenuously parsimonious proposals made by seemingly reliable Machiavellian negotiators.

Despite the empirically demonstrated unreliability of the conventionally enumerated indicia of dishonesty, there are clues that can meaningfully assist people to evaluate the veracity of opposing negotiators.[205] Individuals who plan to make deliberate misrepresentations often emit nonverbal signals that should caution alert observers. Some of these nonverbal messages reflect the stress associated with lying—generated

---

202. *See* Dawson, *supra* note 12, at 257.

203. *See* Navaro, *supra* note 164, at 205–206.

204. Paul Ekman, *Telling Lies* 86–87 (1992). See also Timothy R. Levine, *Duped: Truth-Default Theory and the Social Science of Lying and Deception* (2020).

205. *See* Pamela Meyer, *Lie Spotting* (2010); Bella M. DePaulo, James J. Lindsay, Brian E. Malone, Laura Muhlenbruck, Kelly Charlton & Harris Cooper, "Cues to Deception," 129 *Psychology Bulletin* 74 (2003); David J. Lieberman, *Never Be Lied to Again* (1998); Ford, *supra* note 141, at 201–203, 213; Paul Ekman, Maureen O'Sullivan, Wallace V. Friesen & Klaus R. Scherer, "Invited Article: Face, Voice, and Body in Detecting Deceit," 15 *Journal of Nonverbal Behavior* 125 (1991); Morris, *supra* note 168.

by fear of the truth combined with anxiety regarding the possibility of being caught lying.[206] Other nonverbal behavior is designed to enhance the credibility of the misrepresentations being made. If people are going to engage in mendacious conduct, they want to increase the likelihood they will be believed!

No one signal should be accepted as a definitive indication of deception. Observers must look for *changes* in the speaker's usual behavior and *patterns of behavior* that are consistent with dishonesty. The general anxiety associated with most bargaining encounters may cause someone to exhibit signs of stress, but these should be apparent throughout the critical stages of the interaction. On the other hand, if obvious signs of stress become apparent just before the utterance of a questionable statement, the listener should be suspicious. To further complicate matters, individuals who are afraid that their truthful representations are not going to be believed may exhibit similar signs of stress.[207] Listeners should also be aware of verbal leaks or signal words (*e.g.*, "to be candid", "to be truthful"), which often indicate the presence of deception.[208] Signal phrases, like "to be candid," are used to induce others to listen more intently to the misrepresentations that follow.

It can be especially helpful to establish **baseline behavior** during the Preliminary Stage of interactions with others.[209] Listen carefully for stammers or pauses that might be natural parts of their speech patterns. How quickly do they talk, and what is their natural voice pitch? Ask them seemingly innocuous questions that require them to recall something from their past. While they are thinking, do they look up and to the left or up and to the right? Most right handed persons tend to look up and to the left while trying to *recall* something they have experienced before, while left handed individuals tend to look up and to the right.[210] Ask them to picture something that requires them to imagine something they have not seen before. Do they look up and to the right or up and to the left? Right handed persons tend to look up and to the right when *imagining* something, while left handed individuals tend to look up and to the left. When individuals get to the more significant parts of their interactions and counterparts make statements they suspect might be false, the observers should look for changes in the normal communication patterns of those persons that would suggest deception.

1. Decrease or Increase in Specificity of Statements

When people tell the truth, they fill in the little details as they recall them, adding a substantial amount of incidental information. When individuals fabricate, however, there are no details to remember. As a result, they tend to omit the usual amplifying

---

206. *See* Ekman, *supra* note 204, at 49–64.
207. *See id.*, at 94.
208. *See* Dawson, *supra* note 12, at 263. *See also* Meyer, *supra* note 205, at 94–95.
209. *See* Meyer, *supra* note 205, at 112–115; Hartley & Karinch, *supra* note 156, at 99–124.
210. *See id.*, at 117.

information, providing the bare details of their lie.[211] On the other hand, persons who have prepared elaborate lies may provide an excessive amount of information in an effort to make their fabrication more credible.[212] When they get no response to their misrepresentation, they nervously restate the lie. Specific questions about particular facts can often help to deter or discover whether explicit stories are credible.[213] Individuals find it more reprehensible to lie in response to direct questions, and they find it more difficult to provide believable fabrications in response to inquiries that seek specific information. By being thoroughly prepared for bargaining interactions and by having complete knowledge of the operative factual, economic, and business circumstances, negotiators can greatly enhance their ability to detect deception from persons who distort such factors.[214] Their "situational familiarity" will tip them off to statements that do not appear to be truthful.

2. Partial Shrug

People who shrug their shoulders usually indicate that they are ignorant or indifferent. However, if they are being deceptive, they often exhibit a partial shrug of one shoulder that is only briefly visible.[215]

3. Increased or Reduced Gross Body Movement

When people interact, they move their arms, legs, and torso on a fairly regular basis. Rarely do individuals sit or stand perfectly still. Under stressful circumstances, some persons become more fidgety and move their arms and legs at an increased rate.[216] Some openly fidget or shake. Deceitful people tend to exhibit this behavior as well. However, people may also exhibit contrary behavior when they resort to deceitful tactics. They know that fidgety speakers appear less credible. They attempt to counteract this phenomenon by making a discernible effort to decrease their gross body movement for the purpose of enhancing the trustworthiness of their mendacious comments.[217] Deceitful persons may also exhibit reduced gross body movement as they concentrate on the story they are fabricating.[218] Negotiators should be especially

---

211. *See* DePaulo, et al., *supra* note 205, at 91–92; Aldert Vrij, *Detecting Lies and Deceit* 105 (2000); Ekman, *supra* note 204, at 106.

212. *See* Lieberman, *supra* note 205, at 31.

213. *See* Meyer, *supra* note 205, at 93–94; Maurice E. Schweitzer & Rachel Croson, "Curtailing Deception: The Impact of Direct Questions on Lies and Omissions," 10 *International Journal of Conflict Management* 225 (1999).

214. *See* M.A. Reinhard & S.L. Sporer, "Listening, Not Watching: Situational Familiarity and the Ability to Detect Deception," 101 *Journal of Personality and Social Psychology* 467 (2011).

215. *See* Meyer, *supra* note 205, at 83; Lieberman, *supra* note 205, at 16; Ekman, *supra* note 204, at 102–103.

216. *See* Jeffrey Krivis & Mariam Zadeh, "Back to Deception: 'Winning' Mediation Cases by Understanding Body Language," 24 *Alternatives to the High Cost of Litigation* 123 (2006).

217. *See* Kuhnke, *supra* note 171, at 269.

218. *See* Vrij, *supra* note 211, at 38.

cautious when they evaluate the veracity of statements made by individuals who have obviously increased *or* decreased their gross body movement.

4. Casual Placing of Hand over Mouth

Most people have been raised to believe that prevarication is morally wrong. They suffer from a guilty conscience when they engage in deliberate deception. Psychologists have noticed that liars often place their hand over their mouth when they speak, in a subconscious effort to hold in their morally reprehensible falsehoods.[219] I have frequently observed this behavior when watching negotiators misstate their values or settlement intentions.

5. Unconscious Touching of Nose with Fingertip or Back of Finger; Rubbing One Eye

These gestures are often considered a more subtle equivalent to the "covering of one's mouth" as someone prepares to prevaricate.[220] While these signals may appear in isolation, it is common for deceivers to initially cover their mouth and then quickly touch the side of their nose. Deceitful people may alternatively rub one eye with one or two fingers.[221]

6. Inconsistent Nodding or Shaking of Head

When individuals verbally lie, their heads occasionally give them away.[222] For example, people who say that they are unable to do something may casually nod their heads in an affirmative manner, or persons who state that they want to do something may casually shake their heads in a negative fashion. Their subconscious head movements contradict their misrepresentations and truthfully indicate their intentions.

7. Eyes Looking Up to Wrong Side

When people try to *recall* past events from memory, right handed individuals tend to look up and to the left and left handed persons tend to look up and to the right. On the other hand, when individuals try to *create an image or fact*, right-handed persons tend to look up and to the right and left handed people look up and to the left.[223] When a right handed individual looks up and to the right or a left handed person looks up and to the left, it often means that they are not trying to recall actual circumstances but rather to create a false story.

---

219. *See* Kuhnke, *supra* note 171, at 267–268; Pease & Pease, *supra* note 151, at 148–149; Lieberman, *supra* note 205, at 15.

220. *See* Hartley & Karinch, *supra* note 156, at 88–89; Kuhnke, *supra* note 171, at 269; Pease & Pease, *supra* note 151, at 150–151; Morris, *supra* note 168, at 182.

221. *See* Pease & Pease, *supra* note 151, at 151–152; Morris, *supra* note 168, at 49.

222. *See* Meyer, *supra* note 205, at 74; Ford, *supra* note 161, at 204.

223. *See* Quilliam, *supra* note 154, at 28–29; Lieberman, *supra* note 205, at 162.

8. Dilated Pupils and More Frequent Blinking

When people experience stress, the pupils of their eyes become dilated and their rate of blinking usually increases.[224] Even though business negotiators rarely interact in such close environments that they can observe pupil enlargement, increased blinking should be readily discernible.[225]

9. Involuntary Raising of Inner Portions of Eyebrows

Most individuals are unable to control the muscles that control the movement of their inner eyebrows. Under stressful conditions, however, many people experience an involuntary lifting of their *inner eyebrows or the raising and pulling together of both eyebrows.*[226] These movements tend to be transient and are frequently overlooked, but may be noted by discerning observers.

10. Narrowing and Tightening of Red Margin of Lips

Stress is frequently manifested just before persons speak by the brief narrowing and tightening of the red margin of their lips.[227] Careful viewers can see the lips of prospective speakers tighten into a narrow line across their lower face prior to their utterance of planned misrepresentations.

11. Licking Lips or Running Tongue over Teeth

These are signs of stress and discomfort, and are often associated with deceptive behavior.[228]

12. Heightened Vocal Pitch

People experiencing anxiety often raise their vocal pitch when they speak.[229] Even though intentional prevaricators attempt to control their voice when they talk, listeners can frequently discern this heightened pitch.

13. More Deliberate or More Rapid Speech

Individuals who resort to intentional misrepresentations want to ensure a receptive audience. To accomplish this objective, they often utter their misstatements in a more deliberate manner to be certain that their message is completely received. On the other hand, people experiencing greater stress may speak more rapidly.[230]

---

224. *See* Meyer, *supra* note 205, at 66–67; Krivis & Zadeh, *supra* note 216, at 122; Thompson, *supra* note 65, at 346; Calero, *supra* note 159, at 69–70; Andersen, *supra* note 157, at 147; Ekman, *supra* note 204, at 114, 142.

225. *See* Hartley & Karinch, *supra* note 156, at 86–87.

226. *See* Ekman, *supra* note 204, at 134–136.

227. *See id.,* at 136.

228. *See* Dimitrius & Mazzarella, *supra* note 174, at 60.

229. *See* Meyer, *supra* note 205, at 103; Krivis & Zadeh, *supra* note 216, at 122–123; Thompson, *supra* note 65, at 345; Ford, *supra* note 161, at 213; Ekman, *supra* note 204, at 93.

230. *See* Dimitrius & Mazzarella, *supra* note 174, at 60; Ekman, *supra* note 204, at 93, 122.

14. Increased Number of Speech Errors

Studies have found that people who are attempting to deceive others tend to have a greater number of speech errors. These may manifest themselves as stuttering, the repeating of phrases, the increased presence of broken phrases, the failure to finish sentences, or the inclusion of non-substantive modifiers ("It is clear that ..."; "you know").[231] It is as if their conscience disrupts the communication between the brain and the mouth to prevent issuance of their morally wrongful prevarications.

15. More Frequent Clearing of Throat

The tension associated with deceptive behavior often manifests itself in more frequent throat clearing.[232] As speakers prepare to utter knowingly false statements, they nervously clear their throats in a relatively apparent manner.

16. Change in Frequency of Looking at Listener

As some speakers experience stress associated with their deliberate deception, they become more nervous and look less frequently at their listeners ("gaze aversion").[233] However, other deceivers exhibit the opposite behavior. They realize that people who look others in the eye are perceived as being more credible. To enhance the likelihood that their misrepresentations will be believed, they make an obvious effort to look at their listeners more intently while they are lying.[234]

17. Duping Delight

Some individuals enjoy the challenge of successful deception. When they mislead their listeners, they exhibit a smug contempt toward their targets.[235] These deceivers may also exude signs of pleasure (*e.g.,* self-satisfied smile). These signals are especially likely when these persons are misleading people they think are difficult to fool.

Negotiators should carefully monitor the nonverbal signals emanating from their counterparts. They should be especially alert to signs of stress or increased behavior designed to enhance the credibility of questionable representations. While no single sign should be considered conclusive evidence of deception, observable changes in behavior and the presence of suspicious patterns of conduct should cause listeners to become more circumspect.

If one suspects someone of deceit, they can use silence to enhance the speaker's stress level. If the speaker prattles on nervously and reiterates their story, this may indicate deception. One may also ask specific questions that force the individual to

---

231. *See* Krivis & Zadeh, *supra* note 216, at 123; Andersen, *supra* note 157, at 146; Vrij, *supra* note 211, at 26; Ekman, *supra* note 204, at 121–122.
232. *See* Gifford, *supra* note 58, at 130.
233. *See* Vrij, *supra* note 211, at 38; Lieberman, *supra* note 205, at 13.
234. *See* Andersen, *supra* note 157, at 148.
235. *See id.* at 150; Ekman, *supra* note 204, at 76–79.

fill in details that would be part of any normal story. Difficulty providing these pieces of information is grounds for suspicion.[236]

Since it is difficult to remember and consider all of the different indicators of deception mentioned here, it might be helpful to picture the following absurd scenario. After reviewing this section, readers should ask their spouse or "significant other": "Do you love me?" If their partners increase or stop their fidgeting, look them in the eye, lift their inner eyebrows, place one hand over their mouth, blink more frequently, preface their affirmative response with "to be truthful," and shake their head negatively while answering in a deliberate and higher pitched manner, the relationship is probably in big trouble!

Two other indicators of deception should also be mentioned. People who lie regularly tend to exude a mistrust of others.[237] They think that most people are dishonest and expect others to use the same deceptive tactics they employ. As a result, negotiators who encounter adversaries exhibiting a distrustful predisposition should be circumspect regarding representations made by those participants. They should try to verify critical representations. Verbal leaks may similarly disclose deceptive statements. Since most people feel uncomfortable making direct misstatements, they frequently use modifiers to mask the extent of their dissembling. For example, negotiators who would hesitate to state directly and untruthfully that they cannot go above or below a particular figure may indicate that they are "*not inclined*" to do so. If that figure represented their actual limit, they would be unlikely to use the "not inclined" modifier. counterparts hearing such modifiers should recognize the verbal leak those words represent and be distrustful of the message the speaker appears to be conveying.

§ 9.05. Conclusion

Verbal communication constitutes a critical aspect of the bargaining process. Negotiators should carefully listen for verbal leaks that indicate the true intentions of their counterparts. During the important stages of negotiations, the participants should use definitive language that more forcefully advances the points they are making. Bargainers who mirror the body postures of counterparts, emulate their speech patterns, and reflect their sensory orientations are likely to generate more favorable responses from those people.

Nonverbal signals provide significant clues regarding the true intentions of participants during bargaining interactions. Less controlled nonverbal signs tend to be more trustworthy than more contrived verbal representations. Bargainers should not ignore their "feelings" regarding counterpart intentions. These feelings may be based on an accurate subconscious perception of valid nonverbal signals emanating from their adversaries. Negotiators should look for signs of confidence, sincerity, disinge-

---

236. *See* Lieberman, *supra* note 205, at 119; Ekman, *supra* note 204, at 44–46, 106–107.
237. *See* Lieberman, *supra* note 205, at 40.

nuity, or anxiety, and decide whether these are consistent with or contrary to the verbal messages being conveyed.

Bargainers should be particularly alert for nonverbal indications of stress and nonverbal efforts to enhance the credibility of questionable statements. These factors may indicate the presence of deceptive behavior. Negotiators should be suspicious of the integrity of people who indicate a general mistrust of others, recognizing that dishonest persons tend to expect others to be similarly untrustworthy. They should listen carefully for verbal leaks that undermine the veracity of what speakers appear to be saying.

Chapter 10

Particular Negotiation Issues

Business representatives frequently encounter specific dilemmas during bargaining interactions that should be addressed if the talks are going to progress satisfactorily. It is imperative that bargainers recognize these issues and know how to respond to them effectively.

§ 10.01. Typical Dilemmas

A. Initiating the Negotiation Process

It is amazing how frequently business representatives indicate their reluctance to initiate bargaining discussions. They seem to feel that the party who first suggests these talks will be placed at a disadvantage. This perception may have been fostered by more senior executives who can recall when it was considered inappropriate to directly broach the subject of bargaining. Such a reluctance to be forthright is misplaced today. If your firm is contemplating the sale or purchase of a division or other property, they should not hesitate to contact the appropriate external parties to see if they might be interested in the transaction being contemplated. If your company is thinking of entering into a licensing agreement, you should not be afraid of contacting the patent, copyright, or trademark holder to ask about a possible deal. It is frequently beneficial to be the initiator of such discussions, due to the fact your side will be completely prepared to negotiate from the outset. The side being contacted might not be well prepared, yet they may commence discussions in a naively open manner. By the time they appreciate the need to proceed more cautiously, they may have given up a significant amount of important information.

If someone is contacted by an external party wishing to do business with their firm, they should be careful not to commence serious discussions until they have had the chance to gather the relevant factual, economic, and business information and thought about other parties who might be interested in the arrangements being addressed. This would enable them to become fully aware of the different alternatives that might be available to their company.

B. Weakening Counterpart's Superior Position

Negotiators must remember that bargaining power is rarely defined by objective factors. The strength of each party is determined more by the counterpart's *perception* of the interaction, than by the actual circumstances.[238] If adept negotiators can convince seemingly stronger counterparts that they are unaware of the counterpart's superior strength they may effectively weaken the positions of those parties, causing those persons to suffer a concomitant loss of negotiating confidence.

This phenomenon explains why young children become intuitively gifted negotiators despite their obvious lack of objective bargaining power. When they interact with seemingly omnipotent parents, they disarm their adversaries by ignoring the power imbalance. Since parents are obliged to prevent "child-like" conduct, children also recognize their ability to threaten irrational, self-destructive behavior if they do not achieve their ultimate objectives. Once parents begin to doubt their actual power, they lose confidence and are easy targets for their manipulative offspring!

A factor that significantly influences a party's assessment of its objective power concerns the alternatives that side thinks are available to it if no agreement is achieved during the present negotiations. If several options appear to constitute viable substitutes for bargained results, that party should understand the elevated strength it enjoys. If a counterpart can convince that party that it really does not have as many non-settlement alternatives as it believes or that those options are not as advantageous as it thinks, the power balance can be effectively shifted in favor of the manipulative actor.[239]

Bargainers who are able to use verbal and nonverbal messages to indicate that they do not accord any credence to the actual power possessed by their counterparts can meaningfully undermine counterpart authority. If this strength-diffusing objective is accomplished, adversaries will be rendered incapable of using their objectively superior circumstances to influence the negotiation outcome. Opposing negotiators may be so demoralized by this tactic that they readily accept less beneficial terms than they could otherwise have obtained.

C. Strengthening One's Own Weak Bargaining Position

Representatives who find themselves with apparently anemic bargaining positions should not automatically concede everything. Even when they are unable to ignore the superior power possessed by their counterparts, they may be able to take action that will permit them to artificially enhance their own situations. If they can effectively convince their adversaries that they have adopted an inflexible posture that they cannot reasonably modify, they may be able to force their stronger counterparts to moderate their demands.

Even when weaker parties lack significant power vis-a-vis objectively powerful counterparts, they can enhance their bargaining influence if they can tie weak issues

---

238. *See* Roger J. Volkema, *The Negotiation* Toolkit 7–8 (2006); Cohen, *supra* note 38, at 167, 239; I. William Zartman & Jeffrey Rubin, *Power and* Negotiation 13–14 (2002); Shell, *supra* note 40, at 111.

239. *See* Shell, *supra* note 40, at 149–153.

to specific items the other side values. For example, a firm seeking to establish a business relationship with a large corporation might lack the power to demand significant concessions from that party. On the other hand, so long as the smaller firm possesses something the larger entity needs, it can use "issue specific" power to generate concessions on other issues the other party may not particularly care about.

Some negotiators circumscribe their bargaining freedom through reliance on limited authority. They have their principals provide them with narrowly prescribed discretion, and openly convey these firm constraints to their counterparts. Devious bargainers may combine this Limited Authority practice with the "Mutt and Jeff" approach. They represent their absent principals as the unreasonable parties who must be satisfied before final agreements can be achieved. If they can induce their adversaries to accept the contrived limits under which they appear to be operating, they may persuade those persons to reconsider their own positions. If the other participants seriously want to achieve mutual accords, they may be compelled to reduce their demands below what might otherwise be warranted in light of their actual strength.

When powerful counterparts are confronted by limited authority claims, they may attempt to neutralize the artificially curtailed parameters by suggesting—perhaps with opposing principals in attendance—that the prescribed corporate limits are unreasonably narrow. If the recalcitrant principals can be induced to modify their previous instructions, the use of this ploy by their agents to enhance their negotiating posture will be seriously undermined. It is difficult to employ this technique to generate expanded bargaining agent discretion when those representatives have already taken the time to convince their principals that anything less than the previously formulated and expressed minimum settlement terms should be unacceptable. However, before negotiators decide to lock their principals into uncompromising positions in a desperate effort to enlarge their bargaining power, they should understand the significant risk associated with such indoctrination. If it turns out that their principal's preliminary evaluation of the interaction was incorrect, this approach may preclude agreement.

Some agents try to expand their bargaining authority through the public announcement of minimum "fair" settlements that their constituents should reasonably expect them to achieve. The President occasionally employs this technique when he broadcasts his intention to veto proposed legislation if it fails to conform to certain constraints. Once this position is publicly proclaimed, the Members of Congress recognize that the President would be unlikely to accept the embarrassing loss of face that would accompany any meaningful modification of his previously announced position.

Labor leaders occasionally employ a similar technique to persuade employers of the seriousness of the demands they are making. They openly indicate to their members—sometimes through the news media—that they would not be effectively performing their representational function if they could not achieve certain minimal objectives that are expressly enumerated. Employers then realize that it would be difficult for the union officials who have made these representations to temporize their demands without suffering substantial humiliation and the possible loss of their positions in the next union election. If the employers would prefer to continue their relationship with the present labor leadership, they may accede to more generous employment terms than they had initially contemplated, recognizing the consequences that would likely result if the publicly stated minimum goals were not attained.

Negotiators who find themselves discussing important items over which they possess minimal bargaining leverage may alternatively counteract this deficiency by postponing any final decision on those issues until other matters are explored. They may thus delay final resolution of these matters until other terms are mentioned that the opposing side seriously wants to obtain. They may then be in a position to use their stronger posture with respect to the other items to enhance their less potent situation vis-a-vis the former topics.

If a continuing, symbiotic relationship is involved (*e.g.*, franchisor-franchisee; licensor-licensee, labor-management), a party that temporarily finds itself in disadvantageous circumstances may be able to offset the ephemeral advantage enjoyed by the other party by indicating that any short-term "win" attained by the presently stronger side may result in a mutually destructive Pyrrhic victory. This technique may effectively remind the party with the instant superiority that appropriately moderated demands are necessary to guarantee continued harmonious dealings. A party involved in an ongoing relationship may similarly avoid the consequences of a currently weakened position by postponing negotiations until a more propitious time when the balance of power has shifted more toward equilibrium.

D. Confronting Opposing Side Inflexibility

It can be a frustrating experience to be involved in a negotiation with parties who are unalterably committed to unacceptable positions. It is tempting to challenge their uncompromising stands directly. This approach entails a serious risk that the bargaining process will be irreversibly disrupted by the unwillingness of counterparts to acknowledge openly the unreasonableness of their existing proposals. It is generally more productive to employ a less confrontational technique that provides the other participants with a face-saving means of modifying their obstinate dispositions.[240]

Negotiators should attempt to induce seemingly inflexible counterparts to focus objectively on the underlying needs and interests of their principals. It is usually easier to generate position reappraisals through needs and interests analyses than through discussions focusing exclusively on adamantly articulated positions. Once the underlying objectives have been discerned and explored, it may be possible to formulate alternative solutions that may prove to be mutually beneficial.

During interactions with intransigent counterparts, it is helpful to emphasize the areas of common interest, rather than the zone of disagreement. If they can be induced

---

240. *See* William Ury, *Getting Past No* 90–109 (1991).

to realize the advantageous results their own sides can achieve through agreement on the less controverted items, there is a substantial likelihood they will become more conciliatory with respect to the remaining issues in dispute. As they become psychologically committed to the opportunity to attain mutually beneficial accords, they will be increasingly unwilling to allow a few unresolved topics to preclude overall agreements.

Once previously uncompromising parties have begun to tacitly acknowledge the unreasonable nature of their positions, it is time to employ a face-saving approach that permits a graceful retreat. It would be unwise to expect counterparts to make wholly unreciprocated concessions. This would be tantamount to unconditional surrender. It is preferable to offer some small tokens of exchange that opposing negotiators can use to explain their conciliatory movement to their superiors. The significance of these tokens should be embellished, so that opposing representatives and their principals will feel that they obtained something meaningful in exchange for their truly magnanimous concessions.

E. Dealing with Particularly Difficult Counterparts

Almost all business representatives must occasionally interact with overtly offensive counterparts.[241] These are usually win-lose, competitive/adversarial individuals who only feel successful when they completely annihilate and even humiliate the people with whom they interact. While their behavior generally undermines the interests of their own sides — generating an excessive number of non-settlements and inefficient agreements — they must still be dealt with by opposing parties.

Some of these individuals may be *situationally difficult* people who are behaving badly because of the unusual stress they are currently experiencing as a result of the underlying issues involved or the particular negotiation encounter they are facing.[242] Others may be *strategically difficult* persons who are deliberately using their offensive conduct to intimidate counterparts,[243] while a few may be *simply difficult* individuals who are usually unpleasant.[244] It may be possible to modify the inappropriate behavior of situationally and strategically difficult people, but it is almost impossible to change the conduct of simply difficult individuals.

The first question to ask when someone encounters obstreperous adversaries is whether "attitudinal bargaining" can be employed to modify their conduct. It is wise to politely, but forcefully, indicate one's unwillingness to participate in needlessly unpleasant interactions and to suggest how much more productive professional and civilized negotiations would be. Individuals who are not truly nasty bargainers —

---

241. *See* James Holbrook & Benjamin Cook, *Advanced Negotiation and Mediation* 143–154 (2013).
242. *See* Ron Shapiro & Mark Jankowski, *Bullies, Tyrants, and Impossible People* 20–21, 81–94 (2005).
243. *See* Shapiro & Jankowski, *supra* note 22, at 95–105.
244. *See id.*, at 106–119.

but are affected by unusual stress or have decided to experiment with such an approach — may quickly return to their more agreeable ways.[245]

When dealing with counterparts who are adversely affected by the stress surrounding the current encounter, it is best to empathize with those persons and work to diminish the negative feelings they are experiencing. If they are concerned about the underlying issues, they should be told that those difficulties can be resolved through the bargaining process. If they are afraid to negotiate, they should be reminded that the process need not be unpleasant. If counterparts are using bad behavior as a strategic weapon to advance their bargaining objectives, it can be helpful to let them know their conduct is not working.

If attitudinal bargaining does not produce significant improvement, one should attempt to control the number, and length of these interactions in a way that diminishes the ability of simply nasty persons to bother them. Telephone and e-mail exchanges can be especially effective, since the look of pleasure on the face of an adversary who is being offensive is not visible. This also affords one the opportunity to terminate unpleasant sessions anytime they feel frustrated. It suffices to indicate that there is other more-pressing business to which one must attend.

It is important when dealing with difficult adversaries to try to separate the personalities of the negotiators from the problems that must be addressed.[246] One should set a good example for unpleasant counterparts by being particularly courteous and respectful. Being a good listener who patiently listens to their perspective will break down their counterpart's desire to offend. Placing oneself in their shoes to see if it's possible to discern their underlying concerns and motivations will enable greater understanding of their approach. Are they being driven by unrealistic principal expectations or by adverse economic pressures affecting their firms? Perhaps they are tacitly expressing a personal need to prove their competence. If the problem is associated with unreasonable principal considerations, one may need to help them develop rationales they can use to diminish the expectations of those persons.

Some people apparently believe that everyone else is trying to take advantage of them. If one takes the time to appreciate their perspective — even if one does not agree with it — it may be possible to disarm them. Their discomfort may be associated with the way in which the negotiating issues have been formulated. They may think the issues have been stated in a manner that favors the opposing side. If one takes a few minutes to jointly reframe the problem in a mutually acceptable fashion, it's often possible to negate this potential stumbling block.[247]

During the critical stages of particular negotiations, previously courteous counterparts may become unexpectedly belligerent. They may fear that no agreement is going to be achieved. This is a good time to review the terms that have already been

---

245. *See* Robert S. Adler & Elliot M. Silverstein, "When David Meets Goliath: Dealing with Power Differentials in Negotiations," 5 *Harvard Negotiation Law Review* 1, 90–92 (2000).

246. *See* Fisher, Ury & Patton, *supra* note 11, at 17–40.

247. *See* Ury, *supra* note 240, at 59–85.

tentatively agreed upon and to emphasize how much progress has been made. This may generate a mutual psychological commitment to settlement and induce both sides to become more accommodating with respect to the remaining issues. If the participants are moving too quickly in an effort to compel an agreement, it's beneficial to recess the talks. This permits the parties to reconsider their non-settlement options and the propriety of the positions they are currently asserting.

F. Telephone Negotiations

Since complete reliance upon personal meetings would be unduly expensive and time-consuming, the vast majority of business negotiations are conducted wholly or at least partially on the telephone.[248] Telephone negotiations involve the same stages and conventional bargaining techniques as in-person interactions, but they usually consist of a series of shorter exchanges than in-person transactions, and they preclude visual contact except where video telephones are available. Advocates who make the mistake of treating these electronic exchanges less seriously than they would face-to-face interactions place themselves at a disadvantage.

Time urgency is exacerbated when *cell phone* discussions are involved in public locations. Individuals who call or are called while they are surrounded by other people are often at a disadvantage for several reasons. First, they may be distracted by what is going on around them. Second, individuals on cell phones in open spaces often try to keep the calls short, and this may cause negotiators to try to conclude talks too quickly. This may induce them to give up information or make concessions on an expedited basis. Third, persons may not feel capable of saying in such settings what they would say in private offices. Fourth, they may talk more quietly — and thus less forcefully — to avoid being overheard by strangers. It is thus advisable for persons who must negotiate on cell phones to move to isolated areas in which they can be themselves. If they are called while in public areas, they should not hesitate to ask to return the call when they find a more suitable location to conduct negotiation discussions.

Many individuals speak more loudly on their cell phones than they do on land lines, due to the fact they can hear their own voices on land lines but not on cell phones. When they speak this way when surrounded by strangers, confidential business information may be overheard by those persons. I have often heard important principal information disclosed at restaurants, airports, and train stations while people have been conducting serious business negotiations on their cell phones. It is thus important for persons conducting such interactions to move to areas in which they will not be overheard by others.

Individuals should realize that telephone exchanges are less personal than face-to-face interactions. This factor makes it easier for participants to employ overtly competitive or deliberately deceptive tactics. It also makes it easier for parties to reject proposals being suggested by the other side. Negotiators should recognize that tele-

---

248. *See generally* James Borg, *Persuasion: The Art of Influencing People* 131–159 (2004).

phone discussions tend to be more abbreviated than in-person encounters. It is thus more difficult to create a psychological commitment to settlement through only one or two telephone exchanges. Negotiators who find it difficult to conduct in-person discussions, but who desire more personal interactions than are available through telephone calls, should not hesitate to take advantage of video conferencing. Even though video conferences may not be as intimate as in-person meetings, they can still be conducted in a highly personal manner.

Many people think that telephone conversations are less revealing than in-person talks, because they do not involve visual interactions. They act as if opposing parties cannot perceive nonverbal signals during these transactions. This presumption is incorrect. Some psychologists have suggested to me that many individuals are more adept at reading nonverbal messages during telephone exchanges than they are during in-person interactions. I have found support for this assertion from blind students who have exhibited an uncanny ability to read the nonverbal signals being emitted by others they cannot see. This phenomenon is attributable to the fact that in-person interactions involve a myriad of simultaneous nonverbal stimuli that are often too numerous to be proficiently discerned and interpreted. When people speak on the telephone, however, they are not as likely to be overwhelmed by the various nonverbal clues emanating from the other party. They need only concentrate on the audible messages being received to ascertain the content of the nonverbal messages being communicated.

A substantial number of nonverbal clues are discernible during telephone interactions.[249] Careful listeners can hear changes in the pitch, pace, tone, inflection, rhythm, and volume of speaker voices. A pregnant pause may indicate that a particular offer is being seriously considered by a recipient who did not hesitate before rejecting previous proposals. The initial pause before the most recent position statement was verbally renounced would suggest that the proposal has entered the other party's zone of acceptability. A sigh in response to a new proposal may similarly indicate that the recipient is now confident that some settlement will be achieved.

Voice inflection may be equally informative. People who respond to communicated offers with perceptibly increased levels of excitement may nonverbally suggest that they are more pleased with the proposal than their verbal response might otherwise indicate. Since most negotiators tend to begin the discussions with either their most important or their least important subjects, the topic sequence presented by parties may inadvertently reveal the items they value most. Professor Ekman's seminal book on deception noted that individuals who engage in prevarication tend to speak more deliberately and to utter their misrepresentations with higher pitched voices.[250] Attentive listeners could easily perceive these phenomena.

---

249. *See* Judee K. Burgoon, David B. Buller & William Gill Woodall, *Nonverbal Communication: The Unspoken Dialogue* 4 (1996).

250. *See* Ekman, *supra* note 204, at 92–94.

Individuals engaged in telephone negotiations should listen intently for verbal leaks and nonverbal signals being emitted by their counterparts. They should simultaneously recognize the ability of their adversaries to discern the various verbal leaks and nonverbal messages emanating from themselves. They should thus be as careful to control their verbal leaks and their nonverbal messages during telephone exchanges as they would during in-person encounters. They should additionally note the use of signal words such as "to be candid" or "to be truthful." Many people use them to preface misrepresentations they hope will be unquestioningly accepted. Those participants who ignore this crucial consideration and treat telephone discussions casually may unthinkingly place themselves at a disadvantage. Following each telephonic exchange, a record of negotiation developments should always be entered in the file for future reference.

It is usually more advantageous to be the telephone caller rather than the recipient of the call. The caller has the opportunity to prepare for the exchange.[251] Negotiators who plan to phone counterparts to discuss particular matters should prepare as diligently for these interactions as they would for in-person exchanges. This preliminary effort is usually rewarded. Since they have the opportunity to surprise unsuspecting adversaries with their calls, they may subtly gain the upper hand. The other participants are unlikely to expect their call and are probably unprepared for the conversation that is about to occur. This permits phoning parties to advance more persuasive arguments and to elicit less planned counteroffers than would have been possible during formally scheduled interactions.

Persons are used to communicating with others visually on their cell phones, and they often use this approach when negotiating with counterparts. This approach should enable them to see facial expressions that might provide them with beneficial information. If individuals really want to be able to read facial expressions proficiently when they negotiate visually, studies show that they should do so on their laptop computers. People who negotiate via larger screens generally perform more effectively than persons who do so via cell phones.[252]

Individuals who receive unexpected telephone calls from counterparts should internally assess their degree of preparedness. If they are not fully conversant regarding the pertinent factual circumstances, economic issues, and prior settlement discussions, they should not make the mistake of plunging ignorantly into uncharted waters. They should not hesitate to suggest that they are presently occupied with other matters and unable to talk. They can thereafter peruse the file and telephone the other party when they are completely prepared. When they reach the initial caller, they can say that they are returning that person's call. Their subsequent silence can adroitly return the focus of the interaction to the other party.

---

251. *See* George Ross, *Trump Style Negotiation* 212–213 (2006).
252. See T. Kurtzberg, S. Kang & C. Naquin, "The Effects of Screen Size and E-Communication Richness on Negotiation Performance," 27 *Group Decision and Negotiation* 573 (2018).

Most bargaining techniques that could be used during in-person interactions may be employed with equal efficacy during telephone negotiations. Although it is difficult to walk out during phone calls when people want to graphically demonstrate their displeasure regarding bargaining progress, individuals who are inclined toward such histrionics may accomplish the same result by hanging up on their intransigent counterparts. It must be realized, however, that this tactic may be considered less acceptable than a cessation of in-person talks effectuated by way of a walkout — due to the more contemptuous and discourteous nature of this device. People who wish to terminate current phone interactions should at least inform their counterparts why they are doing so to avoid unnecessary future difficulties.

Many negotiators prefer in-person interactions to telephone discussions.[253] They like the psychological atmosphere they can personally establish, and they believe that they are more proficient readers of nonverbal signals during face-to-face encounters than during telephone talks. They also prefer several longer in-person interactions to numerous brief telephone exchanges. These people should not hesitate to insist on in-person sessions when serious transactions are involved and they think this will provide them with a bargaining advantage.

G. Negotiating via Letters, E-Mail, or Text Messaging

A surprising number of individuals like to conduct their negotiations primarily or entirely through letters, e-mail, or text messaging, especially younger persons who have grown up using e-mail, text-messaging, and similar electronic means of interacting with others.[254] They do not merely transmit written versions of terms orally discussed during earlier interactions. They limit most, if not all, of their transactions to written communications. Most people who endeavor to restrict their bargaining communications to letters and e-mail exchanges are not comfortable with the traditional negotiation process. They do not like the seemingly amorphous nature of that process, and do not enjoy the split-second tactical decision-making that must occur during in-person interactions. They forget that bargaining involves uniquely *personal* encounters that are not easily conducted entirely through written communications.[255]

People contemplating bargaining interactions that will be primarily conducted through the exchange of letters, e-mail, or text messaging should appreciate how difficult it is to establish rapport with counterparts through those lean written mediums that lack facial expressions and general body language signals. It would thus be ben-

---

253. *See* Thompson, *supra* note 65, at 305–307.

254. *See* Lynn A. Epstein & Elena M. Marty-Nelson, *Empowering Negotiators* at 34–38 (2019); H. Ebner, "Negotiating is Changing," 2017 *Journal of Dispute Resolution* 99 (2017); See *generally* Sherry Turklel, *Reclaiming Conversation: The Power of Talk in a Digital Age* (2015); Sherry Turkle, *Alone Together* (2011).

255. *See* Chris Voss, *Never Split the* Difference 136–137 (2016); Leigh Thompson & Janice Nadler, "Negotiating Via Information Technology: Theory and Application," 58 *Journal of Social Issues* 109 (2002).

eficial to initially telephone their adversaries to exchange some personal information and to establish minimal relationships.[256] Individuals who first create mutual relations through such oral exchanges are likely to find their subsequent negotiations more pleasant and more efficient. They are also likely to generate more cooperative behavior and more trusting relationships, and encounter fewer impasses.[257] If telephone exchanges would be difficult, it would be helpful during the preliminary e-mail exchanges to disclose some personal information designed to increase the rapport between the parties.

The use of letters, e-mail, or text messaging to conduct basic negotiations is generally a cumbersome and inefficient process. Every communication has to be drafted and thoroughly edited before being sent to the other side. The counterparts must then read and digest all of the written passages, and formulate their own replies. Due to the definitive nature of written documents, written positions seem to be more intractable than those expressed vocally over the telephone or in person. When people present their proposals orally, their voice inflections and nonverbal signals may indicate a willingness to be flexible with respect to certain items. Written communications rarely convey this critical information. In addition, written encounters tend to produce less efficient outcomes than in-person exchanges, because of the lack of effective cooperative bargaining. People also tend to be less polite—and more confrontational—when communicating through e-mail. They similarly tend to employ more deceptive tactics.[258]

Letter, e-mail, and text exchanges may often be misinterpreted due to the "*attribution bias.*" As the recipients review and evaluate the positions set forth by their counterparts, they tend to read more or less into the stated terms than was actually intended, because they assume that the senders are being manipulative. They may interpret seemingly innocuous language as deliberately inflammatory. As they reread the pertinent passages, they tend to reinforce their preliminary impressions. Their misinterpretations may be compounded by their escalated written responses to the terms they erroneously think their counterparts intended to convey. When the original writers receive their reply, they may not understand the reason for the other side's uncompromising or negative tone, and may further exacerbate the situation with antagonistic responses of their own.[259] This is why e-mail negotiations tend to be less

---

256. *See* Janice Nadler, "Rapport in Legal Negotiation: How Small Talk Can Facilitate E-Mail Dealmaking," 9 *Harvard Negotiation Law Review* 223, 237–247 (2004); Thompson & Nadler, *supra* note 255.

257. *See* Kevin W. Rockmann & Gregory B. Northcraft, "To Be or Not To Be Trusted: The Influence of Media Richness on Defection and Deception," 112 *Organizational Behavior and Human Decision Processes* 107, at 112, 116 (2008); Nadler, *supra* note 256, at 237–247.

258. *See* Rockmann & Northcraft, *supra* note 257, at 112, 116; Kathleen L. McGinn & Rachel Croson, "What Do Communication Media Mean for Negotiators? A Question of Social Awareness," in *The Handbook of Negotiation and Culture* 334, 342–343 (Michele J. Gelfand & Jeanne M. Brett, eds. 2004).

259. *See* Thompson & Nadler, *supra* note 255, at 119; Nadler, *supra* note 256, at 237–238.

cooperative than in-person interactions.[260] If people become especially frustrated by unpleasant e-mail exchanges, they may decide to write negative replies. It may make them feel better to prepare such responses, so long as they remember to click on "cancel" and not "send" when they are done.

It can be highly beneficial for negotiators to telephone their counterparts a day or two after they have sent them written proposals to hear their responses. Slight misunderstandings can often be resolved amicably. More serious disagreements can be discussed in a way that can begin to induce the participants to move toward each other. This more interpersonal approach can be far more accommodating than continued text-based exchanges.

Some complex transactions involve numerous terms that must be carefully formulated to protect the interests of the various parties. In these cases, it is entirely appropriate for the negotiators to exchange draft proposals through letters or e-mails. To avoid communication difficulties, however, each letter or e-mail should be followed by a telephone call. This enables the sending party to ascertain the manner in which the written communication has been received. If it appears that the recipient has read something into the written proposals that was not intended, the misinterpretation can be quickly corrected and the bargaining process can be preserved.

When parties send documents to others in electronic form, they often inadvertently include critical information that is not obvious on the face of those documents — and which they do not intend to share with the document recipients. Every single key stroke, deletion, and addition is recorded in the electronic metadata associated with the file in question. Parties who know how to "mine" electronic files for hidden information may be able to determine exactly how documents were prepared and edited, and even uncover editorial comments made by persons who reviewed earlier drafts. Business persons should use reasonable care when transmitting electronic documents to prevent the disclosure of metadata containing firm confidences. There are several ways they can prevent the unintended transmission of such metadata. They can use one of several scrubbing software programs designed to eliminate metadata from their files before they send the cleansed files to others. They can alternatively send PDF files, or create new files and then insert the existing files into the newly created files. My computer experts indicate that this insertion option eliminates the unintended metadata that were contained in the existing files that were inserted into newly created files. If they are working in Word, they can click on "File" menu, click on "Info," go into "Inspect Document," and finally click on "Remove All."

H. Responding to "Is This Your Final Offer?"

After negotiators articulate new offers, they are occasionally asked by counterparts whether their new positions represent their "final offers." What is the appropriate response to such an inquiry? If the new position actually represents their "final offer," it

---

260. *See* McGinn & Croson, *supra* note 258, at 341.

is beneficial for them to firmly and politely inform the other side of this fact. When doing so, one should avoid any modifiers (*e.g.*, "that's about as far as I can go"; "I don't have much room left"; "we aren't inclined to go higher/lower") which contain verbal leaks indicating that this is not really their final offer. Using unequivocal language and consistent nonverbal signals (*e.g.*, open posture with palms facing outward and sincere eye contact) can ensure that the verbal and nonverbal messages are congruent.

What if the most recent position statement does *not* represent one's final offer? Some negotiators may feel comfortable indicating that there may be more room if the other side modifies its current position. This effectively conveys the need for the other side to make a new offer before one decides whether to make another position change. Other negotiators may prefer to use a blocking technique to avoid a direct response. They might ignore the question and continue to focus on other aspects of the bargaining interaction—hoping their counterpart will forget to restate the unanswered question. They might counter the other party's question with one of their own and ask whether that side's most recent proposal represents *their* "final offer." They might alternatively indicate that this question concerns a confidential matter between them and their principal that they are unwilling to discuss directly. The problem with this response concerns the fact that if when they get to their real bottom line they are willing to disclose this fact, individuals who deal with them regularly will realize that their "no comment" response indicates that they actually possess additional bargaining room.

I. Negotiauctions

When individuals represent entities purchasing or selling goods, services, or even businesses, negotiating licensing agreements, or dealing with similar commodities, they often have the opportunity to interact with several different parties simultaneously. Their final accord may be with a single firm or with two or more companies. If they only consider their bottom lines and agree to contracts as soon as one party proposes terms preferable to those minima, they may forego the opportunity to obtain more beneficial agreements.

Firms that could do business with several different parties need to appreciate the fact they may wish to conduct "negotiauctions."[261] They should begin to interact separately with the relevant entities to learn what they desire and what they are willing to provide in return. They can casually disclose the fact that other parties are being considered, to let their potential partners know that they have to make appropriately beneficial offers if they hope to establish definitive relationships. Even though the parties will be conducting negotiations on a one-on-one basis, they will simultaneously be engaged in separate auctions as the different parties propose terms they think will enable them to obtain the accords they seek.

A perfect example of a "negotiauction" might involve a corporation selling off a division. Several potential buyers may express an interest, and the selling firm could

---

261. *See generally* Guhan Subramanian, Dealmaking: The New Strategy of *Negotiauctions* (2010).

let them know that other parties are involved. Instead of thinking of how much a particular firm should offer to go beyond the bottom line of the selling firm, it has to think about how much others might consider paying. The selling corporation may hope to obtain at least $50 million, and it might seem as if a $55 million offer should be sufficient to seal the deal. On the other hand, if other potential purchasers think the division is worth $60 or $65 million, others will have to offer something in that range if they hope to prevail.

A firm endeavoring to license new technology it has developed could similarly employ a "negotiauction" to maximize its returns. It could induce several interested parties to effectively bid for the exclusive rights to that technology, or it could auction off different geographic areas or different limited uses of the new technology to diverse parties enabling it to generate greater returns for itself.

When company representatives contemplate "negotiauctions," they must appreciate some of the practical and ethical risks involved.[262] If the results of their interactions with others will culminate in on-going relationships, they should be careful not to engage in conduct that might adversely affect those potential relationships. If they whipsaw bidding parties too aggressively, they could create future problems. It thus behooves them to be open and forthright when dealing with other firms during these interactions. They must also appreciate the fact that the highest bidder may not necessarily be the best partner for their own company. Reputational considerations might favor one party over others, as might the potential for greater joint gains in the future.

Substantial ethical issues may surround "negotiauctions." Can a party indicate that it has received an offer from a second firm when it has not obtained such an offer? I believe that such a misrepresentation would constitute fraud since it concerns the intentional distortion of material fact which the other party has the right to rely on. Similar problems could arise if they have received an offer for $52 million and they inform another party they have received a $60 million offer. This would also be a material misrepresentation that the other party would reasonably rely upon to its economic detriment. On the other hand, they could probably indicate truthfully that they have received another offer, and suggest that it will take $60 million to purchase the division in question. If the other party were to ask them how much they have been offered, they could indicate that this issue is confidential and reiterate their $60 million request.

J. Negotiating with Government Agencies

Due to the different value systems involved, when private-sector parties interact with government agencies, they frequently experience cultural difficulties. When pri-

---

262. *See id.*, at 178–195.

vate sector executives evaluate prospective business transactions, they carefully engage in cost-benefit analyses based on the projected costs, the financial benefits to be derived from the transactions in question, and the economic value of their external alternatives. With the primary exception of tax-collecting agencies, most government representatives are not concerned about these factors. They assume a better than average likelihood of prevailing in any resulting litigation, because of the judicial deference accorded to statutes, regulations, and administrative determinations. In addition, government officials tend to ignore the costs associated with litigation, since most agencies are not charged for the legal services involved.

Government administrators recognize the power advantage they enjoy over most private sector parties. They know that most companies do not want to become embroiled in protracted battles with federal or state departments that seem to have unlimited resources. They know they can frighten corporate officials through extensive pre-trial litigation or negotiations that will generate substantial legal fees. They do not hesitate to remind private sector firms that they receive cost-free representation by Justice Department or Attorney General lawyers. If they have the sense that private companies are afraid of possible litigation, they are usually willing to take advantage of this weakness. It is thus necessary for firms to give serious thought to litigation when that course becomes necessary. When government officials realize that they may be forced to defend their actions before judicial tribunals, they often exhibit more accommodating behavior.

Private sector negotiators often find it frustrating to deal with government representatives, because those persons rarely possess significant authority. Agency officials who must assume responsibility for departmental determinations are hesitant to provide their own negotiators with the power those persons require to conclude most interactions. Their bargainers can merely elicit offers from private parties that must be communicated to administrative decision-makers. Government representatives find this just as frustrating as do their counterparts. They would like to be able to resolve matters directly, but must usually function as intermediaries between outside parties and relevant agency officials. Although experienced government negotiators frequently know what they can sell to their superiors, many junior employees do not. Since they do not want to be criticized for overstepping their authority, they tend to be cautious. They feel the need to clear even minor issues with agency officials before they suggest possible solutions to their counterparts.

Agency negotiators do not like to have their recommended settlement proposals overruled by their superiors. When they enter into agreements, they work hard to get them approved. Once private sector agents reach deals with their government counterparts, they should give them the information they need to convince agency officials to accept the final terms. Since the approval process may take some time, private sector parties must be patient and give the agency representatives the time they require to accomplish their objective.

Agency officials normally consider applicable statutes and regulations sacrosanct. People who contemplate challenges to the propriety of these rules are likely to encounter stiff resistance. Most agency representatives are prepared to litigate statutory or regulation challenges to the Supreme Court. It is thus more productive to formulate positions that do not directly attack the legality of agency rules. Company attorneys should look for ways to interpret applicable statutes or regulations in a manner that will produce the desired results. Even strained statutory constructions may be beneficial. They permit agency decision-makers to accede to their demands in a face-saving fashion.

Unlike their private sector counterparts, most government attorneys and administrators are keenly aware of the number of litigated cases they have won and lost. They can usually provide an exact won-loss statistic on a moment's notice. They hate to lose, believing this may adversely affect their agency's reputation. If private sector representatives can convince government representatives that they may lose in court, those legal agents and their superiors are likely to be receptive to settlement discussions. Such discussions may generate final agreements that will preserve their win-loss records.

A common frustration experienced by people dealing with government bureaucracies concerns the seeming unwillingness of many officials to make definitive decisions. This reluctance is based upon the fact that with hundreds or thousands of government personnel, employees rarely stand out for making exemplary determinations. They are more likely to be noticed when they make questionable decisions. To avoid possible criticism, many government officials have modified the plaque that stood on President Truman's desk — "The Buck Stops Here" — to read "Keep the Buck Moving." They recognize that they are unlikely to be chastised for decisions they did not make!

When private sector parties encounter government representatives who are afraid to make decisions, they should use two approaches. They should first try to convince their immediate counterparts that it is in their interest to make the requested decisions. They must not hesitate to give the government representatives with whom they are interacting the information they need to persuade their agency superiors to accept negotiated deals.

When the immediate agency representatives are unwilling to accept proposed solutions, it may be beneficial to approach higher officials who may have the courage to make the necessary decisions. Private firm agents should determine who has the power to grant the results they desire and figure out how to approach those individuals. In some cases, they may wish to have a third person intercede on their behalf to get the process going. Once they get the attention of someone with authority and the fortitude to exercise that power, they should present their positions in the most forceful manner possible.

K. Renegotiating Existing Contracts/Relationships

No matter how carefully parties negotiate and memorialize their agreements, there are times when changed circumstances or unanticipated developments require one or both parties to modify their original understandings.[263] When the new circumstances affect both sides in a similar manner, it is usually easy for both to get together and reassess where they should be now. On the other hand, when the unusual circumstances only impact one side or impact one side far more than the other, it may be more difficult for the adversely affected party to reopen negotiations.

United States business persons are so used to the notion that contractual parties must honor their existing obligations that it may not be easy for one party to induce the other to renegotiate their specified terms. Persons seeking to renegotiate existing relationships should provide the other side with explicit reasons why that side should enter into renegotiation talks. They must explain what that side might lose if it is unwilling to explore the need for new arrangements. The motivating factors may be due to unexpected economic or political occurrences, significant financial changes, the failures of third party suppliers, or even natural disasters. Costs may have escalated, delivery dates can no longer be satisfied, periodic payments may no longer be met, leased space may no longer be needed, unexpected environmental issues may necessitate immediate action, or similar issues may have arisen.

If parties seeking renegotiation try to cover up the real reasons for their requested changes, their partners may become suspicious and refuse to explore possible changes. Only through a direct and truthful explanation regarding the need for relationship modifications can requesting parties hope to achieve their ultimate goals. They must also appreciate the initial inclination of many partners to decline renegotiation requests based upon their belief that contractual obligations are both morally and legally binding. It can be especially helpful to apologize for the present situation and to throw one's self on the mercy of the other side. This approach can greatly diminish the negative emotions initially emanating from the party being asked to renegotiate. The requesting side can also point out how it is virtually impossible for it to honor the existing terms. If operational difficulties are involved, they should explain what has occurred and indicate how soon they may be able to carry out their side's obligations. If financial problems have developed, they should explain how bankruptcy proceedings may be necessary if renegotiations are not successful. Such statements let the other side know that previously promised performance is no longer a possibility. The real issue now is how best to restructure their relationship to enable both to move on successfully. Patience is especially important, because it may take some time before the other side realizes that renegotiation is preferable to inaction. Instead of looking backwards to see who may be responsible for the factors necessitating modified terms, the parties should look forward to determine how best to alter their current arrangements.

If the person asked to renegotiate existing terms is unwilling to participate, it may be necessary to contact someone else in the other side's organization who may be more inclined to do so. If an organizational policy precludes contractual changes, the party seeking the modifications must look for someone who possesses the authority to override that policy. It helps to ask a lot of "who" and "why" questions. Who has the au-

---

263. *See generally* Marc Freeman, *Renegotiate with Integrity* (2006).

thority to renegotiate the current arrangements? Why won't the other side consider modified terms? Why would they prefer a disastrous default to less onerous changes?

It can be beneficial for the party seeking modified terms to explain its underlying reasons and ask the other side how it thinks the parties should proceed. If the other side can be drawn into the problem-solving process, the two sides can begin to work together to restructure their relationship. It is important for both sides to keep open minds. They should look for their respective underlying interests and seek to formulate possible solutions that would meet the basic needs of both. What modifications would enable the defaulting party to carry out its obligations in a manner that would least disadvantage the other side? It is imperative that both sides indicate openly what they have to achieve through renegotiation.

It is often difficult for the individuals who negotiated the original terms to renegotiate the new terms being sought, because the side being asked to change the existing obligations quite reasonably expects performance of what was previously agreed upon. This explains why it can be helpful to have other persons conduct the renegotiation discussions.[264] On the other hand, if the original negotiators have had a long-term relationship and have worked well together, they may still be in the best position to restructure the terms of their arrangement.

Parties being asked to renegotiate existing relationships must carefully weigh their options to be sure they do not end up with situations that are worse than complete default. They must determine their BATRA — their Best Alternative to Renegotiated Agreements. They need to carefully consider their current alternatives and decide what restructured arrangements would be best for them. If they truly believe that terminated relationships or bankruptcy proceedings would be preferable to any modification they would be required to make, they should decline the changes being requested and force the defaulting party into legal proceedings.

Parties willing to restructure their existing arrangements should not hesitate to insist upon provisions that will protect their interests in case the requesting persons are unable to carry out their revised promises. They might insist upon some form of insurance or money placed in escrow that will be forfeited if full compliance with the modified obligations is not met.

§ 10.02. Conclusion

Bargaining power is defined more by participant perceptions than objective reality. Parties may thus undermine counterpart strength by ignoring it and enhance their own weak positions through limited authority and public pronouncements restricting their negotiating freedom. Since the bargaining process involves uniquely personal

---

264. *See id.*, at 142–144.

interactions, individuals should not conduct their negotiation exchanges entirely through written communications.

When negotiators encounter particularly difficult counterparts, they should employ "attitudinal bargaining" to modify their unacceptable behavior. Negotiators can then work to separate the people from the problems that must be solved and start looking for ways to create more cooperative environments.

Telephone negotiations involve the same stages and factors as in-person interactions, with participants being capable in this medium of reading the nonverbal clues associated with voice pitch, pace, tone, and volume. Prepared callers tend to have an advantage over less prepared call recipients. Recognizing the increased use of cell phones, negotiators should be careful to arrange telephone discussions when they will have the other party's undivided attention and there is no risk of being heard by third parties. Individuals who conduct e-mail or text messaging negotiations should use preliminary telephone calls to establish rapport with counterparts, and should phone those persons shortly after they have sent e-mail proposals to *hear* the responses of those recipients. People should also be careful to eliminate the metadata contained in electronic files to be sure their counterparts cannot discern all of the changes they have made in those files.

Private sector individuals who negotiate with government representatives must recognize the inter-cultural aspects of their transactions and key differences between the private and government cultures. There are different value systems involved in these transactions, and agency negotiators rarely possess final settlement authority over the matters being discussed.

Chapter 11

Impact of Gender on Bargaining Interactions

§ 11.01. Impact of Stereotypes

Gender-based stereotypes cause some business persons great difficulty when they interact with individuals of the opposite sex.[265] Males frequently expect females to behave like "ladies" during their interactions. Overt aggressiveness that would be viewed as vigorous advocacy if it were employed by men is likely to be characterized as offensive and threatening when used by women.[266] This is particularly true when the females in question employ foul language and loud voices. Male negotiators who would immediately counter these tactics by other men with quid pro quo responses often find it hard to adopt retaliatory approaches against "ladies." When they permit such an irrelevant factor to influence and limit their use of responsive weapons, they provide their female counterparts with an inherent bargaining advantage. Men who are similarly unwilling to act as competitively toward female adversaries as they would toward male adversaries give further leverage to their female counterparts.

Male bargainers occasionally make the mistake of assuming that female counterparts do not engage in as many negotiating "games" as male adversaries, and they often prefer to negotiate against women instead of men.[267] Even many women er-

---

265. *See generally* Andrea Schneider, "Negotiating While Female," 70 Southern Methodist University Law Review 695 (2017); Deborah Kolb & Jessica L. Porter, *Negotiating at Work* (2015); Yasmin Davidds, *Your Own Terms" A Woman's Guide to Taking Charge of Any Negotiation* (2015); Deborah Kolb, "Negotiating in the Shadows of Organizations: Gender, Negotiation, and Change," 28 *Ohio State Journal on Dispute Resolution* 241, 247–248 (2013); Emily T. Amanatullah & Catherine H. Tinsley, "Punishing Female Negotiators for Asserting Too Much … or Not Enough: Explaining Why Advocacy Moderates Backlash Against Assertive Female Negotiators," 120 *Organizational Behavior and Human Decision Processes* 110,118 (2013); Deborah Kolb & Judith Williams, *The Shadow Negotiation: How Women Can Master the Hidden Agendas That Determine Bargaining Success* (2000); Deborah Kolb & Judith Williams, *Everyday Negotiation: Navigating the Hidden Agendas in Bargaining* (2003).

266. *See* Linda Babcock & Sarah Laschever, *Ask For It* 256–258 (2008); Laura J Kray & Connson C. Locke, "To Flirt or Not to Flirt? Sexual Power at the Bargaining Table," 24 *Negotiation* Journal 483, 485 (2008).

267. *See* Eric Gladstone & Kathleen M. O'Connor, "A Counterpart's Feminine Face Signals Cooperativeness and Encourages Negotiators to Compete," 125(1) *Organizational Behavior and Human Decision Processes* 18 (2014).

roneously assume that other females are unlikely to employ the Machiavellian tactics stereotypically attributed to members of the competitive male culture. Men *and* women who expect their female adversaries to behave less disingenuously and more cooperatively often ignore the reality of their interactions and accord a significant bargaining advantage to women who are in fact willing to employ manipulative bargaining tactics.

Some male negotiators attempt to obtain a psychological advantage against aggressive female bargainers by casting aspersions on the femininity of those individuals. They hope to embarrass those participants and make them feel self-conscious with respect to the approach they are using. Female negotiators should never allow adversaries to employ this tactic successfully. They have the right to use any techniques they think appropriate regardless of the gender-based stereotypes they may contradict. To males who raise specious objections to their otherwise proper conduct, they should reply that they do not wish to be viewed as "ladies," but merely as business representatives involved in transactions in which one's gender is irrelevant.

Women who find that gender-based beliefs may be negatively affecting bargaining interactions may wish to directly broach the subject of negative stereotyping, since this may be the most effective manner of dealing with the influence of these feelings.[268] They may ask counterparts if they find it difficult to negotiate with women executives. While most male adversaries will quickly deny any such beliefs, they are likely to internally reevaluate their treatment of female counterparts. Once both sides acknowledge—internally or externally—the possible impact of stereotypical beliefs, they can try to avoid group generalizations and focus on the particular individuals with whom they must currently interact.

§ 11.02. Perceived Differences

Empirical studies indicate that male and female subjects do not behave identically in competitive settings. Females tend to be initially more trusting and trustworthy than their male cohorts, but they are generally less willing to forgive violations of their trust than are males.[269] People interacting with female negotiators who exhibit verbal and nonverbal signals consistent with these generalities should realize that they may be able to establish trusting and cooperative relationships with them so long as they do not commit unacceptable transgressions. Women often establish relationships

---

268. *See* Catherine H. Tinsley, Sandra I. Cheldelin, Andrea Kupfer Schneider & Emily T. Amanatullah, "Women at the Bargaining Table: Pitfalls and Prospects," 25 *Negotiation Journal* 233, 243 (2009).

269. *See* Daniel Del Gobbo, "The Feminist Negotiator's Dilemma," 33 *Ohio State Journal on Dispute Resolution* 1 (2018); Lee E. Miller & Jessica Miller, *A Woman's Guide to Successful Negotiating* 42–45 (2002); Rubin & Brown, *supra* note 59, at 171–173.

with others more effectively than men, since they tend to make eye contact more frequently and for longer periods of time.[270] On the other hand, men tend to establish higher goals than women in identical situations, often enabling them to obtain more beneficial results.[271]

When men and women prevaricate, they often have different objectives. Males frequently lie on a *self-oriented* basis to enhance their own reputations ("braggadocio"), while females who dissemble are more likely to engage in *other-oriented* lying that is intended to make other people feel better (*e.g.*, "I love your new outfit," or "you made a great presentation").[272] This difference would probably cause males to feel more comfortable than their female cohorts when they engage in deceptive behavior during negotiation encounters to advance their own interests, since such conduct would be of a self-oriented nature.

Studies show that women are more likely than men to avoid competitive situations, less likely to acknowledge competitive wishes, and not likely to do as well in competition.[273] Many women are apprehensive regarding the negative consequences that they associate with competitive achievement, fearing that competitive success will alienate them from others.[274] Males in my Negotiation course have occasionally indicated that they are particularly uncomfortable when women counterparts obtain extremely beneficial results from them. A few have even indicated that they would prefer the consequences associated with non-settlements to the possible embarrassment of "losing" to female counterparts.[275] Even some female students are more critical of women who attain exceptional bargaining results than they are of men who achieve equally advantageous negotiation terms.[276]

---

270. *See* Beall, *supra* note 153, at 60.

271. *See* Russell Korobkin & Joseph Doherty, "Who Wins in Settlement Negotiations?" 11 *American Law and Economics* Review 162 (2009); Laura J. Kray & Linda Babcock, "Gender in Negotiations: A Motivated Social Cognitive Analysis," in *Negotiation Theory and Research* 205 (Leigh Thompson, ed. 2006).

272. *See* Bella M. DePaulo, Deborah A. Kashy, Susan E. Kirkendol, Melissa M. Wyer & Jennifer A. Epstein, "Lying in Everyday Life," 70 *Journal of Personality and Social Psychology* 979, 986–987 (1996).

273. *See* Deborah Kolb, "Too Bad for the Women or Does It Have to Be? Gender and Negotiation Research Over the Past Twenty-Five Years," 25 *Negotiation Journal* 515, 518 (2009); Fiona Greig, "Propensity to Negotiate and Career Advancement: Evidence From an Investment Bank that Women are on a 'Slow Elevator,'" 24 *Negotiation Journal* 495, 496–497 (2008); Muriel Niederle & Lise Vesterlund, "Do Women Shy Away From Competition? Do Men Compete Too Much?" http://www.nber.org/papers/w11474 3, 11–14 (2005); Linda Babcock & Sarah Laschever, *Women Don't Ask* 102–103 (2003).

274. *See* Babcock & Laschever, *supra* note 273, at 32; Tess Wilkinson-Ryan & Deborah Small, "Negotiating Divorce: Gender and the Behavioral Economics of Divorce Bargaining," 26 *Law and Inequality* 109, 115–117 (2008).

275. *See* Miller & Miller, *supra* note 269, at 132.

276. *See* Lloyd Burton, Larry Farmer, Elizabeth D. Gee, Lorie Johnson & Gerald R. Williams, "Feminist Theory, Professional Ethics, and Gender-Related Distinctions in Attorney Negotiating Styles," 1991 *Journal of Dispute Resolution* 199, 233 (1991).

Males tend to exude more confidence than females in performance-oriented settings.[277] Even when minimally prepared, men think they can "wing it" and get through successfully.[278] On the other hand, no matter how well prepared women are, they tend to feel unprepared.[279] I often observe this distinction with my Negotiation students. Successful males think they can achieve beneficial results in any setting, while successful females continue to express doubts about their own capabilities. I find this frustrating, because these accomplished women are as proficient as their accomplished male cohorts.

Male confidence may explain why men like to negotiate more than women,[280] and why they tend to seek more beneficial results when they negotiate than their female cohorts.[281] Men tend to feel more comfortable in risk-taking situations than women.[282] When they bargain, males tend to use more forceful language and exhibit more dominant nonverbal signals (*e.g.*, intense eye contact and louder voices) than females. These gender differences may help to explain why women experience greater anxiety when they have to negotiate than men.[283] In addition, while women tend to seek less than men when they negotiate for themselves, they set higher goals and achieve higher results when they negotiate on behalf of others.[284] On the other hand, while men tend to be more win-lose oriented, women tend to be more win-win oriented, making it easier for them to use cooperative bargaining to expand the overall pie and improve the results achieved by both sides.[285]

Many women feel uncomfortable when they have to negotiate their own terms of employment. I often advise such persons to have an "*out-of-body experience.*" They should behave as if a friend with their CV has asked them to negotiate the terms of employment for that person. They should carefully examine the CV and focus on the positive factors. What terms do they think an individual with that

---

277. *See* Schneider, supra note 265, at 701–702; Kolb, *supra* note 273, at 518; Muriel Niederle & Lise Vesterlund, "Gender Differences in Competition," 24 *Negotiation Journal* 447, 450–56 (2008).

278. *See* Daniel Goleman, *Working With Emotional Intelligence* 7 (1998).

279. *See* Gail Evans, *Play Like a Man, Win Like a* Woman 84–85; 90–91 (2000).

280. *See* Deborah Small, Michelle Gelfand, Linda C. Babcock & Hilary Gettman, "Who Goes to the Bargaining Table? Understanding Gender Variation in the Initiation of Negotiation," 93 *Journal of Personality and Social* Psychology 600 (2007).

281. *See* Babcock & Laschever, *supra* note 266, at 146–47; Babcock & Laschever, *supra* note 273, at 130–35, 140–41; Laura J. Kray, Adam D. Galinsky & Leigh Thompson, "Reversing the Gender Gap in Negotiations: An Exploration of Stereotype Regeneration," 87 *Organizational Behavior and Human Decision* Processes 386, 391 (2002).

282. *See* Babcock & Laschever, *supra* note 266, at 32; Babcock & Laschever, *supra* note 273, at 138.

283. *See* Babcock & Laschever, *supra* note 273, at 113–14.

284. *See* E.T. Amanatullo & M.W. Morris, "Negotiating Gender Roles: Gender Differences in Assertive Negotiating Are Mediated by Women's Fear of Backlash and Attenuated When Negotiating on Behalf of Others," 98 *Journal of Personality and Social Psychology* 256, 258 (2010); Kolb, *supra* note 273, at 521–22.

285. *See* Kolb, *supra* note 273, at 520–521; Babcock & Laschever, *supra* note 273, at 164–172.

background should be able to obtain? If they proceed in this manner, they can usually negotiate far better terms than if they thought they were negotiating for themselves.

Another similar issue frequently raised by women involves a situation which may develop when there are only one or two women at an important meeting dominated by male participants. One of the females makes a proposal which falls on deaf ears. Twenty or thirty minutes later, a man makes the same proposal and is praised for his ingenuity. The person who originally suggested that idea should not allow him to take full credit for their suggestion. They should calmly thank him for supporting their earlier proposal!

During interpersonal transactions, men are more likely than women to employ "highly intensive language" to persuade others, and they tend to be more effective using this approach.[286] Women, on the other hand, are more likely to use less intense language during persuasive encounters, and they are inclined to be more effective behaving in that manner.[287] Females tend to employ language containing more disclaimers ("I think"; "you know") than their male cohorts, which may cause women to be perceived as less forceful. Since women tend to have more acute hearing than men, they often use softer voices than men when interacting with others, and they are more likely than men to view slightly raised voices as aggressive.[288]

When women interact with others, they tend to have a closer spatial distance than when men interact with others.[289] Women also tend to stand or sit directly across from others when they like those persons or are interested in the conversation, while men are more likely to sit or stand at angles with one another. When females interact with males, these differences may induce the women to think that the males are less interested in what they are discussing even though this assumption may be incorrect. It may also induce men to think women are more interested in the discussions than they actually are.

Formal education diminishes the presence of gender-based verbal differences. When individuals receive specific training, male-female communication distinctions are largely eliminated.[290] This factor would explain why male and female business executives tend to employ similar language when endeavoring to persuade others. Nonetheless, even when women use the same language as men, they are often perceived as being less influential. This gender-based factor is offset, however, by the fact that women continue to be more sensitive to verbal leaks and nonverbal signals

---

286. *See* Michael Burgoon, James Dillard & Noel Doran, "Friendly or Unfriendly Persuasion: The Effects of Violations of Expectations by Males and Females," 10 *Human Communication Research* 283, 284, 292 (1983).

287. *See* L.L. Carli, "Gender and Social Influence," 57 *Journal of Social Issues* 725, 732–736 (2001).

288. *See* Linda J. Sax, *Why Gender Matters* 18 (2005).

289. *See* Beall, *supra* note 153, at 19–20.

290. *See* Nancy A. Burrell, William A. Donohue & Mike Allen, "Gender-Based Perceptual Biases in Mediation," 15 *Communication Research* 447, 453 (1988).

than their male cohorts.[291] Woman also tend to ask more questions than men when they interact with others,[292] which makes it easier for them to obtain important information from bargaining counterparts.

There are indications that males and females differ with respect to their views of appropriate bargaining outcomes. Women tend to believe in "equal" exchanges, while men tend to expect "equitable" distributions.[293] These predispositional differences may induce female negotiators to accept equal results despite their possession of greater relative bargaining strength, while male bargainers seek equitable exchanges that reflect relevant power imbalances. Their egalitarian propensity could disadvantage women who hesitate to use favorable power imbalances to obtain more beneficial results for their own sides. On the other hand, when women are put in situations in which they are asked to negotiate on behalf of others—instead of themselves—they work more diligently to obtain optimal results for the persons they are representing.[294]

Gender-based competitive differences may be attributable to the different acculturation process for boys and girls.[295] Parents tend to be more protective of their daughters than of their sons.[296] Most boys are exposed to competitive situations at an early age.[297] They have been encouraged to participate in little league baseball, basketball, football, soccer, and other competitive athletic endeavors. These activities introduce boys to the "thrill of victory and the agony of defeat" during their formative years. "Traditional girls' games like jump rope and hopscotch are turn-taking games, where competition is indirect since one person's success does not necessarily signify another's failure." While directly competitive games teach boys how to resolve the disputes that inevitable arise, girls are less likely to have the opportunity to learn those dispute resolution skills.[298] By adulthood, men are more likely to have become accustomed to the rigors of overt competition. While it is true that little league and interscholastic sports for women have become more competitive in recent years, most continue to be less overtly competitive than corresponding male athletic endeavors.[299]

---

291. *See* Pease & Pease, *supra* note 151, at 13–14; Leigh Thompson, *The Mind and Heart of the Negotiator* 341 (3d ed. 2005); Miller & Miller, *supra* note 269, at 60–61.

292. *See* Michael S. Kimmel, *The Gendered Society* 100 (2013).

293. *See* C. Eckel, C.M. de Oliveira & P. Grossman, "Gender and Negotiation in the Small: Are Women (Perceived to Be) More Cooperative than Men?" 24 *Negotiation Journal* 441 (2008).

294. *See* Hannah Riley Bowles, Linda Babcock & Kathleen L. McGinn, "Constraints and Triggers: Situational Mechanics of Gender in Negotiation," 89 *Journal of Personality and Social Psychology* 951, 958–962 (2005).

295. *See* Carrie Menkel,-Meadow, "Teaching About Gender and Negotiation: Sex, Truths, and Videotape," 16 *Negotiation Journal* 357, 362–364 (2000).

296. *See* Babcock & Laschever, *supra* note 273, at 30–31.

297. *See* Evans, *supra* note 279, at 12–13.

298. *See* Babcock & Laschever, *supra* note 273, at 34–35.

299. *See* Melissa L. Nelken, "The Myth of the Gladiator and Law Students' Negotiation Styles," 7 *Cardozo Journal of Conflict Resolution* 1, at 10 (2006); Evans, *supra* note 279, at 80.

The physical appearance of male and female bargainers may influence the manner in which they are perceived by others.[300] Empirical studies have found that attractive men are likely to be considered more competent than their less attractive male cohorts with respect to their ability to think logically and analytically. Contrary results have been obtained for female subjects. Less attractive women tend to be viewed as more cerebral than their more attractive female colleagues. This stereotypical view of attractive women is frequently based on the theory that good looking females must not have received the same intellectual capacities as their less attractive cohorts. If this assumption were correct, one would expect attractive males to be similarly disadvantaged with respect to their cerebral capabilities. Women with a "less feminine" appearance ("tailored clothes with a jacket, subtle make-up, and either short hair or hair swept away from the face") are similarly more likely to be taken seriously by others and be viewed as more assertive, more logical, and less emotional in critical situations—particularly by male respondents—than are women with a "more feminine" appearance.[301]

Other gender-based stereotypes affect the way in which men and women interact in negotiation settings. Males are expected to be more rational and objective, while females are supposed to concentrate more on relationships.[302] Men tend to define themselves by their achievements, while women tend to define themselves by their relationships.[303] Male negotiators are expected to be dominant and overtly competitive, with women bargainers expected to be passive and submissive.[304] In competitive bargaining situations, participants possessing stereotypically male traits might reasonably be expected to outperform participants possessing stereotypically female traits. In multi-item negotiations, however, the tendency of women to interact more cooperatively should enhance the likelihood of more integrative agreements.[305]

When men and women interact, men tend to speak for longer periods and to interrupt more frequently than women.[306] If females speak half of the time, they tend to be perceived by male participants as domineering. This masculine tendency to dominate male-female interactions could provide men with an advantage during negotiations by enabling them to control the discussions. Men tend to be more direct

---

300. *See* Thomas F. Cash & Louis H. Janda, "The Eye of the Beholder," *Psychology Today* 46, 46–52 (Dec. 1984).

301. *See id.*, at 46–52.

302. *See* Y. Davidds, *Your Own Terms: A Woman's Guide to Taking Charge of Any Negotiation* 21–22 (2015); Laura J. Kray & Linda Babcock, "Gender in Negotiations: A Motivated Social Cognitive Analysis," in *Negotiation Theory and Research* 203, 206–207 (Leigh Thompson, ed. 2006); Malach Pines, Ayala Hamutal Gat & Yael Tal, "Gender Differences in Content and Style of Argument Between Couples During Divorce Mediation," 20 *Conflict Resolution Quarterly* 23, 25–39 (Fall 2002); Laura J. Kray, Leigh Thompson & Adam D. Galinski, "Reversing the Gender Gap in Negotiations: An Exploration of Stereotype Regeneration," 87 *Organizational Behavior and Human Decision Processes* 386, 944 (2002).

303. *See* Babcock & Laschever, *supra* note 273, at 117.

304. *See id.*, at 62–63, 75.

305. *See* Kray & Babcock, *supra* note 302, at 209.

306. *See* Davidds, supra note 302, at 35; Kay Deaux, *The Behavior of Women and Men* 60 (1976).

than women. If a man is hungry, he is likely to say so. On the other hand, if a woman is hungry, she is likely to ask the persons around her if they are hungry, hoping they will suggest the need to get something to eat.[307]

§ 11.03. Evidence Contradicting Behavioral Predictions

Professor Deaux succinctly noted that behavioral predictions based on stereotypical beliefs regarding men and women are likely to be of questionable validity in most settings.

> [D]espite the persistence of stereotypes, the studies of social behavior suggest that there are relatively few characteristics in which men and women consistently differ. Men and women both seem to be capable of being aggressive, helpful, and alternately cooperative and competitive. In other words, there is little evidence that the nature of women and men is so inherently different that we are justified in making stereotyped generalizations.[308]

In light of the fact that most business and economic students are relatively competitive persons and receive extensive academic training, one would certainly expect the traditionally found gender-based differences to be of minimal relevance.[309]

A number of years ago, I compared the results achieved over fifteen years by male and female students in my Legal Negotiating classes. I hypothesized that there would be no meaningful differences, and the statistical results confirmed this belief. There was not a single year for which the average results achieved by men were statistically different from the results attained by women at the 0.05 level of significance.[310] Some people suggested that while the male and female averages might be the same, the individual results would be different with stereotypically competitive males obtaining extremely good or bad results and with stereotypically cooperative females being clustered around the mean. Had the male results been more skewed, the male standard deviations would have been higher than the female standard deviations. My data negated this hypothesis, since the male and female standard deviations were approximately equal throughout the fifteen year period. In 1999, David Barnes and I made the same statistical comparison covering the thirteen years I had taught at George

---

307. *See* Lynn Smith-Lovin & Dawn T. Robinson, "Gender and Conversational Dynamics," in *Gender, Interaction, and Inequality* 122, 124–126 (C. Ridgeway, ed. 1992); Deborah Tannen, *That's Not What I Meant* 71–73 (1986).

308. *See* Deaux, *supra* note 306, at 144; *see generally* Del Gobbo, *supra* note 248; Bobbi Carothers & Harry Reis, "Men and Women Are From Earth: Examining the Latent Structure of Gender," 104 *Journal of Personality and* Analysis," 13 *Texas Journal of Women and the Law* 169 (2003).

309. *See* A.K. Schneider, C.H. Tinsley, S. Chedelin & E.T. Amanatullah, "Likeability v. Competence: The Impossible Choice Faced By Female Politicians, Attenuated by Lawyers," 17 *Duke Journal of Gender and Law* 363, 373–380 (2010).

310. *See* Charles B. Craver, "The Impact of Gender on Clinical Negotiating Achievement," 6 *Ohio State Journal on Dispute Resolution* 1, 12–16 & Table 1 (1990).

Washington University, and we again found no statistically meaningful differences with respect to the negotiation results attained by male and female students.[311] After Professors Russell Korobkin & Joseph Doherty published an article finding that male law students did significantly better than female students with respect to the results achieved on a single negotiation exercise,[312] I decided to explore the sixteen years of data in my Legal Negotiation course since my previous study. I again found absolutely no statistically significant differences with respect to the average results or the standard deviations.[313] If female negotiators are led to believe that women do not usually do as well as males when involved in bargaining interactions, it is possible that this belief could negatively affect their performance due to the impact of "stereotype threat."[314]

During the fall semester of 2015, I decided to perform a slightly different statistical assessment. I initially examined the student results on the first practice exercise to see if there might be any gender-based difference, and I found that average male placement results were higher than average female placement results, with the level of statistical significance at the 0.0276 level.[315] This was consistent with the differences found by Professors Korobkin and Doherty in their earlier study. I thought that with careful training, gender-based differences would disappear, as they had in my prior studies. I was thus surprised when I compared the male and female results on the graded exercises conducted during the second half of the semester. The male placement means were 78.559, while the female placement means were 61.643, with these differences statistically significant at the 0.002 level.

In the final class of the semester, I disclosed my findings and asked the students what might have contributed to these different results. A number of students suggested that some males and a few females had behaved in an aggressive and even adversarial manner to advance their interests, causing more female counterparts to give in than male counterparts. Some female students also indicated that their fear of non-settlements caused them to give in near the end of their interactions to avoid the consequences associated with such "failures."

During the fall 2016, 2017, and 2018 semesters, I focused on the concerns the students had addressed at the end of the 2015 term. We explored ways in which students could effectively counter aggressive and adversarial tactics. I emphasized the fact that when non-settlements resulted, *both sides* generally obtained low exercise scores. I

---

311. *See* Charles B. Craver & David W. Barnes, "Gender, Risk Taking, and Negotiation Performance," 5 *Michigan Journal of Gender and Law* 299 (1999).

312. *See* Korobkin & Doherty, *supra* note 271, at 191–93 (finding that male law students did significantly better than female law students with respect to the results achieved on a single negotiation exercise).

313. *See* Charles B. Craver, "The Impact of Gender on Negotiation Performance," 14 *Cardozo Journal of Conflict Resolution* 339, 354–356 (2013).

314. *See* Robert J. Rydell & Kathryn L. Boucher, "The Effect of Negative Performance Stereotypes on Learning," 99 *Journal of Personality and Social Psychology* 883 (2010).

315. *See* Charles B. Craver, "Formal Training Does Not Always Eliminate Gender-Based Negotiation Differences," 18 *Cardozo Journal of Conflict Resolution* 1, 15 (2016).

indicated that when counterparts threatened non-settlements, all students — especially females — should ask themselves whether they believe that their competitive counterparts would be satisfied with such results. They should thus suggest that they will not give in to such threats.

At the conclusion of the 2016, 2017, and 2018 terms, I compared the average placement scores achieved by male and female students. I found a complete lack of statistical significance between male and female negotiation results.[316] In future years, I will again emphasize the ways in which students can effectively deal with aggressive tactics, and the fact that no rational students want to end up with non-settlements. I am confident that this approach will continue to eliminate any gender-based negotiation differences.

Male negotiators who take female counterparts less seriously than they take male adversaries based upon gender-based stereotypes provide their female adversaries with an inherent advantage. Since they do not expect highly competitive or manipulative behavior from women, they are less likely to discern and effectively counter the use of these tactics by female counterparts. While women bargainers may understandably be offended by such patronizing attitudes, there is an easy way to get even with these male troglodytes. They should clean them out! I have been amazed by the number of proficient female negotiators who have been able to accomplish this objective against unsuspecting male counterparts who had no idea how adroitly they were being fleeced.

One other gender-based phenomenon that continues to unfairly affect women should be noted. When men are successful, their accomplishments are usually attributed to intrinsic factors such as intelligence and hard work.[317] When women are successful, however, their achievements are most often attributed to extrinsic variables such as luck or the actions of others. This phenomenon enhances male self-confidence by permitting them to accept personal credit for their achievements, while it undermines female self-confidence by depriving them of personal credit for their own accomplishments. When superiors are evaluating the work of subordinates or firm officials are reviewing the qualifications of students seeking entry level positions, they should be cognizant of this factor and make sure they give females as much credit for their achievements as they give to equally accomplished males.

§ 11.04. Conclusion

People tend to interact more cooperatively and more openly with persons of the same gender, because they assume common values and do not feel the need to maintain a particular "face." When individuals of different genders negotiate, they should

---

316. *See* Charles B. Craver, "Careful Training Does Eliminate Gender-Based Negotiation Differences," *Cardozo Journal of Conflict Resolution* 583 (2019).
317. *See* Deaux, *supra* note 306, at 30–32, 41.

recognize that stereotypical beliefs may initially impede their interactions and should use an expanded Preliminary Stage to establish beneficial rapport.

Based upon their different acculturation experiences, males are expected to be competitive, forceful, Machiavellian, and abstract, while women are expected to be cooperative, deferential, and more concerned with relationships. Advanced education and specialized training tend to eliminate gender-based dissimilarities. I have found almost no statistically significant differences between the negotiation results achieved by male and female students. Negotiators who underestimate counterparts because of gender-based stereotypes provide those individuals with opportunities. Their adversaries should take advantage of these opportunities.

Individuals tend to over value the success of men, attributing their successes to intrinsic factors such as intelligence and hard work, while they under value the accomplishments of women, attributing their achievements to extrinsic factors such as luck or the assistance of others. Supervisors evaluating the work of subordinates or the records of job applicants should be careful to apply the same standards to both males and females.

Chapter 12

Transnational Business Negotiations

§ 12.01. Increased Significance of Negotiations in a Global World

As instant communications and efficient transportation systems have contributed to the development of a truly global political and economic world,[318] the extent of governmental and private international negotiating has greatly increased. International political bodies—such as the United Nations and its constituent entities and the World Trade Organization (WTO)—and regional political/economic groups—such as the European Union, the Group of Eight (G-8), the expanded Group of 20 (G-20), and the North American Free Trade Zone—have increased the use of bilateral and multilateral governmental interactions. Non-governmental organizations (NGOs) have begun to realize the degree to which they may become involved with matters that were previously addressed solely through governmental channels. The growth of multinational business firms has similarly increased the frequency of private transnational business negotiations. National and international bargaining transactions have many similarities and certain crucial differences.[319] They generally involve the same negotiation stages and many common bargaining techniques—even though identical tactics may be given different names in different nations.

Government representatives are affected by stereotypical views of their political and economic systems and their national cultures—and those of the national groups with which they are interacting. They must be cognizant of the political constraints under which they operate and, in some instances, they may have to be aware of military and security considerations. Private corporate negotiators are similarly influenced by cultural stereotyping. They may also be affected by the need for governmental involvement in what may appear to be wholly private business transactions.

---

318. *See generally* Thomas L. Friedman, *The World Is Flat* (2005).

319. *See generally* I. William Zartman, *International Multilateral Negotiation* (1994); Viktor A. Kremenyuk, *International Negotiation* (2002).

Verbal communication is an indispensable part of the international bargaining process, but written and oral exchanges may be subject to interpretive difficulties— even when the participants think they are using the same language (*e.g.*, United States, British, Canadian, and Australian negotiators). Similar nonverbal signals may have different meanings in diverse cultures. National and regional cultural differences also influence transnational interactions. While a distinct international bargaining culture may have developed among public and private representatives who repeatedly interact with others in European, North and South American, African, and Asian nations, it is rare for most individuals to entirely escape the impact of the cultures in which they were raised and in which they currently reside.[320]

§ 12.02. Official Inter-Government [Track I] Diplomacy

When nations negotiate with one another—"*Track I Diplomacy*"—their discussions may be carried out through formal channels or through informal "back channel" communications.[321] Formal channels are generally used for conventional interactions, while back channels are employed for particularly delicate talks or when the relevant governments do not have direct diplomatic relations.[322] The least complicated internation negotiations involve bilateral interactions between two countries (*e.g.*, United States-Mexico; France-Germany; Japan-China). Multilateral transactions may include three or four countries or a hundred or more nations. They may be conducted on an ad hoc basis involving various countries with common interests or through formal organizations such as the United Nations, the Organization of American States, the World Trade Organization, or the European Union.

Bilateral negotiations are generally conducted under ad hoc procedures agreed upon by the participants for the specific interactions involved. These transactions may concern economic, political, cultural, humanitarian, or military/security issues. For example, governments may be discussing trade restrictions, immigration rules, art exchanges, human rights, and/or regional or global arms limitations. Bilateral interactions may involve participants with relatively equal (*e.g.*, Britain-France; United States-Japan) or wholly disparate (*e.g.*, United States-Cuba; China-Taiwan) economic or military power.

Bilateral agreements usually require approval by the governments of the participating nations before they become operative. When *executive accords* are involved, only the consent of the President or Prime Minister may be necessary, while *treaties* are likely to require legislative ratification. Presidents who fear protracted or divisive

---

320. *See* Michael Watkins & Susan Rosegrant, *Breakthrough in International Negotiation* 73–79 (2001).

321. *See* Anthony Wanis-St. John, "Back-Channel Negotiation: International Bargaining in the Shadows," 22 *Negotiation Journal* 19, 20–29 (2006).

322. *See* Richard H. Solomon & Nigel Quinney, *American Negotiating Behavior* 94–102 (2010).

Senate debate over controversial bilateral pacts often resort to executive agreements that do not necessitate Senate consideration.

Most bilateral accords do not require the approval of other countries before they take effect. In some instances, however, treaty obligations may necessitate the consent of trading partners before trade agreements with other nations may become operative. Bilateral security pacts may first have to be approved by regional groups such as NATO or SEATO. Even when the approval of other nations is not necessary, new bilateral arrangements may directly affect the rights of other countries. For example, nations with "most favored nation" (MFN) trading status may claim the benefit of more generous terms given to another country.

Multilateral interactions are usually far more complex than bilateral discussions. They usually involve numerous issues and many parties. It may be difficult to know which participants will support or oppose which issues. A group hierarchy often develops, with certain individuals leading the talks, certain persons acting as mediators, and certain people undermining progress. The participants playing these roles may vary from issue to issue, depending on the national interests involved.

While multilateral negotiations can be conducted on an ad hoc basis, they are generally carried out through existing international organizations. These interactions usually have formal agendas and specified procedures. On some occasions, a single nation or a group of countries may initiate the discussion process and request the assistance of an appropriate formal organization, while on other occasions the existing entity may itself convene the talks. The interested participants or the sponsoring organization may schedule a pre-conference meeting to define the issues to be addressed, the countries to be invited to participate, the procedural rules, and the final approval process. Countries may try to link issues they hope to obtain to other issues they believe other nations prefer, to enhance the likelihood of success on their preferred items.[323] Some resulting agreements need only be approved by the sponsoring entity to become effective, while other accords must be approved by all or a substantial portion of the participating nations before they become binding. In some instances, domestic legislation must be enacted to effectuate the principles set forth in non-binding international agreements.

When multilateral sessions were previously conducted, the talks tended to be dominated by economically and militarily powerful nations such as the United States and the Soviet Union. Less powerful countries often felt ignored. Over the past several decades, a number of emerging countries have begun to recognize the increased bargaining power they can generate through formal or informal voting blocs.[324] Countries with common interests attempt to align themselves in ways designed to maximize their bargaining influence. They may unite over particular topics or work together with respect to entire agendas. Whenever possible, they try to obtain voting rules that treat large and small nations equally, since this practice may give certain blocs

---

323. *See* Watkins & Rosegrant, *supra* note 320, at 220–221.
324. *See id.*, at 213–215; *see also* Raiffa, *supra* note 34 at 430–449.

veto power. This tactic is frequently employed at the United Nations with respect to issues addressed by the General Assembly. Weaker members try to prevent Security Council consideration, recognizing that any one of the five permanent members (China, France, Britain, Russia, and U.S.) can veto actions in that body. Bloc behavior was critical with respect to the Law of the Sea negotiations to protect the interests of nations that lacked the technology required to exploit seabed resources.

The creation of voting blocs by weaker nations is most effective with respect to deliberations carried out through formal organizations due to the established voting rules that are generally applied. When multilateral negotiations are conducted on an ad hoc basis and the rules are determined by the more powerful participants, weighted voting procedures may be adopted to diminish the capacity of weaker nations to block overall accords. Furthermore, the convening countries can limit the number of participants to reduce the likelihood of bloc formations.[325]

People who represent nations in the international arena must recognize that they are always acting in an official representational capacity. No matter how much they try to develop individual identities, they continue to be viewed as spokespersons for their respective countries. This is true when they are speaking through formal and informal channels. As a result of this phenomenon, American agents tend to be burdened with the stereotypical baggage associated with United States representatives.[326] They are likely to be perceived as arrogant, powerful, uncompromising (*i.e.*, Boulwareistic), unsympathetic, and capitalistic. United States representatives who attempt to dispel these images by disassociating themselves from official U.S. positions are likely to create additional problems. Others will be shocked that U.S. agents would undermine their own country, and will suspect that such disreputable individuals cannot be trusted. It thus behooves U.S. agents to always behave in a manner that furthers the underlying interests of their own country, even when they are working to accomplish seemingly external objectives.

As was noted previously with respect to domestic government agents, designated U.S. representatives generally have circumscribed authority. Strangely enough, while low level agents involved in relatively insignificant meetings may enjoy some degree of negotiating discretion, more visible advocates who are dealing with important matters usually have limited freedom. They may be required to check constantly with the State Department, the White House, the Senate Foreign Affairs Committee, and other groups that have control over the final outcome of the current negotiations. Their actions will be orchestrated by these other entities, severely limiting their ability to do anything spontaneously.

Since bilateral and multilateral international negotiations tend to concern issues of import to different government agencies, it is crucial to engage in thorough *intra-*

---

325. *See* Raiffa, *supra* note 34, at 450–464.
326. *See generally* Richard H. Solomon & Nigel Quinney, *American Negotiating Behavior* (2010).

government planning prior to the external discussions.[327] In order to permit the development of common goals, all interested entities must be asked about their respective interests and objectives. Further, to guarantee the projection of unified national positions, negotiating strategy must also be addressed. If these preliminary planning activities are not carried out, several negative consequences are likely to result. counterparts who sense the lack of a unified approach may try to exploit internal disagreements. In addition, if final terms are agreed upon that do not satisfy the needs of the different U.S. agencies, dissatisfied officials may attempt to undermine the accord. They may contact White House, State Department, or Senate officials in an effort to obtain a renegotiation of the disfavored items. American representatives should thus realize that their *intra-governmental negotiations* may be more contentious and protracted than the subsequent *inter-government bargaining*. People who endeavor to avoid this necessary step usually encounter more difficulties in the long run than if they had engaged in thorough intra-organizational preparation.

When large international conferences are involved, expansive national delegations may be required. When they interact with delegates from other nations, U.S. representatives must try to determine which persons possess real influence with their home governments, which might be destabilizing participants who may try to hinder progress, and which are mediators who will attempt to accommodate competing interests. Means must be found to induce the mediative officials to neutralize the destabilizers in a way that enables the influential agents to agree to the desired objectives.

Inter-nation negotiations at regional or global conferences generally occur at various levels. Preconference discussions between and among key participants are used to define the issues to be addressed and to determine the conference procedures to be followed. Once the conference begins, plenary sessions are used for formal speeches and public debate. Smaller working groups are frequently formed to explore specific topics and to formulate proposals that will ultimately be considered by the entire conference. Informal talks between representatives from critical nations are often employed to ascertain areas of mutual interest. Countries with nonexistent or limited diplomatic relations use back channel communications to exchange ideas in a manner that preserves their public images.

When international negotiations do not progress satisfactorily, it is often beneficial to seek the assistance of neutral intervenors. Mediators from nonaligned nations may use their good offices to move discussions in a productive direction. Some mediators may be selected because of their current positions (*e.g.*, the Secretary General of the United Nations or the Secretary of State of a neutral country). On some occasions, it may be helpful to request assistance from process experts who are not associated with governmental entities (*e.g.*, businesspeople or academics). Just as with domestic negotiations, these individuals can work to reopen clogged commu-

---

327. *See* Salacuse, *supra* note 65, at 29–42.

nication channels, to get the disputants to explore their diverse underlying interests, and to look for alternatives that may simultaneously satisfy the needs of everyone. Once agreements are achieved, the responsible nations must work to ensure their effectuation.

When disputing nations wholly distrust one another because of prior violations of trust, intermediaries cannot hope to induce them to move directly toward final accords. They often have to employ "confidence building" measures that have the parties move in small reciprocal increments until the disputants can restore the mutual trust necessary to allow movement toward final agreements.[328] In such circumstances, each side agrees to take alternative steps toward an overall resolution that will demonstrate their respective good faith. One may agree to pull back slightly from occupied areas, while the other agrees to decrease its troop levels in the region. The first party may then agree to reduce its level of weaponry, while the other recognizes the legitimacy of some of the first party's territorial claims. Once a number of such mutual steps have been taken and bargaining credibility has been restored, the parties may be able to make the overarching commitments needed to resolve the underlying controversy.[329]

§ 12.03. Private Citizen Involvement in Public Matters [Track II Diplomacy]

Certain national or international conflicts may not respond favorably to formal diplomatic intervention by government representatives. The disputants may not trust the countries that are trying to help. Regional or global balances may be undermined by the involvement of external nations. To circumvent these difficulties and fill the diplomatic void, non-governmental organizations (NGOs) have increasingly become involved. For many years, groups affiliated with the Quaker Church—e.g., American Friends Service Committee—have worked in many areas to promote human rights and world peace. In recent years, NGOs like the Institute for Multi-Track Diplomacy and Former President Carter's Peace Institute have provided dispute resolution assistance in areas like Northern Ireland, Cyprus, the Middle East, Yugoslavia, South Africa, and Rwanda.

The involvement of NGOs or private citizens in international conflicts has been labeled "*Track II Diplomacy*."[330] These private entities are not constrained by political considerations affecting official governmental institutions. Unlike State Department personnel who must always speak for their government and further their own nation's

---

328. *See* Watkins & Rosegrant, *supra* note 320, at 167,270.

329. *See generally* Uri Savir, *The Process* (1998) (describing the various steps taken by Israel and the PLO as they worked toward the Oslo Accords); *see also* Tamara Cofman Wittes, *How Israelis and Palestinians Negotiate* (2005); Charles Enderlin, *Shattered Dreams* (2002) (describing more recent Israeli-PLO peace talk developments).

330. *See* John W. McDonald & Diane B. Bendahmane, *Conflict Resolution: Track Two Diplomacy* (1987).

interests, private organizations and private citizens can speak as individuals. They can say things and behave in ways that would be unacceptable for government spokespersons. They do not have to worry about the political ramifications of their actions back home.

Groups and individuals engaged in Track II Diplomacy often interact with private organizations in the host nations. They may be forced to do this because of the unwillingness of government officials to recognize their mediative status. On some occasions, however, they are permitted to meet with government officials and to become directly involved with formal diplomatic efforts.

Despite their freedom from government control, NGO representatives are still subject to cultural stereotyping that may affect the way they are perceived. When United States citizens travel abroad, it is difficult for them to entirely shed their American images. This fact makes it particularly difficult for Americans to mediate disputes that directly involve United States interests. Individuals from countries with competing interests tend to fear that even private U.S. citizens cannot completely ignore the official policies of their home government. While a few groups, like the Quakers, have been able to accomplish this objective, the involvement of the U.S. in specific controversies may necessitate the intervention of private citizens from nonaligned nations such as Sweden, Norway, or Switzerland. It is frequently easier for individuals from these neutral states to earn the trust and respect of the disputing parties.

Experienced negotiators can use Track II Diplomacy to affect inter-nation controversies, such as those between Greece and Cyprus, Rwanda and Burundi, and Israel and Syria. In these areas, they may work in parallel with Track I diplomats representing the United Nations or their home countries. Track II conciliators may also intervene in internal state disputes that threaten human rights—e.g., South Africa and Yugoslavia. While it may be awkward for foreign governments to become directly involved with the internal affairs of other nations, private organizations do not have to worry about this issue. They can easily interact with other private entities within the target country. They may even be able to meet privately with government officials who do not view such discussions as infringements of their national sovereignty.

Track II diplomatic efforts are usually carried out in stages. The preliminary stage involves the establishment of personal contacts with people or organizations in the target nation(s). Once the neutral intervenors have opened communication channels with appropriate persons, they attempt to induce the disputing parties to interact at a minimal level. These efforts frequently take the form of cultural or economic exchanges that are designed to demonstrate that individuals from disputing groups or countries can work together on something. These activities also begin to generate a minimal level of inter-group trust.

Once communications are established with target groups and some cooperative ventures have been attempted, the intervenors try to convene problem-solving workshops that include respected individuals from the disputing entities. The participants are encouraged to get to know each other personally. Cultural differences are explored in an effort to develop mutual respect for the diverse backgrounds involved. Conciliators hope to personalize the disputing parties in a way that humanizes the conflict. When disputants interact—during informal sessions or structured events—they tend to exhibit less hostility toward one another. These preliminary interactions may take a few days or may have to develop over several months. When the time is propitious, group leaders begin to explore the underlying reasons for their conflict and to look for solutions that might be mutually acceptable.

Joint brain-storming sessions can be especially conciliatory experiences, as the disputing parties are induced to work together toward common goals. On some occasions, role reversals can be used to place individuals in the shoes of their counterparts. This technique can help people understand why their adversaries are unhappy and what types of solutions must be formulated to satisfy that side's underlying concerns. If this process functions effectively, the participants begin to move from the adversarial mode to the conciliatory mode, and they look for real solutions to their conflict.

The second stage of this process involves efforts to influence public opinion in ways designed to decrease inter-group tensions and humanize the conflicting factions. Conciliators and group leaders may discuss their differences on television and radio shows or at public gatherings. Written materials may be prepared and disseminated among interested parties. This educational device is especially effective with respect to young people who may not remember past wrongs as strongly as those who lived through them. If public opinion can be generated in favor of peaceful solutions, government officials may begin to participate. Politicians are usually good readers of their constituents, and they are likely to welcome constituent efforts to eliminate strife.

Once tentative resolutions of ongoing conflicts are developed, Track II Diplomacy enters the third stage. This involves the establishment of cooperative educational and economic ventures to unite the prior combatants in common programs. If they can be induced to work together, instead of in conflict, they often develop mutual ties that are difficult for others to sever.

Individuals who attempt Track II Diplomatic efforts must be particularly patient. Most inter-cultural conflicts have taken years to develop, and the disputants are unlikely to change their perspectives quickly. Conciliators who try to hurry the healing process are likely to generate further distrust and undermine settlement efforts. They must start with minimal goals and work slowly but steadily toward final resolutions.

Track II Diplomacy is occasionally employed by government officials to achieve objectives they might not be able to seek through Track I channels. For example, if government representatives could not directly contact outlaw organizations, they may ask private groups or individuals to establish contacts and act as back channel communicators. Once the preliminary Track II efforts become public, State Department representatives may find it safe to participate. Governments may also use Track II intervention to suggest possible settlement options that could not be officially proposed because of their controversial nature. Once these alternatives have been subject to public debate and have generated at least minimal acceptance, they may receive formal political support.

§ 12.04. Transnational Business Negotiations

As national economies have become inextricably intertwined with the economies of other nations, domestic and transnational corporate leaders have had to become more proficient international business negotiators. Creation of the North American Free Trade Zone has generated purchase and sales discussions between United States companies and Canadian and Mexican firms. As other regional economic groups, such as the European Union, are established, American firms will have to negotiate with their member entities. In the coming years, U.S. business officials will regularly bargain about the buying or selling of goods and services with their foreign counterparts in Africa, Asia, Europe, North and South America, Australia, and New Zealand.

Transnational business discussions create unique difficulties for various reasons. Greater distances between negotiating parties often make it necessary for participants to travel to foreign countries. The host organization usually feels comfortable bargaining on its own turf.[331] Visiting negotiators may experience serious jet-lag and fear that their presence in the other firm's territory may be perceived as an indication of their over-eagerness. They may also feel pressure to consummate a deal before they return home. They should try to arrive a day or two before scheduled talks begin—to alleviate jet-lag—and be somewhat flexible regarding their planned return trip home.

Visiting negotiators face other problems. They are likely to stay at foreign hotels that are not as commodious as their home environments. They are away from their families and colleagues, and must adjust to unfamiliar foods. They may have to contend with different foreign cultures and feel embarrassed when they commit faux pas. They must generally accept hospitality from their counterpart-hosts, and this may create feelings of obligation on their part which may induce them to make excessive concessions.

How may visiting negotiators counteract the apparent advantage enjoyed by their foreign hosts? They can try to make their hosts feel beholden to them by reminding them of the difficulty and expense they have assumed in an effort to accommodate the needs of their counterparts. By going to the other side's country, they are demonstrating respect for that party and its culture. They are also indicating their good faith desire to establish a mutually beneficial business relationship. They may try to offset the hospitality extended by their hosts through reciprocal hospitality. They may emulate Japanese bargainers and take small gifts to their hosts. They can arrange to entertain their hosts at local clubs or restaurants. If neither side feels comfortable negotiating at the other party's locale, the participants can agree to meet at a neutral site that would be equally convenient for both sides.

To counterbalance the time pressure usually felt by visiting negotiators, they should remind themselves how much the host firm wants the deal. If that firm were not in-

---

331. *See* Jeswald Salacuse, *Negotiating Life: secrets from Everyday Diplomacy and Deal Making* 151–161 (2013); Jeswald Salacuse, "Your Place or Mine: Deciding Where to Negotiate," 8 *Negotiation* 7 (2005).

terested in a business arrangement, they would not be spending time interacting with their foreign visitors. *Both sides* hope to achieve an accord before the visitors return home. Furthermore, if it appears that no agreement can be attained by that deadline, they can always continue their negotiations after they return home via telephone calls, e-mail, or fax transmissions. Even if these efforts do not generate a current business arrangement, they may lay the groundwork for future deals.

Eastern and Western cultures have historically thought of time quite differently. Western negotiators have traditionally viewed time as a commodity that is costly and should be preserved, while Eastern negotiators have considered time as an unlimited resource. For example, when a Chinese negotiator was being urged by a Western technology sales representative to reach a quick purchase agreement, his reply was incomprehensible to the Western businessperson: "China has been able to do without your technology for five thousand years. We can wait a few years longer."[332]

Transnational business negotiations frequently take longer than domestic business discussions, due to cultural differences and the greater complexity of issues that must be addressed.[333] Some parties try to enhance the negotiation process by breaking their interaction into discrete stages. During the pre-negotiation phase, they attempt to determine whether their contemplated interaction is likely to be mutually beneficial. If circumstances appear propitious, they use the conceptualization phase to create a common agenda for their impending interaction. During the final stage, they address the necessary details of their arrangement. This trifurcated procedure reduces the likelihood of conflict that often results when diverse parties try to achieve complete business transactions through unitary talks.

§ 12.05. Impact of Cultural Differences

What is "culture" and how does it influence bargaining interactions? "*Culture* is an aggregate product of the processes occurring in human society. It typically consists of such social phenomena as beliefs, ideas, language, customs, rules, and family patterns."[334] These factors provide each society with a set of shared values and beliefs that support the underlying assumptions that define the way individuals envision themselves and their societal groups. Culture affects the manner in which group

---

332. Guy Oliver Faure, "International Negotiation: The Cultural Dimension," in *International Negotiation* 392, 407 (Viktor Kremenyuk, ed., 2d ed. 2002).

333. *See* Frank L. Acuff, *How to Negotiate Anything with Anyone Anywhere Around the World*, 89 (1997); Salacuse, *supra* note 65, at 25–27.

334. *See* Michael R. Fowler, *Mastering Negotiation* 267–298 (2017); Salacuse, *Negotiating Life, supra* note 331, at 120–130; Julia A. Gold, "ADR Through a Cultural Lens: How Cultural Values Shape Our Disputing Processes," 2 *Journal of Dispute Resolution* 289, 292–302 (2005); Ilhyung Lee, "In Re Culture: The Cross-Cultural Negotiations Course in the Law School Curriculum," 20 *Ohio State Journal on Dispute Resolution*, 375, 396–400 (2005); Robert A. Rubinstein, "Cross-Cultural Considerations in Complex Peace Operations," *Negotiations Journal* 29, 30–40 (2003); Nancy Alder, *International Dimensions of Organizational Behavior* 16–24 (2002).

members interact with each other and the way in which individuals from different groups relate to one another. These are particularly relevant considerations for negotiating parties, since the behavior of the participants is likely to vary greatly depending on their respective cultural backgrounds.[335] Professional cultures also influence international negotiations, as diplomats, lawyers, and scientists apply different approaches to deal with similar problems.[336]

When Americans interact with other Americans in bargaining situations, they tend to assume similar cultural rules, even when their counterparts are from different geographic regions. Verbal expressions and nonverbal signals have common meanings, and the participants are likely to share common values. On the other hand, when Americans interact with individuals from foreign cultures, they have to recognize the impact of cultural differences.[337] Positive and negative stereotyping may influence their bargaining transactions. Traits may be attributed to individual participants based on their cultural backgrounds that bear no relation to reality. This phenomenon may easily undermine substantive discussions.

Punctuality is more important to the average American than it is to people from other cultures.[338] It would normally be considered unacceptable for an American to arrive more than five or ten minutes late for a business appointment, while a thirty or forty-five minute delay would not be uncommon in various Latin American or Middle-Eastern countries. Americans often separate business and social discussions, while their counterparts in other areas of the world feel comfortable conducting business talks during social functions.[339] Individuals with different time frames may have to discuss this issue and try to generate a mutually acceptable concept of punctuality.

In many Middle Eastern countries, it is considered extremely rude to show the bottom of one's shoe. As a result, persons negotiating in such nations should be careful not to cross their legs in a manner that displays the sole of their shoes. In some Asian countries it is considered disrespectful for people to talk with one another with one or both hands in their pocket. When they interact with others in such nations, outsiders should endeavor to keep both hands outside their pockets.

Spatial and conversational distances vary greatly among persons from different cultures.[340] In North America, it is normally "proper" for interactants who do not know each other well to remain approximately two feet apart, particularly during formal business conversations. While that spatial separation may shrink somewhat

---

335. *See* Tony English, *Tug of War: The Tension Concept and the Art of International Negotiation* 223–226 (2010); Salacuse, *supra* note 65, at 89–115.

336. *See generally* Gunnar Sjöstedt, *Professional Cultures in International Negotiation* (2003).

337. *See generally* Jeanne M. Brett, *Negotiating Globally* (2001); Donald W. Hendon, Rebecca A. Hendon & Paul Herbig, *Cross-Cultural Business Negotiations* (1996); Guy O. Faure & Jeffrey Z. Rubin, *Culture and Negotiation* (1993).

338. *See* Michelle LeBaron, *Bridging Cultural Conflicts* 42 (2003); Edward T. Hall, *The Silent Language* 140–161 (1973).

339. *See* Salacuse, *supra* note 65, at 101–102.

340. *See* Hall, *supra* note 338, at 162–185.

in social environments, Americans rarely feel comfortable with the eight- to twelve-inch distances indigenous to some other cultures (*e.g.*, Middle-Eastern countries). They feel intimidated by such close interactions. Their need for more expansive social distance often causes Americans to be viewed by people from other cultures as cold, withdrawn, or disinterested.

People who do not realize the importance of spatial distance need only consider two situations that commonly arise. Two individuals are engaged in a conversation in which one requires greater physical separation than the other. As the party who prefers a close encounter steps forward, the other person experiences discomfort and moves backward. The first party again moves closer, prompting another reactive retreat. These two participants are likely to continue this seemingly offensive and defensive pattern until the individual who requires greater spatial distance ends up with his or her back literally against a wall! This phenomenon may affect bargaining interactions when one participant gets too close to his or her counterpart—either by standing next to or over that person or by moving his or her chair next to that individual. Negotiators frequently place a table between themselves to avoid this problem.

Another example involves two people eating together at a restaurant. If one invades the other's spatial territory by intentionally or inadvertently moving the salt, pepper, sugar, and other condiments to the other person's side of the table, that individual is likely to exhibit nonverbal signs of discomfort. They may consciously or subconsciously try to alleviate this anxiety by moving some or all of the offending items away from their immediate environment. Similar tensions can be generated during a negotiation, when one of the participants physically invades—with their hands, documents, or briefcase—the other party's side of the bargaining table.

Some cultures are ***individualistic*** (*e.g.*, United States, England).[341] They value individual independence over group cohesiveness. They reward individuals who exhibit autonomous and assertive behavior to advance their own self interests. They value personal privacy and freedom. Societal status is based primarily upon individual, rather than group, accomplishments. People in these cultures work to enhance firm interests more to demonstrate their own capabilities than to contribute to the overall success of the collective business. Managers often possess the authority to make critical decisions on their own. Persons in individualistic cultures tend to enjoy bargaining interactions, because those endeavors allow them to demonstrate their negotiation skills.

Other cultures have a ***collectivistic*** orientation (*e.g.*, Japan, China).[342] People are defined more by their family and business ties than by their own endeavors. They tend to be evaluated by the achievements of their organization rather than by their own accomplishments. Individuals are expected to work together to enhance group interests. Managers consult their colleagues when important decisions have to be made, with

---

341. *See* Joo Seng Tan & Elizabeth Ngah Kiing Lim, *Strategies for Effective Cross-Cultural Negotiation* 20–21 (2004).

342. *See* Gold, *supra* note 334, at 296–297; Tan & Lim, *supra* note 341, at 21–22.

final determinations being made through a consensus process. People in collectivistic cultures often dislike negotiation encounters, because they prefer conflict avoidance and dislike the loss of face associated with the give-and-take of the bargaining process.[343]

Many American negotiators do not hesitate to employ overt power displays to advance their bargaining interests. In other cultures (*e.g.*, Japan), open displays of power are considered crude and unacceptable. Analogous conflicts are encountered with respect to the use of openly aggressive behavior. Since Americans have a reputation for being overly aggressive people, they should attempt to employ less threatening tactics when they interact with persons from less aggressive cultures. They must remember that one can be forceful without being pushy.

Individuals from disparate socio-economic backgrounds may find it difficult to appreciate each other's hopes and fears. People from wealthy nations tend to accept the delayed gratification concept without question, based on the success that has been achieved by their educated ancestors, while persons from poorer countries are less likely to postpone current gratification for the nebulous hope of attaining greater future returns. United States negotiators interacting with persons from emerging nations may have to initially emphasize the short-term benefits over the long-term possibilities if they wish to achieve present agreements.

People from lower socio-economic environments often find it traumatic and intimidating when they first interact with individuals from wealthy backgrounds—especially if they are forced to meet in the gilded offices of their wealthy counterparts. To counteract this factor, individuals representing clients from economically disadvantaged nations may wish to employ a tactic perfected during the 1960s by the late activist Saul Alinsky. He realized that rich and powerful negotiators feel just as uncomfortable in the ghettos occupied by the poor as the latter group members do in upper-class neighborhoods. He thus invited the societal power brokers to bargain with the economically disadvantaged in the areas inhabited by the latter group. For the first time, many wealthy persons began to appreciate the tragic plight of less fortunate people. They felt substantial guilt and discomfort in the pathetic environments occupied by the poor, and were adroitly induced to make significant concessions. Private firm or governmental representatives from emerging countries who think they may embarrass counterparts from wealthy nations by bringing them into their national settings should not hesitate to use this approach to their advantage.

Before U.S. advocates enter into negotiations with people from different countries, they should try to learn about the cultural background of their counterparts.[344] They should study the national histories and cultural practices of those people. Foreigners often criticize Americans for ignoring these factors. They assume that we arrogantly think these influences are irrelevant. When Americans demonstrate both an understanding of and a respect for the historical developments associated with other nations

---

343. *See* Tan & Lim, *supra* note 341, at 34–35.
344. *See* Salacuse, *supra* note 65, at 110–115.

and for the diverse cultures indigenous to those countries, foreign negotiators appreciate the efforts and feel more comfortable interacting with their American counterparts.

Most individuals are significantly influenced by historical developments in their own countries.[345] Do they have a history of unregulated capitalism, limited capitalism, socialism, communism, or another system? Has their economic system been subject to minimal or extensive governmental intervention? Is their government democratic, autocratic, plutocratic, or monarchical? Has their government been relatively stable or unstable? Has their country been invaded by people from other areas and have they been occupied by foreign powers? Persons from nations that have been invaded by major powers—especially those that have been occupied by foreign armies—are likely to be suspicious of what may be perceived as economic invaders. It is thus imperative for American corporate officials to emphasize to persons from less developed and less democratic nations both the mutual relationships they hope to establish with prospective foreign firms and the autonomy those trading partners will continue to enjoy.

American firms negotiating international business deals must consider currency questions.[346] How stable is the relevant foreign currency compared to the U.S. dollar? U.S. firms may wish to avoid the risk of unexpected monetary fluctuations by specifying contract prices in U.S. dollars. Firms that have confidence in the strength of the other company's national currency may decide to specify prices in that currency. Business partners may jointly share the risk of currency changes by relying on the currency of a neutral country. To minimize the impact of currency fluctuations, the parties may use a market-basket unit, such as the Euro created by the European Union. A few parties avoid currency issues through bartering contracts that provide for one side's goods or services to be exchanged for specific amounts of the other party's goods or services.

U.S. business representatives must also determine how foreign firms operate. Do top executives make final decisions alone or must they consult with board members or subordinate groups? Do several people have to be convinced before deals become final or must a substantial number of individuals give their approval?[347] If many persons must be consulted, who are they and how may they be influenced by the American negotiators? When group decision-making is involved, it will usually take longer for consensus to be achieved. U.S. bargainers who ignore this factor and attempt to expedite the approval process are likely to generate suspicion and undermine the entire deal.

American business people must appreciate differences involving the treatment of employees by companies in different countries. In the United States, private employers may usually terminate or lay off workers for good cause, bad cause, or no cause under the employment-at-will doctrine. In most other industrial nations, firms cannot terminate or lay off employees without cause. In countries like Japan, many corporations

---

345. *See id.*, at 117–125.
346. *See id.*, at 165–177; Brett, *supra* note 337, at 188–91.
347. *See* English, *supra* note 335, at 224–226; Brett, *supra* note 337, at 15.

feel a moral obligation to retain employees except when confronted with dire economic circumstances. They are shocked at the short-term perspectives of American executives and their willingness to lay off workers as soon as sufficient profits are realized. Japanese executives tend to have a long-term perspective, and try to avoid arrangements that may necessitate the premature termination of employees. When U.S. advocates attempt to negotiate joint ventures with Japanese firms, they must take these differences into account when describing the partnerships they are seeking.

The government in the United States generally takes a laissez faire approach with respect to the regulation of private business deals. As long as those arrangements do not raise questions under applicable statutes, such as antitrust laws, they do not require government approval. In other countries, however, government bureaucracies may not only have to give final approval to the deals, but may also participate directly in the inter-firm negotiations.[348] When such governmental participation is anticipated, the U.S. negotiators must determine the interests that have to be satisfied before governmental approval can be achieved. The regulatory agencies in question may not focus entirely or even primarily on business considerations. They may be more interested in broader social, political, or environmental issues. It is generally helpful to retain local agents who are familiar with applicable legal doctrines and relevant administrative procedures. They also tend to know the administrative officials to contact when questions arise. If these areas are ignored, beneficial business accords may be thwarted. American negotiators must also prepare themselves and their firms for the months that may elapse during the governmental review process.

In some countries (*e.g.*, China, India, Japan), gifts or gratuities may be expected by government administrators to encourage the expeditious processing of contract approval requests. These are generally not "bribes." They are almost always "facilitation fees" that are not intended to corruptly influence the recipients, but rather to generate faster service. Such facilitation payments are outside the scope of the Foreign Corrupt Practices Act.[349] It is normally preferable to have these payments made by local agents who know the government officials involved and understand how such payments are to be made.

When U.S. firms interact with other companies, they generally try to negotiate binding contractual relationships that are subject to judicial or arbitral enforcement. Each relevant term is explored and defined. Corporations from different cultures, particularly Asian nations, tend to be more relationship-oriented. They hope to create long-term business relationships that are based more on mutual trust and respect than on contractual obligations.[350] As a result, they take longer during their preliminary discussions to get to know each other, and they define their new partnerships in relatively general terms. If one side becomes too specific, they demonstrate a lack of trust that offends the other party. They know that when future questions arise, they

---

348. *See* Brett, *supra* note 337, at 192–194; Jeswald Salacuse, *Making Global Deals* 84–102 (1991).
349. *See* Acuff, *supra* note 333, at 104.
350. *See* Salacuse, *supra* note 65, at 96–97, 103–04.

will work together to resolve those issues. As the interaction develops, patience is important, because cross-cultural encounters tend to take longer than talks between people from the same culture. American business leaders do not feel comfortable with this approach. They fear that general contractual undertakings may not receive judicial acceptance.

When individuals from different cultures interact, it can be helpful for them to employ a prolonged Preliminary Stage to get to know each other and to establish positive relationships.[351] They should take the time to explore their respective national cultures, and to begin to understand each side's idiosyncrasies. During this exploratory period, they should avoid real substantive discussions, focusing instead upon interpersonal considerations. Americans find this part of the process distasteful, because they like to get down to business quickly. Negotiators who patiently establish affirmative relationships based upon mutual respect for each side's different approach to bargaining interactions enhance the likelihood of achieving beneficial, long-term partnerships. Although impatient negotiators may dislike the time it takes to get to know the opposing side, persons who do not do so may either fail to achieve agreements or negotiate terms that are less efficient than those they may have obtained had both sides initially established mutual respect and trust.

When representatives from different cultures interact, they need to use attitudinal bargaining to develop a mutual respect for each side's cultural and legal interests. U.S. negotiators must respectfully explain their need for certain specificity—and they must appreciate the lack of trust indicated by demands for total specificity. They must decide what terms must truly be covered in detail and which may be generally described. This accommodation should enhance the likelihood of beneficial long-term relations. The inclusion of dispute resolution clauses providing for resort to negotiation, mediation, and ultimately arbitration to resolve future disagreements can minimize the fear of judicial intervention.

When negotiators from different cultures interact, language difficulties may arise.[352] Even though most international transactions involving American firms are conducted wholly or at least partially in English, misunderstandings may develop. Foreign representatives may interpret verbal statements and nonverbal signals differently from their American counterparts.[353] Some cultures process information in a highly "rational" linear manner, while others do so in an indirect and more emotional nonlinear fashion.[354] Representatives should speak clearly and more deliberately than they might at home to be certain their message is heard. They should avoid the use of slang expressions that may not be understood by individuals who have not lived in the United States for prolonged periods. They should be especially attuned to any signs of con-

---

351. *See* Nancy Adler, *International Dimensions of Organizational Behavior* 225–227 (2002).

352. *See* R. Rubinstein, "Cross-Cultural Considerations in Complex Peace Operations," *Negotiation Journal* 29, 32–36 (2003); Salacuse, *supra* note 65, at 94–96; Salacuse, *supra* note 331, at 28–36.

353. *See* Adler, *supra* note 351, at 95–96; Raymond Cohen, *Negotiating Across Cultures* 105–130 (1991).

354. *See* Rubinstein, *supra* note 352, at 34–35.

fusion emanating from their counterparts. Do they have puzzling looks on their faces or are they asking questions that suggest they have not fully understood what the speakers intended to convey? Rather than losing patience with counterparts who are experiencing these difficulties, American negotiators must work more diligently to make themselves understood.

On some occasions, international business negotiations must be conducted through interpreters.[355] Even if the foreign corporation provides translators, it is helpful for the U.S. group to have its own language specialist. It is particularly beneficial to have a negotiating team member who is fluent in the foreign language. This helps to diminish the risk of avoidable misunderstandings. U.S. representatives who are not truly fluent in a foreign language should not try to negotiate in that language. While it would certainly be appropriate for them to greet their foreign counterparts in their own language, their efforts to converse in that language during the serious negotiations may create needless problems.

Once transnational accords are achieved, the parties must decide whether the official contract will be expressed in English, the language of the other country, or a neutral third language. This decision may be critical when future disagreements arise, because language differences may be outcome determinative. In some cases, the parties may have official texts in both languages and specify that mediators and arbitrators who may subsequently be employed to help the parties resolve contractual disputes must be fluent in both languages.

Most corporate leaders do not like to subject their firms to foreign laws or the jurisdiction of foreign tribunals. They are concerned that local biases will work to their detriment. They also fear that application of foreign laws will put them at a disadvantage. It is thus common for negotiators from both sides to seek provisions requiring application of their own laws when contract disputes arise. If one party is unable to convince the other to accept its entreaties in this regard, the resulting agreement may not require application of the laws of either nation. It may merely state that legal doctrines generally applied to international business transactions will be employed, leaving it to the ultimate adjudicators to determine which principles should be applied.

Since neither firm is likely to consent to the jurisdiction of courts in the other party's country, international business contracts frequently establish their own dispute resolution procedures.[356] It is beneficial to require the disputing parties to initially use the negotiation process to resolve their conflicts. In many cases, they can reach understandings without the need for third-party intervention. When negotiation efforts are not successful, mediation may be appropriate. They can either list the names of mutually acceptable neutrals or specify an entity that will provide proficient intervenors.

---

355. *See* Hendon, Hendon & Herbig, *supra* note 337, at 58–60.

356. *See* Salacuse, *supra* note 65, at 68–71. *See generally* Claire Mulder, "Commercial Mediation: The United States and Europe," 24 *Dispute Resolution Magazine* 8 (Fall 2017); Thomas J. Stipanowich, "The International Evolution of Mediation: A Call for Dialogue and Deliberation," 46 *Victoria University of Wellington Law Review* 1191 (2015).

When negotiation and mediation efforts are unsuccessful, the parties may have to resort to arbitration.[357] They must specify the arbitrator selection process. Will each name a person and have those two agree upon the neutral chair, or will the disputants try to select a single adjudicator? Will they name a particular individual in their agreement or list an agency — *e.g.*, International Chamber of Commerce, London Court of Arbitration, or the American Arbitration Association — from which they will obtain the names of qualified neutrals? If the latter course is employed, the parties usually strike names alternately from the list until one remains.

§ 12.06. Nation-Specific Negotiating Styles

When negotiators study the cultural backgrounds of foreign — and even domestic — counterparts, they must be careful not to assume that all persons from a specific nation or culture think and act alike.[358] They only have to consider the different traits and personalities associated with persons from their own geographic region to realize how diverse individuals are within the same nation. Even siblings raised in the same household display diverse personal traits. When business representatives have to interact with other people, they must endeavor to determine the relevant personal characteristics indigenous to those individuals. Nonetheless, when they initially encounter persons from different cultures, it may be helpful to consider the behavioral generalizations attributed to people from the pertinent cultural backgrounds. This may provide them with a good point to begin their evaluation of their individual counterparts, and it may enable them to avoid cultural taboos that could adversely affect their interactions.[359]

Professor William Zartman has suggested that national cultural differences have become less important over the past several decades due to the development of an international negotiation culture that is an amalgam of the diverse styles of the regular participants.[360] While it is certainly true that State Department officials who represent their respective governments in the international arena, persons who operate within the structures of formal organizations like the United Nations, the European Union, and the World Trade Organization, and individuals who repeatedly negotiate private transnational business deals have all been influenced by an international or institutional bargaining culture,[361] it is difficult for most people to entirely shed the subtle and

---

357. *See* Salacuse, *supra* note 348, at 128–130.

358. *See* Lothar Katz, *Principles of Negotiating International Business* 9–10 (2008); Adam Kahane, "Dispute Resolution and the Politics of Cultural Generalization," 19 *Negotiation Journal* 5, 13 (2003); James Sebenius, "Caveats for Cross-Border Negotiators," 18 *Negotiation* Journal 121, 123–126 (2002).

359. *See* Michael J. Gelfand & Naomi Dyer, "A Cultural Perspective on Negotiation: Progress, Pitfalls, and Prospects," 49 *Applied Psychology* 62 (2000); Jeswald Salacuse, "Implications for Practitioners," in *Culture and Negotiation* 199–208 (Guy Oliver Faure & Jeffrey Z. Rubin, eds. 1993).

360. *See* I. William Zartman, "A Skeptic's View," in *Culture and Negotiation* 17–21 (Guy Oliver Faure & Jeffrey Z. Rubin, eds. 1993).

361. *See* Faure, *supra* note 332, at 397, 412.

even overt influences of their own cultures.[362] 37 Our fundamental beliefs, customs, value systems, and verbal and nonverbal interpretations continue to be affected by our formative environments and our current surroundings.[363] Our cultural backgrounds significantly affect whether we think we can control our destinies or believe they are predetermined. Our cultures determine how we attempt to resolve problems—deductively, inductively, or in some other manner. Nonverbal signals vary greatly from nation to nation. The identical English words have different meanings in the United States and in England. International negotiators who ignore these differences are likely to encounter both communicational and inter-personal problems.

Sociologists distinguish between *"high context"* and *"low context"* cultures.[364] High context cultures tend to be group-oriented. They value the establishment and preservation of lasting relationships and the perpetuation of group norms. They use face-saving techniques to avoid embarrassing overt capitulations.[365] Individuals from high context cultures often dislike auction bargaining, because of the repeated concessions associated with that process. They communicate more indirectly to avoid placing others in awkward positions. They usually favor emotional appeals enhancing long-term relationships over rational appeals based primarily on objective logic.[366] You often have to consider the setting to understand the precise meaning of particular words or phrases.[367] They are willing to accept ambiguous contractual language that enhances the inter-party relationships involved. They tend to be patient negotiators who prefer to become well acquainted with counterparts before they agree to formal contractual arrangements.

Low context cultures tend to be individualistic and goal-oriented. Low context negotiators are primarily interested in the attainment of legally enforceable contracts They feel comfortable with auction bargaining, believing that compromise leads to common ground. They prefer direct communication that indicates exactly what they want. They are rule-oriented individuals who want to obtain agreements that carefully define all of the relevant terms. They fear that ambiguous language may create future interpretive difficulties.

Individuals feel most comfortable when they interact with persons from same-context cultures. When people from low context cultures interact with others from high context cultures, cross-cultural conflicts may arise.[368] The high context participants may feel their low context counterparts are being too direct, while the low

---

362. *See* Watkins & Rosegrant, *supra* note 320, at 73–79.

363. *See* Jeanne Brett & Michael Gelfand, "A Cultural Analysis of the Underlying Assumptions of Negotiation Theory," in *Negotiation Theory and Research* 175 (Leigh Thompson, ed. 2006); Lee, *supra* note 334, at 388–390; *see generally* LeBaron, *supra* note 338.

364. *See* William H. Requejo & John L. Graham, *Global Negotiation* 58 (2008); Tan & Lim, *supra* note 341, at 30–32; Acuff, *supra* note 333, at 44–48.

365. *See* Cohen, *supra* note 353, at 56–61.

366. *See* Brett & Gelfand, *supra* note 363, at 178–179.

367. *See* Katz, *supra* note 358, at 51–54.

368. *See* Brett, *supra* note 337, at 6–23.

context persons may think their adversaries are unwilling to address the real issues that must be resolved. The low context negotiators cannot understand why their counterparts are hesitant to match their concessions, while the high context participants cannot comprehend why their adversaries wish to openly embarrass them. If the participants are unable to accommodate each other's cultural needs, the likelihood of agreement will be slight.

It tends to be more difficult to achieve mutually efficient agreements during inter-cultural interactions than during intra-cultural encounters. Nonetheless, negotiators from different cultures can maximize their joint gains if certain common values are present. First, a belief in the value of information sharing which enables the parties to appreciate each other's needs and interests. Second, the ability to deal with multiple issues simultaneously, to permit the participants to generate trades that are mutually beneficial. Third, a desire to improve on their present agreement, causing the bargainers to continue to look for ways in which to generate further joint gains. Cultures that do not share these beliefs are less likely to achieve efficient accords.

I will explore the negotiation styles associated with individuals from important American trading partners that have been the subject of scholarly examination. We will begin with a review of the United States style, to permit readers to understand how foreigners view our approach to bargaining. We will then cover countries from Eastern and Western Europe, Asia, Africa, and Latin America. While the nations included are illustrative, they provide negotiators with issues they should evaluate when planning interactions with people from other countries.[369] 44 For a comparison of many cultures with respect to Power Distance Index, Individualism, Masculinity, Uncertainty Avoidance Index and Long Term Orientation, see http://www.geert-hofstede.com. Readers should recognize that the generalizations described do not reflect the behavior of all persons from the same nation.

A. United States

The United States is considered a highly individualistic, low context culture.[370] We are viewed as goal-oriented and impatient.[371] Most U.S. business leaders think in terms of months or calendar quarters, rather than on a long-term basis.[372] State Department officials are under pressure from political leaders who think in two or four year time frames.[373] It is rare to hear American negotiators speak about the next century—unless it is on the immediate horizon—and we never talk about the future of our grandchildren or our great grandchildren. Americans speak fewer foreign lan-

---

369. *See generally* Olegario Llamazares, *How to Negotiate Successfully in 50 Countries* (2008); Terri Morrison & Wayne A. Conaway, *Kiss, Bow, or Shake Hands* (2006) (covering 60 countries).

370. *See* Requejo & Graham, *supra* note 364, at 22–23.

371. *See* Gelfand & Dyer, *supra* note 359, at 66; Cohen, *supra* note 353, at 63–64.

372. *See* Adler, *supra* note 351, at 219–220.

373. *See* Solomon & Quinney, *supra* note 326, at 6.

guages than persons in other countries, and they tend to be less interested in foreign cultures.[374]

We need to take time to get to know the persons with whom we will interact and to establish beneficial relationships with those persons. We need to take the time to literally or figuratively share three cups of tea with them. "The first time you share tea with a Balti, you are a stranger. The second time you take tea, you are an honored guest. The third time you share a cup of tea, you become family, and for our family, we are prepared to do anything, even die."[375]

Americans are considered by many foreigners to be too informal. We get on a first name basis soon after we meet someone. For people from cultures in which first names are reserved for close acquaintances, our behavior in this regard is considered disrespectful. Despite our reputation for informality, we are also viewed as impersonal advocates who are primarily interested in the deal we are negotiating. We only want to interact with our foreign adversaries to the extent necessary to obtain the terms we desire. This tendency causes foreigners to think of us as arrogant and even patronizing. We appear to be disinterested in them personally and in their firms professionally. We do not seem to be concerned about the establishment of long-term business relationships.

United States negotiators tend to feel comfortable with auction bargaining.[376] We often make quick concessions to demonstrate our willingness to compromise. While we think of this as an admirable trait, others frequently view it as a sign of over-anxious weakness. We tend to disclose important information more quickly than individuals from high context cultures who wish to establish more personal relationships before they address substantive matters. Our approach may place us at a disadvantage, because of the excessive information we are divulging. We need to learn to be more patient—especially at the beginning of transnational interactions. We should plan to engage in a prolonged Preliminary Stage to give the participants the opportunity to get to know each other. These exchanges would help us to learn about our counterparts, their negotiating styles, and their underlying needs and interests. We should be careful to avoid substantive discussions until our counterparts are prepared to address these issues. We should particularly avoid one-sided disclosures from us to more taciturn adversaries.

When Americans interact with individuals from other countries, they should err on the side of formality. They should address people by their last names, including any relevant titles. When they interact with younger women, they should use such titles as Senora or Frau, instead of the diminutive Senorita or Fraulein. Since there are not similar diminutive titles for young men, professional women tend to view such titles as sexist. Even when asked to use the other person's first name, Americans should continue to use that person's last name. This formality shows respect for the

---

374. *See* Dawson, *supra* note 12, at 231; Adler, *supra* note 351, at 12.
375. Greg Mortenson & David O. Relin, *Three Cups of Tea* 150 (2006).
376. *See* Cohen, *supra* note 353, at 85–86.

other participant's own culture and will be appreciated. If they really do wish to be addressed on a first name basis, they will insist upon this treatment.

Most foreign negotiators describe Americans as competitive, win-lose bargainers.[377] They think we are only interested in what we can obtain for our own firms, rather than how we might structure mutually beneficial arrangements. When opposing negotiators do not move with sufficient alacrity, American representatives tend to give them "final" concessions which must be quickly reciprocated if the interaction is to continue. This seemingly "take-it-or-leave-it" approach causes many U.S. advocates to be labeled Boulwareistic.[378] It would be helpful if we were more patient. We should not rush the process when it appears that the opposing side cannot move as expeditiously. We should be reluctant to present others with "final" offers, unless we have reasonably concluded that no mutual accords are likely to be achieved. Doubts should be resolved in favor of continued discussions that may enable both sides to reach common ground. When we are uncertain, we should recess talks to give both sides the opportunity to reconsider their underlying needs and interests — rather than terminating the exchanges.

The United States is an extremely legalistic society. Our legal representatives are taught to negotiate agreements that are all-encompassing and unambiguous.[379] We attempt to anticipate every possibility and have clauses covering every contingency. This desire to achieve definitive accords causes many foreign negotiators to think we do not trust them or their companies, and they resent this apparent lack of respect. We should explain our legal system to them and indicate why we are required to be so thorough. If they appreciate our underlying needs in this regard, they are likely to be more accommodating. On the other hand, we need to recognize when we are being overly legalistic and accept the need to leave certain terms unaddressed or defined in general terms. If we can create beneficial relationships, we should have confidence in our mutual ability to resolve future questions in a professional manner.

B. Canada

When foreigners interact with Canadians, they frequently assume that they are interacting with persons who are just like individuals from the United States. They fail to appreciate the subtle and not-so-subtle differences between U.S. and Canadian bargainers.[380] Despite the fact that Canada is the major trading partner of the U.S., Americans know little about the Canadian culture and few studies have attempted to document the differences between the residents of these contiguous nations.

---

377. *See* Frank Acuff, *How to Negotiate Anything with Anyone Anywhere Around the World* 56 (1993).

378. *See* Cohen, *supra* note 353, at 88–89.

379. *See* Solomon & Quinney, *supra* note 326, at 29–32.

380. *See* Nancy J. Adler & John L. Graham, "Business Negotiations: Canadians Are Not Just Like Americans," 4 *Canadian Journal of Administrative Sciences* 211 (1987); Nancy J. Adler, John L. Graham & T.S. Gehrke, "Business Negotiations in Canada, Mexico, and the United States," 15 *Journal of Business Research* 411 (1987).

Canada consists of two major, but quite different, cultures. French Canadians—"Francophones"—make up one-quarter of the population, while English Canadians—"Anglophones"—make up most of the remaining three-quarters.[381] Both groups constitute low context cultures in which they tend to explicitly say what they mean. Francophones are located primarily in Quebec, the French speaking province. They prefer to speak French, even when they are fluent in both French and English. Anglophones usually speak English, even when they are bilingual. Foreigners negotiating with Francophones should always include individuals on their bargaining teams who are fluent in French.

Francophones differ significantly from Anglophones.[382] Francophones reflect their French heritage, while Anglophones reflect their British heritage. Francophones place great emphasis on the need for security, happiness, and self-esteem, while Anglophones respect individual accomplishments and personal autonomy.[383] Francophones value being courageous and being independent less than Anglophones, but value being intellectual more.[384] They like to spend time debating the substantive issues that have to be negotiated. Francophones tend to exhibit a "Catholic ethic" which emphasizes family and de-emphasizes work, while Anglophones tend to exhibit a "Protestant ethic" which emphasizes personal achievement and hard work.[385] Although Anglophones seem similar to Americans, they tend to be more progressive on such issues as national health care, worker rights, and gay marriage. Americans interacting with Anglophones during business negotiations should thus be careful to appreciate the different business philosophies involved.

Francophones tend to employ more competitive negotiating tactics than Anglophones.[386] Their behavior in this regard produces higher individual returns, but lower levels of principal satisfaction.[387] Anglophones tend to employ more cooperative bargaining tactics.[388] If Americans and Anglophones behave too openly and cooperatively with Francophones who are less open and use more competitive tactics, they may achieve less beneficial results for their own sides.

C. Mexico

The establishment of the North American Free Trade Zone has greatly increased the already substantial interaction between Mexican and American business firms. Mexico is a high context culture in which close friendships are valued. Although Mexico has a long and distinguished history, it has been significantly affected by

---

381. *See* Adler, Graham & Gehrke, *supra* note 380 at 412.
382. *See* Adler & Graham, *supra* note 380.
383. *See id.*, at 215.
384. *See id.*, at 222.
385. *See* Adler, Graham & Gehrke, *supra* note 380, at 414.
386. *See* Adler & Graham, *supra* note 380, at 221–222, 229–230; Adler, Graham & Gehrke, *supra* note 380, at 421.
387. *See* Adler & Graham, *supra* note 380, at 229.
388. *See id.*, at 221–222; Adler, Graham & Gehrke, *supra* note 380, at 425.

foreign domination—300 years by the Spanish and French and many years by the United States during the mid-1800s.[389] It still feels understandably aggrieved by the seizure of what is now southern California and the annexation of Texas. Many U.S. negotiators make the mistake of treating Mexican advocates as Spanish-speaking North Americans, ignoring their strong Latin culture.[390] Mexican negotiators appreciate respect shown for their country's history and culture, and for their country's recent economic gains.[391]

Mexico is a nation undergoing rapid economic expansion, and it hopes to use business deals with U.S. firms to advance its economic interests. Nonetheless, it continues to feel dominated by its northern neighbor.[392] It believes that the United States government does not give it the respect it deserves, and it thinks that American business firms are always trying to obtain one-sided deals that only minimally satisfy Mexican interests. They do not like to make overt concessions to U.S. counterparts.[393] U.S.-Mexican relations continue to be strained by efforts by American officials to limit Mexican immigration. Mexican leaders resent the fact the United States shows more respect to other countries. While the inclusion of Mexico in NAFTA has helped to improve relations with the U.S., most Mexicans still feel they are treated as second-class trading partners.

Although most foreigners think that Mexico has a strong central government, the President does not possess the authority to impose his will on the entrenched bureaucracies.[394] Many government agencies are inefficient and suspicious of change. It is thus difficult to get approval for new business deals. When bureaucrats feel that their respective jurisdictions are being threatened by proposed arrangements, they tend to resist them fiercely. In addition, administrative corruption—generated by low compensation levels—causes many bureaucrats to demand "processing fees" to facilitate requests for agency action.[395] People who refuse to accept this reality often encounter approval problems.

Despite the market-place trader image Mexicans have among many Americans, most Mexican business leaders are highly principled negotiators who pride themselves on their integrity. They have a high context communication style and prefer to maintain formal relationships.[396] They generally present a united bargaining front that is difficult for counterparts to exploit. If they are treated with respect, they tend to use a direct style that does not include manipulative tactics. On the other hand, foreigners

---

389. *See* George Grayson, "Mexico: A Love-Hate Relationship with North America," in *National Negotiation Styles* 125–127 (Hans Binnendijk, ed. 1987).
390. *See id.*, at 144.
391. *See* Acuff, *supra* note 333, at 218–219.
392. *See* Cohen, *supra* note 353, at 43–44.
393. *See id.*, at 136–137.
394. *See* Grayson, *supra* note 389, at 136.
395. *See id.*, at 136.
396. *See* Requijo & Graham, *supra* note 364, at 212–213.

who treat them dishonorably are likely to engender hostility and a lack of receptivity. Mexican negotiators occasionally use press "leaks" attributing the lack of bargaining progress to their foreign counterparts to embarrass those people.[397]

Mexico is a relatively macho society in which some males attempt to demonstrate their masculine prowess through ritualistic bluffing. When such efforts are encountered, it is especially important to avoid responsive behavior that may be perceived as disrespectful. Once these rituals are concluded, it is generally beneficial to conduct private negotiating sessions in which concessions can be made with a minimal loss of face. Most bargaining progress tends to be made during these closed discussions.

When Mexicans participate in transnational bargaining, they try to establish good personal relationships with their foreign adversaries.[398] They frequently use informal social events to create positive rapport. They expect their hospitality to be reciprocated and are particularly sensitive to treatment they consider patronizing. They are often offended by impatient American negotiators who seem to consider the preliminary social exchanges a waste of time. Instead of trying to move too quickly toward substantive discussions, American representatives should take the time to get to know their Mexican counterparts. This will facilitate subsequent business discussions and create positive relationships that may continue for many years.

D. Brazil

Brazil is part of the BRIC (Brazil, Russia, India, and China) group of nations expected to have a significant impact on the global economy in the next fifty years. It is the largest nation in Latin America, and the ninth largest economy in the world.[399] Although many Americans think of Brazil as a Hispanic country, Brazilians do not consider themselves to be Hispanic—and they resent being spoken to in Spanish.[400] They prefer to conduct conversations in Portuguese—or English.

In the late 1600s, Portuguese explorers discovered gold in Brazil, and over the next one hundred years, 400,000 Portuguese emigrated to Brazil.[401] When Napoleon occupied Portugal in 1807, the Portuguese royal family fled to Brazil, and Rio de Janeiro became the seat of the Portuguese empire for the next fifteen years. This explains why Portuguese is the official language of Brazil, even though several hundred languages are spoken in different parts of Brazil. Eighty percent of Brazilians are Catholic, with most other residents being Protestant.[402]

Brazilians like to maintain separate private and public lives, and they do not like to discuss private family matters with outside business persons. It can be beneficial

---

397. *See* Grayson, *supra* note 389, at 141–142.
398. *See* Cohen, *supra* note 353, at 53–55; Grayson, *supra* note 389, at 133–135.
399. *See* Llamazares, *supra* note 369, at 22.
400. *See* Morrison & Conaway, *supra* note 369, at 64.
401. *See id.*, at 64.
402. *See id.*, at 66.

to develop local contacts who can schedule meetings with the appropriate persons. Brazilians tend to approach issues indirectly, rather than directly, allowing their feelings to influence their thinking and decision-making.[403] A lack of punctuality is common among Brazilians, who rarely show up for appointments at the scheduled times. Nonetheless, they are professional and serious negotiators.[404]

Individuals negotiating with Brazilians need to be patient, because Brazilians do not like to rush discussions. They do not like to haggle. They like to explore all aspects of potential contracts simultaneously, rather than on an issue-by-issue basis, and they work to develop overall packages covering everything.[405] Most concessions tend to be made near the end of their interactions. They find aggressive tactics offensive, even though they tend to be highly animated negotiators.

When Brazilians interact with strangers, they prefer more formal relationships using formal titles and last names.[406] They like to interact in close proximity with those around them, and frequently touch the hands, arms, and shoulders of others.[407] 80 When they speak, Brazilians tend to be less direct than Americans, but more direct than Japanese or Chinese.[408] They do not like to conduct serious business discussions during meals or social events.[409] Due to the complex nature of the Brazilian legal system, it is helpful to employ the services of local counsel before final agreements are executed. If contracts are to be carried out in Brazil, they will generally be written in Portuguese, but if they are to be carried out in the United States, they are usually written in English.

It is not unusual for Brazilians to conduct discussions with unrelated parties simultaneously.[410] Americans tend to find these distractions frustrating, but they have to accept this style as part of the Brazilian culture. Patience is a virtue when negotiating with Brazilians, to enable them to fully appreciate the entire package being negotiated, and to induce them to feel comfortable with the terms being proposed.

E. Japan

During the past several decades, Japanese and American business firms have become major trading partners. It is likely that these interactions will increase. It is thus beneficial for legal representatives of multinational American enterprises to understand some of the critical cultural aspects of Japanese society.[411] Japan is a high context culture that greatly values long-term relationships and the avoidance of open conflict.

---

403. *See id.*, at 66.
404. *See* Llamazares, *supra* note 369, at 22.
405. *See id.*, at 23; Morrison & Conaway, *supra* note 369, at 66.
406. *See* Morrison & Conaway, *supra* note 369, at 69.
407. *See id.*, at 69.
408. *See* Salacuse, *supra* note 65, at 101.
409. *See id.*, at 47.
410. *See id.*, at 48.
411. *See* Michael Blaker, Paul S. Giarra & Ezra F. Vogel, *Case Studies in Japanese Negotiating Behavior* (2002); James D. Hodgson, Yoshihiro Sano & John L. Graham, *Doing Business with the New*

The Japanese are proud of their distinguished history and culture, and expect foreigners to respect these factors.

Personal introductions are highly regarded by Japanese business leaders and government officials. The initial intervention of respected intermediaries can significantly enhance the likelihood of cordial and productive interactions. It is thus helpful to locate appropriate parties—such as old college friends—who can bring the parties together and establish cooperative environments and trusting relationships.[412] It is usually beneficial to have business cards printed that are in English on one side and Japanese on the other, since the exchange of such status information is expected.[413] When business cards are exchanged, they should be examined carefully and respectfully, and not simply placed in one's briefcase or pocket. The Japanese have a formal culture, and prefer to only use first names with close friends.

Americans tend to have upper level executives conduct their serious negotiations, but Japanese firms tend to use the opposite approach. When top executives attend early bargaining sessions, they are usually there to perform a ceremonial function.[414] They do not expect discussions of a substantive nature, preferring to leave those talks to lower level managers. Japanese firms expect their lower level executives to focus on the specific terms that must be subsequently approved by higher level company representatives through a consensus-building process. Foreign agents who ignore this cultural approach and attempt to negotiate specific terms with upper Japanese executives are likely to depart without accords.

The Japanese language is rather imprecise compared to English. Similar words have very different meanings. "Information comes not through the words but from the social context in which the words are uttered, from an understanding of what the speaker should be saying in contrast to what he is actually saying."[415] For example, while the word "hai" means "yes" in some contexts, it means only "I understand"— not "I agree"—during bargaining encounters.[416] It is thus necessary to engage experienced interpreters who can precisely communicate what each party is saying, and who can read between the lines and comprehend what is really intended.

Japanese negotiators often speak English, but use translators to interpret what their English-speaking counterparts have said. This gives them an advantage, because they first hear the English comments and then have time to plan their responses while the interpreters are translating the English statements into Japanese.[417] Rarely are American business negotiators fluent in Japanese. Having such persons participate

---

Japan (2000); John L. Graham & Yoshihiro Sano, *Smart Bargaining: Doing Business with the Japanese* (1989).

412. *See* Hodgson, Sano & Graham, *supra* note 411, at 3–5, 12–13, 36–37.

413. *See id.*, at 19.

414. *See id.*, at 99–102.

415. Nathanial B. Thayer & Stephen E. Weiss, "Japan: The Changing Logic of a Former Minor Power," in *National Negotiating Styles* 45, 58 (Hans Binnendijk, ed. 1987).

416. *See* Hendon, Hendon & Herbig, *supra* note 337, at 35.

417. *See* Hodgson, Sano & Graham, *supra* note 411, at 419.

on behalf of U.S. firms is both a communication advantage and a way to demonstrate to Japanese company representatives how sincerely U.S. firms wish to establish long-term relationships with Japanese businesses.

Japanese facial expressions can convey various meanings depending upon the particular circumstances involved. "The Japanese smile can be perceived as a mask of politeness, an opaque wall behind which one observes the other. It can express co-operation or denial, joy or anger, certainty or total ignorance, trust or distrust, pleasure or embarrassment. Only some knowledge of the Japanese culture and the reference to the current context of the smile may enable one to get access to its real meaning."[418]

The high context nature of the Japanese culture may explain why Japanese business people prefer to conduct serious negotiations through face-to-face contact.[419] While it may be acceptable to exchange some preliminary information though telephone calls or e-mail communications, foreign representatives should appreciate the importance of personal interactions. They should either travel to Japan or invite their Japanese counterparts to their own countries.

When a Japanese negotiator is contemplating a reply to another party's new proposal, he or she often remains silent for a prolonged period.[420] They have an ancient proverb that "he who knows does not speak, and he who speaks does not know."[421] They thus prefer silence while they determine the appropriate response. Foreign negotiators should not speak during these periods, but should quietly and patiently await their counterpart's reply. They should be especially careful not to bid against themselves by making unreciprocated concessions generated by the other side's silence.

Japanese businesspeople tend to have long-term outlooks.[422] They think in terms of generations, not calendar quarters. They also tend to be less profit oriented. As a result, they exude an inner patience that is based on their belief that, even if they are presently unable to consummate a particular business venture, their successor may be able to accomplish that objective. It is this attitude that many American bargainers find frustrating. These Americans try to complete a proposed transaction within an inordinately curtailed period of time. This sense of time urgency inures to the benefit of their less hurried Japanese counterparts.[423]

The Japanese people tend to be group oriented. They thrive on collective decisions that are achieved through a consensus process known as "ringi."[424] It thus takes more time for them to achieve internally acceptable agreements. Many business transactions must also be approved by appropriate government officials—usually from the Ministry

---

418. *See* Faure, *supra* note 332, at 407.
419. *See* Hodgson, Sano & Graham, *supra* note 411, at 92–93.
420. *See* Calero, *supra* note 159, at 107–108; Hendon, Hendon & Herbig, *supra* note 337, at 63.
421. Hendon, Hendon & Herbig, *supra* note 337, at 63–64.
422. *See* Tan & Lim, *supra* note 341, at 89.
423. *See* Hodgson, Sano & Graham, *supra* note 411, at 10–12.
424. Hendon, Hendon & Herbig, *supra* note 337, at 232–233.

of International Trade and Industry (MITI) when transnational arrangements are involved.[425] During some interactions, government representatives directly participate, while in others they merely have to approve the final accords achieved. This tripartite aspect of Japanese business deals is a time-consuming process. People who attempt to expedite these traditional procedures or endeavor to circumvent them through end runs to higher corporate or government officials are likely to find themselves without business accords.

Americans who negotiate with Japanese business agents must be patient, conciliatory, and respectful. They must take the time to establish trusting and cooperative relationships. During these preliminary social occasions, substantive discussions are considered inappropriate and should be avoided.[426] Direct confrontations should be similarly avoided. They must recognize that, once harmonious relationships have been created, they should be able to achieve lasting agreements that will benefit both sides. American agents who ignore these important cultural considerations will find themselves unable to consummate the types of advantageous business transactions they may otherwise have attained through the development of appropriate intercultural rapport.

Japanese are taught from birth that social conflict must be avoided whenever possible.[427] They have created detailed rituals that are designed to permit them to conduct business dealings through the development of non-confrontational relationships. They do not like the auction process which creates the need for overt position changes. They ask many questions at the beginning of interactions to ascertain the true needs of their counterparts, and they are usually willing to share their own interests. Adversaries who openly respond to these inquiries and who fail to elicit similar information from their Japanese counterparts put themselves at a disadvantage. They frequently conduct serious talks in private to prevent the need for public position changes. Once Japanese negotiators think they have the information they need to assess the situation, they prefer to make initial offers that are realistic and efficient.[428] They are especially resentful of counterparts who disrupt the bargaining process with extreme opening positions. The Japanese participants may even "leak" information regarding their planned opening offers prior to or during the preliminary discussions to avoid embarrassing misunderstandings.

Traditional Japanese hosts feel that it is inappropriate to openly reject proposals suggested by visitors. They generally believe that such overt repudiations cause their guests to suffer a serious loss of face.[429] To avoid such unseemly confrontations, the Japanese often: (1) delay final decisions regarding the matters in question; (2) indirectly discuss the deficiencies associated with the proposals; (3) suggest preferable alternatives; or (4) simply ignore the issues.[430] In some cases they may provide mildly affirmative responses

---

425. *See* Thayer & Weiss, *supra* note 415, at 50–51.
426. *See* Hodgson, Sano & Graham, *supra* note 411, at 20.
427. *See* Tan & Lim, *supra* note 341, at 90; Thayer & Weiss, *supra* note 415, at 54–55.
428. *See* Hendon, Hendon & Herbig, *supra* note 337, at 35.
429. *See* Tan & Lim, *supra* note 341, at 87; R. Cohen, *supra* note 353, at 103.
430. *See* R. Cohen, *supra* note 353, at 112–113.

they hope will be understood as polite rejections.[431] For example, they may indicate a willingness "to seriously consider" or to "do their best" with respect to disfavored topics. While this may give them time to reevaluate the items, they are unlikely to yield on these issues. If they say that something "will be difficult" or they audibly breathe through clenched teeth, they usually mean "definitely not." When foreign visitors do not understand that seemingly affirmative responses are actually indented as polite rejections, they may create problems by directly or indirectly accusing their hosts of deceptive behavior. Proficient interpreters should understand these cultural nuances and provide the visitors with the information they need to avoid communication problems.

It is vital for American business representatives to maintain a noncombative, harmonious tone during their dealings with Japanese agents. Anger and indignation should not be openly displayed, due to the loss of face associated with these expressions. Overt threats rarely work and generally exacerbate bargaining relationships. Americans should not attempt to negotiate ironclad contracts that specifically cover every possible contingency that may arise. This approach is likely to be perceived as an indication that they doubt the sincere intent of their Japanese counterparts to honor their agreements. The Japanese view business contracts very differently from American businesspeople:

> [T]he Japanese envision such a business transaction as an ongoing, harmonious relationship between parties committed to creating and maintaining a mutually beneficial business relationship ... [T]he Japanese do not really negotiate contracts but rather business relationships themselves.[432]

Written agreements are thus expected to be somewhat vague and amorphous. Japanese business agents do not fear noncompliance, since "a person who owes the duty to another is under a strict moral obligation to fulfill it."[433] Any questions regarding the meaning and application of indefinite contractual terms are to be resolved amicably through mutual consultations.

Americans must recognize that some older Japanese businessmen are not accustomed to interacting with women in business environments. As a result, female representatives may initially find it difficult to establish traditional business relationships with their male Japanese counterparts. As Japanese businessmen have increasingly interacted with foreign businesswomen, they have become more flexible with respect to this issue, despite the continuation of the traditional male-female distinctions within their own society.

F. China

The Chinese, like the Japanese, are a high context culture.[434] They are also particularly proud of their extraordinary history and expect others to respect their past ac-

---

431. *See* Thayer & Weiss, *supra* note 415, at 57–59.
432. Elliott Hahn, "Negotiating with the Japanese," *California Lawyer* 21, 22 (1982).
433. R.E. Watts, "Briefing the American Negotiator in Japan," 16 *International Lawyer* 597, 604 (1982).
434. *See* Robert M. March & Su-Hwa Wu, *The Chinese Negotiator* 81 (2007).

complishments. They are a relatively entrepreneurial people who enjoy the opportunity to establish economically beneficial business relationships — "guanxi."[435] As in Japan, governmental ministries may become directly or indirectly involved with transnational business negotiations.

Observers have noted that "the Chinese negotiator is a blend of Maoist bureaucrat, Confucian gentleman, and Sun Tzu-like strategist."[436] The bureaucrat is cautious and tries to follow established government policy. The Confucian seeks to create mutual trust, harmony, and cooperative dealings.[437] The Sun Tzu strategist employs manipulative tactics for their own gain. In many negotiations with Chinese representatives, all three influences may be seen at different times during the same interaction.[438] They tend to distrust strangers, thus it is important for foreigners to develop close relationships before they try to negotiate business deals.[439] Chinese negotiators like to use an expanded Preliminary Stage to get to know their counterparts before substantive issues are discussed.

Chinese negotiators frequently try to remind counterparts how much those parties need Chinese participation. They attempt to develop feelings of friendship in their counterparts, and they manipulate those feelings to their own advantage.[440] They also try to create feelings of guilt in adversaries by reminding them of previous transgressions. They like to play counterparts off against one another, as they did the United States and the Soviet Union for many years.

Chinese negotiators are usually thoroughly prepared for bargaining encounters.[441] During preliminary bargaining discussions, Chinese participants often work to obtain the commitment of opposing parties to general principles that are favorable to them. They use those basic tenets to generate the results they prefer.[442] Chinese negotiators also like to employ protracted talks to induce less patient participants to make unreciprocated concessions.[443]

Chinese negotiators find the auction process distasteful, viewing repeated position changes as a sign of weakness.[444] Once they think they have extracted sufficient in-

435. *See* Sujin Lee, Jeanne Brett & Ji Hyearn Park, "East Asians' Social Heterogeneity: Differences in Norms Among Chinese, Japanese, and Korean Negotiators," 28 *Negotiation Journal* 429, 431–432, 446 (2012).

436. March & Wu, *supra* note 434, at 45; Tony Fang, *Chinese Business Negotiating Style* 272 (1999).

437. *See* Cheng C. Qian, "The Culture of China's Mediation in Regional and International Affairs," 28 *Conflict Resolution Quarterly* 53, 54 (2010).

438. *See generally* Bee Chen Goh, *Negotiating with the Chinese* (1996).

439. *See* Requejo & Graham, *supra* note 364, at 220–224; March & Wu, *supra* note 434, at 192; Tan & Lim, *supra* note 341, at 46.

440. *See* Hendon, Hendon & Herbig, *supra* note 337, at 37, 51–52; Richard Solomon, *Chinese Negotiating Behavior* 3–4 (1999).

441. *See* Hendon, Hendon & Herbig, *supra* note 337, at 232.

442. *See* Solomon, *supra* note 440, at 4–5.

443. *See* March & Wu, *supra* note 434, at 20, 56; R. Cohen, *supra* note 353, at 101.

444. *See* R. Cohen, *supra* note 353, at 93–95.

formation and as many preliminary concessions as possible from counterparts, they tend to develop firm positions they do not plan to alter significantly.[445] They announce their offers sternly and move quickly toward closure. Their uncompromising attitudes and expeditious movement toward agreement may catch unsuspecting counterparts off guard. Once counterparts appreciate their unwillingness to make further concessions, they must either accept or reject the proposed terms.

Once business deals have been arranged, they usually require the approval of government bureaucrats. This can be a time-consuming process that may be facilitated through "gifts" to the requisite ministry representatives. After agency consent is obtained, the foreign participants think the negotiation is finished. They are surprised when the Chinese representatives discover "ambiguities" in the applicable agreements that enable them to reopen bargaining over seemingly closed issues.[446] Adept Chinese negotiators frequently employ this "Nibble" technique to extract additional concessions from naive and unprepared adversaries who are afraid to walk away if that becomes necessary. People who encounter this tactic should remember to demand reciprocal concessions from their Chinese partners.

G. South Korea

South Korea is an economically powerful Asian country. It has a long history, but was occupied by the Japanese during the first half of the twentieth century. Following World War II, it was divided into Communist North Korea and democratic South Korea. Korean is the official language, but English is widely spoken. Korea is a Confucian culture, which considers the family to be the basic unit of society.[447] Although Korea has no *official* religion, Buddhism is the predominant religion.

Koreans can be difficult negotiators.[448] Although it is a collectivist culture, where decisions tend to be made by group consensus, Koreans are more individualistic than the Japanese or the Chinese.[449] As a result, they are the most direct of Asian negotiators.[450] When they negotiate with others, they strive for harmony. Foreigners should be careful to avoid hurting their feelings, especially in public, to prevent a loss of face.

Since Koreans value established relationships, it can be beneficial for foreigners to make initial contacts through mutual acquaintances. The common greeting with foreigners involves a hand shake and a slight bowing of the head. Small gifts are usually exchanged, along with business cards that should be in Korean on one side and English

---

445. *See* Hendon, Hendon & Herbig, *supra* note 337, at 86–87; Cohen, *supra* note 353, at 66–67, 85.

446. *See* March & Wu, *supra* note 434, at 81; Tan & Lim, *supra* note 341, at 55, 65; Hendon, Hendon & Herbig, *supra* note 337, at 37.

447. *See* Morrison & Conaway, *supra* note 369, at 460.

448. *See* Lee, Brett & Park, *supra* note 435, at 435–435; Llamazares, *supra* note 369, at 188.

449. *See* Morrison & Conaway, *supra* note 369, at 461.

450. *See* Llamazares, *supra* note 369, at 188.

on the other.[451] When someone receives a Korean business card, they should examine it carefully, never write on it, and put it away respectfully.[452] Koreans are punctual people, and guests should always arrive for meetings at the scheduled times. Initial meetings are usually used to establish professional relationships.[453] Small talk should be used to establish rapport, with serious business discussions postponed for later sessions.

Koreans are highly respectful of older persons and individuals of higher social and professional rank.[454] When individuals enter a room, senior members should enter first, followed by higher ranking members of the party. First names are rarely used unless the individuals are very close. As with other Asian cultures, a Korean's surname comes first. They should be addressed as Mr. or Mrs. _____. Foreigners preparing for bargaining interactions with Koreans should try to determine who will participate for the Korean firms and plan to have persons of equal rank present on their own side.

Koreans tend to begin negotiations with relatively extreme positions, and they expect repeated position changes during the bargaining process.[455] They are more aggressive and more direct than Japanese or Chinese negotiators, but still try to avoid open losses of face. They tend to smile or laugh when they are embarrassed, and silences are often an indication they are confused. When this occurs, others should not directly ask them if they do not understand, because such inquiries would embarrass them.[456] It is preferable to carefully restate what was said earlier in a manner designed to clarify what they may be finding difficult to comprehend.

Although Koreans can be more direct than Japanese or Chinese negotiators, they often hesitate to openly reject offers articulated by foreigners. When they say "yes" or nod their heads affirmatively, this does not always mean yes; it often means maybe.[457] When they say "maybe," this usually means no, and if they say "that would be difficult," they mean definitely not.

H. India

India is rapidly becoming a significant economic power. A Goldman-Sachs study recently predicted that by 2035, the Indian economy will be the third largest in the world, surpassed by only the economies of the United States and China.[458] More than one-third of the Fortune 500 companies have outsourced some of their software re-

---

451. *See id.*, at 189.
452. *See id.*, at 189.
453. *See* Morrison & Conaway, *supra* note 369, at 462.
454. *See id.*, at 462.
455. *See* Llamazares, *supra* note 369, at 188.
456. *See* Morrison & Conaway, *supra* note 369, at 463–464.
457. *See id.*, at 464.
458. *See* Rajesh Kumar, "Negotiating with the Complex, Imaginative Indian," *Ivey Business Journal* 1 (March/April 2005).

quirements to Indian firms, and more businesses are expected to negotiate similar arrangements.[459] Despite the recent economic developments, however, India continues to be a relatively poor country, with a per capita GDP of $2200.

Indian negotiators exhibit a high context communication style.[460] They do not like to reject proposals as overtly as their American counterparts, and frequently use ambiguous language to avoid this necessity. Foreigners interacting with Indian negotiators should recognize the need to appreciate the surrounding circumstances and nonverbal signals to understand the verbal message actually being conveyed. Individuals who try to interpret Indian presentations literally will find it difficult to comprehend what has actually been said. Nonverbal signals may have different meanings. For example, Indians often shake their heads from side-to-side when they mean "yes," which causes many Americans to misinterpret the actual message being communicated.[461] India is also a highly relationship-oriented culture.[462]

India is a vast and culturally diverse nation.[463] Each state has its own cultural norms and value system. Although 80 percent of Indians are Hindu, there are 105 million Muslims, making India one of the largest Islamic countries in the world. There are also 22 million Christians. Religious beliefs influence social, economic, and political activities throughout the country.

India is also a linguistically diverse nation. Although Hindi, the national language, is spoken by 20 percent of the Indian people, there are eighteen official languages and 1600 secondary languages and dialects.[464] Nonetheless, English is the language most often used in business dealings involving people from other nations.

Persons living in South India tend to be quite different from individuals residing in North India. South Indians tend to value punctuality and efficiency, while North Indians tend to be more casual regarding these factors. South Indians tend to be more straightforward when they negotiate than North Indians. South Indians tend to focus more on basic objectives than their North Indian counterparts, with the latter more likely to focus on the development of relationships rather than mere contracts. North Indians like to use bargaining interactions to develop long-term relationships. This is why it often takes longer to negotiate with North Indians than with South Indians. The Preliminary Stage should be carefully employed in North Indian territories to develop good working relationships before the serious discussions begin. Food and drinks are likely to be provided to advance this process.

Indians consider it very inappropriate for persons to touch something of value with their feet or shoes. It is thus improper for someone to sit with their feet on their desk or table. It is similarly unsuitable to touch a briefcase or book with one's feet.

---

459. *See* Tan & Lim, *supra* note 344, at 122.
460. *See* Requejo & Graham, *supra* note 364, at 195; Tan & Lim, *supra* note 341, at 151–152.
461. *See* Calero, *supra* note 159, at 115.
462. *See* Requejo & Graham, *supra* note 364, at 194–195.
463. *See* Tan & Lim, *supra* note 341, at 123–126.
464. *See id.*, at 125–126.

As in the Middle East, the bottom of one's feet should not be displayed to others, since this is thought to demonstrate a serious lack of respect.

India has historically had a caste system that was reinforced by over 250 years of British rule.[465] The Indian people tend to believe that their positions in life have been irreversibly determined by the fortuity of birth which is reflective of their prior lives and reincarnations. They think their personalities and socio-economic circumstances cannot be altered during their lifetimes. This perspective tends to make them fatalistic, based upon the assumption that they cannot move from their caste of birth. There are four main castes in India. The Brahmins, comprised of priests and intellectuals, are at the top, followed by the Kshatriyas, comprised of warriors, rulers, and states-men.[466] Traders, merchants, and artisans are Vaishyas, with laborers in the lowest Shudras caste.

Indians tend to follow a hierarchical system in their business dealings, with senior managers being respected and obeyed by less senior personnel.[467] When firm or de-partmental decisions are being made, the most senior persons are expected to speak. Less senior individuals tend to remain silent, especially if they do not agree with what has been said. When foreign representatives negotiate with Indian business groups, they should carefully work to understand the concerns of silent subordinates who will have to effectuate the terms finally agreed upon since they may passively fail to do what is expected of them.[468]

India tends to be a collectivistic, rather than an individualistic, culture similar to Japan and China.[469] Group interests and long-term relationships tend to take prece-dence over individual considerations. On the other hand, Indians can be more openly competitive than their Japanese or Chinese counterparts.[470] In this regard, their be-havior may seem more like the individualistic style of people from countries like the U.S. or Germany. Indian negotiators like to decide what is good for their organizations, then use positional bargaining to achieve optimal results for their own side.[471] This approach may seem schizophrenic to counterparts who cannot understand the overtly competitive behavior by seemingly relationship-oriented people.

Indians consider bargaining interactions as part of a long-term process which must be developed deliberately.[472] They like to obtain detailed information and carefully analyze those data before they address substantive issues. They work to create good relationships with their business partners, and view the initial agreement as the end of the Preliminary Stage. They often rely upon ambiguous contractual language to allow them to reopen negotiations on seemingly final provisions to enable them to

---

465. *See* Kumar, *supra* note 458, at 2; Tan & Lim, *supra* note 341, at 126.
466. *See* Tan & Lim, *supra* note 341, at 127.
467. *See id.,* at 128.
468. *See id.,* at 151.
469. *See id.,* at 150.
470. *See* Kumar, *supra* note 458, at 2.
471. *See* Tan & Lim, *supra* note 341, 151.
472. *See id.,* at 125, 142.

enhance their own returns. It is this passive-aggressive style, combined with the "nibble" technique, that causes foreign negotiators to become frustrated by Indians who appear to have said "yes," but who then fail to carry out what appears to have been agreed upon. As a developing nation, Indians especially think that advanced countries like the U.S. should provide them with more generous terms simply to offset the economic imbalance involved, and they frequently employ this factor to extract greater concessions from representatives from such nations.[473]

People negotiating business deals with Indian firms should use prolonged Preliminary Stages to create beneficial professional and personal relationships before the substantive issues are addressed, especially when dealing with North Indians. When the actual contract terms are discussed, they should appreciate the high context Indian culture and not expect precise responses. They should also recognize that the provisions initially agreed upon are not final. As the business deal unfolds, the Indian representatives will work to renegotiate ambiguous provisions to their advantage.

Indian government officials are likely to become involved in international business negotiations.[474] Certain business arrangements must be approved by administrative agencies, and the approval process may be time consuming. Foreign firms must be patient and allow this process to evolve. If they try to expedite or circumvent this stage, the entire deal may be lost. Indians have historically been expected to make payments to government officials to enhance the approval process. Many outsiders consider these payments to constitute "bribes" designed to corrupt the administrative process. In recent years, Indian leaders have worked diligently to eliminate this practice, and foreigners should refuse to make payments that are clearly improper.

I. Russia

Despite long periods of domination by Czars and Communist leaders who attempted to impose diverse concepts of social order, Russia is a relatively low context culture.[475] As a result of centuries of government censorship, Russians have a penchant for secrecy, valuing individuals who possess confidential information.[476] To circumvent strong, undemocratic leaders, they developed deceptive means of achieving their objectives. They continue to respect people who use indirect—*i.e.*, passive-aggressive—techniques to attain their goals, even when more direct measures would be effective.[477]

Russians continue to be suspicious of outsiders, probably because of both their traditional geographical isolation and the number of times their country has been

---

473. *See* Kumar, *supra* note 458, at 5.

474. *See id.*, at 1; Tan & Lim, *supra* note 341, at 132–138.

475. *See* Dawson, *supra* note 12, at 244.

476. *See* Leon Sloss & M. Scott Davis, "The Soviet Union: The Pursuit of Power and Influence Through Negotiation," in *National Negotiating Styles* 17, 19–20 (Hans Binnendijk, ed. 1987).

477. *See generally* Jerold L. Schecter, *Russian Negotiating Behavior* 1 (1998).

invaded by foreign powers.[478] Throughout the 1960s, 1970s, and 1980s, World War II documentaries were regularly shown on Russian television, to remind citizens of the millions of casualties suffered during those hostilities. Just as many Americans were concerned throughout the Cold War of possible Russian invasion, Russians shared similar fears vis-a-vis the United States. With the collapse of the former Soviet Union and the demise of traditional Communism, Russians are experimenting with free market economic ideas. Westerners must realize that Russians now fear capitalist invasion from Western European and North American powers. Corporate leaders interested in joint ventures with Russian business firms must move slowly to create feelings of trust in host participants who are afraid their authority may be supplanted by foreign domination.

As a result of centuries of strict government market regulation, most Russians have not developed any significant entrepreneurial spirit.[479] While most are relatively competitive people who still see life as a class struggle—previously between Communists and others and now between capitalists and others—the majority are not overly ambitious. Years of what Chinese have referred to as the "Communist or iron rice bowl" chilled their belief in individual accomplishment. Instead of trying to emulate the successes of others, many prefer to thwart such advances. For example, if their neighbor were to get two cows and they were asked what they would like to see, many would respond—not with a desire for their own cows—but rather with a wish for the death of their neighbor's animals.

Russians have historically had an oligarchical decision-making system in which small groups of leaders made most fundamental decisions.[480] Most Russian negotiators still possess minimal authority and must obtain final approval of proposed agreements from higher government or firm officials. This protracted approval process often frustrates impatient foreign negotiators. With the demise of the Communist system, Russians fear being viewed as a second-class power. They very much want to be respected for their economic and military capabilities.

Russians have traditionally considered open compromise as a sign of weakness, and they admire individuals who can employ confrontational tactics to generate counterpart concessions.[481] They frequently use intransigence and protracted bargaining sessions to induce careless counterparts to make unilateral concessions.[482] No matter how slowly progress is being made, they like to continue interactions with expectations of future gains. Opposing parties must be especially patient to wait for the serious negotiations to begin. People who rush matters are likely to make unreciprocated concessions that will inure to the benefit of their more patient Russian adversaries.[483] Once the real exchanges commence, Russian negotiators tend to make concessions

---

478. *See* Sloss & Davis, *supra* note 476, at 18–19.
479. *See* Dawson, *supra* note 12, at 243; Acuff, *supra* note 333, at 82–84.
480. *See* Sloss & Davis, *supra* note 476, at 20–23.
481. *See id.,* at 32.
482. *See* Hendon, Hendon & Herbig, *supra* note 337, at 41.
483. *See* Sloss & Davis, *supra* note 476, at 32–36.

in small increments because of their distaste for overt capitulation. counterparts must either move slowly with them, or they will find themselves bidding against themselves in a losing endeavor.

Once common ground is achieved, Russians tend to prefer general language, rather than specific provisions. This allows them to reopen negotiations later as "ambiguities" are discovered. Whenever possible, it is beneficial to include language that expressly defines the basic terms involved. When this cannot be accomplished and Russian bargainers subsequently attempt to claim additional items for themselves — the "Nibble" technique — counterparts should remember to demand appropriate reciprocal concessions from their Russian counterparts.

J. United Kingdom

Although many Americans think of England as the United Kingdom, the UK actually consists of England, Wales, Scotland, and Northern Ireland.[484] In addition, while most Americans consider England to be part of Europe, most English persons think of their country as a separate entity.[485] This is why England decided to leave the European Union on January 31, 2020. Americans and the English seem to speak a common language, but there can be subtle differences in meaning that can cause confusion.[486] For example, to "table a matter" in the UK means to deal with it immediately, while the same phrase in the United States means the opposite. Even within UK nations, there are a number of different dialects that can be especially confusing for outsiders.[487]

The English tend to be a more formal culture than the United States. They generally begin relationships with polite handshakes, but some women still prefer to avoid such contacts.[488] They prefer greater spatial distance than Americans, and do not like physical contact beyond initial handshakes. Although they are becoming less formal, they often prefer to use last names until they get to know others well. English business persons prefer formal and conservative dress. They are quite unemotional, and seemingly distant individuals. Unlike most Americans, they do not feel comfortable talking with strangers, and they generally avoid asking — and do not like being asked — personal questions.[489] United Kingdom countries continue to be rather class conscious.

It can be beneficial to establish contact with English business executives through mutual acquaintances.[490] They expect others to be punctual, but not early. They like to commence business interactions with patient small talk, using an extended Pre-

---

484. *See* Llamazares, *supra* note 369, at 224, Morrison & Conaway, *supra* note 369, at 534.
485. *See* Llamazares, *supra* note 369 at 223, Morrison & Conaway, supra note 369, at 535.
486. *See* Llamazares, *supra* note 369, at 226, Morrison & Conaway, *supra* note 369, at 537.
487. *See* Morrison & Conaway, *supra* note 369, at 537.
488. *See* Llamazares, *supra* note 369, at 225, Morrison & Conaway, *supra* note 369, at 542.
489. *See* Dawson, *supra* note 12, at 235; Morrison & Conaway, *supra* note 369, at 541.
490. *See* Llamazares, *supra* note 369, at 224, Morrison & Conaway, *supra* note 369, at 540.

liminary Stage to establish pleasant environments.[491] They tend to be impassive during initial bargaining sessions, and they are masters of understatements.[492]

UK business persons tend to have a highly individualistic style, which causes them to accept responsibility for their own actions.[493] Like Americans, they are more interested in short-term results, than in long term outcomes.[494] Although they have historically been less legalistic than Americans, they do have prescribed rules for most things and they now resort to legal proceedings more than they did in previous years.[495]

English business persons are quite direct when they interact with others in the style of low context cultures.[496] They are usually highly educated, and they like to process information in an abstract and objective fashion.[497] Although they tend to be quite time-oriented, they like to make decisions in a slow and deliberative manner.[498] It is thus important for others not to rush them when decisions have to be made.

English business representatives do not like prolonged haggling, and it can be counterproductive for others to begin with greatly exaggerated positions that will necessitate drawn out discussions.[499] They particularly dislike aggressive tactics Most English business executives consider American negotiators to be rather slick, and view them with suspicion.[500] It is thus important for American firm representatives to establish beneficial relationships during the Preliminary Stage and to avoid the use of tactics that might be considered deceptive.

K. France

France is a high context, legalistic culture, but not as high context as countries like China and Japan.[501] The French people are especially proud of their great cultures and diplomatic accomplishments and find it hard to accept their reduced stature in the international community.[502] They can be especially difficult when dealing with Americans, because they do not wish to acknowledge the superior economic and political power possessed by the U.S. today.[503] They appreciate efforts by foreign visitors to partake of their extraordinary museums and their historical achievements. During the Preliminary Stage, foreign negotiators should take the time to establish beneficial working relationships with their French counterparts, since the French appreciate

---

491. *See* Llamazares, *supra* note 369, at 224.
492. *See id.* at 224.
493. *See* Morrison & Conaway, *supra* note 369, at 538.
494. *See* Llamazares, *supra* note 369, at 225; Morrison & Conaway, *supra* note 369, at 540.
495. *See* Morrison & Conaway, *supra* note 344, at 538–539.
496. *See* Llamazares, *supra* note 369, at 225; Morrison & Conaway, *supra* note 369, at 540.
497. *See* Morrison & Conaway, *supra* note 369, at 538.
498. *See id.*, at 530.
499. *See* Llamazares, *supra* note 369, at 225.
500. *See* Dawson, *supra* note 12, at 236.
501. *See* Charles Cogan, *French Negotiating Behavior* 125–127 (2003).
502. *See id.*, at 104–105.
503. *See id.*, at 130–131.

such personal efforts.[504] Nationalistic considerations often cause French citizens who are fluent in English to refuse to converse in that language with foreigners from the United States, Canada, or England. They insist that French be spoken, through interpreters if necessary.

The French, tend to be individualistic people, but to a lesser extent than Americans.[505] They dislike overt compromise, and are well known for bargaining stalemates that continue for years due to the unwillingness of either side to make new offers.[506] They would prefer no agreement to one that may cause a loss of face or status. The French are highly analytical people who try to use unemotional logic to determine the appropriate results.[507] They appreciate presentations based on abstract principles more than displays of economic or political power. They like to initially agree upon general principles that will guide the subsequent focus on specific issues.[508] They frequently endeavor to wear down impatient counterparts through shear intransigence. They do not view bargaining as a process involving a series of distinct stages, but tend to see such interactions as a battle of wills.[509] They dislike compromise, and often make concessions at the last minute when agreement seems impossible to achieve.[510]

French advocates tend to be positional, rather than interest-based, bargainers who become enamored with their stated positions.[511] They are often accused of Boulwareistic negotiating because of the fact they begin with offers they are reluctant to modify.[512] Their frequent failure to plan fall-back positions makes it difficult for them to gracefully modify their stated bargaining positions. They are usually accepting of the status quo and work diligently to avoid significant changes in their current situations. Opposing negotiators must be extremely patient when interacting with French representatives. If they display signs of time urgency, their French counterparts are likely to take advantage of the temporal imbalance.

French administrators are highly legalistic. They exercise their authority in an abstract and impersonal manner, maintaining a safe distance from those being affected by their decisions.[513] French institutions rely on elaborate rules to govern their business relationships. In this regard, they are similar to stereotypical American government bureaucrats who like to rely on agency regulations to guide their actions.[514]

---

504. *See id.*, at 246–247.

505. *See id.*, at 44–45.

506. *See id.*, at 135–137.

507. *See id.*, at 11, 48–51; Hendon, Hendon & Herbig, *supra* note 337, at 30.

508. *See* Salacuse, *supra* note 65, at 4.

509. *See* Cogan, *supra* note 501, at 107–108.

510. *See id.*, at 152–153.

511. *See id.*, at 11–12, 120–121.

512. *See* Michael M. Harrison, "France: The Diplomacy of a Self-Assured Middle Power," in *National Negotiating Styles* 75, 88–89 (Hans Binnendijk, ed. 1987).

513. *See id.*, at 80–81.

514. *See* Cogan, *supra* note 501, at 111–115.

L. Germany

Contemporary Germany is an economically and industrially advanced nation.[515] Although the German language is rather precise, most foreign negotiators lack the fluency to negotiate in that language. Since most German business leaders are fluent in English, international business negotiations tend to take place in English. German industrial officials tend to be technologically advanced, yet pragmatic.[516] Germany is a low context culture.[517] Germans are direct in their approach to interpersonal dealings, and tend to state explicitly what they are thinking. German agents thoroughly prepare for bargaining encounters, and often surprise foreign visitors by the knowledge they possess about the company being represented by the United States representatives.[518] They expect their foreign counterparts to be equally prepared, and to be familiar with their German firms.

German negotiators like to develop comprehensive rationales to support their bargaining positions (*Gesamtkonzept*) which they use to explain the issues being addressed.[519] During their opening statements, they use the *Gesamtkonzept* to provide a detailed philosophical basis for the points they articulate.[520] Their initial positions usually reflect not only their own interests, but also those of opposing parties which they have explored during their thorough preparation. This part of the encounter can be drawn out, as the speakers exhaustively explain why they deserve what they are requesting. Individuals negotiating with Germans should be thoroughly prepared, and develop logical explanations to support the positions they take.[521] As interactions develop, they should listen carefully for verbal leaks, as the Germans often use subtle signals to indicate their receptiveness to possible position changes.

German negotiators tend to be quite formal, preferring the use of last names, instead of first names, and the use of formal titles—Herr for men and Frau for women including younger, unmarried females.[522] Foreigners speaking German should be careful to always use the formal pronoun *sie* instead of the informal pronoun *du*. Even though younger German business negotiators feel more comfortable with the use of first names, they continue to be more formal than Americans and do not like the use of nicknames. They do not like to discuss personal issues, such as family matters, with strangers.

Germans are serious negotiators who do not appreciate the use of humor by others. They are very direct when they articulate their positions, and do not like emotional arguments.[523] As the bargaining process develops, they recognize the need

---

515. *See* Hendon, Hendon & Herbig, *supra* note 337, at 148.
516 . *See id.*, at 154.
517. *See id.*, at 31, 66.
518. *See* W.R. Smyser, *How Germans Negotiate* 58–59 (2003).
519. *See id.*, at 60.
520. *See id.*, at 72–73.
521. *See id.*, at 200–202.
522. *See id.*, at 107.
523. *See id.*, at 82–83.

to make concessions, but work to maintain positions that are consistent with the underlying *Gesamtkonzept*.[524] They thus provide highly principled explanations for their position changes, and they appreciate counterparts who provide overarching rationales to support their own positions. They tend to negotiate deliberately to be certain they do not make inappropriate position changes.[525] They can be gracious hosts during social events, but they do not like to conduct bargaining discussions during such occasions.[526]

Decision-making in German companies tends to be hierarchal and centralized.[527] It is thus important for foreign negotiators to develop contacts with top level officials while inter-firm negotiations are being conducted. Once tentative agreements are achieved, they will be scrutinized by higher executives who must give their approval before they become final. If appropriate relationships have already been established, this process should go smoothly. Germans are precise people who prefer legalistic and detailed contracts.[528]

German firms are substantially unionized and have codetermination laws which require larger companies to consult with worker representatives both at the corporate board level and at the plant level with respect to matters of interest to employees.[529] Workers are rarely laid off except for proper business reasons. Foreign investors who wish to establish joint ventures with German corporations must consider these factors before they decide to enter into commitments that will necessarily create long-range obligations.

Germans tend to be tough bargainers.[530] They focus on specific terms and attempt to obtain agreements that favor their companies. Foreign representatives must be prepared for competitive interactions, and individuals who fail to heed this admonition are likely to leave with inferior agreements.

M. Saudi Arabia

Saudi Arabia is an important nation because it possesses one of the world's largest oil reserves and it produces more oil than any other members of the Organization of Petroleum Exporting Countries (OPEC).[531] It is a high context culture in which people try to avoid open confrontations. As a result, they are not always open about their actual thoughts.[532] They place a premium on appearances and the maintenance of a favorable social image. They are formal people who prefer to address individuals by

---

524. *See id.*, at 85–86.

525. *See id.*, at 112.

526. *See id.*, at 117–119.

527. *See id.*, at 121–22; Hendon, Hendon & Herbig, *supra* note 337, at 156.

528. *See* Hendon, Hendon & Herbig, *supra* note 337, at 113.

529. *See id.*, at 157.

530. *See id.*, at 155–156.

531. *See id.*, at 165. *See also* Llamazares, *supra* note 369, at 170.

532. *See id.*, at 175.

their titles.[533] They can be expansive people who often speak in raised voices, and frequently gesticulate with their hands.[534]

Saudi Arabians are greatly influenced by family ties, their Islamic religion, and the House of Saud.[535] They maintain close family relationships, and often conduct business through various relatives. It is important for foreign negotiators to take the time to establish beneficial relationships that will continue for many years.[536] It is helpful to obtain introductions from local agents with close ties to the families with whom you wish to do business. Since it is considered extremely rude to display the bottom of one's foot to another in Saudi Arabia, foreigners should never sit with the soles of their shoes exposed to others.[537] Women have historically been limited in their access to education and business positions without the express approval of their guardians, but these practices have been changing. Many women now study abroad, and a number have been allowed to work in the business world.

The Saudis believe that their Muslim religion provides them with a comprehensive guide to govern their personal and business lives. The words of the Prophet Muhammad are set forth in the Koran, and they consult this document for guidance on most important questions.[538] Most Muslims pray five times per day, and businesses are closed during these periods. Persons wishing to conduct business with Saudi business and government leaders should be careful not to propose anything that would be contrary to Islamic principles.

Muslim cultures frequently use the past as the standard to guide present decisions.[539] They tend not to function on "clock time" as do most Western negotiators. They do not consider it rude to show up late for appointments, and they do not like to rush the decision-making process. It is thus critical for foreign negotiators to be patient. They should not berate Saudi negotiators who show up late for meetings,[540] nor should they seek to generate expeditious decisions. The more significant the issues to be resolved, the more protracted the discussions tend to be.

Muslims believe that future events are within the hands of Allah. It is thus beneficial not to indicate that future occurrences are controlled by the negotiating parties themselves. Muslims regularly use the phrase "in sha'a Allah" [God willing] when they talk about what might happen in the future to show respect for Allah's control over such occurrences.[541] They thus appreciate it when foreign negotiators respect their Muslim heritage and suggest that future developments will take place "God willing."

---

533. *See* Acuff, *supra* note 333, at 287.

534. *See id.* at 288. *See also* Llamazares, *supra* note 369, at 171.

535. *See* Hendon, Hendon & Herbig, *supra* note 337, at 167–170.

536. *See* I. Alon & J. Brett, "Perceptions of Time and Their Impact on Negotiations in the Arab-Speaking Islamic World," 23 *Negotiation Journal* 55, 60–61 (2007).

537. *See* Morrison & Conaway, *supra* note 369, at 435; Acuff, *supra* note 308, at 288.

538. *See* Hendon, Hendon & Herbig, *supra* note 337, at 168.

539. *See* Alon & Brett, *supra* note 536, at 64.

540. *See* Morrison & Conaway, *supra* note 369, at 432.

541. *See id.*, at 66–67.

One other factor that causes consternation among Western negotiators is the fact that Saudi Arabians following the ancient teachings of Muhammad believe that it is contrary to Islamic law to conduct business on credit.[542] They often characterize sales transactions in different terms to avoid the appearance of credit, even though credit is effectively being extended. It behooves foreign negotiators to accept these formulations if they wish to consummate the deals being discussed.

The House of Saud has ruled Saudi Arabia for many decades.[543] Family members occupy positions throughout government agencies. Since Saudi Arabia has a centralized decision-making process, House of Saud members tend to exercise influence over most significant business transactions. It is important for foreigners to establish personal relationships with House of Saud members, whenever possible. These family members respect personal integrity, and place great faith in their own impressions of others.

Bargaining with Saudi Arabians traditionally commenced with inflated demands, followed by a series of ritualistic concessions,[544] but more modern Saudis tend to begin with more modest positions. Patience is especially important, because it takes time for the negotiation process to unfold. Apparent deadlines are frequently ignored. Saudis have historically maintained an open door policy for business partners, and they are often visited by outsiders when conducting significant business negotiations with others.[545] It is not unusual for Saudis to conduct independent negotiations with different parties simultaneously.

Once Saudi Arabians reach agreement, many confirm it orally or with a handshake,[546] but increasing numbers draft written agreements in the Western style. They do not like lengthy and detailed contracts, which they view as a sign of distrust. As a result, their accords tend to contain general language that does not precisely define the actual terms agreed upon. They generally expect international accords to be expressed in both English and Arabic.

The Saudi Arabian government requires foreign firms to either have partnership relationships with Saudi companies or be represented by local commercial agents.[547] Many transnational arrangements have to receive government approval. It is quite common for "facilitation fees" to be paid to expedite the processing of government approval requests. While United States corporate leaders may fear that these payments would contravene the Foreign Corrupt Practices Act, there is little evidence to suggest that these payments are intended as corrupting bribes.[548] As mere facilitation payments, they are outside the scope of the FCPA.

---

542. *See id.*, at 65.
543. *See* Hendon, Hendon & Herbig, *supra* note 337, at 169.
544. *See* Acuff, *supra* note 333, at 289.
545. *See* Morrison & Conaway, *supra* note 369, at 432; Hendon, Hendon & Herbig, *supra* note 337, at 175.
546. *See id.*, at 173.
547. *See id.*, at 176.
548. *See id.*, at 179.

N. Egypt

Egyptians are part of a high context culture. They are understandably proud of their great history and culture, viewing themselves as the cradle of civilization.[549] Egyptians value personal and national honor, with these concepts being important in their interpersonal dealings. Egyptians consider themselves an economically advanced people, and resent being treated as citizens from another third-world Arab country.

Egypt has been an independent Arab nation that has demonstrated a willingness to break with Arab unity to advance its own national interests.[550] On the other hand, it considers itself to be an important part of the Arab world, with a predominantly Muslim population. Egypt has a pharaonic tradition of strong leaders who are empowered to act without consultation with others. If others can convince Egyptian officials that certain agreements would be in their nation's interest, it is often easy to obtain binding commitments pertaining to future relations.

Egypt has a history of entrenched and overlapping bureaucracies that must be satisfied before certain actions can be approved.[551] The administrative approval process is complicated and protracted. Even Egyptian leaders find it difficult to gain bureaucratic consent to proposed action that requires administrative acceptance. Foreigners frequently use back channel contacts with governmental leaders to circumvent foreign ministry delays. The assistance of presidential aides can be especially helpful in this regard. Private intermediaries may also be employed to facilitate the approval process.

Egypt is greatly affected by problems associated with over-population, decreasing natural resources, and an aging and deteriorating infrastructure.[552] Although it has often been dependent on assistance from foreign powers, it still remembers the British colonialism that limited Egyptian freedom throughout the first half of the twentieth century. Egyptian leaders are thus careful to avoid international entanglements that may infringe on their country's national sovereignty.

Egyptian negotiators continue to be influenced by tribal traditions that encourage preliminary posturing, ritualistic confrontation, and lofty rhetoric.[553] These stages are then followed by face-saving arrangements that are designed to preserve the honor of all participants. They tend to begin bargaining interactions with elaborate ritual — formal coffee and tea — intended to permit the establishment of personal relationships.[554] It is important for foreign negotiators to graciously accept this generous hospitality to create a beneficial atmosphere of trust and cooperation. Egyptians resent the rudeness and impatience exhibited by many foreign bargainers, especially those from the United States.

---

549. *See* William B. Quandt, "Egypt: A Strong Sense of National Identity," in *National Negotiating Styles* 105 (Hans Binnendijk, ed. 1987).

550. *See id.*, at 106–107.

551. *See* Cohen, *supra* note 353, at 100; Quandt, *supra* note 549, at 107–108.

552. *See* Quandt, *supra* note 549, at 109–110.

553. *See id.*, at 118–119.

554. *See* Cohen, *supra* note 353, at 86–87.

Egyptian advocates usually begin with extreme positions and anticipate prolonged haggling as the parties attempt to ascertain each other's true needs and interests.[555] They like to rely on seemingly neutral principles to support their claims. Impatient counterparts frequently pay a high price for their unwillingness to permit the process to develop in a deliberate manner. They are unable to discern the true interests of their Egyptian adversaries and often make unnecessarily large concessions in an effort to achieve expeditious accords. When progress is not being made, Egyptian negotiators may request assistance from respected intermediaries.

Final deals are usually expressed in general terms. This allows Egyptian representatives to make subsequent demands for additional concessions as the parties are forced to clarity "ambiguities" that are discovered in their agreements. This device can be minimized through the negotiation of specific contractual provisions. When this technique does not prevent post-contract renegotiating, foreign advocates should be sure to request reciprocal concessions from Egyptian representatives as prerequisites to acceptance of their demands for changed conditions.

§ 12.07. Conclusion

As communication and transportation systems have created a global political and economic world, the extent and importance of private and public international negotiations have increased. Although national and transnational bargaining interactions have many similarities, language and cultural differences become important, and stereotypical impressions may influence interactions.

Inter-governmental negotiations ("Track I Diplomacy") may be conducted through formal channels or through informal back channels, and may involve bilateral or multilateral interactions. Multilateral interactions tend to be conducted under the auspices of existing international organizations (*e.g.*, the United Nations) — which may define the issues and specify the procedures to be followed — and voting blocs may be used by weaker nations to enhance their bargaining power. Private individuals and non-governmental institutions are becoming increasingly involved in foreign political controversies, with such "Track II Diplomacy" being employed where formal governmental participation may not be acceptable to the affected parties.

With the development of a global economic system, the frequency of transnational business negotiating has greatly increased, forcing American firm representatives to become better acquainted with foreign cultures and foreign negotiating styles. Even though individual negotiating styles vary greatly even among people from the same background, it is beneficial when first interacting with foreign counterparts to study their national cultures and their traditional negotiating styles.

---

555. *See* Quandt, *supra* note 549, at 119–120.

Chapter 13

Dispute Resolution Procedures

Many persons think of dispute resolution procedures as tools employed by lawyers and clients to help parties resolve legal disputes. Although mediation and arbitration systems have been established by federal and most state courts to decrease the need for adjudications, these methods can also be of significant assistance to business people when they endeavor to establish new relationships or deal with difficulties arising under existing relationships.

When individuals are seeking to purchase or sell businesses, structure licensing agreements, buy or sell goods or services, develop joint ventures, and generate other similar arrangements, they may encounter some bargaining difficulties. Neither side may want to initiate the requisite discussions for fear of appearing too eager. Once the talks have commenced, the parties generally over and under state the value of different terms for strategic purposes. They endeavor to hide their weaknesses and exaggerate their strengths. As a result, the bargaining parties may either find it impossible to achieve any agreement, or they may agree to terms that are inefficient due to the fact that different items ended up on the wrong side of the bargaining table.

It can be highly beneficial for transactional negotiators to employ the services of neutral facilitators to help those persons initiate interactions and to assist them with their discussions. A party wishing to structure a deal with another firm could ask a neutral third person to suggest to both sides the possibility of mutually beneficial talks. This would allow the relevant individuals to commence their interaction without either appearing to be the initiator. As the discussions unfold and the participants encounter substantive difficulties, the mediator could help them to explore options that might prove to be mutually beneficial. Once they are able to achieve tentative agreements, the neutral facilitator would further work to insure that they have agreed to terms that maximize their joint returns. When disagreements arise regarding the interpretation of specified terms, the parties can also employ neutral facilitators to help them resolve their conflicts.

Business persons need to understand the role of neutral facilitators, so they can properly prepare themselves and their principals for mediation sessions and maximize the benefits to be derived from third-party intervention. They must familiarize themselves with the styles and techniques employed by successful conciliators. This will enable them to understand which types of neutral to use, and know what they should be doing during mediated sessions.

§ 13.01. Mediation as Assisted Negotiation

The inability of negotiators to achieve mutual accommodations of their competing interests does not necessarily mean that they are better off with no agreements. Inexperienced participants may have failed to initiate the negotiation process. Each side could have simply been waiting for the other to broach the subject. One or both parties may have employed disingenuous tactics that discouraged counterparts. One or both may have over or under stated what they required to attain mutual accords. The participants may have reached unyielding positions that neither could modify without appearing weak and losing face. Communication channels may have been disrupted because of the intense pressure on the participants. This disruption could have caused parties to ignore areas of potential overlap. Cultural differences may have generated personal misunderstandings due to different communication approaches, different value systems, different group orientations, and other similar factors.[556] If their bargaining deficiencies could be alleviated, the participants might realize that negotiated arrangements would still be preferable to non-settlements.

A significant consideration involves the concern of some experts that women and minorities who have traditionally lacked economic and social equality might be at a disadvantage when participating in dispute resolution procedures compared to Caucasian males.[557] Subtle biases might cause such persons to accept settlement terms that are less beneficial than they economically and psychologically deserve. Recent empirical studies have found, however, that women and minorities are able to negotiate as effectively as their white male counterparts.[558] Most contemporary mediators are aware of this concern, and they endeavor to advance the interests of all parties on an equal basis.

Parties afraid that conciliators may impose unwanted terms on them do not understand the mediation process. Mediators lack the authority to dictate agreements. They are merely empowered to *assist* parties with *their own* negotiations.[559] While neutral intervenors may enhance communication and help advocates develop innovative alternatives not previously considered, the final authority always rests with the parties. They must consent to any proposed arrangements. No matter how diligently mediators seek to encourage agreements, clients always control their own final destinies.[560]

---

556. *See generally* Michael LeBaron, *Bridging Cultural Conflicts* (2003).

557. *See* Richard Delgado, "Fairness and Formality: Minimizing the Risk of Prejudice in Alternative Dispute Resolution," 1985 *Wisconsin Law Review* 1359 (1985).

558. *See* Charles B. Craver, "Do Alternative Dispute Resolution Procedures Disadvantage Women and Minorities?" 70 *Southern Methodist University Law Review* 891 (2017).

559. *See* Robert A. Baruch Bush & Joseph P. Folger, *The Promise of Mediation* 2–3 (1994); Robert A. Baruch Bush & Joseph P. Folger, *The Promise of Mediation* 8 (2d ed. 2005) (primarily a response to evaluations of concepts set forth in first edition).

560. *See* Robert M. Ackerman, "Disputing Together: Conflict Resolution and the Search for Community," 18 *Ohio State Journal on Dispute* Resolution 27, 75–78 (2002); Stephen K. Erickson & Marilyn S. McKnight, *The Practitioner's Guide to Mediation* 205, 216–217 (2001).

Firm representatives should recognize that mediation is essentially ***assisted negotiation***.[561] Conciliators effectively employ bargaining skills to facilitate inter-party negotiating and encourage the attainment of mutual accords.[562] The negotiation stages and techniques remain the same, but the interaction becomes more complex due to the participation of neutral intervenors. The representatives must negotiate with the mediator, through the mediator with each other, directly with each other, and with their own principals—who may decide to interact directly with each other or with the mediator. Nonetheless, the parties continue to exchange ideas and proposals, as they were previously doing alone, and the advocates retain control over any final terms agreed upon.

Successful conciliation efforts can significantly enhance the psychological wellbeing of negotiating parties. Mutually beneficial agreements avoid the anxiety, trauma, and uncertainty associated with the premature breakdown of transactional discussions. More importantly, mediated solutions enable the parties to participate directly in the formulation of their own final arrangements.[563] Mutually developed results are generally preferable to terms imposed on people through external factors such as market constraints and judicial determinations.

An additional psychological factor concerns the degree to which parties believe that conciliation procedures have been fair.[564] The more the participants feel their voices have been heard and valued, and their underlying interests have been fairly considered, the more pleased they tend to be with the overall process and the final accords that are achieved.[565] It is thus crucial for neutral facilitators to treat all parties with respect and dignity, and to make sure everyone feels they had the opportunity to fully express their viewpoints and to be heard. Even at the conclusion of the discussions, it can be beneficial to ask the participants if there is anything else they would like to say. They usually have nothing to add, but seem pleased to have been asked.

Bargaining parties often lock themselves into unyielding "principled" positions and refuse to consider objectively the proposals being propounded by counterparts.[566] Adept conciliators can frequently induce these individuals to reconsider their own underlying needs and interests and to more realistically evaluate the proposals being suggested by their counterparts.[567] This phenomenon significantly enhances the likelihood of negotiated solutions.

---

561. *See* Harold Abramson, *Mediation Representation* 67 (2004).

562. *See* Kimberlee K. Kovach, *Mediation: Principles and Practice* 26–27 (2004); Linda Singer, *Settling Disputes* 79–80 (1994).

563. *See generally* Ackerman, *supra* note 561.

564. *See* David A. Hoffman, "Mediation, Multiple Minds, and Managing the Negotiation Within," 16 *Harvard Negotiation Law Review* 297, 321 (2011); Nancy Welsh, "Remembering the Role of Justice in Resolution: Insights From Procedural and Social Justice Theories," 54 *Journal of Legal Education* 49, 52–53 (2004).

565. *See* Keith Allred, "Relationship Dynamics in Disputes," in *The Handbook of Dispute Resolution* 83, 90–92 (Michael L. Moffitt & Robert C. Bordone, eds. 2005).

566. *See* Gary L. Kaplan, *Executive Guide to Managing Disputes* 26–40 (2009).

567. *See* Michael Watkins & Susan Rosegrant, *Breakthrough in International Negotiation* 91–92

Corporate officers discussing possible business transactions often terminate their interactions prematurely. If their articulated positions are far apart, they begin to think that no agreement is likely and they look for other opportunities. They focus so intently on their areas of disagreement that they fail to discern areas of possible joint gain.[568] With the assistance of skilled mediators, they may begin to appreciate the areas of positional overlap and how their areas of conflict may be transformed into mutually beneficial arrangements.[569] It should not take long for effective conciliators to induce seemingly deadlocked transactional negotiators to explore their joint interests. In many instances, these efforts will enable pessimistic participants to achieve beneficial business arrangements they never thought possible. Mediation efforts can also assist business partners who have decided to dissolve their relationships.[570]

§ 13.02. Different Mediator Styles

Proficient mediators tend to possess common characteristics no matter what styles they employ.[571] They are objective individuals who are cognizant of their own biases. They have excellent communication skills — *i.e.*, they are both good, empathetic listeners and assertive speakers. They are adept readers of nonverbal signals. They have good interpersonal skills that enable them to interact well with people from diverse backgrounds and different personalities.[572] They understand the negotiation process and the way in which conciliators can enhance that process. They can even modify their usual styles when particular dispute circumstances suggest the need for a different approach. The introduction of an individual with these skills to an otherwise stalemated negotiation can be of great benefit.

Both neutrals and business representatives must recognize that mediator personalities directly influence intervenor behavior. Since mediators lack the authority to impose final terms on parties, they must rely upon their powers of persuasion and their reputations for impartiality and fairness to encourage mutual accords.[573] Neutral intervenors should not merely emulate the styles employed by other people. If they copy the behavior used by individuals with different personalities, they are likely to experience discomfort and ineffectiveness. Naturally aggressive individuals tend to feel most comfortable with relatively assertive mediation techniques, while laid back people tend to prefer low key approaches. Neutrals must candidly evaluate the manner

---

(2001).

568. *See* F. Bannink, "Solution-Focused Mediation: The Future With a Difference," 25 *Conflict Resolution Quarterly* 163, 167 (2007).

569. *See* Peter D. Ladd, *Mediation, Conciliation, and Emotions* 18–19 (2005).

570. *See* James C. Freund, "Anatomy of a Split-Up: Mediating the Business Divorce," 52 *The Business Lawyer* 479 (1997).

571. *See* Abraham P. Ordover & Andrea Doneff, *Alternatives to Litigation* 54–55 (2002); Erickson & McKnight, *supra* note 560, at 144–145, 198–201); *see generally* Laurence J. Boulle, Michael T. Colatrella & Anthony P. Picchioni, *Mediation: Skills and Techniques* (2008).

572. *See generally* Jeffrey Krivis, *Improvisational Negotiation* (2006).

573. *See* Rubin & Brown, *supra* note 59, at 62.

in which others have traditionally responded to them and develop mediative styles consistent with those assessments. Once they find an approach they feel comfortable using, mediators should try to maintain a consistent style that parties can anticipate when they retain their services. Neutrals who exhibit erratic behavior are unlikely to generate client confidence.

Mediators tend to employ one of three diverse styles.[574] Most mediators are facilitative/elicitive. They seek to reopen blocked communication channels and to encourage direct inter-party negotiations that will enable the parties to formulate their own final terms. Other neutral facilitators focus primarily on the substantive terms being discussed. They try to determine the provisions they think the parties will jointly accept and work to induce the participants to agree to the packages they have formulated. An innovative group of conciliators are relationship-oriented. They endeavor to empower the participants and generate mutual respect that will enhance the ability of disputants to solve their own problems. These styles are not always distinct and separate, with many competent mediators behaving in a facilitative, evaluative, or transformative manner when they think the particular circumstances warrant such behavior.[575]

A. Facilitative/Elicitive Mediators

Facilitative/elicitive mediators attempt to regenerate party-to-party discussions to enable the participants to structure their own deals.[576] They believe that temporary bargaining impasses are the result of communication breakdowns and/or unrealistic expectations. They work to reopen communication channels and to induce negotiating parties to reevaluate the reasonableness of their respective positions. They use questions in an elicitive manner to generate position reconsiderations and to induce parties to explore new areas. Once facilitative/elicitive intervenors generate meaningful bargaining exchanges, they let the parties determine what is best for themselves. They like to use joint meetings during which the parties engage in face-to-face bargaining. Separate sessions are reserved for crisis intervention when the disputants are unable to talk directly to one another.[577] These conciliators function like orchestra leaders.

Communication between facilitative/elicitive mediators and advocates is designed to reestablish inter-party discussions. The following dialogue is typical of the exchanges one might observe during separate caucus sessions:

---

574. *See* Michael Leathers, *Negotiation: Things Corporate Counsel Need to Know But Were Not Taught* 156–157 (2017); Bush & Folger (2005), *supra* note 559; Peter D. Ladd, *Mediation, Conciliation, and Emotions* 30–31 (2005).

575. *See* H. Jay Folberg & Dwight Golann, *Lawyer Negotiation Theory, Practice, and Law* 298–299 (2011); Dorothy J. Della Noce, "Evaluative Mediation: In Search of Practice Competencies," 27 *Conflict Resolution Quarterly* 193, 195, 202–205 (2009).

576. *See* Michael L. Moffitt & Andrea Kupfer Schneider, *Dispute Resolution* 85–86 (2011).

577. *See* Deborah Kolb *The Mediators*, 46–47 (1983).

MEDIATOR (to Negotiator A): You appear to be making significant progress. Both sides appear to be favorably disposed toward Items P and Q. How do you feel about these developments?

NEGOTIATOR A: While we could live with Items P and Q, we would prefer to obtain Item X or Y.

MEDIATOR: Would you be willing to give up Item P or Q if you could get X or Y?

NEGOTIATOR A: We certainly would.

MEDIATOR: Would you be willing to reconsider your prior refusal to move with respect to Items R and S if necessary to obtain Item X or Y?

NEGOTIATOR A: If we had to. We would prefer to exchange Item P or Q for X or Y, but would reassess our position on Items R and S if need be.

* * *

MEDIATOR (to Negotiator B): We appear to have agreement with respect to Items P and Q. How do you feel about this?

NEGOTIATOR B: Okay, but we would prefer to explore Items R and S more thoroughly before we finalize any agreement.

MEDIATOR: Would you be willing to trade Item P or Q for Item R or S?

NEGOTIATOR B: Yes.

MEDIATOR: I'm not sure whether Side A would be amenable to any reconsideration of Items R and S—unless you would be willing to reassess your view regarding Items X and Y. Would you do so if necessary to get movement on Items R and S?

NEGOTIATOR B: We should probably stay with Items P and Q, and contemplate mutual exchanges involving Items R and/or S for Items X and/or Y.

Facilitative/elicitive mediators are especially appreciated by proficient negotiators who want minimal bargaining assistance and wish to control their own bargaining outcomes.

B. Evaluative/Directive Mediators

Evaluative/directive mediators are typically used to interacting with relatively inexperienced negotiators who have difficulty achieving their own agreements.[578] They tend to encounter negotiators who either do not know how to initiate meaningful negotiations or are unable to explore the different issues in a manner likely to generate mutual accords. As a result, evaluative/directive neutrals feel the need to control the bargaining interactions they encounter. During the 1960s and 1970s, following the enactment of various public sector labor relations statutes giving government em-

---

578. *See* Moffitt & Schneider, *supra* note 576, at 86–87.

ployees the right to engage in collective bargaining, it was common to encounter evaluative/directive mediators who thought they had to direct the negotiations being conducted by inexperienced advocates.

Transactions conducted by evaluative/directive mediators tend to resemble parent-child interactions. The "parent"-like neutrals attempt to ascertain the needs and interests of the "child"-like participants so they can tell those individuals what they *should* accept. These mediators determine the substantive terms they believe would best resolve the underlying controversy and use a directive style to persuade the parties to accept their proposed provisions. When parties object to their suggestions, evaluative/directive mediators try to convince the parties that the proposed terms are the best they can achieve. They consider themselves "deal makers" who must decide what is best for the parties. They prefer to use separate sessions during which they probe underlying party needs and work to convince the participants to accept the terms they have formulated.

Most of the communication between evaluative/directive mediators and negotiators is one-sided — carefully controlled by the neutral intervenors. Typical exchanges during separate caucus sessions conducted during the latter stages of interactions may be seen in the following dialogues:

MEDIATOR (to Negotiator A): I have been able to determine what is acceptable to both sides. I think Side B can live with Items P and Q, but definitely not with Items X or Y.

NEGOTIATOR A: We were hoping to obtain Item X or Y, even if we had to give up Item P or Q or reconsider our prior rejection of Items R and S.

MEDIATOR: I understand your concerns, but must emphasize the need for you to recognize the realities of the situation. You are fortunate that I have been able to get you Items P and Q. That was not easily accomplished. If you insist on Item X or Y, I'm certain the whole deal will unravel. Would you prefer to lose everything at this point?

NEGOTIATOR A: If I could meet with Negotiator B and directly raise these concerns, perhaps I could convince him/her of our significant interest in Items X and Y.

MEDIATOR: Don't you understand how diligently I have worked to explore these issues with Negotiator B? If these items were available, I would certainly have sought to get them for you. If you seek joint negotiations pertaining to Items X and Y, the great progress we have made will be lost.

* * *

MEDIATOR (to Negotiator B): After lengthy discussions with both sides, have come to the conclusion that the parties can jointly agree upon Items P and Q. Any effort to modify these terms would be likely to destroy everything.

NEGOTIATOR B: During our earlier discussions, I got the impression that Side A might be amenable to an exchange that would give us either Item R or S. We might even be willing to reevaluate our position regarding Items X and Y if necessary. Don't you think we should explore these possibilities further?

MEDIATOR: I do not. It was an arduous process to find the common ground with respect to Items P and Q. If you insist on further talks involving Items R and S—and X and Y—I think the negotiations will stalemate. Please remember how hard I have worked to protect your interests. Do you want to risk a non-settlement at this crucial point?

NEGOTIATOR B: I wish we could explore these other issues more fully, but I appreciate your concern. I guess we'll have to live with what you've been able to get for us.

Empirical studies have found that disputants who settle controversies with the assistance of evaluative/directive mediators often feel they have been denied "procedural justice" even if the substantive terms are fair.[579] They have not had the opportunity to express their underlying feelings and be heard by the mediator and their counterparts. They also feel disrespected by the undignified process imposed upon them.

Parties that are uncertain regarding the appropriate way in which to achieve negotiated agreements and who desire substantive guidance from experienced intervenors may appreciate the assistance provided by evaluative/directive conciliators. They should carefully select substantive experts who are likely to understand their particular interests. In the end, these mediators are going to directly influence the actual terms agreed upon. Individuals who prefer to control their own destinies do not usually feel comfortable with such evaluative/directive intervention.[580]

C. Relationship-Oriented/Transformative Mediators

In their thoughtful book, Robert Baruch Bush and Joseph Folger discuss a novel approach to mediation.[581] They reject evaluative/directive and facilitative/elicitive intervention in favor of a relationship-oriented/transformative approach that is designed to transform disputants into relatively self-sufficient problem solvers. They believe that mediators should strive to empower weaker parties by demonstrating the rights and options available to the participants through settlement and non-settlement op-

---

579. *See* Nancy Welsh, "Making Deals in Court-Connected Mediation: What's Justice Got to Do With It?" 79 *Washington University Law Quarterly* 787, 851–853 (2001).

580. *See* Nancy Welsh, "Reconciling Self-Determination, Coercion, and Settlement in Court Connected Mediation," in *Divorce and Family Mediation: Models, Techniques, and Applications* 420, 427 (H. Jay Folberg, Ann L. Milne & Peter Salem, eds. 2004).

581. *See* Bush & Folger (1994), *supra* note 559.

tions, and to generate mutual respect among the competing parties.[582] They contend that empowered participants who truly appreciate the interests and viewpoints of their counterparts can optimally work to achieve their own mutually acceptable solutions. Even when immediate agreements are not attained during relationship-oriented intervention, Bush and Folger maintain that empowered parties will be better able to handle future bargaining interactions due to their new found problem-solving skills.[583]

Unlike evaluative/directive and facilitative/elicitive mediators who are particularly interested in resolution of the underlying disputes, relationship-oriented/transformative conciliators are primarily interested in future party relationships. While they are pleased when their efforts generate current agreements, they prefer to help disputants understand how they can effectively resolve their own future controversies. To accomplish this objective, relationship-oriented/transformative intervenors focus on two basic issues—party *empowerment* and inter-party *recognition*. They endeavor to show each side that it possesses the power to order its future relationships even if they do not reach an agreement with respect to the current matter. They simultaneously attempt to generate inter-party empathy by inducing each side to appreciate the feelings and perspectives of their adversaries.

A study of professional mediators in Israel found some interesting gender differences with respect to mediator styles. Female mediators were more likely to prefer a more facilitative and transformative approach than their male cohorts who tended to favor a more directive style.[584] Nonetheless, both male and female mediators considered more important the opportunity to help disputing parties achieve final agreements that would enable them to end their conflicts. These findings would suggest that while female mediators may employ more transformative techniques and male mediators may be more directive, both tend to use these somewhat different styles to generate final agreements.

Exchanges between relationship-oriented/transformative mediators and advocates are quite different from those involving facilitative/elicitive and evaluative/directive neutrals. Instead of focusing primarily on the bargaining process, as do facilitative/elicitive neutrals, or substantive issues, as do evaluative/directive mediators, these innovative intervenors focus on the disputants themselves. They attempt to encourage participant deliberations and decision-making. They try to demonstrate to emotionally drained and dispirited parties that they have options they can pursue if negotiations do not prove fruitful. Typical empowerment and recognition exchanges involving relationship-oriented/transformative mediators might include:

582. *See* Richard McGuigan & Nancy Popp, "The Self in Conflict: The Evolution of Mediation," 25 *Conflict Resolution Quarterly* 221 (2007).

583. *See* Bush & Folger (2005), *supra* note 559, at 22–39; Bush & Folger (1994), *supra* note 559, at 200–201.

584. *See* Noa Nelson, Adi Zarankin & Rachel Ben-Ari, "Transformative Women, Problem-Solving Men? Not Quite: Gender and Mediators' Perceptions of Mediation," 26 *Negotiation Journal* 287, 302 (2010); *see also* Long Charkoudian & Ellen Wayne, "Fairness, Understanding, and Satisfaction: Impact of Mediator and Participant Race and Gender on Participants' Perception of Mediation," 28 *Conflict Resolution Quarterly* 23, 26–27 (2010) (suggesting the same gender differences in the U.S.).

MEDIATOR (to Negotiator A): We've discussed how the parties might resolve their underlying differences. You do not appear to be entirely satisfied with the proposals suggested by Side B. What other issues would you like to have addressed? How would you like to have them resolved?

NEGOTIATOR A: I feel as if I must reach an agreement with Side B or else. I don't believe Side B is being fair to me. They seem to think they can force me to accept anything they offer. They don't care about my feelings regarding this matter.

MEDIATOR: Side B cannot force you to accept anything. You always have the right to walk away from these talks if you do not like the way they are progressing. If you are unable to reach an agreement with Side B, what other options would be available to you? What could you do on your own to limit the impact of the current controversy?

* * *

MEDIATOR (to Negotiator A): Why do you think Side B has behaved the way it has? What do you think are Side B's concerns here? If you were in Side B's shoes, what would you be trying to achieve through these negotiations?

* * *

MEDIATOR (to Negotiator B): Side A is not satisfied with the way these talks are progressing. Why do you think Side A is upset? What are their concerns? If you were in Side A's situation, what would you expect to achieve from these negotiations?

Many facilitative/elicitive mediators believe that they work to preserve inter-party relationships when they perform their usual conciliation functions. As they attempt to enhance the negotiation process and create optimal problem-solving environments, they simultaneously endeavor to respect party empowerment. They truly wish to assist parties to structure their own agreements, and this objective can most effectively be accomplished if the participants believe they possess the power to influence the final terms agreed upon. Parties that feel impotent lack the capacity to negotiate meaningfully, and they feel they are being forced to accept the provisions proposed by their counterparts or recommended by the mediators. This result would not please facilitative/elicitive neutrals who hope to encourage joint problem-solving.

Facilitative/elicitive mediators recognize that most negotiated agreements require future party interaction as the participants effectuate the terms of their arrangements. If the parties do not have sufficient mutual trust and respect, problems are likely to arise. Dissatisfied individuals may attempt to undermine the terms agreed upon.

People who feel a lack of counterpart respect may attempt to evade contractual obligations in an effort to retaliate against their disrespectful adversaries.

Facilitative/elicitive mediators differ from Bush/Folger relationship-oriented/ transformative neutrals in one critical respect. They would prefer to generate final agreements than to merely preserve inter-party relationships. While relationship-oriented/ transformative intervenors would rather forego agreements if necessary to enhance party empowerment and recognition, facilitative/elicitive mediators would place final accords ahead of empowerment and respect. This is why Bush and Folger maintain that mediators cannot function as facilitative/elicitive and relationship-oriented/ transformative intervenors simultaneously.

§ 13.03. Timing of Initial Mediation Intervention

The timing of initial mediation efforts can be crucial. If neutral intervention occurs prematurely, the parties may be unreceptive. They may not even be sufficiently prepared to participate meaningfully in mediation sessions. On the other hand, if conciliatory attempts begin in a belated manner, the parties may be locked into unyielding positions that would be difficult to alter. Business parties are usually able to initiate bargaining discussions. If talks are progressing well, there may be no need for mediative assistance. Nonetheless, if problems are encountered, the parties should acknowledge the benefits that may be derived from neutral intervention. Too often, business firms that are unable to achieve mutual accords on their own give up and walk away. If they continue to believe that mutually beneficial deals could be structured, they should not hesitate to request mediative assistance.

What functions could transactional mediators perform?[585] They could assist parties to reopen blocked communication channels. They could obtain confidential information the parties would not be willing to share directly with each other, enabling the neutral facilitators to look for ways to optimize joint gains. To avoid the impact of "reactive devaluation" when proposals are advanced by interested participants, mediators could suggest terms they think might be mutually beneficial. When emotional conflicts arise, the neutral persons could reframe difficult issues to neutralize their impact and help the parties preserve their relationships.

When transactional discussions are not fruitful, the parties should not wait until a complete cessation of talks before they ask for neutral intervention. Once unyielding final positions are reached, the parties are likely to give up on the current negotiations and contemplate discussions with other business partners. It thus behooves business negotiators to seek mediative help *before* they become wholly unreceptive to further discussions.

---

585. *See* Scott Peppet, "Contract Formation in Imperfect Markets: Should We Use Mediators in Deals?," 19 *Ohio State Journal on Dispute Resolution* (2004).

§ 13.04. Mediator Selection

When negotiating parties seek the assistance of neutral intervenors, they should carefully evaluate the type of mediation assistance they desire.[586] Do they want the help of a facilitative/elicitive neutral, an evaluative/directive neutral, or a relationship-oriented/transformative neutral? Individuals who wish to control their own interactions — but who feel a strong need to achieve agreements — would probably prefer a facilitative/elicitive style that provides bargaining assistance but permits the parties to determine their own final terms.[587] These parties do not want mediators who try to dictate terms. They instead wish to obtain the assistance of individuals who merely enhance the bargaining process through an elicitive approach.

Parties who are inexperienced negotiators and have difficulty with the give-and-take inherent in the bargaining process may appreciate the assistance of evaluative/directive mediators.[588] These neutrals can take charge of the interactions and steer the discussions in the appropriate direction. If directive neutrals are to be used, it is imperative that the parties have complete faith in the judgment and integrity of those intervenors. Only then will the negotiators be willing to accept their recommendations with confidence.

Individuals who feel a lack of control over their personal destinies may benefit from the help of relationship-oriented/transformative intervenors. This type of intervention is especially appropriate with respect to truly personal controversies generating strong emotional feelings. Disputes involving family members, business partners, and employer-employee relationships frequently fall within this category — particularly when unequal financial or emotional relationships are present. These people would most likely resent attempts by evaluative/directive mediators to control their bargaining outcomes. They might also fear that facilitative/elicitive neutrals are insufficiently attuned to the unequal relationships involved. They would thus benefit from the attention to empowerment and recognition issues they would expect to receive from relationship-oriented/transformative intervenors.

Once parties determine the type of mediation assistance they prefer, they must decide how many mediators they need. In the vast majority of negotiation situations, one proficient neutral is sufficient. As long as that individual has the respect of both parties, they should be capable of providing the requisite help. In some cases, however, multiple mediators may be beneficial. If unusually technical business or economic issues are involved, the parties may want neutral intervenors who are both substantive experts and process experts. Since they may not be able to find both qualities in the same person, they may wish to use two or three neutrals who may each provide different expertise.

---

586. *See* Abramson, *supra* note 561, at 129–143.

587. *See* Jeffrey H. Goldfien & Jennifer K. Robbennolt, "What If the Lawyers Have Their Way? An Empirical Assessment of Conflict Strategies and Attitudes Toward Mediation Styles," 22 *Ohio State Journal on Dispute Resolution* 277, 300–301 (2007).

588. *See id.*, at 302–303.

Multiple neutrals may also be required in cases in which mutual distrust or significant cultural differences would preclude the selection of a single mediator. In these instances, the parties may each name a preferred neutral and have those two individuals select a third person who would be relatively acceptable to both sides. For example, international business controversies may concern firms from diverse areas of the world that do not trust neutrals from the opposing company's culture. Each firm could select a neutral from its own culture, and authorize those two to select the third from a neutral nation.

§ 13.05. Party and Mediator Preparation

Parties frequently fail to appreciate the fact that mediation is *assisted negotiation*. As a result, they go to conciliation sessions unprepared. This lack of planning causes many bargainers to be less forceful than they could have been. It also undermines the capacity of neutral intervenors to perform their functions effectively.

Parties should prepare for mediation as they would for any negotiation.[589] They must be thoroughly familiar with the operative factual, economic, and business issues. They should also review the previous bargaining sessions with their counterparts, to comprehend how their interaction has developed and why they may have been unable to achieve mutually acceptable terms on their own. They must appreciate the underlying needs and interests of their own principals and those of the other side. They must remember the negotiating styles of their counterparts. Firm representatives must realize the need to be prepared *to negotiate* during the impending mediation sessions — with the neutral intervenor, through that person with their adversaries, and directly with their counterparts.

Negotiators should formulate principled opening positions that can be divided into components and be rationally defended on a component-by-component basis during their mediation sessions. They may decide to prepare formal pre-mediation position statements they can either send to the mediator ahead of time or take to the initial group session. They must reconsider their initially established goals in light of their previous negotiation exchanges with their adversaries. They should either reconfirm the propriety of their prior bargaining objectives, or develop rationales to support their modified goals. They must finally review their non-settlement alternatives to ensure they do not make the mistake of accepting mediator-generated terms that are actually worse than what would happen if no agreement was achieved. This error occasionally happens when parties try to please the neutral participants and forget about their own needs and interests. Parties must always remember that no agreement is preferable to one that is less beneficial than their best non-settlement option.

---

589. *See* Dwight Golann & H.T. Folberg, *Mediation: The Roles of Advocate and Neutral* 233–264 (2011); Abramson, *supra* note 561, at 153–217.

Negotiators should attempt to become familiar with the mediation style of the designated conciliator. Is that individual evaluative/directive, facilitative/elicitive, or relationship-oriented/transformative? Are they likely to be an active or a passive participant? Are they going to ask general or specific questions regarding each side's circumstances? If they have not dealt with this person before, negotiators should not hesitate to ask other persons about the mediation style of the neutral participant.

If principals are expected to attend the initial mediation session, the negotiators must prepare those individuals for what may be expected to occur.[590] Principals should be especially cautioned about neutral intervenors who like to directly challenge the positions and opinions of the parties. This minimizes the likelihood principals will be unduly intimidated by that kind of behavior. Principals should generally be instructed not to speak when their representatives and the mediator are directly interacting. Instead of making open statements that may undermine their own interests, they should be told to communicate in private with their own agent. Principals should also be cautioned about nonverbal signals, to minimize the likelihood they will inadvertently disclose confidential information to their counterparts.

Is the mediator someone who likes to interact directly with the principals themselves? If yes, each principal must be prepared for this possibility. In some instances, it may be beneficial to give the principal a mini-course on negotiating to enable that person to forcefully advance his or her own interests when asked to do so. This type of preparation is particularly important with respect to mediators who ask the designated negotiators to leave the room so that he or she may discuss the transaction with the principals alone. If a negotiator thinks that his or her principal would be at an unfair disadvantage if he or she had to negotiate alone, the representative should refuse to leave the principal alone.

Designated mediators should also prepare for scheduled sessions to the extent possible.[591] They should review any written materials given to them by the parties to familiarize themselves with the basic issues, the current party positions, and apparent party interests. Neutrals dealing with transactional controversies may be given copies of prior proposals and supporting position statements. These can be quite informative.

Mediators should think about how they plan to conduct their initial session with the parties, and how they plan to conduct subsequent joint sessions.[592] How do they plan to help the parties define the relevant issues and explore their underlying needs and interests? How do they hope to use separate caucus sessions to further their problem-solving function?

---

590. *See* Dwight Golann, *Mediating Legal Disputes* 67–68 (2009); Abramson, *supra* note 561, at 229–237; G. Nicholas Herman, Jean M. Cary & Joseph E. Kennedy, *Legal Counseling and Negotiating: A Practical Approach* 329–331 (2001).

591. *See* Kovach, *supra* note 562, at 142–151.

592. *See* Christopher Moore, *The Mediation Process* 102–117 (2003).

§ 13.06. Conducting the Initial Session

Most mediators prefer to conduct the initial meeting at a neutral location—the mediator's office or another non-party site. They reasonably fear that if they meet at the offices of one of the parties, the other side may feel intimidated or disrespected. Nonetheless, when the parties themselves express a desire to meet at one side's place of business, neutrals normally honor that request.

An ideal meeting room has enough space to accommodate all of the participants, is sufficiently private to preclude unwanted interruptions, and has external space that may be used for separate caucus sessions by the parties alone or with mediator involvement. The furniture should be arranged in a non-confrontational configuration.[593] When bargaining adversaries who have been unable to achieve mutual accords interact, they tend to sit directly across from one another in a highly combative configuration. They often sit with their arms folded across their chests and with their legs crossed—highly unreceptive postures. Neutral intervenors should endeavor to create more conciliatory atmospheres. Appropriate seating arrangements can also diminish the impact of power imbalances that may exist.

Mediators should make sure the disputants initially shake hands and take seats that are not directly across from one another. A round table may be used with the mediator on one side and the parties situated relatively close to each other along the same portion of the table. If a square or rectangular table is used, the parties should be positioned along adjoining sides in an "L" configuration or adjacent to one another along the same side. Whenever possible, the participants should be encouraged to address each other on a first name basis to reinforce the informal and personal nature of the interaction. It is generally easier for people to disagree with impersonal counterparts than personalized adversaries. In addition, the creation of positive moods in the participants increases the likelihood of cooperative behavior and decreases the probability of competitive conduct.

Mediators generally assume control over the sessions. Someone must determine how the discussions are going to proceed, and the neutral participants are in the best position to do this. If they fail to assume a leadership role, the negotiations may deteriorate into unproductive adversarial exchanges. The establishment of mediator control also enhances the ultimate capacity of the neutral intervenors to generate discussions that are likely to produce beneficial results. Mediators generally assume an optimistic demeanor that encourages the disputants to think of settlement as a mutually beneficial outcome.

As soon as the parties are comfortable, the mediator explains the conciliation process.[594] This is especially important when inexperienced negotiators or principals are present. The neutral intervenors should emphasize their impartiality and the fact

---

593. *See id.*, at 154–156.

594. *See* Boulle, Colatrella & Picchioni, *supra* note 571, at 61–75; Susan Oberman, "Mediation Theory vs. Practice: What Are We Really Doing? Resolving a Professional Conundrum," 20 *Ohio State Journal on Dispute Resolution* 775, 793–794 (2005); Ordover & Doneff, *supra* note 571, at 61–62.

they lack the authority to impose any terms on the parties. This is especially important, because many people who participate in mediated discussions feel that they lack control over the outcomes that may be agreed upon.[595] The mediators are merely present to encourage inter-party bargaining and facilitate the consideration of alternative proposals. The parties will have the final say with respect to any terms that may be agreed upon. The mediator should explain the use of joint sessions and the possible use of separate caucus sessions to promote the mediation process. When necessary, the mediator may articulate behavioral guidelines designed to ensure full party participation in an orderly and non-disruptive manner.[596]

Individuals who participate in mediated settlement discussions judge the fairness of those procedures not only by the substantive terms agreed upon, but also by their perception of the procedural fairness involved.[597] "The presence of four particular process elements results in heightened perceptions of procedural justice: the opportunity for disputants to express their 'voice,' assurance that a third party considered what they said, and treatment that is both even-handed and dignified."[598] Mediators should always emphasize the fact that the parties will have the chance to express their concerns fully in circumstances that guarantee careful consideration by both the other parties and the neutral facilitators.[599] They should also make it clear that the mediation process will be completely even-handed and conducted in a dignified and impartial manner. By articulating these critical safeguards at the outset, mediators can begin to enhance disputant perceptions of procedural justice.

Confidentiality is a crucial aspect of the mediation process. It is also important for mediators to establish trust—both in themselves and the mediation process. These factors encourage the participants to speak openly about their interests, concerns, and desires. If they thought that their candid disclosures could be used against them in subsequent interactions, few participants would be forthcoming and little progress could be made.

Confidentiality is especially important with respect to disclosures made during separate caucus sessions conducted by the mediator with each side. Neutral intervenors must emphasize the fact that all information disclosed during separate caucuses will remain confidential—unless the interested party authorizes the mediator to convey that knowledge to the other side.

---

595. *See* Nancy Welsh, "Disputants' Decision Control in Court-Connected Mediation: A Hollow Promise Without Procedural Justice," 2002 *Journal of Dispute Resolution* 179, 183–184 (2002).

596. *See* Moore, *supra* note 592, at 219–220.

597. *See* Carol Izumi, "Implicit Bias and the Illusion of Mediator Neutrality," 34 *Washington University Journal of Law & Policy* 71, 140–141 (2010); Welsh, *supra* note 592, at 184–185; Welsh, *supra* note 579, at 791–792, 817–830.

598. Welsh, *supra* note 595, at 185.

599. *See* Mary Beth Howe & Robert Fiala, "Process Matters: Dispute Satisfaction in Mediated Civil Cases," 29 *Justice Systems Journal* 85, 86–87, 93–94 (2008).

Once the fundamental guidelines have been established, mediators generally ask the parties to summarize their respective positions.[600] Each side is given the opportunity to accomplish this objective free from counterpart interruptions.[601] Whenever one side objects to something contained in the other side's presentation, they are gently but firmly told they will have the chance to express their views once this party has finished speaking. During these summaries, mediators usually take brief notes, and they occasionally ask questions to clarify uncertain points. They want to be certain they fully comprehend the underlying issues and interests.[602] They also want to be certain each side has heard the other's perspective. Mediators should carefully listen for allusions to hidden agendas that are not being openly discussed by the parties, but will have to be addressed before mutual accords can be achieved.[603]

Mediators should recognize the different types of interests being expressed.[604] Some will be the type of *substantive* issues negotiating parties openly discuss. These may involve money or the way in which a contractual provision should be resolved. Mediator assisted negotiation should enable the parties to address these matters in an objective and detached manner. The mediation process should diminish the impact of these concerns by providing both parties with a fair and open interactive process. Others may relate to *psychological* issues that concern emotional needs, such as a desire for respect or sympathy. These matters may be addressed during cathartic expressions that enable each side to indicate how they feel regarding the way in which they have been treated.

Full party disclosure may be enhanced through "active listening."[605] Nonjudgmental but empathetic interjections such as "I understand," "I see," "I understand how you feel," "um hum," etc. can be used to encourage participant openness.[606] Warm eye contact and an open face can also be beneficial. This approach encourages both sides to thoroughly express their underlying feelings and beliefs in a relatively sympathetic atmosphere.[607] The mediator is actively listening to their circumstances, and each party feels that the opposing side is finally being forced to appreciate their side of the matter.

---

600. *See* Boulle, Colatrella & Picchioni, *supra* note 571, at 75–82; Kovach, *supra* note 533, at 162–167. Although mediators have traditionally used these joint sessions to explore the relevant issues with both parties together, an increasing number of contemporary neutral facilitators prefer to skip these joint sessions and move directly into separate caucus sessions. See Jay Folberg, "The Shrinking Joint Session: Survey Results," 2016 *Dispute Resolution Magazine* 12, 14–17 (2016). This approach may significantly diminish the cathartic benefits often generated during initial joint sessions.

601. *See* Moore, *supra* note 592, at 221–231; Allison Taylor, *The Handbook of Family Dispute Resolution* 134–136 (2002).

602. *See* David R. Hoffman, "Mediation, Multiple Minds, and Managing the Negotiation Within," 16 *Harvard Negotiation Law Review* 297, 323–324 (2011); Lucinda E. Sinclair & William D. Stewart, "Reciprocal-Influence Mediation Model: A Guide for Practice and Research," 25 *Conflict Resolution Quarterly* 185, 204–207 (2007).

603. *See* Jay Folberg & Allison Taylor, *Mediation* 42–43 (1984).

604. *See* Boulle, Colatrella & Picchioni, *supra* note 571, at 86.

605. *See* Boulle, Colatrella & Picchioni, *supra* note 571, at 124–126; Kovach, *supra* note 562, at 52–53; Golann, *supra* note 590, at 75–76.

606. *See* Moore, *supra* note 592, at 175–177, 197–198; Kovach, *supra* note 562, at 52–55.

607. *See* Hoffman, *supra* note 602, at 320; Dorothy Della Noce," Seeing Theory in Practice: An Analysis of Empathy in Mediation," 15 *Negotiation Journal* 271, 283–286 (1999).

When emotionally-charged controversies and relationships are involved, cathartic "venting" may permit the dissipation of strong feelings that may preclude the realistic consideration of possible solutions.[608] The mediator should allow the requisite venting in an environment that is likely to minimize the creation of unproductive animosity.[609] While candid feelings may be expressed, intemperate personal attacks must not be tolerated. Extreme statements can be adroitly reframed to make them more palatable to the other side.[610] For example, "I don't think that referring to X as a 'total jerk' or an 'asshole' is likely to induce X to consider your position with an open mind. Let's focus instead on the specific issues that are bothering you." Once both sides have been allowed to participate fully in the cathartic process, they may be able to put their emotional baggage behind them and get on with more productive discussions. This phenomenon explains why mediators must be attuned to emotional intelligence that enables them to deal with disputing party emotional feelings.[611]

To enhance the cathartic process, it is important for principals to attend initial mediation sessions.[612] Even if opening statements are made on their behalf by their representatives, the principals should be asked if they wish to speak. They often disclose personal feelings that must be heard and addressed before they will be ready to seek closure of their disputes through settlement agreements. If their need for cathartic venting is not recognized, they may feel dissatisfied with the final terms agreed upon even when those terms are substantively fair. In some cases, if their agents have done a good job of expressing their feelings, the principals will decline the opportunity to speak for themselves and be perfectly satisfied with the procedural fairness of the mediation process.

One way to enhance the healing process concerning a controversy between business partners involves the use of a sincere apology at the conclusion of the cathartic process.[613] This does not require one party to admit culpability. They may merely indicate how sorry they are that the other side has suffered a loss, recognizing the financial or emotional trauma sustained. They may alternatively state how sorry they are their counterpart feels the way he or she does, acknowledging that party's feelings. On some occasions, a full admission of responsibility and a forthright apology may be necessary to enable the disputing parties to get beyond their current controversy.

---

608. *See* Folberg & Golann, *supra* note 575, at 300–301.

609. *See* Hoffman, *supra* note 602, at 302–304; Ladd, *supra* note 569, at 35–60; Kovach, *supra* note 562, at 64–69.

610. *See* Ladd, *supra* note 569, at 35–37.

611. *See* Jessica Katz Jameson, Andrea Bodtker, Dennis Porch & William Jordan, "Exploring the Role of Emotion in Conflict Transformation," 27 *Conflict Resolution Quarterly* 167 (2009); Ladd, *supra* note 569.

612. *See* Welsh, *supra* note 579, at 845, 852–855.

613. *See generally* Jennifer K. Robbennolt, "Attorneys, Apologies, and Settlement Negotiation," 13 *Harvard Negotiation Law Review* 349 (2008); Jennifer K. Robbennolt, "Apologies and Settlement Levers," 3 *Journal of Empirical Legal Studies* 333 (2006).

During their frequently protracted one-on-one negotiations, parties that have been unable to achieve mutual accommodations of their competing interests often lock themselves into unalterable "principled" positions. They reach the point at which they are merely reiterating their respective positions in a non-conciliatory manner. They are so intent on the advancement of their own interests that they fail to listen meaningfully to the representations and suggestions being articulated by their counterparts.

When mediators become involved in the negotiation process, they must initially endeavor to reestablish meaningful communication between the parties.[614] If conciliation efforts are to have a beneficial impact, the participants must be induced to listen carefully to one another and to the neutral intervenor. They must be persuaded to appreciate the underlying interests and fundamental objectives of each other. During the initial joint session, the mediator must assist the parties to reopen blocked communication channels. If the parties cannot agree upon the precise issues to be resolved and if each prefers its own often value-laden formulations, the neutral should reframe the underlying problems in a way that is acceptable to both sides.[615] This neutral reformulation of the underlying issues can induce the participants to begin to view the controverted items in a more dispassionate manner.

Communication problems occasionally arise from unrealistic principal expectations. Mediators should be cognizant of direct or indirect indications that negotiators are having difficulty moderating excessive principal aspirations. For example, although representatives may acknowledge the reasonableness of opposing party positions, they may suggest that their principal is unwilling to consider those terms. Other agents may merely express principal opposition to opposing side proposals without providing any support for their side's intransigence. When it becomes apparent that principals do not appreciate the factual, economic, and/or business realities involved, neutral intervenors should attempt to enlighten those people in a fashion that does not embarrass them or their representatives.[616]

During some introductory conciliation meetings, the parties begin to negotiate meaningfully with one another. If they appear to be making actual progress, it is a propitious moment for the neutral participant to engage in passive mediation. The intervenor should smile benignly at the person speaking, until they are finished. If the mediator then turns toward the other party for a response, they are likely to generate further discussion. As long as the parties continue to exchange information and ideas, the mediator should maintain a low profile and permit the advocates to conduct their own talks. When inter-party communication begins to lag, the conciliator may interject questions designed to stimulate further negotiation progress or suggest alternatives the participants may not have contemplated.

---

614. *See* Moore, *supra* note 592, at 196–200; James K. Lawrence, "Mediation Advocacy: Partnering with the Mediator," 15 *Ohio State Journal on Dispute* Resolution 425, 436–437 (2000).

615. *See* Moore, *supra* note 592, at 236–242; Kovach, *supra* note 562, at 180–181.

616. *See* Golann, *supra* note 590, at 145–177, 249–252.

§ 13.07. Using Subsequent Sessions to Explore Innovative Alternatives

Negotiators who have reached an impasse during their own negotiations frequently focus exclusively on their own stated positions causing them to ignore other possible options. Neither party is willing to suggest new alternatives, lest they be perceived as weak. Neutral intervenors can significantly enhance the bargaining process by encouraging the parties to explore other formulations in a non-threatening manner under circumstances that do not require either side to make overt concessions.[617] If the way in which particular issues are phrased appears to impede open discussions, the mediator can either reframe them in a manner both parties find palatable or divide those issues into manageable subparts.[618]

A special meeting may be scheduled for the express purpose of permitting the exploration of alternative settlement options.[619] The conciliator should encourage the parties to explain their needs, interests, and objectives. The parties should be prompted by careful, gentle probing to discuss these critical issues. What does each side really hope to achieve? What do the parties fear might occur if they do not attain their goals or if they accede to certain proposals being suggested by their counterpart? If the participants can be induced to express themselves in a candid fashion, this substantially enhances the likelihood of negotiated resolutions. Whenever possible the mediator should introduce objective standards the parties can use to guide their evaluations and exchanges.[620]

An effective needs and interests analysis stimulates the disclosure of information not previously divulged.[621] Communication channels are usually reopened, and stalled negotiations are revitalized in a way that does not cause either party to suffer a loss of face.[622] Mediator patience is crucial during this phase, because it takes time for the participants to move from the adversarial mode to the cooperative mode. If the neutral facilitator attempts to rush things, the problem-solving process is likely to break down. Once relatively cooperative communication has been reestablished, conciliator silence, accompanied by supportive smiles and gestures, may be sufficient to encourage the parties to engage in meaningful bargaining. When necessary, the interjection of nonthreatening inquiries and suggested options may be employed to maintain a positive negotiating environment.

Transactional negotiators should be encouraged to examine unarticulated alternatives.[623] If parties discussing an international business arrangement cannot agree

---

617. *See* Moore, *supra* note 592, at 252–268; Lawrence, *supra* note 614, at 432–433; Folberg & Taylor, *supra* note 603, at 49–53.

618. *See* Moore, *supra* note 592, at 236–242; Kovach, *supra* note 562, at 236–238.

619. *See* Moore, *supra* note 563, at 252–259; Fisher, Ury & Patton, *supra* note 11, at 58–83.

620. *See* Moore, *supra* note 592, at 252–259; Fisher, Ury & Patton, *supra* note 11, at 58–83.

621. *See* Sam Kagel & Kathy Kelly, *The Anatomy of Mediation* 123–124 (1989).

622. *See* Folberg & Taylor, *supra* note 603, at 53–57.

623. *See* Golann, *supra* note 590, at 78–81.

whether to specify contractual payment in the currency of the seller or the purchaser, they may consider the use of a market-basket currency such as that of the European Union. Parties disagreeing on the official language to govern their relationship may agree upon a dual language approach or the use of a neutral third language. Parties negotiating the sale of business assets may disagree about the one to assume the risk of unknown liability. The buyer typically wants to exclude responsibility for unknown liabilities, while the seller wants the buyer to assume these risks. These firms can resolve their controversy by establishing an escrow account funded by the seller. This account would cover unknown liabilities for a specified period of time. The excess escrow funds would be returned to the seller at the expiration of that time period.

Reasonable substitutes for articulated demands should be sought during these brainstorming sessions. The participants should be encouraged to think of options that would beneficially satisfy the underlying needs and interests of both sides.[624] They need to engage in cooperative problem-solving that is designed to generate "win-win" results. Significant issues must be distinguished from less important matters, and the parties must be induced to focus primarily on those topics that have to be resolved if a final accord is to be achieved. How might the critical needs of each side be satisfied or protected by different options? Which alternatives acceptable to one side would least trammel the interests of the other party?

It is occasionally helpful to have the negotiators engage in *role reversal*. Once the underlying needs and interests of the parties have been discerned, each representative can be asked to indicate the ways in which his or her counterpart's rights may be optimally protected.[625] This technique may generate options that have been previously ignored. It should simultaneously induce each side to develop a greater appreciation for the needs of the other side.

Mediators should try not to place disputants in positions in which they would be required to make overt capitulations. A face-saving means of compromise should be provided whenever possible. For example, a significant concession by one side may be counterbalanced by a seemingly reciprocal relinquishment by the other side to preserve the aura of mutuality. Negotiators should be provided with rationales they can use to convince their principals of the reasonableness of proposals their principals might otherwise be reluctant to accept.

Conciliators must be particularly wary of passive-aggressive individuals who do not directly reject suggested solutions advanced during mediation discussions. They indirectly undermine the negotiation process either by obliquely undercutting apparently reasonable offers ("*Yes*, that is a generous proposal, *but* it does not sufficiently advance the interests of my particular principal because …"), or by employing pro-

---

624. *See* Michael D. Lang & Allison Taylor, *The Making of a Mediator* 27–28 (2000); Folberg & Taylor, *supra* note 603, at 49–53.

625. *See* Jeffrey Hartje, "Lawyer's Skills in Negotiations: Justice in Unseen Hands," 1984 *Missouri Journal of Dispute Resolution* 119, 161 (1984).

crastination or tardiness to subvert the talks. These people usually find negotiations and the concomitant auction process distasteful, but are unable to express these feelings overtly.

It is frequently beneficial to ask passive-aggressive negotiators to articulate the specific objectives of their respective principals, to compel them to state definitive positions that may provide the basis for further discussions. These individuals must be forced to participate actively in the conciliation process as formulators of alternative proposals and not merely as critics of suggestions made by others. On the other hand, if a number of participants are involved in the particular transaction, a passive-aggressive impediment to settlement may be temporarily ignored until the others have agreed upon specified terms. These conditions can then be presented to the passive-aggressive person as a fait accompli that he or she would be likely to accept due to the absence of viable alternatives.

Joint conciliation sessions do not always move inexorably toward mutual accords. Mediators must be cognizant of those verbal and nonverbal signals that indicate that joint meetings are approaching an irreconcilable impasse.[626] The parties are continuing to place exaggerated emphasis on unyielding positions designed more to impress their respective principals than to influence their counterparts. They may have changed their seating arrangement from a cooperative setting into a more confrontational configuration — sitting directly opposite each other. The participants may be wringing their hands and/or gnashing their teeth in utter frustration regarding the lack of progress, or they have crossed their arms and legs in a wholly unreceptive manner. When these negative signs are perceived, it may be time to suggest separate mediation sessions.

§ 13.08. Conducting Separate Caucus Sessions

When joint meetings do not achieve fruitful results, it is frequently beneficial to propose separate caucuses that will enable neutral participants to meet individually with each side.[627] Since separate encounters can only be effective when undertaken with the cooperation and confidence of the parties, mediators generally ask the participants if they would be amenable to a bifurcated approach. If one side is really opposed to this technique, it would be unlikely that separate sessions would be productive. In most instances, the parties readily consent to separate caucuses, and their commitment to this process enhances the likelihood of success.

Mediators who are considering the use of segregated discussions should explain at a joint session that they would like to explore the matter with each side individually. The conciliators should emphasize the fact that they do not intend to support either side as such. They merely wish to explore each party's underlying needs, interests,

---

626. *See* Lang & Taylor, *supra* note 624, at 25–27.
627. *See* Boulle, Colatrella & Picchioni, *supra* note 571, at 106–113; Moore, *supra* note 592, at 369–377; Herman, Cary & Kennedy, *supra* note 590, at 337–338.

and objectives in an environment that may be more conducive to candor than a joint meeting. They must expressly promise to maintain the confidences shared by the participants during private discussions—except when they are specifically authorized to divulge the information in question. Once these basic guidelines are established, the disputants are ready for separate mediation sessions.

During the separate meetings, conciliators endeavor, in a non-judgmental manner, to ascertain the true underlying interests and beliefs of the respective participants.[628] Most mediators also begin to determine the minimal goals each side hopes to achieve. When they first meet with each participant, they reaffirm the fact that all discussions will remain confidential unless they are expressly given permission to convey certain information to the other side.

When separate caucus meetings commence, it is often advantageous for the neutral intervenors to ask each participant what they—as mediators—should know that they were unable to learn during the joint discussions.[629] This inquiry acknowledges the fact that disputing parties are frequently willing to divulge information to conciliators in confidence that they would be unwilling to disclose in the presence of their adversaries. This question must be propounded in an open and wholly non-threatening manner to encourage the desired candor. At this stage, mediators try not to put participants on the defensive by asking them to explain their behavior. It is more productive to ask them about their aspirations and their concerns.

Mediators can use private caucus sessions to control the flow of information between the parties. There are times when full disclosure of certain facts or thoughts can be an impediment to negotiation success. While the disputants may be willing to disclose such information to a neutral facilitator in a confidential setting, they would not wish to have it communicated to their counterparts. Mediators must be careful not to disclose things that might undermine settlement discussions, and to rephrase disclosures of an emotional or accusatory nature that might offend the other side.

There are occasions when negotiating parties are a great distance apart and neither is willing to make a unilateral concession of a meaningful nature lest this action be perceived as a sign of weakness.[630] For example, a business seller may be demanding $50 million, while the prospective buyer is only offering $30 million. When this type of situation arises, some mediators use "*conditional offers*" to get the parties moving. They begin by asking the seller, in a separate caucus session, if it would be willing to move to $45 million *if* the buyer was willing to come up to $35 million. He then raises this topic with the buyer, asking it if it would move up to $35 million *if* the seller reduced its demand to $45 million.

The risk to the Seller is minimal. If buyer refuses to accept the seller's conditional offer and responds with an offer of $32 million, the seller can withdraw its conditional

628. *See* Karl A. Slaikeu, *When Push Comes to Shove: A Practical Guide to Mediating Disputes* 91–109 (1996).
629. *See* Golann, *supra* note 590, at 25.
630. *See* Anderson J. Little, *Making Money Talk* 121–183 (2007).

offer and counter with an offer of $48 million. This approach clearly indicates that no real movement will be forthcoming until the buyer accepts the need for more significant position changes.

If the seller's conditional offer is accepted, the mediator asks the seller to make another conditional offer of $42 million if the buyer will counter with $38 million. After several rounds of such conditional offers, the parties may reach positions where the seller is demanding $41 million and the buyer is offering $39 million. The parties have made great progress, and they are now only $2 million apart. The mediator should be able to help them achieve a deal approaching $40 million.

During the early portion of separate sessions, it is often instructive to ask the participants to explain any concerns they may have regarding the ramifications they associate with specific terms that are being considered. One or both parties may think that a negotiated agreement on the current issues may prejudice another matter involving the same participants or adversely affect some other relationship. If these concerns are well founded, they will have to be addressed before any resolution of the immediate controversy can be amicably obtained. For example, a business firm may fear that an agreement with respect to the instant matter may affect other contracts that contain "most favored nation" (MFN) clauses requiring it to give equally advantageous terms to other contractual partners. A rearrangement of the relevant terms may take care of the concerns of the corporation with MFN clauses in other contracts by avoiding the inclusion of provisions that would be affected by those MFN obligations.

It is not unusual for mediators to conclude that the fears expressed in private by negotiating parties appear to be unfounded. A thoughtful and empathetic assessment of the real consequences of bargained results may help to alleviate the anxiety that is preventing a mutual resolution of the current issues. This must be done with sensitivity to the feelings of the concerned participants and in a manner designed to induce those parties to recognize the fact that their fears are unrealistic. The following example may be instructive:

SIDE A NEGOTIATOR:	If we enter into a ten year lease with Side B, we may lose out on a better deal that may arise in the coming years. Yet Side B is unwilling to enter into a lease of shorter duration, and this is the building we would really like to lease.
MEDIATOR:	Haven't you been looking for new space for several years now?
SIDE A NEGOTIATOR:	Yes, we have.
MEDIATOR:	Have you noticed a lowering of rents over that period of time?
SIDE A NEGOTIATOR:	As a matter of fact, we haven't. Rents have actually been rising at the rate of two to three percent per year.
MEDIATOR:	Do you really think Side B will be giving other parties lower rents in the next several years?
SIDE A NEGOTIATOR:	Now that you mention it, I doubt that will happen.

If the concerns expressed by Side A regarding possible future rent reductions were valid, then the mediator would have to explore options that might assuage those fears:

MEDIATOR: I can understand why you would not like to lock your firm into a ten year rent commitment. Would you be willing to do so if Side B agreed to include a clause promising to give your firm the benefit of any future rent reductions given to other companies? What if Side B agreed to a clause providing for the reopening of the rent issue after the first five years of the lease?

While meeting separately with the participants, mediators must look for possible *intra-group* difficulties that may impede negotiations.[631] What constituencies must be satisfied before any accord can be approved? What are their underlying interests and how may they be addressed? Are all interested constituencies currently represented at the negotiation table? If not, how might that objective be accomplished? Advocates who are ignoring constituent conflicts must be convinced of the need for full intra-group participation if the assisted discussions are to be successful.

During some separate sessions, parties may continue to assert wholly unrealistic positions. If mediators were to directly challenge those views, the parties would probably become defensive and more intransigent. It is more productive to explore these positions in a nonthreatening manner. This can be accomplished through the use of *probing questions*.[632] The conciliator takes out a writing pad and explains how helpful it would be for them to fully comprehend the way in which that particular party has calculated its current position. The mediator wants to induce that side to break its overall demand/offer into components that must be valued on an individualized basis.

The probing questions initially pertain to the more finite aspects of the party's position to leave minimal room for puffing. How has that side valued the real property? If the response is realistic, the neutral intervenor writes it down and goes on to the value of the building and equipment. If it is unreasonable, the conciliator may cite a recent property appraisal that is substantially different from the one being offered, followed by a seemingly innocent question regarding the way in which the participant determined its valuation. In most cases, the party will feel embarrassed and be induced to provide a more realistic figure.

Most advocates advancing unreasonable positions are unprepared for component-by-component evaluations. When they are forced to provide explanations for each aspect of their overall positions, they tend to give more defensible numbers. Once this questioning process is finished, the final figure is often one-fourth or one-fifth of what was being demanded or four or five times what was being offered. This technique can greatly narrow the distance between the disputants.

When negotiators reach impasses, they are usually focusing almost entirely on their areas of disagreement. As a result, they frequently fail to consider other areas where

---

631. *See* Slaikeu, *supra* note 628, at 24–25, 56–57.
632. *See* Erickson & McKnight, *supra* note 560, at 64.

their interests may overlap. Mediators must be especially attuned to the issues in which the interests of the parties are not diametrically opposed.[633] These items should be highlighted, because they may provide the basis for cooperative solutions that may simultaneously enhance the needs of both sides. Points of immediate confrontation can be minimized through the development of alternative formulations that emphasize the areas of common interest and downplay the areas of direct conflict.

As the parties tentatively resolve the less controverted issues, they become psychologically committed to an overall settlement. Their focus on the mutually agreeable terms begins to convince them that the conflicted items are not as important as they initially thought. They do not want to permit their substantial progress on the cooperative issues to be negated through impasses on the few remaining terms. As a result, both sides become more amenable to settlement, making the mediator's job easier. Once the underlying needs and interests have been determined and possibly acceptable alternatives have been explored with the individual parties, mediators generally attempt to formulate comprehensive proposals they hope will lead to final agreements. They may first review the strengths and weaknesses of the terms being proposed by each side to demonstrate the significant risks associated with non-settlement.[634] Financial and emotional transaction costs may also be noted. At this point, the parties are likely to be most receptive to mediator-generated formulations.

When a number of different issues are involved, some conciliators employ the *single text approach*. When the time is ripe, the neutral intervenors draft a single document that reflects the areas of discerned commonality.[635] After the single text is prepared, the mediator shares that document with each party during separate sessions. The neutral listens carefully to each side's criticisms and suggestions, and then redrafts the appropriate provisions. Even when parties submit their own proposed terms, the conciliator incorporates those suggestions into the single text. In this manner, the mediator retains control over the drafting process, and he or she is only required to work with a single official document. This avoids the problems that are often created when each participant attempts to work from its own written submission.

The single-text approach enables the conciliator to negate two frequent impediments to final agreements. Advocates tend to be suspicious of proposals suggested by their adversaries. They assume that counterparts are attempting to obtain provisions that satisfy their own interests.[636] The single-text format generates an overall draft formulated by the neutral intervenor who has no reason to favor one party over the other. The participants are thus more receptive to terms coming from the unbiased mediator.

---

633. *See* Golann, *supra* note 590, at 244–246.

634. *See* Lawrence, *supra* note 614, at 438–43; Slaikeu, *supra* note 628, at 104–105.

635. *See* Slaikeu, *supra* note 628, at 123–129.

636. Regarding this "reactive devaluation" tendency, see Russell Korobkin, "Psychological Impediments to Mediation Success: Theory and Practice," 21 *Ohio State Journal on Dispute Resolution* 281, 316–318 (2006); Raiffa, *supra* note 34, at 282–283; Lawrence, *supra* note 614, at 440–441.

The single-text device also enables the neutral intervenor to formulate proposals that appear to provide *gains*, rather than *losses*, for both sides. Since people tend to accept a *sure gain* over a possibly greater gain but reject a *certain loss* they might possibly avoid, final proposals that seem to guarantee *sure gains* for both sides are more likely to be found acceptable by the negotiating parties.[637]

As the single text provisions are being explored and redrafted, the mediator engages in "shuttle mediation." That person goes back and forth between the parties refining their suggestions. Different style mediators behave somewhat differently during this part of the process.

Facilitative/elicitive mediators generally use the closing phase of the resolution process to generate mutually formulated provisions. During the separate caucuses, they listen carefully to the actual desires of the parties. They then endeavor to encourage joint problem-solving. Even though these neutral intervenors are functioning as communication facilitators between the parties, they try to limit their messages to the actual intentions of the interested participants. Instead of imposing final provisions, these neutrals merely want to participate in *assisted negotiations* in which the parties continue to control their own destinies. When they think it beneficial, they even schedule joint sessions at the end to enable the parties to structure their final terms together. The continuing presence of the neutral intervenor minimizes the likelihood that these joint discussions will deteriorate into unproductive confrontations.

Evaluative/directive neutrals often use this stage of the mediation process to formulate the terms they believe the parties would be willing to accept. Most mediators do not feel comfortable dictating final terms to negotiating parties, and they attempt to incorporate provisions the participants appear to desire. These neutrals would only employ a more directive approach when required by the inability of inexperienced negotiators to comprehend their own needs. A few mediators with extensive business market experience occasionally put together overall packages they strongly encourage the parties to accept.[638] These neutrals have ascertained the respective needs and interests of the parties from the separate caucus session discussions, and they have sought to put together overall deals they believe would be most acceptable to both sides.

Relationship-oriented/transformative conciliators tend to focus less on bargaining substance and more on the underlying inter-party relationship. During the separate sessions, they attempt to accomplish two objectives. They hope to generate sufficient participant empowerment to enable them to resolve their own issues They demonstrate the options available to each side, and indicate how non-settlements are not necessarily negative. They simultaneously endeavor to induce each side to recognize the feelings, perceptions, and motives of the other. They try to get each party to place itself in the shoes of its counterpart. They believe that this recognitional process enhances

---

637. *See* Russell Korobkin & Chris Guthrie, "Psychological Barriers to Litigation Settlement: An Experimental Approach," 93 *Michigan Law* Review 107, 129–138 (1994).

638. *See* Freund, *supra* note 570, at 169–184; 219–228.

the parties' mutual relationship and increases their ability to interact successfully with each other and with others in the future.

Once the parties have agreed upon the terms contained in the mediator's text, the neutral drafter carefully reviews the items agreed upon to be sure that there are no misunderstandings. They are also certain that the specified terms satisfy the critical underlying interests of both sides.[639] If the conciliator is concerned that a party may subsequently attempt to modify or reject some of the pertinent provisions, they can ask the participants to indicate their assent to everything by initialing each term. The mediator may also avoid future difficulties by agreeing to prepare the final settlement agreement for the parties. This function should not entail much additional work, because the accord would be based on the final text approved by the disputants. The neutral participant would merely have to clarify ambiguous language and clean up inartfully drafted provisions.

When separate caucus discussions begin to break down, conciliators frequently recess the talks to give the parties time to reconsider their current positions and to permit time constraints to enhance settlement pressure. To avoid future scheduling difficulties, it is generally preferable to agree now to future joint or separate meeting dates, instead of trying to do this after the present sessions have ended. In addition, parties that have been asked to supply information to the mediator or to the other side should be given specific instructions regarding the accomplishment of this task.

When mediation efforts are not moving expeditiously toward settlement, neutral intervenors must be patient. If they attempt to rush the parties, unproductive intransigence is likely to result. It takes time for locked in parties to reconsider the merits of established positions and reevaluate their real non-settlement alternatives. It is unlikely that meaningful settlement discussions can again occur until the participants have had the chance to reassess their respective situations.

§ 13.09. Moving toward Final Terms

Near the end of most mediations, the parties begin to realize that mutually beneficial agreements can be achieved. How should they move from their present positions toward settlement?[640] First, they can move incrementally from their current positions toward a compromise result approximately half way between their existing offers. Each side may be hesitant to make larger concessions without being certain of counterpart reciprocity. By moving together in increments, they can avoid unreciprocated position changes. Although this approach may lead to final accords, the moving parties often forego the possibility of integrative bargaining that would enable them to expand the overall pie and simultaneously improve their respective situations.

---

639. *See* Slaikeu, *supra* note 628, at 156–157.
640. *See* Moore, *supra* note 592, at 309–318.

A second closure technique may involve a unilateral or joint leap to a conclusion, as either one side or both sides move directly from their current positions to a mutually acceptable result. This technique is most likely to occur after extended and often difficult negotiations, when the parties begin to appreciate the obvious result that will be acceptable to both. They no longer wish to continue incremental position changes, and one or both suggest a result they are almost certain will resolve their dispute.

A third closure device relies upon objective criteria or a consensus process to achieve final accords. With mediator assistance, the parties agree upon general principles that should guide their discussions. The parties then apply these principles to their specific issues and reach final terms. They may alternatively agree upon a formula to be used to accomplish the same result.

When disputes involve parties with on-going relationships, the attainment of agreements on substantive terms may not fully resolve the controversy. One or both parties may still feel a need for psychological closure.[641] Mediators should be cognizant of this phenomenon and work to achieve a complete closure that will optimally preserve the parties' relationship. The party or parties who are perceived as having acted wrongfully should be asked to go through a multi-step healing process. They must initially acknowledge what has occurred to disrupt the relationship. They must then accept responsibility for the role they played in this disruption, and affirm their interest in the maintenance of a positive and mutually beneficial relationship. They should offer a sincere apology for the harm they may have caused, and request forgiveness for their behavior. At this point, the parties should engage in a joint act of reconciliation that will allow their relationship to continue to flourish in the future.

§ 13.10. Regulation Negotiation/Mediation

When large federal, state, and municipal agencies oversee particular areas, the regulation adoption/amendment process may be protracted, contentious, and expensive. Administrative procedure statutes require the publication of proposed regulations, the holding of public hearings, and documented agency deliberations. Once this process is finished and new regulations are issued, adversely affected parties frequently request judicial intervention. The resulting court proceedings may continue for several years. If agency reconsideration is ultimately directed, five or more years may elapse before rules become final.

When highly contentious issues are involved, the regulatory process is usually lengthy. This is almost always guaranteed when controversial environmental changes are involved or visible zoning modifications are considered. Some government officials have begun to recognize that it may be advantageous to use the negotiation process prior to the regulation adoption stage to avoid subsequent administrative and judicial

---

641. *See id.*, at 332–346.

proceedings. Instead of merely publishing proposed regulations, agencies initially determine the interest groups most likely to be affected by the contemplated rules. Representatives of these different groups are then asked to participate in what has become known as a "*regulation-negotiation proceeding*" — a "*reg.-neg. proceeding*" for short.

Despite the reg.-neg. characterization, most regulation-negotiation proceedings are really "*regulation-negotiation-mediation*" proceedings, due to the participation of neutral facilitators. Respected neutral experts are asked to solicit the participation of the relevant interest groups, ranging from business organizations and administrative officials to public interest spokespersons. The process can only function effectively if all interest groups are adequately represented. It is thus better to err on the side of inclusion, rather than exclusion.

Once the diverse participant groups are selected, neutral facilitators attempt to elicit the information they need to determine and define the issues that must be addressed. When technical, scientific, environmental, and/or economic issues are involved, respected experts may be asked to provide their insights. The individuals selected must be viewed as unbiased and enjoy general acceptability among the different groups if their opinions are to be persuasive.

When substantial questions must be overcome, it is often beneficial to appoint subcommittees comprised of representatives from each group. These subcommittees focus on specific issues or groups of issues. They try to agree upon the precise problems that must be addressed and look for alternatives that may prove mutually acceptable. It is especially important for the participants to explore options that minimize the adverse impact on any group. Even if the final terms are not considered perfect by any constituency, the fact that these provisions are generally acceptable to everyone may prove to be more important to the overall success of the reg.-neg. process.

The neutral facilitators must ensure that each group's interests receive thoughtful consideration. This helps to generate mutual respect among the different participants and is conducive to the development of amicable solutions. If diverse participants can be induced to appreciate the concerns of opposing parties, this can significantly reduce distrust and enhance the dispute resolution process. Use of the single-text approach can be especially beneficial during reg.-neg. discussions, to minimize problems that might otherwise result from the presence of diverse participants and contentious issues.

After the participants have had the opportunity to define the relevant issues and evaluate the options available to them, they must begin to look for common ground. Whenever possible, decisions should be made by consensus, rather than by majority vote. Even when most participants support a particular proposal, if one group is unalterably opposed to that suggestion, it may be able to prevent the adoption of that provision or delay effectuation of that term through protracted litigation. It thus behooves the parties to respect the rights and interests of all representative groups.

When mutually acceptable regulations are drafted, they are recommended to the governing agency for final approval. Even when no overall agreement can be achieved, the reg.-neg. process may narrow the pertinent issues and induce the different groups to agree upon numerous factual matters. If these ideas are carefully considered by the agency during the formal rule-making process, it decreases the likelihood of subsequent legal challenges by parties dissatisfied with the promulgated regulations. Furthermore, even if litigation were to occur, a prior narrowing of the factual and legal issues should make the resulting legal proceedings more efficient. The enactment of the Negotiated Rulemaking Act of 1990 encouraged federal agencies to make greater use of the reg.-neg. process.[642] The basic provisions of that temporary statute were permanently codified in the Administrative Dispute Resolution Act of 1996.

§ 13.11. Use of Arbitration to Avoid Judicial Litigation

Business parties with on-going relationships occasionally develop strong disagreements regarding whether their contractual obligations are being entirely satisfied. When this occurs, the dissatisfied party frequently files a law suit seeking redress. These proceedings can be time-consuming, expensive, and detrimental to their relationships. To minimize the impact of such proceedings, many parties include arbitration provisions in their contracts that substitute private arbitral proceedings for public court adjudications. The parties either designated specific individuals they have selected to serve as arbitrators, or provide for the joint selection of such persons if disagreements arise. They often agree to follow the procedures established by the American Arbitration Association for disputes involving United States partners, and indicate the state legal principles to be applied.

When transnational parties are involved, they almost always include arbitration provisions in their agreements, due to the fact that neither is willing to subject itself to jurisdiction of courts in the other party's home nation. Since the parties may not be able to agree to the national laws to be applied before such tribunals, they frequently specify that the arbitrator(s) will apply generally accepted legal principles applied internationally to such controversies.

§ 13.12. Use of Cyber Mediation and Arbitration

The substantial expansion of cyber commerce has created a need for efficient ways to resolve disputes that arise between electronic purchasers and sellers of goods and services who may be located in different states or countries.[643] Many e-business sites have adopted cyber mediation programs that use neutral facilitators and e-mail ex-

---

642. *See* Singer, *supra* note 562, at 148.

643. *See* Amy J. Schmitz & Colin Rule, "Online Dispute Resolution for Smart Contracts," 2019 *Journal of Dispute* Resolution 103 (2019); Alyson Carrel & Noam Ener, "Mind the Gap: Bringing Technology to the Mediation Table,: 2019 *Journal of Dispute Resolution* 1 (2019); Sarah R. Cole &

changes to resolve conflicts. The parties describe their difficulties through e-mail communications, and they are assisted by conciliators who participate in their exchanges. When cyber mediators think that over-reliance upon e-mail channels is creating negotiation difficulties, they should use one-on-one and conference telephone calls to reestablish rapport and diminish the mistrust that may have developed because of the impersonal means of communication being employed. When cyber mediation efforts are unsuccessful, many e-commerce companies require customers to resort to private arbitral procedures that may be conducted electronically or in person.

Individuals representing e-business firms should consider the efficiency of cyber mediation systems. These programs should be specifically described in the home pages of the firms involved to apprise prospective purchasers of their obligation to resort to cyber mediation procedures before they seek further redress—either through private arbitral procedures or external legal channels. Such procedures can help them to avoid claims that the procedures imposed are unconscionable.[644] When prospective e-customers register on Internet sites, they expressly agree to use the dispute resolution procedures described to them. People assisting principals with e-business disputes should initially contact opposing parties through telephone calls to establish some rapport and to see if direct oral communications may expeditiously resolve the underlying issues. If not, they may wish to use e-mail exchanges to define the problem and search for possible solutions. Cyber mediation participants should appreciate the impersonal nature of e-mail communications and the fact that people are far more likely to flame other persons through e-mail than they would in person or via the telephone.[645] They are also more likely to be suspicious of the motives and trustworthiness of other e-mail communicators. Resort to occasional telephone calls can often correct these communication difficulties. The use of cyber mediation may also provide the neutral facilitators with more control over inter-party communications than they would have with in-person mediation.[646] This is why some experts have suggested a need for explicit ethical standards to regulate the manner in which cyber dispute resolution programs are conducted.[647]

Kristen Blankley, "Online Mediation: Where Have We Been, Where Are We Now, and Where Should We Be," 38 *University of Toledo Law Review* 193 (2006); Ethan Katsh, "Online Dispute Resolution," in *The Handbook of Dispute Resolution* 425 (Michael L. Moffitt & Robert C. Bordone, eds. 2005); Llewellyn J. Gibbons, Robin M. Kennedy & Jon M. Gibbs, "Cyber-Mediation: Computer-Mediated Communications Medium Massaging the Message," 32 *New Mexico Law Review* 27 (2002). Compare Robert Condlin, "Online Dispute Resolution: Stinky, Repugnant, or Drab," 18 *Cardozo Journal of Conflict Resolution* 717 (2017).

644. *See generally* Lucille M. Ponte, "Getting a Bad Rap? Unconscionability in Clickwrap Dispute Resolution Clauses and a Proposal for Improving the Quality of These Online Consumer 'Products,'" 26 *Ohio State Journal on Dispute Resolution* 118 (2011).

645. *See* Janice Nadler, "Electronically-Mediated Dispute Resolution and E-Commerce," *Negotiation Journal* 333, 338 (Oct. 2001).

646. *See* David Allen Larson, "Technology Mediated Dispute Resolution (TMDR): Opportunities and Dangers," 38 *University of Toledo Law Review* 213, 234–235 (2006).

647. See Susan Nauss Exon, "Ethics and Online Dispute Resolution: From Evolution to Revolution," 32 *Ohio State Journal on Dispute Resolution* 609 (2017).

Firms doing electronic business with persons around the world are increasingly using cyber mediation systems to help them resolve their disputes amicably. Mediators often use phone calls and video conferencing technologies (*e.g.*, Skype, Google Video Chat, Gotomeeting, or Webex) to establish rapport with the disputing parties. E-mail exchanges can also be used to explore possible settlement options. When language differences are involved, the parties can use technologies such as Google Translator to translate messages from one language to another.[648] When different Internet communications are being employed, it can be especially difficult to maintain the confidentiality of mediation exchanges. When disputing parties are unwilling or unable to get together at the same location, cyber mediation procedures may be able to help them achieve mutual resolutions of their issues where it might be difficult for the courts in either country to resolve these matters conclusively and in mutually beneficial ways.

Computer programs can also assist disputing parties achieve efficient resolutions of their underlying conflicts.[649] Negotiators can be asked a series of questions that are designed to determine the issues that must be addressed. When larger issues are involved, the program can elicit additional information that will help divide expansive terms into subissues. The parties are then asked to assign point values to the various subissues, with each side given a total of 100 or 200 points to be allotted. The computer program then explores ways to maximize and equalize the relative values to be given to each side. The computer program explores the different ways in which the parties have valued the various terms and endeavors to maximize the joint returns achieved.

§ 13.13. Conclusion

When transactional negotiations break down, it is frequently beneficial to ask mediators to facilitate the bargaining process. Mediators may be primarily facilitative/elicitive, evaluative/directive, or relationship-oriented/transformative. Parties should initially decide which form of neutral intervention they would prefer.

Parties should prepare for mediation sessions as thoroughly as they would for negotiation meetings, knowing that they will negotiate with the neutral participants, as well as through mediators, and directly with their counterparts. Mediators should also prepare for scheduled interactions by reviewing available party documents and by determining the optimal way to proceed with settlement discussions.

Most mediators initially schedule joint sessions to explain their facilitative function, their impartiality and lack of capacity to impose terms, and the confidential nature of participant communications. When joint sessions do not produce accords, mediators generally schedule separate caucuses that enable them to explore underlying

---

648. *See id.*, at 316–317.

649. *See* Orna Rabinovich-Einy & Ethan Katsh, "Technology and the Future of Dispute Systems Design," 17 *Harvard Negotiation Law Review* 151 (2012); Arno R. Lodder & John Zeleznikow, "Developing an Online Dispute Resolution Environment: Dialogue Tools and Negotiation Support Systems in a Three-Step Model," 10 *Harvard Negotiation Law Review* 287 (2005).

needs and interests confidentially with each party. During both joint and separate sessions, mediators look for areas of joint interest and encourage the generation of alternative formulations that may be mutually beneficial.

Regulation-negotiation procedures can be used by government agencies to facilitate the drafting and approval of controversial regulations. Neutral facilitators get all of the interested parties together and endeavor to generate mutually acceptable provisions.

Arbitration procedures are frequently used by business partners to resolve disputes that may arise. Parties located within the United States usually specify the applicable law to govern such proceedings. Where transnational parties are involved, they typically provide for arbitrators to apply the legal principles applied internationally to such controversies.

Business firms with electronic customers located around the world are increasingly using cyber mediation and arbitration procedures to resolve disputes that may be raised by their customers.

Chapter 14

Benefits from Post-Negotiation Assessments

§ 14.01. Importance

Most business persons negotiate their way through life without ever trying to learn from their encounters. They complete one bargaining interaction and move directly to another. If they want to improve their negotiation skills, they have to learn from their prior encounters.[650] After their more significant bargaining interactions, they should take a few minutes to ask themselves how they did.[651] Which techniques worked well, and which did not? What new tactics did they encounter, and how might they have countered those techniques more effectively? Whether they think they did well or not so well, each time individuals complete a significant negotiation they should briefly review the manner in which that particular interaction developed. It is only through objective post-mortems focusing on every negotiating stage that individuals can continuously enhance their negotiating capabilities.[652]

Empirical studies show that negotiators tend to under estimate how high or low their counterparts are actually willing to go before they begin their serious discussions, causing them to over-estimate how well they have performed once agreements have been achieved.[653] Because of this over confidence, they often see no reason to objectively evaluate their performances. It is thus important — even when individuals think they have done well — to do post negotiation assessments with an open mind. They really need to determine the degree to which they may have erroneously estimated during their preparation how high or low the other side was really willing to go, and think about whether they could have obtained even more advantageous terms.

---

650. *See* Charles B. Craver, "The Benefits to Be Derived From Post-Negotiation Assessments," 14 *Cardozo Journal of Conflict Resolution* 1 (2012); John Lande, "Getting Good Results for Clients by Building Good Working Relationships with Opposing Counsel," 33 *La Verne Law* Review 107, 131–132 (2011).

651. See Jeff Weiss, *HBR Guide to Negotiating* 167–170 (2016).

652. *See* Michael Watkins, *Shaping the Game* 153–163 (2006); Fisher & Shapiro, *supra* note 56, at 177–182.

653. *See* Richard P. Larrick & George Wu, "Claiming a Large Slice of a Small Pie: Asymmetric Disconfirmation in Negotiation," 93 *Journal of Personality and Social Psychology* 212 (2007).

§ 14.02. Asking Questions about All Stages

A. Preparation Stage

The first analysis should focus on the Preparation Stage, which is usually the most important part of the bargaining process. Did they thoroughly gather the relevant factual, economic, and business information? Did they determine which items were "essential," "important," and "desirable"? Did they carefully evaluate their non-settlement options (*i.e.*, their *bottom line*) and the non-settlement alternatives available to their *counterparts*? Did they establish an appropriate aspiration level for *each issue* to be addressed? Did they plan a beneficial and principled opening offer which they could rationally support? Did they develop a strategy designed to take them from where they began to where they hoped to end up? Did their pre-bargaining prognostications prove to be accurate? If not, what might have been done to provide a better preliminary assessment? Which party dictated the contextual factors such as time and location? Is it likely that these seemingly ancillary considerations influenced the substantive aspects of the transaction? Could they have been handled in a more advantageous fashion?

B. Preliminary Stage

Did the participants have a good Preliminary Stage? Did they take the time to establish rapport with each other? This is an especially important stage when parties from different cultures interact. Did they try to personalize their relationship, and create a positive bargaining environment? If one side did not like the way their adversary began the interaction, did they employ "attitudinal bargaining" to modify their behavior? If they planned to conduct most of their interaction via e-mail exchanges, did they take the time to meet in person or talk on the telephone to get to know each other?

C. Information Stage

The Information Stage must be similarly explored to determine if the parties efficiently generated a good joint surplus to be divided. How well was the Information Stage developed? Did they ask their counterpart many open-ended, information-seeking questions? As they got further into the interaction, did they ask "what" and "why" questions to ascertain counterpart needs and interests? Were both parties relatively candid or were they unusually circumspect? Did the unreciprocated candor of one side adversely affect its position during the subsequent discussions? Were unintended disclosures inadvertently made through verbal leaks or nonverbal signals? If so, how might they have been prevented? Were the participants able to ascertain the knowledge they needed to permit an efficient and productive Competitive/Distributive Stage? Were they able to use Blocking Techniques to avoid the disclosure of sensitive information? What other pertinent information should have been divulged, and when and how should it have been revealed?

D. Competitive/Distributive Stage

Which party made the first *real* offer? Were appropriate explanations used to support the precise proposals articulated—*i.e.*, were *principled* opening positions stated? Could different rationales have been employed more persuasively to support those positions? How did the counterparts react to the preliminary offer and its accompanying elucidation? Did they appear to be genuinely surprised, or did the proffered terms seem to be close to what they had apparently anticipated? Did the participant who made the initial offer make another proposal without receiving any definitive offer from the other side first? If so, what precipitated this conduct? How did the concession pattern develop and what caused each side to move toward the other?

E. Closing Stage

How did the Closing Stage evolve? Did it develop deliberately, with the parties moving together toward the final agreement or did one participant close an excessive amount of the distance remaining between the parties? Did the bargainers continue to use the techniques that got them to this stage of the interaction, or did they resort to less effective tactics? Participants should similarly ask themselves whether they exuded sufficient patience to induce over-anxious counterparts to move more quickly and more carelessly toward closure than they did. What ultimately induced them and the opposing side to accept the terms agreed upon or to reject the final offers that were made before the discussions were terminated?

F. Cooperative/Integrative Stage

Did the parties attempt to employ the Cooperative/Integrative Stage to maximize their joint gains achieved? Was a tentative accord clearly achieved before the initiation of cooperative bargaining? Did the Cooperative/Integrative Stage significantly enhance the return to each party? Were the Cooperative/Integrative Stage participants relatively candid about their respective needs and interests, or did a counterproductive competitive atmosphere permeate this portion of the interaction? How might the cooperative experience have been improved?

§ 14.03. Topics to Consider

A. Review of Concession Pattern

It is informative to explore the concession patterns of the two sides. Which party made the first concession and how was it generated? Were subsequent concessions by each side matched by reciprocal movement from the other party, or were either excessive or consecutive concessions made by one side? If so, were they inadvertently made? Was each concession accompanied by an appropriate explanation—*i.e.*, were "*principled*" *concessions* articulated? What was the exact size of each concession? Did successive position modifications involve consistently decreasing increments? If not, did one party unsuccessfully attempt to establish a false resistance point that could not be sustained? How close to the mid-point between the opening offers was the final settlement?

B. Influence of Time Pressures on Parties

How did time pressures influence the negotiation process? Did one party appear to be operating under greater time pressure than the other? If so, why? Was the party with less time pressure able to take advantage of this situation? Did the time factor generate a greater number of concessions or more sizable position changes as the impending deadline approached?

C. Specific Bargaining Techniques Used

What specific bargaining techniques were employed by their counterparts? How were they countered? Could they have been more effectively neutralized? Participants should ask themselves which particular tactics they used to enhance their own positions. Did their counterparts appear to recognize those tactics? What countermeasures did their counterparts adopt to undermine those tactics? What different approaches might participants have employed to advance their position more forcefully? What other tactics might counterparts have used more effectively against them? How could they have minimized the impact of these counterpart measures?

D. Deceitful Tactics

Did either side resort to deceitful tactics or deliberate misrepresentations to advance its position? Did these involve acceptable "puffing" and "embellishment," or inappropriate mendacity? If so, how were these devices discovered and how were they countered? What impact would these tactics have on future interactions involving the same participants?

E. Knowing Who Achieved More Beneficial Results and Why

Negotiators should always ask whether one side appeared to obtain more beneficial results than the other party. They should not merely ask whether their own side was satisfied with the final accord, since winning and losing participants tend to express equal satisfaction with the agreement achieved. If one side seemed to fare better than the other, what did it do to produce this outcome? What might the less successful bargainer have done differently? Did principal constraints contribute to an unequal result? If so, what might have been done to minimize the impact of this factor? If no settlement was ultimately attained, was principal recalcitrance the primary factor? Were principal expectations unduly elevated? If the principal rejected a final proposal that you thought should have been accepted or accepted final terms you thought should have been rejected, how might you have more effectively educated the principal regarding the negotiation process and the substantive merits of their situation?

F. Impact of Attribution [Self-Serving] Bias

When we evaluate how we have done, we are often influenced by self-serving attributions.[654] When we are successful, we tend to attribute our success to our own skill and efforts. On the other hand, when we do not do so well, we tend to attribute our results to external factors beyond our control. For example, when students achieve good grades, they usually say "I got an A." When they do not do very well, they say "Craver gave me a C." It is as if they had nothing to do with the C they earned.

Individuals analyzing bargaining interactions should be careful not to give themselves too much credit for their successes and too little responsibility for their shortfalls. When they do not achieve good results, they should really examine what they personally may have done wrong. Were they insufficiently prepared? Did they fail to put themselves in the shoes of the other side? Did they fail to establish beneficial aspiration levels and sufficiently persuasive arguments supporting those positions to generate confidence in the positions they were taking? What else could they have done to advance their side's interests? Even if the other side possessed greater bargaining power and/or skill, what could these persons have done to have had a greater beneficial impact on the interaction?

G. Dealing with Mistakes/New Tactics Encountered

Bargainers should finally ask two critical questions. What did they *do* that they wish they had not done? This inquiry relates to a mistake they may have made. If it were a mere tactical error, they should realize that their counterparts were probably unaware of their mistake. Negotiators should never do anything to alert unsuspecting counterparts to errors they may have made, hoping to cover up those errors. On the other hand, if true mistakes are made—such as mathematical errors—the best way to deal with them is directly. It is best that the participant confess the mistake, apologize, and make the necessary modification(s) in the originally stated position.

Advocates should similarly ask themselves what they did *not do* that they wish they had done. This question usually relates to a new tactic they encountered that they did not think they handled well. They should ask their colleagues if they ever encountered this approach. If so, how did they deal with it? If not, how would they try to counter such behavior? The more negotiators plan effective responses to counterpart tactics they may encounter during future interactions, the more effectively they should deal with those techniques when they next experience them. Individuals who fail to consider possible counter-measures to innovative tactics—hoping not to see them again—rarely handle them more effectively when they are forced to deal with them again.

---

654. *See* Malhotra & Bazerman, *supra* note 42 at 135–136.

Although it is helpful for negotiators to ask both what they did that they wish they had not done and what they did not do that they wish they had done, it is interesting to note that studies indicate that the latter question is more likely to enhance their future negotiations than the former inquiry.[655] This difference is due to the fact that individuals who think about what they *did not do* are able to incorporate the missing element(s) in their *future interactions*. On the other hand, persons who think about what they *had done* that they think they should not have done can omit such behavior from future encounters, but this information will not necessarily induce them to understand what they should do now instead. It is thus critical for people conducting post-negotiation assessments to focus carefully on the actions they did not take which they believe would benefit them in future interactions.

H. Use of Checklist

Through the use of the brief checklist set forth in the Table at the end of this chapter, negotiators may readily review almost any bargaining interaction. While it is certainly true that experience can be an excellent teacher, it must be remembered that experience without the benefit of meaningful post-transaction evaluation is of limited value. The time expended during the appraisal process should be amply recouped through improved future performance.

§ 14.04. Conclusion

At the conclusion of their more significant negotiations, participants should review their performance to ascertain what they did well and what they should strive to improve. Even though experience can be an excellent teacher, individuals who fail to analyze their prior negotiation experiences are unlikely to learn from those transactions and tend to repeat the same mistakes in their future interactions.

Negotiators should carefully evaluate how the bargaining process unfolded. They must consider the Preparation Stage, the Preliminary Stage, the Information Stage, the Competitive/Distributive Stage, the Closing Stage, and the Cooperative/Integrative Stage to determine whether the entire process evolved in an efficient manner.

Proficient bargainers are generally able to learn from previous mistakes by increasing the influence of their efficacious behavior and by decreasing the impact of their less effective conduct. When they review bargaining interactions, advocates should ask themselves what they did that they wish they had not done and what they did not do that they wish they had done.

---

655. *See* Laura J. Kray, Adam D. Galinsky & Keith D. Markman, "Counterfactual Structure and Learning from Experience in Negotiations," 45 *Journal of Experimental Psychology* 979 (2009).

Post-Negotiation Evaluation Checklist

1. Was your *pre-negotiation* preparation sufficiently thorough? Were you completely familiar with the operative factual, economic, and business issues? Did you fully understand your firm's value system and non-settlement alternatives? Did you calculate your side's Best Alternative to a Negotiated Agreement? Did you carefully place yourself in the shoes of the other side and estimate your *counterpart's* non-settlement options?

2. Was your *initial* aspiration level high enough? Did you establish a firm goal for *each issue* to be addressed? If you obtained everything you sought, was this due to the fact you did not establish sufficiently elevated objectives? Did you prepare a beneficial and principled opening offer?

3. Did your *pre-bargaining* prognostications prove to be accurate? Did your counterpart begin near the point you thought he/she would begin? If not, what caused your miscalculations?

4. Which party dictated the *contextual* factors such as time, day, and location? Did these factors influence the negotiations?

5. Did you use the *Preliminary Stage* to establish rapport with your counterpart and to create a positive negotiating environment? Did you employ *Attitudinal Bargaining* to modify inappropriate counterpart behavior? If you negotiated primarily through electronic exchanges, did you initially telephone the other side to establish a beneficial relationship, and telephone that party shortly after you e-mailed proposals to enable you to hear their response and to clarify any misconceptions they might have had?

6. Did the *Information Stage* develop sufficiently to provide the participants with the knowledge they needed to understand their respective needs and interests and to enable them to consummate an optimal agreement? Did you use *broad, open-ended questions* to determine what the other side wanted, and use *what* and *why* questions to ascertain their needs and interests? Did you disclose your own important information in response to counterpart inquiries to induce them to listen more carefully to those disclosures and accord them greater respect?

7. Were any unintended *verbal leaks* or *nonverbal disclosures* made? What precipitated these revelations? Were you able to use *Blocking Techniques* to prevent the disclosure of sensitive information?

8. Who made the *first* offer? The first "*real*" offer? Was a "*principled*" initial offer articulated by you? By your counterpart? How did your *counterpart* react to *your* initial proposal? How did *you* react to your *counterpart's* opening offer?

9. Were *consecutive* opening offers made by one party before the other side disclosed its initial position? What induced that party to engage in this conduct?

10. What specific *bargaining techniques* were employed by your coun*terpart* during the *Distributive/Competitive Stage* and how were these tactics countered

by you? What else might you have done to counter these tactics more effectively?

11.   What particular *negotiation devices* were employed by *you* to advance your position? Did your counterpart appear to *recognize* the various techniques you used, and, if so, how did he/she endeavor to minimize their impact? What *other tactics* might you have used to advance your position more forcefully?

12.   Which party made the *first concession* and how was it precipitated? Were *subsequent concessions* made on an *alternating basis*? You should keep a record of each concession made by you and by your counterpart throughout the interaction.

13.   Were *"principled"* concessions articulated by you? By your counterpart? Did *successive position* changes involve decreasing increments and were those increments relatively reciprocal to the other side's concomitant movement?

14.   How did the parties use the *Closing Stage* to achieve an agreement once they realized that they had overlapping needs and interests? Did either side appear to make greater concessions during the *Closing Stage*?

15.   Did the parties resort to *Cooperative/Integrative Bargaining* to maximize their aggregate returns?

16.   How close to the *mid-point* between the initial *real offers* was the final settlement?

17.   How did *time pressures* influence the parties and their respective concession patterns? Try not to ignore the time pressures that affected your counterpart.

18.   Did either party resort to *deceitful tactics* or deliberate misrepresentations to enhance its situation? Did these pertain to material law or fact, or only to the speaker's value system or settlement intentions?

      If you sent files to the other side by e-mail, did you initially cleanse those files to eliminate the electronic metadata containing information you did not want the other side to see?

19.   What finally induced you *to accept the terms* agreed upon or *to reject* the final offer made by the other party?

20.   Did *either* party appear to obtain *more favorable terms* than the other side, and if so, how was this result accomplished? What could the *less successful participant* have *done differently* to improve its situation?

21.   If *no* settlement was achieved, what might have been done differently with respect to principal preparation and/or bargaining developments to produce a different result?

22.   What did you do that you *wish* you had *not done*? Do you think your counterpart was aware of your error? How could you avoid such a mistake in the future?

23.   What did you *not do* that you *wish you had done* to advance your own interests or to counteract unexpected counterpart behavior? What should you plan to do differently in your future interactions?

Chapter 15

Ethical Considerations

§ 15.01. Negotiation as a Deceptive Process

On the one hand the negotiator must be fair and truthful; on the other he must mislead his opponent. Like the poker player, a negotiator hopes that his opponent will overestimate the value of his hand. Like the poker player, ... he must facilitate his opponent's inaccurate assessment. The critical difference between those who are successful negotiators and those who are not lies in this capacity both to mislead and not to be misled.... [A] careful examination of the behavior of even the most forthright, honest, and trustworthy negotiators will show them actively engaged in misleading their opponents about their true positions.... To conceal one's true position, to mislead an opponent about one's true settling point is the essence of negotiation.[656]

Over the past 30 years, most business schools and many economic departments have developed courses designed to teach students how to negotiate, in recognition of the fact that business persons employ this skill throughout their careers. Professors explore the various concepts relevant to bargaining interactions, and assign students various negotiation exercises designed to demonstrate the concepts being taught. Many students worked hard on these exercises to achieve results beneficial to their own sides. Many teachers became uncomfortable with such student competition. They apparently felt that students should not be exposed to the types of bargaining environments they would encounter when they deal with real world situations. The teachers feared that overtly competitive interactions would be too traumatic for sensitive students. These teachers thus developed what has become known as the communitarian approach.

The communitarian style is based on the integrative bargaining concepts developed over one hundred years ago by Mary Parker Follett[657] and explored in the mid-1960s

---

656. James J. White, "Machiavelli and the Bar: Ethical Limitations on Lying in Negotiation," 1980 *American Bar Foundation Research Journal* 926, 927–28 (1980). "Deceitful or not, lies about price, value, and some other matters are practically sacrosanct to conventional negotiation. If lawyers were forbidden from engaging in these lies, they would be at a tremendous disadvantage when negotiating with any nonlawyer," Walter W. Steele, Jr., "Deceptive Negotiating and High-Toned Morality," 39 *Vanderbilt Law Review* 1387, 1395 (1986).

657. *See* Joan C. Tonn, *Mary P. Follett* 360–388 (2003).

by Professors Walton and McKersie.[658] This approach gained general acceptance following the publication of *Getting to Yes* by Roger Fisher and William Ury.[659] This style is based on the theory that most negotiations do not involve conflicted issues. If negotiators go behind the stated positions, which often appear to be opposite, and explore the underlying interests of the parties, they can discover solutions beneficial to both sides. Two persons are trying to decide how to divide an orange they both want. It may seem fair to divide it in half, until they discover that one wants the pulp to make juice while the other wants the rind to make zest. This discovery permits them to give one all of the pulp and the other all of the rind.[660]

Communitarians believe "that negotiation is a moral and ethical process, worthy of deep philosophical, political, legal, and human respect."[661] Their approach requires negotiating parties to be completely open and honest with each other with respect to their true interests and settlement intentions.[662] Each side must candidly indicate the terms they desire and the true value placed on each, to enable the parties to achieve Pareto optimal agreements which satisfy the underlying interests of each — *i.e.*, "win-win" agreements instead of what are often characterized by commentators as "win-lose" accords that favor one side over the other. If negotiators are not entirely truthful with respect to their real interests and values, inefficiencies result or potentially beneficial accords are not achieved.

Communitarians do not like to engage in conventional distributive bargaining in which the opposing parties use deceptive tactics to enable them to claim more than a fair share for themselves. They have thus created a world in which negotiators have underlying interests that do not conflict with each other.[663] Side A gives Side B what it prefers to have, while Side B gives Side A what it wants. The negotiators use a cooperative/problem-solving style which generates mutually beneficial and jointly efficient accords, instead of a competitive/adversarial style which produces one-sided and inefficient agreements.

Communitarians eschew deceptive bargaining tactics. They believe that professionals should not be allowed to over or under state the way they actually value the different terms being exchanged, they do not think that individuals should be

---

658. *See* Richard E. Walton & Robert B. McKersie, *A Behavioral Theory of Labor Negotiations* (1965).

659. Fisher, Ury & Patton, *supra* note 11.

660. *See id.* at 76.

661. Carrie Menkel-Meadow, "The Ethics of Compromise," in *The Negotiator's Fieldbook* 155, 156 (Andrea Kupfer Schneider & Christopher Honeyman, eds. 2006). See also Carrie Menkel-Meadow, "The Evolving Complexity of Dispute Resolution Ethics," 30 *Georgetown Journal of Legal Ethics* 389 (2017).

662. *See* Michael R. Fowler, *Mastering* Negotiation 361–362 (2017); Mark Young, "Sharks, Saints, and Samurai: The Power of Ethics in Negotiations," 24 *Negotiation Journal* 145, 150 (2008) (exhorting negotiators to always behave honorably simply because counterparts *deserve* to be treated fairly).

663. *See generally* Robert J. Condlin, "Bargaining with a Hugger: The Weaknesses and Limitations of a Communitarian Conception of Legal Dispute Bargaining, or Why We Can't All Just Get Along," 9 *Cardozo Journal of Conflict Resolution* 1 (2007).

permitted to misrepresent their true settlement intentions, and they believe that such tactics as bluffing should be proscribed.[664] This approach is based upon the naïve belief that business world bargaining interactions are primarily integrative, with few conflicting interests. It assumes that business representatives rarely have to deal with distributive items that both sides value and wish to claim for themselves. It ignores the fact that in business interactions, "opportunities for integrative bargaining are not nearly as pervasive as sometimes authoritatively asserted,"[665] due to the fact that monetary issues tend to dominate such circumstances.

> [M]ost negotiations are "mixed motive"; they include both opportunities for joint gain, and opportunities for grabbing more from the other side … [S]trategies that are wise for creating are often opposite from those that are wise for claiming (*e.g.*, deception about positions and power is necessary for claiming, while deception about interests is disruptive for creating). But all negotiations include both elements, and few negotiations occur where a wise negotiator would not employ at least some of each set of behaviors. Indeed, one of the more interesting challenges faced by negotiators is how to balance both of these elements.[666]

When I teach negotiation skills to practicing attorneys and business persons, I often ask if they can lie during their interactions. They usually respond negatively. I then talk about two persons engaged in a negotiation where Side A is authorized to accept anything over $1,000,000 while Side B is authorized to pay anything up to $1,300,000. We thus have a $300,000 zone of possible agreement between the $1,000,000 and $1,300,000 positions. The parties begin with small talk, then move on to the serious discussions. At an appropriate point, Side A says it can't accept anything less than $1,600,000, and Side B responds that it can't go a penny over $700,000. Both sides are pleased that they have begun the process successfully, yet they have both begun with bald-faced lies.

Audience members become uncomfortable. They all recall times they have commenced bargaining encounters with exaggerated position statements they did not expect their counterparts to take literally. I then quote from Model Rule 4.1 which provides that "a lawyer shall not knowingly make a false statement of material fact or law to a third person." Rule 4.1 is a paragon of clarity: A lawyer may not lie. When is a lie not a lie? When it is by a lawyer! Comment 2 acknowledges that attorneys involved in bargaining interactions have different expectations.

> Whether a particular statement should be regarded as one of fact can depend on the circumstances. Under generally accepted conventions in

---

664. *See generally* Robert C. Bordone, "Fitting the Ethics to the Forum: A Proposal for Process-Enabling Ethical Codes," 21 *Ohio State Journal on Dispute Resolution* 1 (2005). *See also* Chris Provis, "Ethics, Deception and Labor Negotiation," 28 *Journal of Business Ethics* 145 (Nov. 2000).

665. Gerald B. Wetlaufer, "The Limits of Integrative Bargaining," 85 *Georgetown Law Journal* 369, 372 (1996).

666. Raymond A. Friedman & Debra Shapiro, "Deception and Mutual Gains Bargaining: Are They Mutually Exclusive?" 11 *Negotiation Journal* 243, 247 (1995). *See* Gerald Wetlaufer, "The Ethics of Lying in Negotiation," 75 *Iowa Law Review* 1219, 1245–48 (1990).

negotiation, certain types of statements ordinarily are not taken as statements of material fact. Estimates of price or value placed on the subject of a transaction and a party's intentions as to an acceptable settlement of a claim are ordinarily in this category....

Although Rule 4.1 unequivocally proscribes lawyer prevarication, Comment 2 excludes puffing, embellishment, and dissembling with respect to a negotiator's true settlement objectives.[667] This Comment acknowledges the reality of bargaining interactions between legal practitioners.

> [N]egotiation often cannot take place if the parties must reveal ... their true asking price, or their intention regarding settlement throughout the bargaining process. Deception concerning value as well as deception concerning settlement point in particular are consistent with functionalism because they are recognizable as bargaining techniques and allow accurate information to be achieved through bargaining.[668]

The ironic aspect of this exception to Rule 4.1 concerns the fact that there are really only two things that are truly material when attorneys and business persons negotiate. The legal, factual, economic, business, and cultural issues are all secondary. What each participant must ascertain is the degree to which the other side values each of the items being discussed and the amount of each that must be conceded if an agreement is to be achieved. Nonetheless, most professional negotiators do not expect such candor.

Business persons recognize that serious risks are associated with inappropriately dishonest negotiating conduct. Whether they function as generalists in smaller communities or specialists in larger metropolitan areas, they begin to see the same persons repeatedly. If someone is discovered misrepresenting what the other side has the right to know, their reputation will suffer.[669] The persons who discern the violation of trust are likely to tell others in their own firms. They and their colleagues will often tell friends in other firms. They may even place their picture and name on the Internet to let millions of persons know these individuals cannot be trusted. When negotiators can no longer be trusted with respect to representations pertaining to material factual, economic, or business issues, they will find it difficult to interact with others.[670] Instead of accepting what such individuals say, counterparts have to

---

667. *See* Ronald D. Rotunda, *Professional Responsibility* 167–168 (1995); Gary T. Lowenthal, "A General Theory of Negotiation Process, Strategy, and Behavior," 31 *Kansas Law* Review 69, 101 (1982); Geoffrey C. Hazard, Jr., "The Lawyer's Obligation to Be Trustworthy When Dealing With Opposing Parties," 33 *South Carolina Law Review* 181, 183 (1981); Raymond A. Friedman & Debra L. Shapiro, "Deception and Mutual Gains Bargaining: Are They Mutually Exclusive?" 11 *Negotiation Journal* 243, 245 (1995).

668. Eleanor Holmes Norton, "Bargaining and the Ethic of Process," 64 *New York University Law Review* 493, 537 (1989).

669. *See* Greg Williams (with Pat Iyer), *Body Language Secrets to Win More Negotiations* 185 (2016); Peter C. Cramton & J. Gregory Dees, "Promoting Honesty in Negotiation: An Exercise in Practical Ethics," 3 *Business Ethics Quarterly* 359, 369 (1993).

670. *See* Epstein & Marty-Nelson, *supra* note 254, at 68–69.

verify everything they assert. Instead of relying on literal or figurative handshakes, all agreements have to be reduced to writing and signed. The negotiation process is substantially undermined, and bargaining interactions take longer and are more difficult.

If firm representatives misrepresent material fact relied upon by other parties to their economic detriment, those parties may sue the responsible companies for fraud. Such situations would not only be monetarily costly, but would also negatively affect the business reputations of the responsible firms.

When I teach my Negotiation class, I have the Model Rules in force. If a student is accused of a violation, a trial would take place in front of the class. In all the years I have taught my course, I have never had to conduct a trial. Instead of filing formal charges of deceit, the accusers simply raise the issues informally before the class. The accusers and the accused are permitted to explain their positions, and I ask class members whether they think the conduct in question was appropriate or inappropriate. In most instances, students suggest that the challenged statements involved mere "puffing" or acceptable "embellishment." On rare occasions, however, they indicate a belief that the misrepresentations were improper. By the end of the semester, the students being discussed end up with one or two non-settlements simply because their future counterparts do not trust their representations and are hesitant to enter into agreements with them. If they cannot be sure of the fundamental information being conveyed by these persons, they do not feel comfortable interacting with them.[671] These results graphically demonstrate to everyone the importance of relative honesty. While puffing and embellishment do not undermine future interactions, inappropriate mendacity makes it difficult for disreputable actors to achieve future accords.[672]

Basic trust is essential to bargaining interactions.[673] The participants have to be willing to disclose their true needs and interests if the negotiators hope to achieve mutual accords—especially if they hope to generate efficient agreements.[674] If one

---

671. *See* Carol M. Rose, "Lecture: Trust in the Mirror of Betrayal," 75 *Boston University Law Review* 531, 539–541 (1995).

672. *See* Debra L. Shapiro, Blair H. Sheppard & Lisa Cheraskin, "Business on a Handshake," 8 *Negotiation Journal* 365, 366–367 (1992) (discussing the degree to which mutual trust enables business partners to interact with each other efficiently and with minimal need for monitoring); Menkel-Meadow, *supra* note 609, at 160 ("[L]awyers who are perceived as unethical are also perceived as ineffective."). *See also* David A. Lax & James K. Sebenius, "Three Ethical Issues in Negotiation," 2 *Negotiation Journal* 363, 364 (1986): "[A] lie always leaves a drop of poison behind, and even the most dazzling diplomatic success gained by dishonesty stands on an insecure foundation, for it awakes in the defeated a party a sense of aggravation, a desire for vengeance, and a hatred which must always be menace to his foe ..." (quoting Francois de Callieres).

673. *See generally* Roy Lewicki, "Trust and Distrust," in *The Negotiator's Fieldbook* 191, 196–199 (Andrea Kupfer Schneider & Christopher Honeyman, eds. 2006). "[H]igher levels of trust make negotiation easier, while lower levels of trust make negotiation more difficult." *Id.* at 197.

674. *See* Lee Ross & Constance Stillinger, "Barriers to Conflict Resolution," 7 *Negotiation Journal* 389, 391 (1991); Catherine H. Tinsley, Jack J. Cambria & Andrea Kupfer Schneider, "Reputations in

side does not trust the other, it will be hesitant to disclose its own confidential information and underlying values, fearing exploitation by manipulative and less candid counterparts. On the other hand, negotiators must be careful, even when interacting with honest counterparts, not to be too forthcoming, lest they naively permit skilled adversaries to claim an excessive share of the surplus involved.[675]

§ 15.02. Overt Misrepresentations, Partial Disclosures, Nondisclosures, and Deceptive Conduct

When I teach negotiating skills to lawyers and business persons, I often indicate that I have never participated in a negotiation — as an advocate or mediator — where both sides did not lie, yet I have encountered almost no bargainers I thought were dishonest.[676] This seeming contradiction is based upon the fact that they have all engaged in "puffing" and "embellishment." They have over and under stated client values, and misstated their true settlement intentions, but have almost never misrepresented other factual or legal issues of a material nature.

> In certain bargaining situations, we ... play ... mutually deceptive roles; ... [F]alse claims are a convention; ... If buyers and sellers bargain knowingly and voluntarily, one would be hard put to regard as misleading their exaggerations, false claims to have given their last bid, or words of feigned loss of interest. Both parties have then consented to the rules of the game.[677]

A. Overt Misrepresentations

Suppose a corporate representative is negotiating the sale of a business. The owner of the firm would like to obtain $50 million, but would seriously consider offers in the $40 to $45 million range. Could the business negotiator tell a prospective buyer that her client would not accept anything less than $55 million? The answer is clearly yes, since this statement concerns client *settlement intentions* that do not constitute *material* information. Could she state that other parties will undoubtedly be interested in this firm, even if no one else has yet contacted her client about a possible purchase?

Negotiation," in *The Negotiator's Fieldbook* 203, 207–209 (Andrea Kupfer Schneider & Christopher Honeyman, eds. 2006).

675. *See* Scott R. Peppet, "Lawyers' Bargaining Ethics, Contract, and Collaboration: The End of the Legal Profession and the Beginning of Professional Pluralism," 90 *Iowa Law Review* 475, 482–483 (2005); Geoffrey M. Peters, "The Use of Lies in Negotiation," 48 *Ohio State Law Journal* 1, 32, 36 (1987); Chris Provis, "Ethics, Deception and Labor Negotiation," 28 *Journal of Business Ethics* 145, 147 (2000).

676. "Bargaining is a unique process in which the parties engage in stylized strategic behavior and use practices such as bluffing, puffing, and withholding information as a matter of course." Norton, *supra* note 636, at 506.

677. Sissela Bok, *Lying: Moral Choice in Public and Private Life* 138 (1978).

Most bargainers would consider such a statement to be mere puffing and permissible under acceptable negotiation ethical standards, even though such misstatements would be likely to help the speaker obtain an advantage at the bargaining table.[678] It would similarly be acceptable to most persons for the seller's representative to talk generally about the golden future of the business, even if she somewhat over-states the actual situation, since such embellishments are normally not considered to concern statements of material fact.[679]

If the firm representative obtains a $42 million offer from one party, may she indicate that her side has an offer from a different party when they have not received any such offer? When I have discussed this question with corporate counsel at continuing legal education programs, the vast majority suggest that such a misstatement would not be appropriate. It is not mere puffery, but concerns an issue of *material fact*—whether another party has made a definitive offer to purchase the business in question. I agree with this viewpoint. While it is almost certainly acceptable to indicate that other parties would have an interest in the firm, with such a general statement constituting mere puffery, it is inappropriate for the representative to make a knowingly false statement regarding the existence of another bidder.

Suppose the seller receives an offer of $45 million form another party. Could the firm representative tell the $42 million bidder that they have received a $50 million offer? I believe that such a deliberate misrepresentation would expose her client to a suit for fraud based on the clearly material nature of this misrepresentation.[680] On the other hand, she could probably state that they have received another offer and suggest to the $42 million bidder that it will cost $50 million to purchase the business. When this statement is made, the negotiator is not disclosing the actual value of the

---

678. *See* Alan Strudler, "Incommensurable Goods, Rightful Lies, and the Wrongfulness of Fraud," 146 *University of Pennsylvania Law Review* 1529, 1540–41 (1998).

679. *See, e.g.*, Royal Business Machines v. Lorraine Corp., 633 F.2d 34, 42 (7th Cir. 1980); Vaughn v. General Foods Corp., 797 F.2d 1403 (7th Cir. 1986); Vulcan Metals Co. v. Simmons Mfg. Co., 248 F. 853 (2d Cir. 1918).

It is common knowledge and may always be assumed that any seller will express a favorable opinion concerning what he has to sell; and when he praises it in general terms, without specific content or reference to facts, buyers are expected to and do understand that they are not entitled to rely literally upon the words.

Restatement (Second) of Torts § 542 cmt. e. While statements of opinion do not usually give rise to actionable fraud, more specific statements upon which listeners may reasonably rely may be actionable. *See, e.g.*, James v. Lifeline Mobile Medics, 792 N.E.2d 461 (Ill. App. Ct. 2003) (misrepresentation regarding defendant's pending bankruptcy during settlement negotiations actionable, since such a specific statement involved more than mere statement of opinion).

680. *See* Kabatchnick v. Hanover-Elm Building Corp., 103 N.E.2d 692 (Mass. 1952) (actionable fraud for real estate owner to tell lessee he had an offer from a third party for an exaggerated rental amount in an effort to induce the lessee to enter into a new lease at an unwarranted rental rate). *See generally* Perschbacher, *supra* note 4, at 90, 127–29; Anne M. Burr, "Ethics in Negotiation: Does Getting to Yes Require Candor?" 17 *Negotiation Journal* 8, 10–11 (2001); G. Richard Shell, "Bargaining With the Devil Without Losing Your Soul," in *What's Fair: Ethics for Negotiators* 57, 58–65 (Carrie Menkel-Meadow & Michael Wheeler, eds. 2004).

other offer. She is truthfully indicating that they have received another offer, and is engaging in mere puffery when she indicates that it will take $50 million to purchase her firm. Since the latter point clearly concerns the settlement intention of her principal, it is nonmaterial information. What could she ethically say if the other party directly asks her if they have received a $50 million offer from the other party? She may not answer this inquiry affirmatively, because they have not received such an offer, and such a misrepresentation would concern material fact. She could, however, indicate that such information is confidential and reiterate that it will take $50 million to purchase her firm.

B. Misleading Partial Disclosures

Negotiators often use selective disclosures to enhance their positions. They discuss the economic information and business considerations beneficial to their situations and withhold the circumstances that are not helpful. In most instances, these selective disclosures are expected by counterparts and are considered an inherent aspect of bargaining interactions. When negotiators emphasize their strengths, opposing parties must work to ascertain their hidden weaknesses. Probing questions can be effectively employed to explore areas not being discussed.

There are times when the partial disclosure of information is improper, because of legal obligations requiring full disclosure. For example, securities regulations generally require stock and bond sellers to disclose certain financial information to prospective purchasers. The housing laws in many states require sellers to disclose serious defects, even if they are not asked about such circumstances. When such affirmative obligations are imposed, negotiators are obliged to disclose the requisite information or expose their firms to liability.

Under some circumstances, partial statements may mislead opposing parties as effectively as overt misrepresentations. For example, the plaintiff in *Spaulding v. Zimmerman*[681] sustained cracked ribs and fractured clavicles in an automobile accident. After the ribs and clavicles had healed, the defendant had the plaintiff examined by his own medical expert who found an aorta aneurysm that neither the claimant nor his attorney knew about. Although the defendant was under no ethical obligation to voluntarily disclose the existence of the aneurysm and could ignore questions regarding the independent medical examiner's findings, he could certainly not overtly misrepresent the doctor's diagnosis by indicating that everything had healed. Would it be ethical for the defendant to respond to plaintiff questions regarding this matter by stating that "the ribs and the clavicles have healed"? Would such a partial disclosure constitute a deliberate misrepresentation of material fact due to the fact the defendant realized that the claimant would interpret such a statement as an indication that

---

681. 116 N.W.2d 704 (Minn. 1962).

everything had healed? Comment 1 to Rule 4.1 expressly addresses this issue when it indicates that "[m]isrepresentations can also occur by partially true but misleading statements ... that are the equivalent of affirmative false statements."[682] Although the defendant counsel could most likely say nothing about the aneurysm, he could not provide a statement that, while true, is clearly misleading to the claimant. Negotiators must thus forego statements that are facially true, but which they know are misleading to listeners who do not appreciate the inherent deception involved, since such statements could subject their side to law suits for fraud.

C. Nondisclosure of Information

In the absence of special relations imposing fiduciary obligations or express contractual or statutory duties, negotiators are normally not obligated to divulge relevant factual or economic information to their counterparts.[683] This doctrine is premised upon the duty imposed upon negotiators to conduct their own factual investigations. If they fail to perform such research, they have no right to expect the opposing party to assist them in this regard, absent special circumstances.

D. Deception by Disingenuous Conduct

Suppose two parties are negotiating and one provides the other with a written proposal. The recipient of the proposal looks disappointed, tears up the written document, and walks out of the room. If the terms set forth in the proposal are actually within the settlement range of the recipient, would that person's actions be fraudulent since designed to mislead the offeror? Most negotiators would answer in the negative, on the ground the misleading demonstrative behavior concerns their underlying settlement intentions that are considered nonmaterial fact. Such threats or bluffs are part of many bargaining interactions. They may hinder effective integrative negotiations, but they may be effectively employed by individuals seeking to claim value for themselves.[684] Only communitarian-oriented theorists who believe that no deceitful conduct should be permitted during bargaining interactions would be likely to consider such actions to be improper.[685]

---

682. *See generally* Donald C. Langevoort, "Half-Truths: Protecting Mistaken Inferences by Investors and Others," 52 *Stanford Law Review* 87 (1999).

683. *See* Barry R. Temkin, "Misrepresentation by Omission in Settlement Negotiations: Should There Be a Silent Safe Harbor?" 18 *Georgetown Journal of Legal Ethics* 179 (2004); Deborah A. DeMott, "Do you Have the Right to Remain Silent? Duties of Disclosure in Business Transactions," 19 *Delaware Journal of Corporate Law* 65 (1994). *See also* Alan Strudler, "Moral Complexity in the Law of Nondisclosure," 45 *U.C.L.A. Law Review* 337 (1997).

684. *See generally* Debra L. Shapiro & Robert J. Bies, "Threats, Bluffs, and Disclaimers in Negotiations," 60 *Organizational Behavior & Human Decision Processes* 14 (1994).

685. *See* Reed Elizabeth Loder, "Moral Truthseeking and the Virtuous Negotiator," 8 *Georgetown Journal of Legal Ethics* 45, 79–81 (1994–95).

§ 15.03. Conclusion

Business persons negotiate frequently, but many feel uncomfortable with the deception inherent in most bargaining interactions. They do not like to exaggerate their positions for personal gain or to misrepresent their side's true settlement intentions. Although Model Rule 4.1 prohibits the knowing misrepresentation of *material fact* by attorneys, Comment 2 expressly notes that due to accepted bargaining conventions, advocate statements regarding *client values* and *client settlement intentions* do not concern "material fact." Courts similarly decline to find that misstatements by business persons concerning such matters constitute actionable fraud. These exceptions are actually quite narrow. They merely permit "puffing" and "embellishment," but no overt or subvert misstatements of true material fact. Negotiators who misrepresent material information risk the loss of reputations for integrity, which will significantly undermine their ability to conduct future bargaining interactions. In addition, their firms may be held liable for fraud.

Whenever negotiators are contemplating behavior they think might be inappropriate, they should ask themselves one critical question. If such conduct was engaged in by their counterparts, would they consider it to be acceptable "puffing" or "embellishment," or unacceptable deception? If they think that it would be fine for their adversaries to employ such tactics, it would most likely be appropriate for them to do so, but not if they believe it would be improper.

Appendix

The following negotiation exercises have been included both to demonstrate the concepts covered in the book and to allow individuals who work on these exercises to see how differently individuals assess identical bargaining situations. Participants should be divided into groups of two or four, with half assigned to one side and half assigned to the other side. Everyone should read the *General Information* provided, but should only read the *Confidential Information* pertaining to their assigned side. Point values are assigned to different items in two of the exercises, with these points representing the value systems of the opposing sides. When the parties interact, they may discuss the specific factual, economic, and business information set forth in their respective sets of Confidential Information, but they may **not** talk about the **points** assigned to each particular issue. For example, it is fine to indicate that you value Item 1 twice as much as Item 2, but you may not indicate that Item 1 is worth 100 points, while Item 2 is worth 50 points. This is to ensure that the negotiating parties behave just as they would if they were actually representing the parties in question.

The SINGLEPART-LARGECORP EXERCISE concerns a typical buy-sell negotiation involving a large firm seeking to acquire a small firm. There are various issues that must be addressed, and participants should endeavor to generate efficient agreements which maximize the joint gains achieved.

The NERD-SOFTWARE TECH EXERCISE involves a negotiation between a major programmer and the firm he desires to leave. The parties have to decide the terms on which he may depart and the limitations that should be placed upon him once he is employed at another company.

The CHINESE JOINT VENTURE EXERCISE concerns the formation of a joint venture between a Chinese firm and a United States firm. They have to decide upon the financial support to be provided by the American company, and the degree to which that company will exercise influence over the joint venture.

Following each exercise is a summary of the different issues from both sides' perspective, to enable the parties to see how efficiently they divided the items they had to share with each other. If they did not do a good job of maximizing their joint results, what should they have done differently? Did they fail to employ the Cooperative/Integrative Stage effectively? Did they hide or misrepresent their underlying value systems to such a degree that they were unable to locate areas for joint gains?

The MODIFIED NASA DECISION MAKING EXERCISE is included to demonstrate the manner in which group decisions are made and the way in which competitive tendencies often influence what seem to be wholly cooperative interactions. This Exercise is especially instructive for corporate leaders who must regularly interact with managers from other departments within their own organizations. Since the stranded moon explorers must endeavor to survive together, there is no reason for either detail or its members to view the other detail or its members as competitors. Nonetheless, when this exercise is conducted, counterproductive competitive behavior is usually discernible. During the initial phase, each participant should be given five to ten minutes to individually rank the fifteen items in order of perceived importance.

During the second phase of this Exercise, details from eight to twelve persons must be formed. Each detail must then engage in an intra-detail negotiation that is designed to achieve a group consensus with respect to the ranking of the fifteen items—and whether the entire detail would prefer to hike to the parent ship or remain behind and allow the other detail to go for help. I usually provide each detail with about fifteen minutes for this purpose, to make them feel some degree of urgency. It is interesting to watch for "leaders" to emerge. They may be selected by their detail because of their personal backgrounds or simply because of their physical location in the group (e.g., the head of the table). Participants should observe the way in which leaders and others attempt to minimize group conflict and maximize group harmony. How do these persons work (mediate) to resolve disputes regarding particular items?

The final phase of the Exercise involves inter-detail negotiations. Pairs are given fifteen to twenty minutes to resolve two basic issues: (1) which entire detail will hike to the parent ship to get assistance and which entire detail will remain behind; and (2) which of the different items will be assigned to the group hiking to the parent ship and which will be given to the detail which remains behind. By having details of eight to twelve persons, each group must initially decide whether they will all participate in the inter-detail negotiations or will select one or two representatives to speak for them.

When NASA created this exercise about fifty years ago, we still believed that due to the rotation of the moon, one side was exposed to the sun while the other remained dark. We now know that this assumption was incorrect and that most of the moon has bright times and dark times each day. I usually instruct the participants to assume that the rover vehicle went 200 miles into the dark side of the moon so they will appreciate the assumption that the solar powered transmitter will not work until the traveling detail gets near the parent ship.

Singlepart-Largecorp Purchase Agreement
General Information

Fifteen years ago, Singlepart, Inc., a stereo speaker component manufacturer, was started in a garage. Today, Singlepart, a privately held company, has 50 employees, including 8 electrical engineers, and 32 well-paid assembly line workers. Singlepart owns numerous patents, and has an outstanding reputation. HIGH TECH. NEWS has praised Singlepart "for being on the cutting edge of technology, continually innovating and improving its products, and having a unique approach to component manufacture." While many companies make similar components, Singlepart components are considered the best available.

Six months ago, Largecorp initiated efforts to acquire Singlepart. Preliminary negotiations have been completed. A purchase concept outlining the selling price, the items to be transferred, and other basic terms has been orally agreed to by both parties. Largecorp representatives were instructed to draft a formal Agreement for Sale of the business.

A Largecorp representative wrote the attached Agreement for Sale of the business and sent it to Bill Stewart, the President and Owner of Singlepart, and to the Chairman and CEO of Largecorp for their approval. Stewart and the CEO of Largecorp have instructed their representatives to meet one last time to finalize the precise terms and sign the agreement. As soon as the final terms are agreed upon and the closing date is specified, the Agreement for Sale will become binding.

Agreement For Sale of Business

This agreement is between *Largecorp*, Buyer, and *William Stewart*, Seller.

A. Seller is the owner of certain real property, including land, buildings, and improvements, located at 110 Main Street, Neeto City, West Dakota, referred to as "the property."

B. Seller is the owner and operator of Singlepart, Inc., a stereo speaker component manufacturer, operated on the property ("the business").

C. Buyer and Seller desire to enter into this agreement for the purchase and sale of the property and business.

D. Therefore, the parties agree as follows:

Section One—Offer

Buyer agrees to buy from Seller and Seller agrees to sell to Buyer the property and the business, subject to the conditions set forth herein.

Section Two—Description of Property and Business

The legal description of the real estate included in the property is set forth on page 147 of Book 173 of the Record of Deeds, which is incorporated by reference. The property also includes Singlepart, Inc., the building, equipment, furniture, fixtures, and other improvements located on the described land. The business includes all customer lists, telephone listings, licenses and permits, business and professional memberships, the trade name, patent rights, and all other tangible and intangible property, used in or related to the operation of Singlepart, Inc.

Section Three — Purchase Price and Terms

The purchase price for the property, business, inventory and supplies is $_____.

Section Four — Non-Competition Obligation

Seller agrees that neither Seller nor any entity in which Seller has an interest as owner, officer, or manager, will open, operate, or in any way become involved in any stereo component research, development, manufacture, or sales business for a period of 5 years after the closing.

Section Five — Warranty and Indemnification Provisions

[To be agreed upon during final negotiations between parties]

Section Six — Closing Matters

Buyer and Seller will close this sale on or before _____ (date) subject to the satisfaction of all conditions set forth in this agreement. Seller will transfer possession of and title to the property and the business to Buyer at the closing.

Section Seven — Signatures

_____   _____
Buyer   Seller

Confidential Information for Singlepart Representatives

1. Stewart, the President and sole stockholder, has thought about selling Singlepart for many years but resisted because it was his own creation. Largecorp's offer is rather generous, and Stewart has decided to sell his assets, take time off, and travel. Stewart is proud of his accomplishment with Singlepart. The company weathered the 2000 economic downturn without layoffs, and few workers have left voluntarily—the employees are loyal and deeply committed to their work. Stewart set up specialized management, engineering, and manufacturing work groups, and is convinced that this structure has been the key to Singlepart's success. His greatest concern is that a sale may result in layoffs or splitting up of the long-standing work groups.

2. Several Singlepart employees were interviewed by Largecorp. They were asked numerous questions regarding the effectiveness of the work groups and how they felt about working in new groups. Steward suspects that Largecorp intends to break up Singlepart by changing the management and engineering groups and laying off administrative staff. There is a rumor that six Largecorp engineers would work on projects presently staffed by Singlepart. This is a new development that Stewart wants you to raise today. He is infuriated and may call off the deal—unless he is assured that his work over the past 15 years will not be dismantled by Largecorp. Stewart has also hinted that if the work groups are eliminated and component quality suffers, he may decide to go back into the stereo speaker business.

3. Largecorp is Singlepart's primary customer, and Stewart is concerned that if negotiations are unsuccessful, Singlepart will lose Largecorp's business. As a result, if you fail to reach a final purchase-sales agreement with Largecorp, you will have failed Stewart and be placed at the **bottom** of Singlepart groups.

4. The following is an up-to-date outline of the terms that have been tentatively agreed upon. Stewart realizes that negotiations regarding job protections for his employees may require some changes in the agreement. He has instructed you to finalize the deal as quickly as possible.

EMPLOYEES (the most important issue):

The first choice is to include a clause in the sale agreement guaranteeing each employee (including administrative staff) a minimum **5-year** employment contract **and** maintaining the existing work group structure. If you obtain **both** of these guarantees, score **plus 100 pts.**

The second choice is a clause guaranteeing each employee a minimum 5-year employment contract, but permitting changes in the existing work group structure. If you obtain this promise, score **plus 50 pts.**

For an employment guarantee of **4 years plus 40; of 3 years plus 30;** and of **2 years plus 20** (regardless of whether the existing work group structure is to be maintained).

Anything with **less** than a **2-year** employment contract guarantee is unacceptable, no matter what concessions Largecorp offers with respect to the maintenance of the existing work group structure. For any employment guarantee of <u>less than</u> 2 years, score **minus 50 pts.**

PRICE (the second most important concern):

$10,000,000 was Stewart's initial asking price, and he would still like to get more than the $7,500,000 that is presently being offered by Largecorp. Score **plus 1 pt.** for <u>each</u> **$20,000**, or part thereof, you obtain <u>over</u> $7,500,000.

Anything less than $7,500,000 is unacceptable. Score **minus 5 pts.** for <u>each</u> **$10,000**, or part thereof, agreed to <u>below</u> $7,500,000.

NON-COMPETITION (the third most important concern):

Although Stewart would prefer to avoid any non-competition obligation, he would be willing to bind himself to a term of no more than 3 years duration, since he would not be likely to return to the stereo component business during that period.

If you eliminate the non-competition obligation entirely, score **plus 25 pts.** If you agree to a non-competition clause of **no more** than **3 years**, score **plus 15 pts.** If you agree to a non-competition clause of <u>over</u> 3 years, score **minus 10 pts.** for <u>each</u> year, or part thereof, agreed to <u>in excess</u> of 3 years.

Warranty and Indemnification Provisions

Singlepart believes that Largecorp will request a Warranty Clause stating that Singlepart warrants that there are **no known** environmental problems. Since Singlepart officers are aware of no such problems, you **lose no points** for such a warranty. On the other hand, if you agree to a warranty provision stating that there are **no known or unknown** environmental problems, score **minus 75 points.**

Largecorp may also request an Indemnification Provision obliging Singlepart to indemnify it for any environmental problems discovered on the former Singlepart premises in the coming years. Score **minus 30 points** for an Environmental Indemnification Provision of **up to 2 years** in duration and **minus 100 points** for any Environmental Indemnification Provision **exceeding 2 years** in duration.

Largecorp may request a Liquidated Damage Provision that would apply to its discovery—prior to the closing date—of any financial misrepresentations by Singlepart agents. Since you believe that all financial representations have been accurate, score **minus 10 points** for any liquidated damage clause—of **up to $150,000**—pertaining to financial misrepresentations by Singlepart agents. For a liquidated damage clause **exceeding $150,000**, you must score **minus 50 points.**

5. Do not forget to discuss the **closing date**. Stewart is in no hurry to turn over the company, so if Largecorp wants to wait three or four months, that's fine with him—the South Pacific is warm and sunny all year long. Stewart would like some time to prepare his employees for the change. Score **plus 5 pts.** for <u>each</u> **month**, or part thereof, you post postpone the closing date—up to a maximum or 6 months.

Confidential Information for Largecorp Representatives

1. Largecorp hopes that this acquisition will (1) reduce its costs by enabling it to produce the components it is currently purchasing from Singlepart and (2) improve firm efficiency and creativity by inculcating Singlepart's corporate philosophy throughout Largecorp. Largecorp has interviewed members of various Singlepart work groups to gather information about how Singlepart works and why it has been so successful. The interviewers detected some hostility towards change and concern about future employment security, and you are surprised that employment contracts and office organization have not been part of the negotiations. You hope these issues won't be raised today. Largecorp would like to select a closing date, shake hands, and sign the contract as quickly as possible.

2. If some unexpected issues arise, you must remain pleasant because if negotiations turn bitter and the deal falls apart, Singlepart may refuse to sell to you in the future. Should you fail to achieve a final sales-purchase agreement, you will have failed Largecorp and be placed at the **bottom** of Largecorp negotiating groups.

3. Largecorp's CEO likes the agreement as it stands. If concessions need to be made, he wants to compromise as little as possible. The following issues are the most important to him.

PRICE (most important issue):

Largecorp initially offered $7,500,000, but this was not accepted. After interviewing some of Singlepart's employees, you realized that Singlepart is worth much more—up to $10,000,000. You are thus willing to go somewhat above the original $7,500,000 figure if necessary to close the deal. For **each $20,000**, or part thereof, **over $8,500,000**—up to $10,000,000—agreed to, score **minus 1 pt.** In addition, for **each $10,000**, or part thereof, **over $10,000,000**, score **minus 5 pts.**

NON-COMPETITION (second most important issue):

Since Largecorp is purchasing Singlepart to reduce the cost of high-quality components, it would like as little future competition from Stewart as possible. Largecorp fears that Stewart will soon be bored and reenter the stereo component business as a competitor (perhaps even rehiring his former engineers). Largecorp is willing to pay a premium to keep Stewart out of the market. A Largecorp attorney informed you that long-term non-competition clauses are frowned upon by the courts of this state. She told you that a court would almost certainly strike down any non-competition clause in excess of 5 years.

Largecorp and Stewart have tentatively agreed to a five-year term. In five years, start-up costs will have skyrocketed and technology will have advanced so that new companies would have a difficult time breaking into the market. If a shorter period were specified, there would be a risk that Stewart would begin a new venture.

If you obtain a non-competition clause of **5 years** in length, score **plus 75 pts.** If you agree to a non-competition clause of **at least 2 years** but **less than 5 years**, score **plus**

20 points—<u>plus</u> an **additional 10 points** for **each year**, or part thereof, **over 2 years**. If you fail to obtain a non- competition clause of **at least 2 years**, you **lose 25 points**.

EMPLOYEES (third most important issue):

Largecorp is still not sure how best to use Singlepart's employees. It has explored various options such as breaking up Singlepart and reassigning its employees and resources throughout the existing Largecorp structure, leaving Singlepart as an independent entity (a wholly-owned subsidiary), and different "in-between" ideas that would maintain some of Singlepart's existing work groups and break up others. Largecorp executives want to acquire Singlepart first and then try different options to determine which one works best. They like the fact the contract does not specify which Singlepart employees will be retained and for how long and how Singlepart's work groups should be structured. If Singlepart tries to obtain more precise agreements on these issues, you should try to maintain as much flexibility for Largecorp as possible.

Should you agree to any future employment guarantees or work group maintenance obligations, you will be scored as follows:

If you include <u>no</u> continuing **employment guarantees** for former Singlepart employees, **plus 40 pts.**

If you guarantee Singlepart employees employment for no more than 3 years, **0 pts.**

For any employment guarantee <u>in excess</u> of **3 years**, score **minus 10 pts.** for <u>each</u> **year**, or part thereof, <u>over</u> **3 years**.

Largecorp would like to retain discretion concerning future **work group configurations**. If you restrict Largecorp's discretion with respect to future work group configurations, **minus 20 pts.**

Warranty and Indemnification Provisions

Largecorp is always concerned about possible environmental problems discovered after it has purchased other companies. Score **plus 25 pts.** for a Warranty Provision from Singlepart stating that there are **no known** environmental problems. Score **plus 50 pts.** for a Warranty Provision stating that there are **no known or unknown** environmental problems.

Largecorp would like to obtain an Indemnification Provision obliging Singlepart to indemnify Largecorp for any environmental problems discovered on the former Singlepart premises in the coming years. Score **plus 50 pts.** for an Environmental Indemnification Provision of **2 years duration**. Score **plus 75 pts.** for an Environmental Indemnification Provision of **5 years duration**.

Largecorp would like to obtain a Liquidated Damage Provision that would require Singlepart to give it $100,000 in case it discovers—prior to the closing date—any financial misrepresentations by Singlepart agents. Score **plus 30 pts.** for such a Liquidated Damage Provision.

Don't forget to decide on the **closing date**. Largecorp would like to close the deal quickly, but recognizes that it may take several months for Stewart to finalize everything. You thus lose **no points** for an agreement to postpone the closing for **up to three months**. Score **minus 8 pts.** for <u>each</u> **month**, or part thereof, you postpone the final closing date **past the third month** — up to 6 months **from now**. For <u>each</u> **month**, or part thereof, <u>**beyond**</u> **6 months**, score **minus 25 pts.**

SINGLEPART/LARGECORP. EFFICIENCY POINTS

	SINGLEPART	*LARGECORP*
PRICE	+1/$20,000 over $7.5 mill.	−1/$20,000 $8.5−10 mill.
	−5/$10,000 under $7.5 mill.	−5/$10,000 over $10 mill.
$8.5 mill.:	+50 Singlepart	0 Largecorp
	[+1 & −1 per $20,000 from $8.5 mill. to $10 mill.]	
NONCOMPET.	No Non-Comp. Cl. +25	If no cl. of at least 2 yrs. −25
	Up to 3 Yr. Limit +15	Between 2–5 yrs. +20 **plus** +10/yr. Over 2 yrs.
	Over 3 yrs. −10/yr. Over 3	5 Yr. Non-Comp. Cl. +75
5 yr. Cl.	−20 Singlepart	+75 Largecorp
EMPLOYEE	5 yr. Contract and Same Work	No Guarantees +40
GUARANTEES	Grps. +100 5 yr. Contract/Changed Grps. +50 Guarantee Less than 5 yrs. (Same Or Changed Grps.): 2yrs. +20; 3 yrs. +30; 4 yrs. +40 Guarantee less than 2 yrs. −50	Up to 3 yr. Guarantee 0 Guarantee over 3 yrs. −10/yr. Over 3 Restriction on Work Grps. −20
Same Grps. 5 Yr. Term	+100 Singlepart	−40 [−20 & −20]
WARRANTY/	*No Known Problems 0	*No Known Problems +25
INDEMNIF.	No Known/Unknown −75 *Indemnif. up to 2 yrs. −30Indemnif.over 2 yrs. −100*Liq. Dam. up to $150k −10Liq. Dam. over $150k −50	No Known/Unknown +50 *Indem. for 2 yrs. +50Indem. for 5 yrs. +75*Liq. Dam. of $100k +30
CLOSING	+5 /mo. Up to 6 mo. Delayed	−8/mo. Delayed past 3 mo.
DATE		−25/mo. Delayed past 6 mo.
3 Mo. Delay	+15 Singlepart	0 Largecorp

Harry Nerd — Software Tech Corp.: General Information

Software Tech is an innovative software production firm that has developed many original computer programs for clients throughout the world. Although it began ten years ago in the basement of a house owned by its founder George Gates, it has grown into a billion dollar company with several hundred employees. It is located in Metropolis, East Dakota.

Harry Nerd joined Software Tech five years ago as a programmer. He demonstrated extraordinary software capabilities and designed some of the most sophisticated software ever developed. His efforts have generated tens of millions of dollars for the firm. Nerd is presently the Vice President in charge of United States operations. Last year, Nerd began to develop a new software coding system that would make it almost impossible for hackers to obtain entry into computer software systems. Although he was sure that his coding system was the best then available, Gates decided to place this project on hold because of his merger with a small company that had perfected its own security coding system. Nerd was very displeased with this decision, and he and Gates had several unpleasant conversations over it.

Over the past several weeks, Nerd has experienced a distinct coldness from Gates. On a couple of occasions, Gates even made negative comments regarding Nerd's work in front of individuals who work in Nerd's department. This has created great tension between Nerd and Gates and between Nerd and the people he directs.

Nerd and Gates have agreed to meet to discuss their future relationship. Gates hopes the two of them can work out their differences and reestablish the wonderful relationship they enjoyed before their recent disagreement over the coding software.

Confidential Information for Harry Nerd Representatives

You have been asked by Nerd to accompany him to the meeting with Gates to assist him with the negotiations he would like to conduct. He is tired of the bickering that has been taking place between Gates and himself, and he thinks that Gates has become too commercial. Gates appears to be more interested in business expansion, through the acquisition of, or merger with, smaller firms. Nerd prefers the cutting-edge work this firm did before it became so large. As a result, he would like to immediately sever his employment relationship with Software Tech.

Nerd has been approached by a recently-established East Dakota software company—Zenox Corporation—that would like him to become the Executive Vice President of its software development operations. His present compensation package with Software Tech generates $2,500,000 per year for Nerd. Although his base salary with Zenox would only pay him $500,000 per year to start, he anticipates generous stock options which, when the company goes public, could generate tens of millions of dollars for Nerd. Zenox is located 1500 miles from Software Tech.

Nerd would like to accept the Zenox offer, but he has a legal problem—his employment contract with Software Tech has two years to run *and* it contains both a Non-Compete Clause which forbids him from working for a competing firm within the United States for five years after he leaves Software Tech and it contains a Trade Secrets Clause which forbids him from disclosing any trade secrets he obtained while working for Software Tech including programming experiments that did not pan out and any information pertaining to firm clients. Nerd hopes you can help him extricate himself from Software Tech and allow him to relocate to Zenox. Should you fail to achieve an acceptable agreement on his behalf immediately ending his employment relationship with Software Tech, you will have failed an important client and be placed at the **bottom** of all Nerd groups.

East Dakota court decisions have allowed the enforcement of non-compete agreements, so long as they are reasonable in terms of geographical scope and duration. Although Nerd would like to relocate to Zenox immediately, he is willing to take a one or even two year hiatus before joining that company, because he has saved sufficient funds to allow him to travel and work on his own projects. He realizes that the Non-compete Clause limits his employment rights for five years, but hopes Software Technologies may release him from several of those years since East Dakota judicial decisions have usually limited the duration of such clauses to two or three years. Score **plus 200 points** if Nerd is allowed to join Zenox immediately; score **plus 150 points** if Nerd is allowed to join Zenox after only one year; score **plus 100 points** if he is required to wait two years before joining Zenox. Since Zenox is unlikely to wait more than two years, score **minus 500 points** if Nerd is not allowed to join Zenox within the next two years.

Nerd has no intention of using any trade secrets he obtained while at Software Tech, because they have all been patented and/or copyrighted and such usage would be illegal. He is thus perfectly willing to agree that he will not disclose any such **beneficial trade secret information**, and you **lose no points** for such a promise. He would, however, like the right to indirectly share information concerning software projects he worked on while at Software Tech that did **not pan out**. This information would not be made public, but it would save him and Zenox millions of dollars. Score **plus 50 points** if Software Tech will permit Nerd to share these **unsuccessful results** with his new employer.

Nerd would like to be able to reveal some Software Tech client information, since Zenox is developing a new client base and would benefit greatly from such information. You **lose 30 points if you agree that Nerd may not disclose any Software Tech client information.**

Nerd is prepared to compensate Software Technologies for the right to move to Zenox and to obtain release from the five year portion of the Non-Compete Clause and the portion of the Trade Secrets Clause pertaining to failed software undertakings. Score **minus 3 point** for each $10,000, or part thereof, Nerd agrees to pay to Software Tech *up to $1,000,000*. Score **minus 6 points** for each $10,000, or part thereof, Nerd agrees to pay *over $1,000,000*. If you can possibly convince Software Tech to pay Nerd money to depart, score **plus 2 points** per $10,000, or part thereof, they agree to pay Nerd to leave.

Over the past several years, Nerd had been working on a specialized software system for one of Software Tech's primary clients. If he were to depart now, Software Tech may want him to continue to assist their other programers on a part-time, consulting basis. Since such consulting work might detract from Nerd's other endeavors, you **lose 25 points** if you agree to such an arrangement. If Nerd does agree to work for Software Tech as a consultant and Software Tech agrees to compensate Nerd for this work, score **plus 2 points** for each $1,000, or part thereof, they agree to pay him to work as a consultant during the next year.

Confidential Information for
Software Tech Representatives

The relationship between Nerd and Gates rapidly deteriorated over the past few months. They clearly have different views concerning the future of Software Tech. Gates has been building a multinational enterprise that is moving into every region of the world. After Software Tech went public several years ago, Gates began to be more business-oriented. Nerd, on the other hand, has wanted to continue the speculative, cutting-edge work they previously undertook. Gates has finally decided that it is time for Nerd to look for work elsewhere, and he is willing to compensate him generously if he agrees to depart discretely. If you are unable to obtain an agreement inducing Nerd to leave Software Tech right now, you will have failed a significant client and be placed at the **bottom** of all Software Tech groups.

Nerd has two years to go on his current employment contract. His compensation package with Software Tech generates $2,500,000 per year. With his extraordinary skills, Nerd could easily locate a position with another software firm, but not one which compensates him so generously. To induce Nerd to depart, you have been authorized to pay him $500,000 and you lose **no points** for agreeing to such a sum. If you agree to pay Nerd *more than $500,000*, you **lose 1 point** for each $10,000, or part thereof, you agree to pay **between $500,000 and $1,000,000; you lose 2 points** for each $10,000, or part thereof, you pay **between $1,000,000 and $1,500,000**; and.you **lose 10 points** for each $10,000, or part thereof, you pay **over $1,500,000**.

Nerd's employment contract contains a Non-Compete Clause precluding Nerd from working for a competing firm within the United States for five years after he leaves Software Tech. East Dakota judicial decisions have not permitted the enforcement of such expansive non-compete restrictions. They have limited such clauses both geographically—most often to East Dakota and adjacent states—and in terms of duration—refusing to sustain such prohibitions for more than two or three years. Although Software Tech would be happy to get rid of Nerd, Gates would like to prevent him from working for another software development firm for a year or two. Score **plus 100 points** if Nerd agrees not to work for a competing firm for one year; score **plus 150 points** if Nerd agrees to such a limitation for two years.

Nerd's employment contract also contains a Trade Secrets Clause forbidding him to disclose any trade secrets he obtained while working for Software Tech, including programming experiments that did not pan out and any information pertaining to firm clients. Gates wants to be certain that Nerd not be allowed to disclose any client information. Score **plus 50 points** if Nerd agrees not to disclose any Software Tech client information. Score **plus 50 points** if Nerd also agrees not to disclose any trade secrets—both beneficial trade secrets *and* trade secrets pertaining to unsuccessful software initiatives—he obtained while working at Software Tech. If Nerd agrees not to disclose beneficial trade secrets, but is allowed to disclose trade secret information pertaining to *unsuccessful software initiatives*, score **plus 20 points**.

Over the past several years, Nerd had been working on a specialized software system for a prime Software Tech client. If he were to depart now, Software Tech would like him to continue to assist with this project on a part-time **consulting basis.** Score **plus 50 points** if Nerd agrees to work in such a consulting capacity. Gates is perfectly willing to compensate Nerd for this consulting work. You lose **no points** for an agreement to pay Nerd **up to $50,000** for such consulting work over the next year. Score **minus 5 points** for each $1,000, or part thereof, you agree to pay Nerd for such work over the next year **in excess of $50,000.**

NERD-SOFTWARE TECH EFFICIENCY POINTS

NERD		SOFTWARE TECH
Money Paid TO Nerd	+2/$10k	0 Up to $500,000 −1/$10k $500k–$1.0 Mill. −2/$10k $1 Mill.– $1.5 Mill. −10/ $10k OVER $1.5 Mill.
Money Paid BY Nerd	−3/$10k to $1 Mill. −6/ $10k over $1 Mill.	00
Can Work Zenox NOW	+200	0
Can Work Zenox 1 Yr.	+150	+100
Can Work Zenox 2 Yr.	+100	+150
Must Wait More Than 2 Yrs.	−500	0
No Client Info. Disclosure	−30	+50
May Disclose Failed Efforts	+50	+20
Will Work as Consultant	−25	+50
Payment to Consult	+2/$1000	−5/$1000 Over $50k

General Information — Chinese Joint Venture

The Eastern Electric Light Company, a Delaware Corporation, has been manufacturing light bulbs and small electrical appliances since 1923. Eastern Electric has been doing well financially in recent years, with gross revenues for the last fiscal year of $350,000,000. It has been thinking of entering the expanding market in the People's Republic of China ("China"), but is unwilling to enter that market alone. It would thus like to develop a joint venture with a Chinese firm. It was recently contacted by Mu Electronics, a three-year old limited liability company headquartered in Beijing. Mu Electronics also manufactures light bulbs and small electrical appliances, but its factory consists of an antiquated facility that was formerly owned and operated by the Chinese Government. Despite the inefficiencies associated with such an old plant, Mu Electronics has been doing remarkably well for a newly-formed company. Last year, it had gross sales of $10,000,000. The Mu Electronics managers think that they could generate much greater revenues if they could obtain an infusion of foreign funds, modernize their existing facility, and develop a national sales campaign.

Representatives of Eastern Electric and Mu Electronics are endeavoring to negotiate the terms of a mutually acceptable joint venture. They must agree upon the financial support to be provided by Eastern Electric, the percentage of Mu Electronics stock Eastern Electric is to acquire, the collateral Eastern Electric is to be given in case the joint venture fails or the Chinese Government decides to nationalize Mu Electronics, the official language to be used in the official joint venture documents, the applicable law to govern future contractual disputes, the dispute resolution procedures to be used to resolve any such controversies, and any other matters the representatives consider important.

Confidential Information — Eastern Electric Representatives

Mu Electronics provides Eastern Electric with the exact target of opportunity it has been seeking. It is a new, but already successful, firm with outstanding managers and a well-trained labor force. Eastern Electric believes that the infusion of new capital should enable a modernized Mu Electronics to greatly expand its currently limited production. You have thus been instructed to reach a joint venture agreement with Mu Electronics if at all possible.

Eastern Electric realizes that Mu Electronics will require an initial infusion of approximately $25,000,000 to modernize the production facility and will probably require about $10,000,000 per year for the next few years to develop a national sales campaign. If these goals are achieved, it is believed that Mu Electronics could increase its current $10,000,000 gross revenues to the $50–75 million range. You have thus been authorized to agree to the $25,000,000 initial outlay and to $10,000,000 per year thereafter for the following four years. You should be extremely reluctant to promise financial support above these figures over the first five years, and should refuse to make any definitive commitments beyond the first five years of this joint venture — unless absolutely necessary. If the projected joint venture revenue figures are not met during this time frame, Eastern Electric would be hesitant to contribute further financial support.

Chinese businesses do not like to have foreign firms hold majority ownership in Chinese corporations. If possible, Eastern Electric would like to obtain a fifty percent share that would give it the same power possessed by Mu Electronics. It would also like to have the name of the joint venture firm changed to "Mu-Eastern Electronics." If you are unable to achieve a 50-50 share division, you must at least obtain a promise that Eastern Electric will be given one-quarter of Mu Electronics shares by the end of the first year and one-third of Mu Electronics shares by the end of the initial five year period. Eastern Electric would also like to be guaranteed the right to immediately name one-quarter of the Mu Electronics Corporate Board members and to name one-third of the Board by the end of the initial five-year period. It would also like to be able to immediately name one Executive Vice President of Mu Electronics and to be able to name a second Executive Vice President within the next five years. (Mu Electronics currently has seven Executive Vice Presidents.)

Eastern Electric would like to be guaranteed fifty percent of Mu Electronics profits. If it is unable to achieve this profit division, it would like to be promised a profit split in proportion to its share of Mu Electronics shares.

Eastern Electric is concerned about the uncertain fate of the free market system in China in the coming years. If Communist hard-liners regain control, they may outlaw private firms and nationalize existing businesses. To protect Eastern Electric interests, you have been instructed to seek a provision giving Eastern Electric a secured interest in the building, equipment, and real property of Mu Electronics. It would also like to obtain the right to petition the Chinese Government for just compensation for any Mu Electronics property that is nationalized.

You must agree with Mu Electronics whether English, Chinese, or some third language is to be the official contract language. Although you would prefer English to govern, you recognize that Mu Electronics will probably reject this option. If you are unable to obtain English as the official language, you would prefer to have English and Chinese texts govern jointly. If compelled, however, you may reluctantly agree to Chinese as the official language.

You must also agree upon the legal doctrines to govern the interpretation and application of your joint venture agreement. Eastern Electric would prefer to have United States law and the Delaware Corporate Code govern and is unalterably opposed to reliance on Chinese law due to the uncertainty surrounding the evolving Chinese law regulating private business arrangements. If you cannot obtain an agreement to apply United States law, you would like to get Mu Electronics to agree to the application of European Union doctrines. If this proposal is unacceptable to Mu Electronics, you would then prefer language merely stating that the terms of your joint venture agreement will be interpreted according to business doctrines that are generally applied by the international community when resolving transnational business controversies.

Since Mu Electronics is unlikely to submit itself to jurisdiction of United States courts and Eastern Electric is unwilling to subject itself to the jurisdiction of Chinese judicial tribunals, you must agree upon a mutually acceptable procedure to resolve contractual disputes that may arise. You would like to specify that the Presidents, or their designates, of Eastern Electric and Mu Electronics will initially endeavor to negotiate an acceptable resolution of any disagreement regarding the interpretation and application of the joint venture agreement. In case these efforts are not successful, you would like to specify a list of three or four respected international conciliators who would be used on a rotating basis to mediate any disputes. In case conciliation efforts are unsuccessful, you would like to use binding arbitration procedures to resolve the matter. You would prefer a tripartite system under which Eastern Electric and Mu Electronics representatives would each appoint their own arbitrator, with these two individuals attempting to agree upon a third neutral arbitrator. Should the designated arbitrators be unable to agree upon the neutral arbitrator, you would like to require the parties to follow the appointment procedure used by the International Chamber of Commerce. You would like a requirement that all designated mediators and arbitrators be fluent in both English and Chinese.

Confidential Information — Mu Electronics Representatives

Mu Electronics desperately requires external financial support. Although it has experienced great financial success during its first three years of existence, it needs millions of dollars to modernize its antiquated manufacturing facility. With new financial support, Mu Electronics could probably expand sales throughout China and increase gross annual revenues from the current $10,000,000 to the $75,000,000 or even $100,000,000 range. Since no other firms have expressed an interest in a joint venture with Mu Electronics, it is imperative that you achieve a mutually acceptable arrangement with Eastern Electric.

Mu Electronics has estimated that it will take an initial investment of at least $15,000,000 to modernize its existing production plant. To provide some leeway, you have been instructed to seek as much over this $15,000,000 initial investment figure as possible. After the first year plant changes, Mu Electronics believes that it will take a minimum of $5,000,000 per year to generate a national sales campaign. If you could obtain commitments in excess of this $5,000,000 per year figure, this would greatly enhance the future prospects of Mu Electronics. You would like to obtain such an annual commitment for nine years following the plant modernization year, but would be willing to accept a shorter commitment if necessary. If you cannot get a full nine-year commitment, you would like to obtain a general promise that Eastern Electric will endeavor to continue this annual support so long as annual revenues are increasing.

Chinese corporations generally do not agree to majority ownership of Chinese firms by foreign interests. Mu Electronics is thus unwilling to allow Eastern Electric to hold over fifty percent of the Mu Electronics shares. While Eastern Electric may seek a fifty percent share interest, this would be wholly unacceptable to Mu Electronics which insists on maintaining majority interest. You may grant a thirty percent interest to Eastern Electric as soon as the joint venture is agreed upon. Assuming Eastern Electric continues to provide annual financial support of at least $5,000,000, you may also agree to grant that firm a forty percent interest by the end of the fifth year of the new relationship. You should only exceed forty percent with great reluctance, and you may not grant more than a forty-five percent share under any circumstances. Since your firm is named after Mr. Mu, the founder of the business, you would like to retain the Mu Electronics name in future years.

It is likely that Eastern Electric will demand the right to select several members of the Mu Electronics Board of Directors. Since that firm will hold at least a quarter of Mu Electronics shares, you would be perfectly willing to let Eastern Electric name one-quarter of the Corporate Board members. By the end of the initial five-year period, you may even permit Eastern Electric to name up to forty percent of the Corporate Board. You may not, however, allow that company to name over forty percent.

Mu Electronics currently has seven Executive Vice Presidents. It assumes that Eastern Electric will insist on the right to name one, two, or possibly even three Executive Vice Presidents to protect its economic interest in Mu Electronics. Since such a request is common in joint ventures, you are authorized to agree to Eastern Electric control over one or even two Executive Vice Presidencies. Since Mu Electronics has been planning to expand the number of Executive Vice Presidents from seven to ten, you may agree to let Eastern Electric name three Executive Vice Presidents, so long as this is done after the total number is expanded to ten.

You anticipate that Eastern Electric will demand the right to half of the profits generated by Mu Electronics following the joint venture. Your firm considers this an excessive figure, and will not accept any deal that gives Eastern Electric more than forty percent of Mu Electronics profits. You have been authorized to give Eastern Electric a profit share equal to the percent of Mu Electronics shares held by that firm — i.e., up to thirty percent at the outset and up to forty percent by the end of the initial five year period.

Mu Electronics recognizes that Eastern Electric is concerned about the uncertain future of the free market in China. You suspect that Eastern Electric will ask for a secured interest in the building, equipment, and real property of Mu Electronics. You are perfectly willing to agree to such a provision.

Mu Electronics would like to have the Chinese draft of the joint venture contract constitute the official draft and will not permit the English draft to govern. If you are unable to obtain an agreement specifying that the Chinese draft is controlling, you would be willing to allow the English and Chinese texts to govern jointly.

The parties must agree upon the legal doctrines that will govern the interpretation and application of their joint venture agreement. Mu Electronics would like to have Chinese law apply, but realizes the hesitancy of foreign firms to agree to such an arrangement due to the evolving nature of Chinese private venture legal doctrines. Mu Electronics is unalterably opposed to the application of United States law to contractual matters, because it fears the law will favor U.S. companies. You have been authorized to agree to the application of European Union doctrines, and if this is unacceptable, to a provision merely stating that the terms of the joint venture agreement will be interpreted according to business doctrines generally applicable by the international community when resolving transactional business disputes.

Mu Electronics is unwilling to submit itself to jurisdiction of United States courts and assumes that Eastern Electric would be unwilling to submit to Chinese judicial jurisdiction. As a result, the parties must agree upon a mutually acceptable dispute resolution procedure. You are willing to allow the assistance of internationally respected mediators, and would even be willing to submit unresolved controversies to an international arbitral panel. You are flexible regarding the exact arbitrator selection procedures, so long as the procedures would guarantee the selection of qualified neutrals who are fluent in Chinese.

EFFICIENCY DISTRIBUTION CONSIDERATIONS

	EASTERN ELECTR.	MU ELECTR.
INIT. INVEST.	UP TO $25 MILL.	AT LEAST $15 MILL.
PER YEAR	$10 MILL. PER TO 4 YRS AVOID LONGER COMMIT.	$5 MILL./YR. FOR 9 YRS SHORTER TERM ACCEPT.
CORP. CONTROL	GOAL: 50/50 SHARE SPLIT	INITL. 30% SHARE SPLIT
	AT LEAST 25% BY 1ST YR.	40% BY END OF 5TH YR.
	"MU-EASTERN ELECTR." POSSIB.	KEEP MU NAME IF POSSIB MU-EASTERN IF NEED BE
	NAME 1/4 CORP. BD. NOW	NAME 1/4 CORP. BD. NOW
	1/3 BD. BY END OF 5TH YR.	UP TO 40% BY 5TH YR.
EXEC. VPs NOW	NAME 1 EXEC VP NOW	NAME 1 OR 2 VPs NOW
	NAME ANOTHER BY YR. 5	UP TO 3 WHEN 10 VPs.
PROFITS	50% IF POSSIB.	% OF SHARES HELD
	AT LEAST % OF SHARES	30% NOW
	HELD	40–45% BY 5TH YR.
SECURED INT.	BLDG., EQUIP. & REAL PROP.	BLDG., EQUIP. & REAL PROP.
OFFICIAL DRAFT	1) ENGLISH 2) JT. ENG.-CHIN. 3) CHINESE IF NEC-ESSARY	1) CHINESE 2) JT. ENG. CHINESE
LEGAL RULES	1) U.S./DEL. CORP. CODE	1) CHINESE RULES
	2) EU DOCTRINES	2) EU DOCTRINES
	3) BUS. DOCTRINES GEN.	3) BUS. DOCTRINES GEN.
	APPLIED INTL. BUS. COM.	APPLIED INTL. BUS. COM
DISP. RES. PROC.	1) FIRM PRES. TO DISCUSS	
	2) LIST OF 3–4 INTL. MEDS.	1) ASST. OF INTL. MEDS.
	3) BINDING TRI-PARTITE ARB.	2) INTL. ARB. PANEL
	IF NEUTRAL ARB. NOT AGREED	
	TO APT. BY INTL. CHAMB.OF COMMERCE ALL NEUTRALS FLUENT IN ENG. & CHINESE	FLEXIBLE RE ARB. SELEC-TION RULES NEUTRALS FLUENT IN CHINESE

Modified NASA Decision Making Exercise*

INSTRUCTIONS: You are a member of one of two space details assigned to the mission ship "Galaxy," which was originally scheduled to rendezvous with the parent ship "Angel" on the lighted surface of the moon. Due to mechanical difficulties, however, the Galaxy was forced to land on the dark side of the moon some 200 miles from the rendezvous point. During piloting and landing, some of the crew and both Detail A and Detail B captains died. Much of the equipment aboard was damaged. No one knows for sure how long the ship's life support systems will last because all gauges were broken. Detail A piloted the mission and Detail B was to explore the surface before returning to the parent ship. *Survival of both Details is crucial.* Below are listed the 15 items left intact and undamaged after landing. Your task is to *individually rank* them in order of their importance to the survival of the remaining crew of the mission ship, Galaxy. Place the number 1 by the most important item, the number 2 by the second most important, and so on through number 15, the least important.

Modified NASA Decision Making Exercise
Inventory of Undamaged Material

— Ten Blankets

— 100 Cartons of Food Concentrate (20-day Ration for Each Crew Member)

— 150 Feet of Nylon Rope

— Parachute Silk From 3 Parachutes

— One Portable Heating Unit that is Self-Lighting

— Two .45 Caliber Loaded Pistols

— One Case Dehydrated Milk

— Three 100 lb. Tanks of Oxygen (Each Holds 20-Day Supply for Each Crew Member)

— One Stellar Map of the Moon's Constellation

— One Life Raft

— One Magnetic Compass that Functions on the Moon

— 5 Gallons of Water (Normally a 10-Day Ration for Each Member of the Crew)

— Five Light Flares Containing Their Own Oxidizing Agent

— First Aid Kit Containing Injection Needles

— Solar-Powered FM Receiver-Transmitter

---

* Department of Education and Training/American Arbitration Ass'n. Reprinted by permission of the American Arbitration Association. When this exercise was formulated many years ago, it was believed that the moon rotated in a manner that kept one side light and the other dark. We now know that this belief was incorrect. Nonetheless, for the purposes of this exercise, participants should assume that one side is still primarily light and the other primarily dark.

Modified NASA Decision Making Exercise
Decision by Consensus

INSTRUCTIONS: This is an exercise in group decision-making. Your Detail is to use the method of group consensus in reaching its decision. This means that the ranking for each of the 15 survival items *must* be agreed on by each Detail member before it becomes a part of the group decision. Consensus is difficult to reach. Therefore, not every ranking will meet with everyone's complete approval. Try, as a Detail, to make each ranking one with which all group members can at least partially agree. Here are some guides to use in reaching consensus:

1. Avoid arguing for your own individual judgments. Approach the task on the basis of logic.

2. Avoid changing your mind merely to reach agreement and avoid conflict. Only support solutions with which you at least partially agree.

3. Avoid "conflict-reducing" techniques such as majority vote, averaging, or trading in reaching decisions.

4. View differences of opinion as helpful rather than as hindrances in decision-making.

Modified NASA Exercise — Detail Consensus Form									
ITEMS	A	B	C	D	E	F	G	H	AGT
Ten Blankets									
100 Cartons of Food Concentrate									
150 Feet of Nylon Rope									
Parachute Silk from Three Parachutes									
One Portable Heating Unit									
Two .45 Caliber Loaded Pistols									
One Case of Dehydrated Milk									
Three 100 lb. Tanks of Oxygen									
One Stellar Map of Moon Constel.									
One Life Raft									
One Magnetic Compass									
Five Gallons of Water									
Five Light Flares									
One First Aid Kit									
Solar Powered FM Receiver/Transm.									

On the Modified NASA Consensus Form place the individual rankings made earlier by each group member.

Modified NASA Decision Making Exercise
Decision by Negotiation

INSTRUCTIONS: Detail A will attempt to *survive* while *waiting for help* from the parent ship "Angel."

Detail B will attempt to *survive* and *make* the rendezvous with the parent ship "Angel."

This is an exercise in group decision-making. Your Detail is to use the method of group negotiations in reaching its decision. Both groups must decide which Detail will remain with the disabled mission ship "Galaxy" (*i.e.*, which group will be designated "Detail A") and which group will endeavor to rendezvous with the parent ship "Angel" (*i.e.*, which group will be designated "Detail B"). Both groups must also agree upon the division of the inventoried items between Details A and B (*i.e.*, which items will remain with Detail A and which will be taken with Detail B).

Modified NASA Negotiated Agreement Form is provided to list the terms of your negotiated agreement.

Modified NASA—Negotiated Agreement Form		
ITEMS	DETAIL A	DETAIL B
Ten Blankets		
100 Cartons of Food Concentrate		
150 Feet of Nylon Rope		
Parachute Silk from Three Parachutes		
One Portable Heating Unit		
Two .45 Caliber Loaded Pistols		
One Case of Dehydrated Milk		
Three 100 lb. Tanks of Oxygen		
One Stellar Map of Moon's Constellation		
One Life Raft		
One Magnetic Compass		
Five Gallons of Water		
Five Light Flares		
One First Aid Kit		
Solar Powered FM Receiver/Transmitter		

Index

[References are to sections.]

A

Agencies, Government
Negotiating with, 10.01[J]
Aggressive Behavior
Generally, 8.02[M]
Alleged Expertise/Snow Job Technique
Generally, 8.02[Q]
Arbitration
Cyber mediation and, use of, 13.12
Judicial litigation, use of arbitration to avoid, 13.11
Asymmetrical Time Pressure
Use of, 8.02[B]
Attribution Bias
Post-negotiation assessments, impact on, 14.03[F]

B

Bargaining
Attitudinal bargaining to counter negative behavior, 4.02
Boulwareism/best offer first bargaining, 8.02[E]
Electronic devices, turning off before in-person, 4.03
Gender on bargaining interactions, impact of (See Gender on Bargaining Interactions, Impact of)
Numerically superior bargaining team, 8.02[A]
Post-negotiation assessments, 14.03[C]

Power bargaining tactics (See Distributive and Closing Stages, Claiming Value through, subhead: Power bargaining tactics)
Proficiency, importance of, 1.01
Weak bargaining position, strengthening one's own, 10.01[C]
Belly-Up Approach
Generally, 8.02[W]
Body Posture/Speech Pattern Mirroring
Generally, 9.02
Boulwareism/Best Offer First Bargaining
Generally, 8.02[E]
Bracketing Technique
Generally, 8.02[R]
Brazil
Negotiating styles in, 12.06[D]
Brer Rabbit (Reverse Psychology)
Generally, 8.02[U]

C

Canada
Negotiating styles in, 12.06[B]
Checklist
Post-negotiation assessments, 14.03[H]
China
Negotiating styles in, 12.06[F]
Classic Signs (See Nonverbal Signals, subhead: Classic signs)